TEN STEPS TO IMPROVING COLLEGE READING SKILLS

TEN STEPS TO IMPROVING COLLEGE READING SKILLS

SECOND EDITION

JOHN LANGAN

ATLANTIC COMMUNITY COLLEGE

TOWNSEND PRESS   Marlton, NJ 08053

The Other Books in the Townsend Press Reading Series:

GROUNDWORK FOR COLLEGE READING
GROUNDWORK FOR COLLEGE READING II
TEN STEPS TO BUILDING COLLEGE READING SKILLS
TEN STEPS TO ADVANCING COLLEGE READING SKILLS

Books in the Townsend Press Vocabulary Series:

GROUNDWORK FOR A BETTER VOCABULARY
BUILDING VOCABULARY SKILLS
IMPROVING VOCABULARY SKILLS
ADVANCING VOCABULARY SKILLS
BUILDING VOCABULARY SKILLS, SHORT VERSION
IMPROVING VOCABULARY SKILLS, SHORT VERSION
ADVANCING VOCABULARY SKILLS, SHORT VERSION

Supplements Available for Each Book:

Instructor's Manual
Test Bank and Computer Guide
Set of Computer Disks (Apple, IBM, or Macintosh)

Copyright © 1992 by Townsend Press, Inc.
Printed in the United States of America
ISBN 0-944210-52-X

Send book orders and requests for desk copies or supplements to:

Townsend Press, Inc.
Pavilions at Greentree—408
Marlton, New Jersey 08053

For even faster service, call us at our toll-free number:
1-800-772-6410

Or FAX your request to:
1-609-772-9611

ISBN 0-944210-52-X

LB2395 3 L36 1992

CONTENTS

Preface to the Instructor

We all know that many students entering college today do not have the reading skills needed to do effective work in their courses. A related problem, apparent even in class discussions, is that students often lack the skills required to think in a clear and logical way.

The purpose of TEN STEPS TO IMPROVING COLLEGE READING SKILLS, Second Edition, is to develop effective reading *and* clear thinking. To do so, Part I presents a sequence of ten reading skills that are widely recognized as essential for basic and advanced comprehension. The first five skills concern the more literal levels of comprehension:

- Using vocabulary in context
- Recognizing main ideas
- Identifying supporting details
- Understanding transitions
- Understanding patterns of organization

The remaining five skills cover the more advanced, critical levels of comprehension:

- Distinguishing facts from opinions
- Making inferences
- Understanding purpose and tone
- Detecting propaganda
- Evaluating arguments

In every chapter in Part I, the key aspects of a skill are explained and illustrated clearly and simply. Explanations are accompanied by a series of practices, and each chapter ends with three review tests. The last review test includes a reading selection, so that students can apply the skill just learned to real-world reading materials, including newspaper and magazine articles and textbook selections. Together, the ten chapters provide students with the skills needed for basic and more advanced reading comprehension.

Part II is made up of six mastery tests for each of the ten skills, as well as six combined skill tests. The tests progress in difficulty, providing students with the additional practice and challenge they may need for the solid learning of each skill. While designed for quick grading, the tests also insure that students must think carefully before answering each question.

Part III consists of ten additional readings that will help improve both reading and thinking skills. Each reading is followed by *Basic Skill Questions* and *Advanced Skill Questions* so students can practice all of the ten skills presented in Part I and reinforced in Part II. In addition, an *Outlining, Mapping, or Summarizing* activity after each reading helps students think carefully about the basic content and organization of a selection. Finally, *Discussion Questions* provide teachers with an opportunity to engage students in a variety of reading skills and to deepen their understanding of a selection.

Important Features of the Book

• **Focus on the basics.** The book seeks to explain in an extremely clear, step-by-step way the essential elements of each skill. Many examples are provided to ensure that students understand each point. In general, the focus is on *teaching* the skills—not just on explaining them and not just on testing them.

• **Frequent practice and feedback.** In the belief that it is largely through abundant practice and careful feedback that progress is made, this book includes numerous activities. Students can get immediate feedback on the practice exercises in Part I by turning to the limited answer key at the back. The answers to the review tests in Part I, the mastery tests in Part II, and the readings in Part III are in the Instructor's Manual.

The limited answer key increases the active role that students take in their own learning. They are likely to use the answer key in an honest and positive way if they know they may be tested on the many activities and selections for which answers are not provided. (Answers not in the book can be easily copied from the manual and passed out at the teacher's discretion.)

• **High interest level.** Dull and unvaried readings and exercises work against learning. Students need to experience genuine interest and enjoyment in what they read. Teachers as well should be able to take pleasure in the selections, for their own good feeling can carry over favorably into class work. The readings in the book, then, have been chosen not only for the appropriateness of their reading level but also for their compelling content. They should engage teachers and students alike.

• **Ease of use.** The straightforward sequence in each chapter—from explanation to example to practice to review test—helps make the skills easy to teach. The book's three distinct parts also makes for ease of use. Within a single class, for instance, teachers can work on a new skill in Part I, review skills with one or more mastery tests in Part II, and provide variety by having students read one of the selections in Part III. The limited answer key at the back of the text also makes for versatility: it means that the teacher can assign some chapters for self-teaching. Finally, the mastery and combined skill tests—each on its own tear-out page—make it a simple matter for teachers to test and evaluate student progress.

• **Integration of skills.** Students do more than learn the skills individually in Parts I and II. They also learn to apply the skills together through the reading selections that close the chapters in Part I, through the combined-skill tests in Part II, and through the readings in in Part III. They become effective readers and thinkers through a good deal of practice in applying a combination of skills.

• **Thinking activities.** Thinking activities in the form of outlining, mapping (using a map, or diagram, to organize material in a highly visual way), and summarizing are a distinctive feature of the book. While educators agree that such organizational abilities are important, they are all too seldom taught. From a practical standpoint, it is almost impossible for a teacher to respond individually to entire collections of class outlines or summaries. This book seeks, then, to create activities that truly involve students in outlining and summarizing—in other words, that truly make students *think*—and yet that enable a teacher to give feedback. Again, it is through continued practice *and* feedback on challenging material that a student becomes a more effective reader and thinker.

• **Supplementary materials.** The three helpful supplements listed below are available at no charge to instructors using the text. Any or all can be obtained quickly by writing or calling Townsend Press (Pavilions at Greentree—408, Marlton, New Jersey 08053; 609-772-6410).

1   An *Instructor's Edition*—chances are you are holding it in your hand—is identical to the student book except that it also provides all of the following: 1) hints for teachers (see the front of the book); 2) answers to all the practices and tests; and 3) comments on many answers.

2   A combined *Instructor's Manual, Test Bank, and Computer Guide* consists of the following:

   a Suggestions for teaching the course, a model syllabus, readability levels, and writing activities for each reading selection.

b Four additional mastery tests for each of the ten skills, and four additional combined-skill tests—all on letter-sized sheets so they can be copied easily for use with students.

c A computer guide that reproduces the two additional mastery tests for each skill that are on the computer disks available with the book

3 A *set of computer disks* (in Apple, IBM, and Macintosh formats) that contain two additional mastery tests for each of the ten skill chapters in the book. The disks are self-booting and contain a number of other user- and instructor-friendly features: brief explanations of answers, a sound option, frequent mention of the user's first name, a running score at the bottom of the screen, and a record-keeping score file.

Since the disk tests are reproduced in the *Computer Guide*, teachers can readily decide just how to use the materials without having to work through each test on the computer. And teachers without a computer lab can copy these tests for use in class as additional mastery tests.

• **One of a sequence of books.** This is the intermediate text in a series that includes two other books. TEN STEPS TO BUILDING COLLEGE READING SKILLS is the basic book in the series, and TEN STEPS TO ADVANCING COLLEGE READING SKILLS is an advanced text.

The BUILDING book is a lower-level book suited for a first college reading course. The IMPROVING book is appropriate for the core developmental reading course offered at most colleges. The ADVANCING book is a slightly higher developmental text than the IMPROVING book. It can be used as the core book for a more advanced class, as a sequel to the intermediate book, or as a second-semester alternative to it.

A companion set of vocabulary books, listed on page iv, has been designed to go with the TEN STEPS books. Recommended to accompany this book is IMPROVING VOCABULARY SKILLS or IMPROVING VOCABULARY SKILLS, SHORT VERSION.

Together, the books and their full range of supplements form a sequence that should be ideal for any college reading program.

To summarize, then, TEN STEPS TO IMPROVING COLLEGE READING SKILLS, Second Edition, provides ten key reading skills to help developmental college students become independent readers and thinkers. Through an appealing collection of readings and a carefully designed series of activities and tests, students receive extensive guided practice in the skills. The result is an integrated approach to learning that will, by the end of a course, produce better readers and stronger thinkers.

Changes in the Second Edition

I am grateful for the helpful comments from the many teachers who have either written or spoken to me at conferences about the book over the last couple of years. Based on their suggestions and my own classroom use of the text, I have made some major changes:

- *More progression in the mastery tests from easier to more difficult material.* Students are given a greater challenge, especially with the fifth and sixth tests, which usually feature textbook excerpts.

- *Integration of the individual comprehension skills with the reading selections.* A reading selection now follows each chapter in Part I, so students can apply immediately the skill they have learned to an actual reading. As students move from one chapter to the next, they both apply the new skill learned and review the skills covered in earlier chapters.

- *More tests and practice materials.* There are now six mastery tests instead of five, and there are twenty reading selections, compared to seventeen in the first edition. Completely new are brief content tests for each of the ten skills chapters in Part I; these tests begin the final review test in each chapter. Also new are six combined-skill tests—short reading passages followed by questions on a variety of skills. The passages and tests approximate those in typical standardized reading tests. These combination tests will help prepare students for such standardized tests, which are often a requirement at the end of a semester.

- *Many revisions and additions throughout the text.* Users of the first edition will note, for example, that a second color is now used to make the content more readable and visually appealing. They will see that thirteen of the readings are new; that maps as well as outlines now dramatize the patterns of organization; that the inferences chapter has been expanded to include literary materials; that bias has been moved out of the propaganda chapter to a spot where it more logically belongs, in the fact and opinion chapter; that the first half of the argument chapter is completely new; and that there have been changes of some kind on virtually every single page of the text.

- *An* Instructor's Edition *of the book.* In the special teacher's version of the book, users now have at their fingertips the answers to all of the tests and practices. Included as well are comments that may help in explaining to students why a given answer is correct and why other answer options are not. There is also a series of teaching hints that may be of help—especially for people teaching a reading course or using this book for the first time.

Acknowledgments

I am grateful to Carol H. Bader and Harley F. Anton of Middle Tennessee State University, who carefully worked through every practice and test in the book and made suggestions for changes. I am especially indebted to two of my colleagues at Townsend Press. Thanks to the exceptional design and editing skills of Janet M. Goldstein, this book, which was prepared on a Macintosh computer, enjoys a remarkably clear and "user-friendly" format. Her work also made possible the creation of the *Instructor's Edition*, complete with answers and marginal glosses, that now accompanies the book. I value equally the exceptional editorial role played by Carole Mohr, who has worked closely with me for many months on every page of the book. Thanks to her many insights into the nature of each skill and her unfailing sensitivity to the needs of students, the text is significantly better than it would have been otherwise. It has been a special pleasure to work with colleagues who aspire toward excellence. With them, I have been able to create a much better book than I could have managed on my own.

John Langan

How to Become a Better Reader and Thinker

The chances are you are not as good a reader as you should be to do well in college. If so, it's not surprising. You live in a culture where people watch on the average of *over seven hours of television every day!!!* All that passive viewing does not allow much time for reading. Reading is a skill that must be actively practiced. The simple fact is that people who do not read very often are not likely to be strong readers.

• How much TV do you guess you watch on an average day? _____

Another reason besides TV for not reading much is that you may have a lot of responsibilities. You may be going to school and working at the same time, and you may have a lot of family duties as well. Given a hectic schedule, you're not going to have much time to read. When you have free time, you're exhausted, and it's easier to turn on the TV than to open up a book.

• Do you do any regular reading (for example, a daily newspaper, weekly magazines, occasional novels)? ___yes___

• When are you most likely to do your reading? ___late night___

A third reason for not reading is that our public school system may have soured you on it. One government study after another has said that our schools have not done a good job of turning people on to the rewards of reading. If you had to read a lot of uninteresting and irrelevant material in grade and high school, you may have decided (mistakenly) that reading in general is not for you.

• Do you think that school made you dislike reading, rather than enjoy it?

___no___

Here are three final questions to ask yourself.

- Do you feel that perhaps you don't need a reading course, since you "already know how to read"? _____ _yes_ _____

- If you had a choice, would you be taking a reading course? (It's OK to be honest) _____ _probably   it   doesn't matter_

- Do you think that a bit of speed reading may be all you need? ____?____

Chances are that you don't need to read *faster* as much as you need to read *smarter*. And it's a safe bet that if you don't read much, you can benefit enormously from the reading course in which you are using this book.

One goal of the book is to help you become a better reader. You will learn and practice ten key reading comprehension skills. As a result, you'll be able to better read and understand the many materials in your other college courses. The skills in this book have direct and practical value: they can help you perform better and more quickly—giving you an edge for success—in all of your college work.

The book is also concerned with helping you become a stronger thinker, a person able not just to understand what is read but to analyze and evaluate it as well. In fact, reading and thinking are closely related skills, and practice in thoughtful reading will also strengthen your ability to think clearly and logically. To find out just how the book will help you achieve these goals, read the next several pages and do the brief activities as well. The activities are easily completed and will give you a quick, helpful overview of the book.

HOW THE BOOK IS ORGANIZED

The book is organized into three parts:

Part I: Ten Steps to Improving College Reading Skills (Pages 7-208)

To help you become a more effective reader and thinker, this book presents a series of ten key reading skills. They are listed in the table of contents on page v. Turn to that page to fill in the skills missing below:

1   Vocabulary in Context

2   _main ideas_

3   Supporting Details

4   _transitions_

5   Patterns of Organization

6   Fact and Opinion

7   Inferences

8   _purpose + tone_

9   Propaganda

10   _argument_

    Each chapter is developed in the same way. First of all, clear explanations and examples help you *understand* each skill. Practices then give you the "hands-on" experience needed to *review* the skill.

- How many practices are there for the second skill, "Main Ideas" (pages 24-48)? _5_

Closing each chapter are three review tests.

- On which pages are the first two review tests for "Main Ideas"? _41 - 44_

The third review test always consists of two parts: a review of the chapter and a reading selection that gives you a chance both to practice the skill learned in the chapter and to review skills learned in earlier chapters.

- How many questions are asked about the "Main Ideas" chapter (page 44)? _5_

- What is the title of the reading on page 45? _Here's To Your Health_

Part II: Mastery Tests (Pages 209-342)

    This part of the book provides mastery tests for each of the ten skills in Part I.

- Look through pages 211-330. How many mastery tests are there for each skill? _6_ .

    The test pages are perforated and can be torn out and given to your instructor. There is a scorebox at the end of each test so you can track your progress. Your score can also be entered in the "Reading Performance Chart" at the back of the book.

- Exactly where is this chart located? _On the inside of the cover_

Part III: Ten Reading Selections (Pages 345-438)

    The ten reading selections that make up Part III are followed by activities that give you practice in all of the skills studied in Parts I and II. Turn to the table of contents on page vi and answer the following question:

- Which selection is probably about good eating habits? _The No-Fat Nation_

Each reading begins in the same way. Look, for example, at "The Yellow Ribbon," which starts on page 345. What are the headings of the two sections that come before the reading itself?

- _preview_
- _words to watch_

Note that the vocabulary words in "Words to Watch" are followed by the numbers of the paragraphs in which the words appear. Now look at the first reading (345-347) and explain how each vocabulary word is marked in the reading itself:

- _a circle to the upper rt. side of the word._

Activities Following Each Reading Selection

After each selection, there are four kinds of activities to improve your reading and thinking skills. Look at those following "The Yellow Ribbon" (pages 347-351). Note that the first activity consists of **basic skill questions**. The second consists of (fill in the missing words) _Advanced Skill Questions_. The third activity involves **outlining, mapping,** or **summarizing**. The fourth consists of (fill in the missing words) _discussing questions_.

- Look at the **basic skill questions** for "The Yellow Ribbon" on pages 347-348. You'll see that there are ten questions covering five basic skills. Note that there are always one to three questions for each skill. The questions give you a chance to practice the skills you learned in Part I and strengthened in Part II. How many questions deal with the skill of understanding transitions? _3_

- Look at the **advanced skill questions** on pages 348-350. Again, there are ten questions, covering the five more advanced skills. How many questions here deal with making inferences? _3_

- The third activity is always **outlining, mapping,** or **summarizing**. Any one of these will sharpen your ability to get to the heart of a piece and to think logically and clearly about what you read. What kind of activity is provided for the reading titled "Urban Legends" on page 359? _mapping_

Note that a **map,** or diagram, is a highly visual way of organizing material. Like an outline, it shows at a glance the main parts of a selection.

- Write down how many **discussion questions** there are for "Urban Legends" (page 360)—and for every other reading: _____4_____. The questions provide a chance for you to deepen your understanding of each selection.

HELPFUL FEATURES OF THE BOOK

1   The book centers on *what you really need to know* to become a better reader and thinker. It presents ten key comprehension skills, and it explains the most important points about each skill.

2   The book gives you *lots of practice.* We seldom learn a skill only by hearing or reading about it; we make it part of us by repeated practice. There are, then, numerous activities in the text. They are not "busy work," but carefully designed materials that should help you truly learn each skill.

   Notice that after you learn each skill in Part I, you read a selection in Review Test 3 that enables you to apply that skill. And as you move from one skill to the next, you continue to practice and reinforce the ones already learned.

3   The selections throughout the book are *lively and appealing.* Dull and unvaried readings work against learning, so subjects have been carefully chosen for their high interest level. Almost all of the selections here are excellent examples of how what we read can capture our attention. For example, take a look at the textbook selection, "Preindustrial Cities," on page 429. Despite its unexciting title, it is full of fascinating details about city life before modern food distribution and sanitary facilities.

4   The readings include six *selections from college textbooks.* Therefore, you are practicing on materials very much like the ones in your other courses. Doing so will increase your chances of transferring what you learn in your reading class to your other college subjects.

HOW TO USE THE BOOK

1   A good way to proceed is to read and reread the explanations and examples in a given chapter in Part I until you feel you understand the ideas presented. Then carefully work through the practices. As you finish each one, check your answers with the "Limited Answer Key" that starts on page 439.

For your own sake, don't just copy in the answers without trying to do the practices! The only way to learn a skill is to practice it first and *then* use the answer key to give yourself feedback. Also, take whatever time is needed to figure out just why you got some answers wrong. By using the answer key to help teach yourself the skills, you will prepare yourself for the review tests at the end of each chapter as well as for the mastery tests and the reading selection tests in the book. Your instructor can supply you with answers to those tests.

If you have trouble catching on to a particular skill, stick with it. In time, you will learn each one.

2   Read the selections with the intent of simply enjoying them. There will be time afterwards for rereading each selection and using it to develop your comprehension skills.

3   Keep track of your progress. In the "Reading Performance Chart" on the inside back cover, enter your scores for the mastery tests in Part II. In addition, fill in the "Check Your Performance" chart at the end of each reading in Part III. These scores can also be entered on the inside-back-cover chart, giving you a good view of your overall performance as you work through the book.

In summary, TEN STEPS TO IMPROVING COLLEGE READING SKILLS has been designed to interest and benefit you as much as possible. Its format is straightforward, its explanations are clear, its readings are appealing, and its many practices will help you learn through doing. *It is a book that has been created to reward effort*, and if you provide that effort, you will make yourself a better reader and a stronger thinker. I wish you success.

John Langan

Part I

TEN STEPS TO IMPROVING COLLEGE READING SKILLS

1

Vocabulary in Context

If you were asked to define the words *torrid*, *ascertain*, and *euphoria*, you might have some difficulty. On the other hand, if you saw these words in the sentences, chances are you could come up with fairly accurate definitions. To illustrate, see if you can define the words in *italics* in the three sentences below. Circle the letter of the meaning you think is correct.

To avoid the burning sun in *torrid* climates such as deserts, many animals come out only at night.

Torrid means
a. familiar   b. extremely hot and dry   c. very bright

The officer tried to *ascertain* the truth about the accident by questioning each witness separately.

Ascertain means
a. create   b. avoid   c. find out

In their *euphoria,* the fans of the winning team danced in the stadium aisles and chanted victory songs, until their intense joy was dampened by a sudden downpour.

Euphoria means
a. intense joy   b. hurry   c. disappointment

In the sentences above, the *context*—the words surrounding the unfamiliar word—provides clues to each word's meaning. You may have guessed from the context that a *torrid* climate is an extremely hot and dry one, that *ascertain* means "find out," and that *euphoria* is "intense joy."

Using context clues to understand the meaning of unfamiliar words will help you in several ways:

- It will save you time when reading. You will not have to stop to look up words in the dictionary. (Of course, you won't always be able to understand a word from its context, so you should always have a dictionary nearby as you read.)

- After you figure out the meaning of the same word more than once through its context, it may become a part of your working vocabulary. You will therefore add to your vocabulary simply by reading thoughtfully.

- You will get a good sense of how a word is actually used, including its shades of meaning.

TYPES OF CONTEXT CLUES

There are four common types of context clues:

1   Examples

2   Synonyms

3   Antonyms

4   General Sense of the Sentence or Passage

In the following sections, you will read about and practice using each type. The practices will sharpen your skills in recognizing and using context clues. They will also help you add new words to your vocabulary.

1   Examples

If you are given *examples* of an unknown word, you can often figure out its meaning. To understand how this type of clue works, read the sentences below. An *italicized* word in each sentence is followed by examples that serve as context clues for that word. These examples, which are in **boldfaced** type, will help you figure out the meaning of each word. Circle the letter of each meaning you think is correct.

Note that examples are often introduced with such signal words and phrases as *including* and *such as*.

1.   *Nocturnal* creatures, such as **bats and owls**, have highly developed senses that enable them to function in the dark.

Nocturnal means
a. feathery   b. flying   c. active at night

2.   The *adverse* effects of this drug, including **dizziness, nausea, and headaches,** have caused it to be withdrawn from the market.

   Adverse means
   a. deadly   b. harmful   c. expensive

3.   Common *euphemisms* include **"final resting place"** (for *grave*), **"intoxicated"** (for *drunk*), **and "comfort station"** (for *toilet*).

   Euphemisms means
   a. unpleasant reactions   b. answers   c. substitutes for offensive terms

In the first sentence, the examples given of nocturnal creatures—bats and owls—may have helped you to guess that nocturnal creatures are those that are active at night, since bats and owls do come out at night. In the second sentence, the unpleasant side effects mentioned are clues to the meaning of *adverse*, which is "harmful." Finally, as the examples in sentence three indicate, *euphemisms* means "substitutes for offensive terms."

➤ *Practice 1*

In each of the sentences below, underline the examples of the italicized word. Then circle the letter of the meaning of the word in italics.

1.   The *meager* meal, consisting of only a spoonful of rice and a few beans, was the most the neglected boy had eaten all day.

   Meager means
   a. small   b. sweet   c. filling

2.   Some mentally ill people have *bizarre* ideas. For instance, they may think the TV is talking to them or that others can steal their thoughts.

   Bizarre means
   a. very strange   b. realistic   c. creative

3.   There are several common *gambits* used in singles bars, such as "What sign are you?" "How do you like this place?" and "You remind me of someone."

   Gambits means
   a. questions   b. conversation starters   c. steps

4.   Since my grandfather retired, he has developed such *avocations* as gardening and long-distance bike riding.

   Avocations means
   a. hobbies   b. vacations   c. jobs

5.   In biology class today, the teacher discussed such *anomalies* as two heads and webbed toes.

Anomalies means

a. groups   b. illnesses   c. abnormalities

2 Synonyms

Context clues are often found in the form of *synonyms*: words that mean the same as the unknown word. Synonyms may be purposely included by an author to help readers understand a less familiar word. In such cases, the synonyms are usually set off by special punctuation within the sentence, such as commas, dashes, or parentheses; and they may be introduced by *or* ("Nuptials, or weddings, . . .") and *that is* ("Woolies, that is, knitted wool underwear . . ."). A synonym may also appear anywhere in a sentence as a restatement of the meaning of the unknown word.

In each of the following sentences, the word to be defined is italicized. Underline the synonym for the italicized word in each sentence.

1.   Are you *averse*—opposed to—the decision?

2.   His *naivete*, or innocence, was obvious.

3.   The salesperson tried to *assuage* the angry customer's feelings, but there was no way to soothe her. (*Hint:* Here, a synonym of the italicized word is used later in the sentence to restate the word's meaning.)

You should have underlined "opposed to" as a synonym for *averse*, "innocence" as a synonym for *naivete*, and "soothe" as a synonym for *assuage*. (Remember, by the way, that you can turn to your dictionary whenever you want to learn to pronounce an unfamiliar word.)

➤ *Practice 2*

Each sentence below includes a word or phrase that is a synonym of the italicized word. Underline the synonym of the italicized word in each case.

1.   My friend Julie is a great *procrastinator*—she's a person who habitually postpones doing things, from household chores to homework.

2.   Because my father had advised me to *scrutinize* the lease, I took time to carefully examine all the fine print.

3.   The presidential candidate vowed to discuss *pragmatic* solutions to the nation's problems; the American people, he claimed, want practical answers, not empty theory.

4. A common public-health measure is *quarantine*, or isolating infected patients to prevent their diseases from spreading.

5. Father Gordon decided to lecture on *euthanasia* to the Nurses' Association because there is a great deal of interest in mercy-killing these days.

3 Antonyms

Antonyms—words and phrases that mean the opposite of a word—are also useful as context clues. Antonyms are often signaled by words and phrases such as *however, but, yet, on the other hand*, and *in contrast*.

In the sentences below, underline the words that mean the *opposite* of the italicized words; then circle the letter of the meaning of the word in italics.

1. My sister Kathy is lively and outgoing; however, I am rather *introverted*.

   Introverted means
   a. friendly and helpful   b. quiet and withdrawn   c. strong and athletic

2. Religions in America are not *static*, but changing, especially in this period of shifting values.

   Static means
   a. unchanging   b. unknown   c. shifting

3. Many people have pointed out the harmful effects that a working mother may have on the family, yet there are many *salutary* effects as well.

   Salutary means
   a. well-known   b. beneficial   c. hurtful

In the first sentence, *introverted* is the opposite of "lively and outgoing"; *introverted* means "quiet and withdrawn." In the second sentence, the opposite of *static* is "changing"; *static* means "unchanging." Last, *salutary effects* are the opposite of "harmful effects"; *salutary* means "beneficial."

➤ Practice 3

Each sentence below includes a word or phrase that is an antonym of the italicized word. Underline the antonym of the italicized word in each case. Then, based on these clues, circle the letter of the meaning of the word in italics.

1. He was born to a family that possessed great wealth, but he died in *indigence*.

   Definition of *indigence*:
   a. a hospital   b. an accident   c. poverty

2.   Many politicians do not give *succinct* answers to questions, but long, vague ones.

   Succinct means
   a. brief and to the point   b. accurate   c. complete

3.   "I've caught several students *surreptitiously* checking answer sheets during my exams," said the professor. "However, until today I never saw one openly lay out a cheat sheet on his desk."

   Surreptitiously means
   a. legally   b. secretly   c. loudly

4.   In the early days of automobile manufacturing, *stringent* laws controlled motorists' speed; in contrast, the laws designed to protect consumers from faulty products were extremely weak.

   Stringent means
   a. informal   b. not effective   c. strong

5.   While Irma's house is decorated plainly, her clothing is very *flamboyant*.

   Flamboyant means
   a. inexpensive   b. flashy   c. washable

4   General Sense of the Sentence or Passage

Sometimes it takes a bit more detective work to puzzle out the meaning of an unfamiliar word. In such cases, you must draw conclusions based on the information given with the word. Asking yourself questions about the passage may help you make a fairly accurate guess about the meaning of the unfamiliar word.

Each of the sentences below is followed by a question. Think about the answer to each question, and then circle the letter of the meaning you think is correct.

1.   A former employee, *irate* over having been fired, broke into the plant and deliberately wrecked several machines. (What would be the employee's state of mind?)

   Irate means
   a. relieved   b. very angry   c. undecided

2.   Despite the *proximity* of Ron's house to his sister's, he rarely sees her. (What about Ron's house would make it surprising that he didn't see his sister more often?)

   Proximity means
   a. similarity   b. nearness   c. superiority

3. The car wash we organized to raise funds was a *fiasco*, for it rained all day.
    (How successful would a car wash be on a rainy day?)

    Fiasco means
    a. great financial success   b. welcome surprise   c. complete disaster

The first sentence provides enough evidence for you to guess that *irate* means
"very angry." *Proximity* in the second sentence means "nearness." And a *fiasco*
is a complete disaster. (You may not hit on the exact dictionary definition of a
word by using context clues, but you will often be accurate enough to make
good sense of what you are reading.)

➤ Practice 4

Try to answer the question that follows each item below. Then use logical
guesses based on each answer to help you circle the letter of the meaning you
think is correct.

1. Larry didn't want to take the time to tell Anne the entire plot of the movie
    so far, so he just gave her the *gist* of the story.
    (What kind of information would Larry give Anne?)

    Gist means
    a. ending   b. title   c. main idea

2. The lizard was so *lethargic* that I wasn't sure if it was alive or dead. It
    didn't even blink.
    (How active is this lizard?)

    Lethargic means
    a. green   b. inactive   c. big

3. After the accident, I was angered when the other driver told the police
    officer a complete *fabrication* about what happened. He made it seem that
    I was the only person at fault.
    (How truthful was the other driver's information?)

    Fabrication means
    a. lie   b. description   c. confession

4. The public knows very little about the *covert* activities of CIA spies.
    (What kind of activities would the CIA spies be involved in that the public
    wouldn't know much about?)

    Covert means
    a. public   b. secret   c. family

5. Whether or not there is life in outer space is an *enigma*. We will never know for sure until we are capable of space travel or aliens actually land on our planet.
   (What would we call something to which we have no answer?)

   Enigma means
   a. reason   b. certainty   c. mystery

A NOTE ON TEXTBOOK DEFINITIONS

You don't always have to use context clues or the dictionary to find definitions. Very often, textbook authors provide definitions of important terms. They usually follow a definition with one or more examples to ensure that you understand the word being defined. Here is a short textbook passage that includes a definition and example:

> People do not always satisfy their needs directly; sometimes they use a substitute object. Use of a substitute is known as **displacement**. This is the process that takes place, for instance, when you control your impulse to yell at your boss and then go home and yell at the first member of your family who is unlucky enough to cross your path.

Textbook authors, then, often do more than provide context clues: they define a word and provide examples as well. When they take the time to define and illustrate a word, you should assume that the material is important enough to learn.

More about textbook definitions and examples appears in the "Patterns of Organization" chapter on page 102.

➤ *Review Test 1*

A. Using context clues for help, circle the letter of the best meaning for each word in italics.

1. *Nepotism* is commonplace where I work: the boss's daughter is vice-president of the company, her husband runs the order department, and their son has just started working in the warehouse.

   a. Good managerial practice   c. Arguments among employees
   b. Favoritism to relatives   d. Confusion among management

2. The students thought the professor's explanation of his course requirements was *nebulous*, but no one asked him to make himself clear.

   a. vague   c. fascinating
   b. boring   d. brief

3. The bank robber was apparently so *nondescript* that none of the witnesses could think of any special characteristics that might identify him.

   a. poorly disguised   c. memorable
   (b.) lacking distinctive qualities   d. cruel

4. The lake water was so *murky* that my hand seemed to vanish when I dipped it only a few inches under the surface.

   a. cold   (c.) dark
   b. dangerous   d. inviting

5. During the Revolutionary War, the English hired German *mercenaries* to help fight the Americans.

   a. hired soldiers   c. rebels
   (b.) traitors   d. recent immigrants

B. Using context clues for help, write the definition for each word in italics. Choose from the definitions in the box below. Each definition will be used once.

provided ✓	doubtful ✓	discouraged ✓
out of the ordinary ✓	nag ✓	

6. Bruce is quite *eccentric*. For example, he lives in a circular house and drives to work on a motorcycle, in a three-piece suit.

   Definition of *eccentric*: ___out of the ordinary___

7. Nature has *endowed* hummingbirds with the ability to fly backward.

   Definition of *endowed*: ___provided___

8. Opponents of the death penalty say it has never actually *deterred* anyone from committing murder.

   Definition of *deterred*: ___discouraged___

9. Around the age of two or three, small children like to *badger* their parents with endless questions beginning with the word "why."

   Definition of *badger*: ___nag___

10. While four-year-old Rita claimed she was going to stay up until midnight on New Year's Eve, her parents were *dubious* of her ability to stay awake that late.

    Definition of *dubious*: ___doubtful___

➤ Review Test 2

A. Five words are italicized in the paragraphs below. Write the definition for each italicized word, choosing from the definitions in the box. (Three definitions will be left over.)

lacking ✓	admired	guilty ✓
looked down upon ✓	clever plans ✓	rain
directed	animals that hunt ✓	

Fire extended humans' geographical boundaries by allowing them to travel into regions that were previously too cold to explore. It also kept *predators* away, allowing early humans to sleep securely. Fire, in fact, has been a significant factor in human development and progress in many ways. Obvious benefits of fire are its uses in cooking and in hunting. Probably even more important, however, is that learning to control fire allowed people to change the very rhythm of their lives. Before fire, the human daily cycle coincided with the rising and setting of the sun. With fire, though, man gained time to think and talk about the day's events and to prepare *stratagems* for coping with tomorrow.

1. Definition of *predators*: ___animals that hunt___

2. Definition of *stratagems*: ___clever plans___

Although mysteries and science fiction may seem like very different kinds of writing, the two forms share some basic similarities. First of all, both are action-*oriented*, emphasizing plot at the expense of character development. Possibly for this reason, both types of literature have been *scorned* by critics as being "mere entertainment" rather than "literature." But this attack is unjustified, for both mysteries and science fiction share a concern with moral issues. Science fiction often raises the question of whether or not scientific advances are of benefit to humanity. And a mystery story rarely ends without the *culpable* person being brought to justice.

3. Definition of *oriented*: ___directed___

4. Definition of *scorned*: ___looked down upon___

5. Definition of *culpable*: ___guilty___

B. Use context clues to figure out the meaning of the italicized word in each of the following sentences, and write your definition in the space provided.

6. When you're broke, you find that many things you thought were *indispensable* are not so necessary after all.

   Definition of *indispensable*: _things that can't be gotten rid of._

7. It's amazing that Rosalyn always appears *immaculate*, yet her apartment is often quite dirty.

   Definition of *immaculate*: _clean and neat_

8. When I spilled soda on Pablo's shirt—an action that was purely *inadvertent*—he refused to believe it was not intentional.

   Definition of *inadvertent*: _accidental_

9. I thought selling cosmetics door-to-door would be a *lucrative* part-time job, but in my first month I earned only twenty-nine dollars.

   Definition of *lucrative*: _worthy_

10. Doctors should *alleviate* the pain of terminally ill patients so that their final days are as comfortable as possible.

    Definition of *alleviate*: _relieve_

➤ Review Test 3

A. To review what you've learned in this chapter, complete each of the following sentences.

1. Often, a reader can figure out the meaning of a new word without using the dictionary—by paying attention to the word's _____.

2. One type of clue that helps readers figure out the meaning of a new word is the general sense of a _____.

3. In the sentence below, which type of context clue is used for the italicized word?

   a. example   b. antonym   c. synonym

   You can't take certain courses unless you've taken a *prerequisite*; for instance, you can't take Spanish Literature I unless you've taken Spanish III.

4. In the sentence below, which type of context clue is used for the italicized word?

    a. example   b. antonym   c. synonym

    There are thick pine forests at the foot of the mountain, but higher up, the trees become *sparse*.

5. Often when textbook authors introduce a new word, they provide you with

    a _____ and follow it with _____

    that help make the meaning of the word clear.

B. Here is a chance to apply the skill of understanding vocabulary in context to a full-length selection. Read the story below, which first appeared in *The National Observer*, and then answer the questions that follow.

Words to Watch

Following are some words in the reading that do not have strong context support. Each word is followed by the number of the paragraph in which it appears and its meaning there.

smudged (2): dirty with streaks or stains
boondocks (3): a rural region
maneuvers (3): military exercises
oblivious (7): unaware

NIGHT WATCH

Roy Popkin

The story began on a downtown Brooklyn street corner. An elderly man had   1
collapsed while crossing the street, and an ambulance rushed him to Kings County
Hospital. There, during his few returns to consciousness, the man repeatedly called
for his son.

From a smudged°, oft-read letter, an emergency-room nurse learned that the   2
son was a Marine stationed in North Carolina. Apparently, there were no other
relatives.

Someone at the hospital called the Red Cross office in Brooklyn, and a request   3
for the boy to rush to Brooklyn was relayed to the Red Cross director of the North
Carolina Marine Corps camp. Because time was short—the patient was dying—the
Red Cross man and officer set out in a jeep. They located the sought-after young man
wading through marshy boondocks° on maneuvers°. He was rushed to the airport in
time to catch the one plane that might enable him to reach his dying father.

It was mid-evening when the young Marine walked into the entrance lobby of   4
Kings County Hospital. A nurse took the tired, anxious serviceman to the bedside.

"Your son is here," she said to the old man. She had to repeat the words several   5
times before the patient's eyes opened. Heavily sedated because of the pain of his
heart attack, he dimly saw the young man in the Marine Corps uniform standing
outside the oxygen tent. He reached out his hand. The Marine wrapped his toughened
fingers around the old man's limp ones, squeezing a message of love and
encouragement. The nurse brought a chair, so the Marine could sit alongside the bed.

Nights are long in hospitals, but all through the night the young Marine sat   6
there in the poorly lighted ward, holding the old man's hand and offering words of
hope and strength. Occasionally, the nurse suggested that the Marine move away and
rest a while. He refused.

Whenever the nurse came into the ward, the Marine was there, oblivious° of   7
her and night noises of the hospital—the clanking of an oxygen tank, the laughter of
night-staff members exchanging greetings, the cries and moans and snores of other
patients. Now and then she heard him say a few gentle words. The dying man said
nothing, only held tightly to his son through most of the night.

Along toward dawn, the patient died. The Marine placed on the bed the lifeless   8
hand he had been holding, and went to tell the nurse. While she did what she had to
do, he smoked a cigarette—his first since he got to the hospital.

Finally, she returned to the nurse's station, where he was waiting. She started to   9
offer words of sympathy, but the Marine interrupted her. "Who was that man?" he
asked.

"He was your father," she answered, startled.   10

"No, he wasn't," the Marine replied. "I never saw him before in my life."   11

"Why didn't you say something when I took you to him?" the nurse asked.   12

"I knew right off there'd been a mistake, but I also knew he needed his son,   13
and his son just wasn't here. When I realized he was too sick to tell whether or not I
was his son, I figured he really needed me. So I stayed."

With that, the Marine turned and left the hospital. Two days later a routine   14
message came in from the North Carolina Marine Corps base informing the Brooklyn
Red Cross that the real son was on his way to Brooklyn for his father's funeral. It
turned out there had been two Marines with the same name and similar serial
numbers in the camp. Someone in the personnel office had pulled out the wrong
record.

But the wrong Marine had become the right son at the right time. And he   15
proved, in a uniquely human way, that there are people who care what happens to
their fellow man.

Vocabulary Questions

Use context clues to help you decide on the best definition for each italicized
word. Then circle the letter of each choice.

1. The word *relayed* in the sentence on the next page means
   a. hidden.
   b. passed along.
   c. made a gift.
   d. ignored.

Someone at the hospital called the Red Cross office in Brooklyn, and a request for the boy to rush to Brooklyn was relayed to the Red Cross director of the North Carolina Marine Corps camp. (Paragraph 3)

2. The words *enable him* in "He was rushed to the airport in time to catch the one plane that might enable him to reach his dying father" (paragraph 3) mean
   a. stop him.
   b. encourage him.
   c. know him.
   d. make him able.

3. The word *sedated* in the excerpt below means
   a. spoken loudly.
   b. wide awake.
   c. armed.
   d. drugged with a pain reliever.

"Your son is here," she said to the old man. She had to repeat the words several times before the patient's eyes opened. Heavily sedated because of the pain of his heart attack, he dimly saw the young man. . . . (Paragraph 5)

4. The word *limp* in "The Marine wrapped his toughened fingers around the old man's limp ones" (paragraph 5) means
   a. lacking strength and energy.
   b. equally tough.
   c. long.
   d. bleeding.

5. A clue to the meaning of *limp* in the sentence above is the antonym

   _____.

6. The word *startled* in the excerpt below means
   a. very pleased.
   b. with admiration.
   c. angry.
   d. surprised.

"Who was that man?" he asked. "He was your father," she answered, startled. (Paragraphs 9–10)

7. The word *dimly* in "She had to repeat the words several times before the patient's eyes opened. Heavily sedated because of the pain of his heart attack, he dimly saw the young man" (paragraph 5) means
   a. clearly.
   b. unclearly.
   c. rarely.
   d. often.

8. The words *uniquely human* in "he proved, in a uniquely human way, that there are people who care what happens to their fellow man" (paragraph 15) mean
   a. impossible for humans.
   b. scary to humans.
   c. done only by humans.
   d. sudden by human standards.

2

Main Ideas

Read the following paragraph:

> Many bosses share two weaknesses. First, they are often poor communicators. They tell people what to do and how and when to do it, without explaining the reasons for their rules, and they do not welcome feedback or questions. In addition, many bosses are not well-rounded people. Their jobs tend to be their lives, and they expect everybody who works for them to think and act the way they do. These bosses frown upon hearing that a family matter will keep an employee from working late, and they come out of their office looking irritated if there is too much talk or laughter during a coffee break.

More than any other skill, the key to good comprehension is recognizing the main idea. The basic question you must ask about any selection that you read is, "What is the main point the author is trying to make?" To answer such a question, it is often useful first to determine what topic is being discussed. In the above paragraph, for example, the topic is "many bosses"; the main idea about the topic "many bosses" is that they "share two weaknesses." The rest of the paragraph then supports that idea by detailing the two weaknesses.

The purpose of this and the following chapter is to give you a solid sense of the key parts in any communication: the *topic*, the *main idea* about the topic, and the *supporting details* that develop the main idea.

AN OVERVIEW: TOPIC, MAIN IDEA, SUPPORTING DETAILS

To fully understand any selection that you read, it is important to find the main idea and its supporting details. One way to find the main idea is to use a two-step process:

1 Find the topic.

2 Then find the writer's primary point about that topic. You will now have the main idea.

Any selection that you read will be about a particular *topic*. The topic is a selection's general subject. The topic of a paragraph, for example, might be "My Roommate."

Topic: My Roommate

In contrast, the *main idea* is the writer's primary point *about* the subject. The main idea of the paragraph on the roommate might be that the roommate is messy.

Topic: My Roommate
Main Idea: My roommate is messy.

The rest of the paragraph might be a few sentences that give examples of the messiness. Imagine that you have a sloppy roommate. Write down in the space below two examples of his or her behavior:

Topic: My Roommate
Main Idea: My roommate is messy.
Supporting Details:

_____

_____

Compare what you have written with my experience. I had a messy dorm roommate in my first year at college. He threw his dirty laundry under his bed and let it stay there for weeks. He brought with him to school his collection of a hundred-plus copies of *Playboy* magazines, and they were everywhere in the room: on the bed, chairs, his desk, chest of drawers, the floor. He also piled on any horizontal surface his clothes, empty soda cans, notebooks, crumpled pizza boxes, letters, newspapers, and so on. He was a nice enough guy who did not quite have his life under control, and he disappeared from school by mid-semester.

I could easily write a paragraph about my roommate. The topic would be my roommate, the main idea would be that he was messy, and the evidence would be supporting details such as the ones I provide above. My paragraph would be typical of paragraphs in general: it would have a topic, a main idea about the topic, and details that develop the main idea.

Note that in longer selections made up of many paragraphs, such as articles or textbook chapters, there is an overall main idea called the *central point* or *thesis*. There may also be a number of intermediate and smaller main ideas within a long selection.

This chapter focuses on finding the main idea in a paragraph, and the next chapter focuses on identifying supporting details. Once you can identify main ideas and details on the level of the paragraph, you can begin to identify them as well in the longer selections that are included in this book.

MORE ON USING THE TOPIC TO FIND THE MAIN IDEA

Remember that the *topic* is the subject of a selection. It is a general term that can usually be expressed in a few words. Textbooks typically give the overall topic of each chapter in the title of the chapter; they also provide many topics and subtopics in boldface headings within the chapter. Most magazine and journal articles, as well, give you the topic in the title of the piece.

To find the topic of a selection for which there is no title, ask the simple question, "Who or what is the selection about?" Ask this question as you read carefully the paragraph that follows. Then write, on the line below, what you think the topic is.

Topic: _____

Extrasensory perception, or ESP, is an area that fascinates people. However, ESP is not documented by any convincing evidence. For instance, it would seem that ESP would be an excellent way of winning at games of chance, such as are played at gambling casinos. But casino owners in Las Vegas and Atlantic City report no problem with "psychics" winning great sums of money. For another thing, although great publicity is generated when a psychic helps police solve a crime, such a thing rarely happens. Much more often, psychic tips are worthless, and a case is solved through traditional police work. And while audiences may be amazed at the feats of "mind readers," there is rarely any ESP at work there. Instead, mind readers use simple psychological tricks to exploit their audiences' willingness to believe.

The first sentence suggests that the topic of this paragraph is extrasensory perception. And as you read the paragraph, you see that everything has to do with ESP. Thus your first impression in this case was correct—the topic is ESP. Once you have the topic, your next step is to ask, "What is the author's primary point about the topic?" The answer will be the main idea of the paragraph. Read the ESP paragraph again, and then write down in the space below the author's point about ESP:

Main Idea: _____

The main idea about the topic, ESP, is that it is not documented by any convincing evidence. Here as in other paragraphs, the main idea is a general idea that summarizes what the entire paragraph is about. In other words, the main idea is an "umbrella" statement under which the other material in the paragraph fits. In this case, the other material is in the form of several examples that back up the main idea. The parts of the paragraph can be shown as follows:

Topic: ESP

Main Idea: The evidence for ESP has not been convincing.

Supporting Details:

1. There have been no reports of "psychics" winning great sums at casinos.

2. Most crimes are solved by police work, not psychic tips.

3. Mind readers use simple psychological tricks, not psychic ability.

The following activities will sharpen your sense of the difference between the topic of a selection and the main idea of that selection.

➤ *Practice 1*

Circle the letter of the correct topic of each paragraph. (To find the topic, remember to ask yourself, "Who or what is the paragraph about?") Then circle the letter of the main idea—the author's main point about the topic.

1. According to one scientist who has studied aging, there are ways to remain healthy in old age. The key, he believes, is to continue to find mental and physical challenges. In addition, he recommends that people stick to a balanced, low-cholesterol diet and a reasonable exercise program throughout their lives. He also cautions people about the dangers of smoking.

    Topic:
    a. Science
    b. Mental and Physical Challenges

    c. Health in Old Age
    d. A Balanced Diet

    Main Idea:
    a. A balanced diet helps the elderly stay healthy.
    b. According to one researcher, health in old age can be achieved in various ways.
    c. Science includes the study of aging.
    d. A scientist who has studied aging cautions people about the dangers of smoking.

2.   A good way to find a part-time job is to create one yourself. Two high school students, for example, realized that many people prefer not to leave their pets at a kennel. Those students started a business of feeding and exercising pets while their owners are on vacation. And a housewife runs her own pet-taxi service, for which she drives people's caged pets to the vet or the kennel.

Topic:
(a.) Finding a Part-time Job   c. Animal Care
b. Student Jobs   d. A Pet-Taxi Service

Main Idea:
a. Many people work in animal care.
b. One good part-time job is running a pet-taxi service.
c. Many students as well as people in general need part-time jobs.
(d.) One way to get a part-time job is to create one that fills a need.

3.   Some people believe that if you spill salt, you must toss a pinch of salt over your left shoulder "into the Devil's face" in order to avoid bad luck. That is just one of many superstitions that cover everyday events. Others are the beliefs that umbrellas should not be opened indoors and that people should leave a friend's house by the same door they entered.

Topic:
a. Spilling Salt   (c.) Superstitions
b. Umbrellas   d. Bad Luck

Main Idea:
a. People are afraid of bad luck.
b. Some people consider opening an umbrella indoors to be bad luck.
(c.) Many superstitions are about everyday events.
d. According to one superstition, if you spill salt, you should toss a pinch of salt over your shoulder.

4.   Instinct, rather than learning, is the strongest influence on animals' behavior. One common example of instinct is the spider's spinning of its intricate web. No one teaches a spider how to spin; its inborn instinct allows it to accomplish the task. Another example of instinctive behavior is the salmon's struggle to swim upstream to lay its eggs. It would be much easier for the salmon to follow the current downstream, but instinct overrides all other considerations.

Topic:
a. Learned behavior   c. The salmon's upstream struggle
b. Spiders   (d.) Instinct

Main Idea:
a. One type of behavior is learned behavior.
b. Spiders spin intricate webs without being taught to do so.
c. Salmon swim upstream to lay their eggs.
d. Instinct is the strongest influence on animal behavior.

THE TOPIC SENTENCE

In a paragraph, authors often give readers the main idea in a single sentence called the *topic sentence.* For example, look again at the paragraph on bosses:

> Many bosses share two weaknesses. First, they are often poor communicators. They tell people what to do and how and when to do it, without explaining the reasons for their rules, and they do not welcome feedback or questions. In addition, many bosses are not well-rounded people. Their jobs tend to be their lives, and they expect everybody who works for them to think and act the way they do. These bosses frown upon hearing that a family matter will keep an employee from working late, and they come out of their office looking irritated if there is too much talk or laughter during a coffee break.

As we have already seen, the topic of this paragraph is "many bosses," and the primary point about bosses is that they "share two weaknesses." Both the topic and the point about the topic are expressed in the opening sentence, which is therefore the topic sentence. All the sentences that follow provide details about the weaknesses which bosses share. The parts of the paragraph can be shown as follows:

Topic: Many bosses

Main Idea (expressed in the topic sentence): Many bosses share two weaknesses.

Supporting Details:
1. They are poor communicators
2. They are not well-rounded people

Now read the paragraph on the next page and try to find the topic sentence that states its main idea. Test a statement that you think is the main idea by asking, "Is this statement supported by all or most of the other material in the paragraph?" Write the number of the sentence you choose in the space provided. Then read the explanation that follows.

Topic sentence: _____

> ¹Bad health habits can persist for a number of reasons. ²One is childhood fears; if people are afraid as children to go to the dentist, they might avoid dental checkups when they are adults. ³In addition, poor health habits mày persist if they are defense mechanisms. ⁴An overweight teenager, for example, could be holding onto that baby fat to avoid the pressure of competing for dates. ⁵It's easier to blame loneliness on twenty extra pounds than to slim down and face potential rejection. ⁶A third reason is low self-esteem. ⁷People who smoke or subsist on junk foods may simply not care enough about themselves to go to the trouble of improving their habits.

After thinking about the paragraph, you may have decided that the first sentence is the topic sentence. If so, you should have checked yourself by asking, "Does the other material in the paragraph support the idea that 'Bad health habits can persist for a number of reasons?'" In fact, the rest of the paragraph does provide three reasons why bad health habits may persist. The specific details about childhood fears, defense mechanisms, and low self-esteem all develop the general idea expressed in the first sentence. By asking and answering a basic question, you have made it clear that the first sentence is indeed the topic sentence.

The important hint given above for finding the topic sentence and main idea is worth repeating: *Always test yourself on an idea you think is the main idea by asking the question, "Is this statement supported by all or most of the other material in the paragraph?"*

➤ Practice 2

This exercise will give you more practice in distinguishing between a topic (the general subject), a main idea (the primary point being made about the subject), and the specific ideas that support and develop the main idea. Each group of statements on the next page includes one topic, one main idea (topic sentence), and two supporting ideas. In the space provided, label each item with one of the following:

T	(for *Topic*)
MI	(for *Main Idea, expressed in a topic sentence*)
SD	(for *Supporting Detail*)

Group 1

SD a. Teachers cause stress by asking children to copy and recopy their work until it is perfect.

SD b. The children are afraid of getting a low grade for their work.

T c. Children's fears of writing in school.

MI d. Children's fears of writing in school have several causes.

Group 2

SD a. The horned toad and the glass snake are both really lizards, and the crayfish isn't a fish, but a relative of the lobster.

T b. The names of some animals.

SD c. Neither the ring-tailed cat nor the civet cat are actually cats: the ring-tailed cat is related to the raccoon, and the civet cat is related to the mongoose.

MI d. Some animals' names are misleading.

Group 3

MI a. Antibiotics have helped cure children of certain infectious diseases.

T b. Childhood diseases that used to be fatal.

SD c. Better hygiene has helped to control infectious diseases from spreading.

SD d. Many childhood diseases that used to be fatal are now almost unknown in the United States because of scientific advances.

Group 4

T a. How vitamin C can cause scurvy.

SD b. When a person takes large doses of vitamin C, the body speeds up its process of eliminating the excess.

MI c. Taking large amounts of vitamin C and quitting suddenly can cause scurvy, a vitamin-deficiency disease.

SD d. The body continues to rid itself of the vitamin for some time even after the large dose is discontinued, and a shortage results.

LOCATIONS OF THE TOPIC SENTENCE

In two of the paragraphs considered in this chapter, the topic sentence has been the first sentence of the paragraph: "Many bosses share two weaknesses" and "Bad health habits can persist for a number of reasons." That is a common pattern, but not the only one. Topic sentences may also appear within the paragraph. For example, the topic sentence of the ESP paragraph ("However, ESP is not documented by any convincing evidence") is the second sentence. Topic sentences may also appear at the very end of a paragraph. Or they may even appear twice—at the beginning and the end.

Within a Paragraph

```
Introductory Detail
Topic Sentence
Supporting Detail
Supporting Detail
Supporting Detail
```

When the topic sentence appears somewhere *within* a paragraph, it is preceded by one or more introductory sentences that may relate the main idea to the previous paragraph, arouse the reader's interest, or give background for the main idea. Here is an example of a paragraph in which the topic sentence is somewhere in the middle. Try to find it, and then write its number in the space provided. Then read the explanation that follows.

Topic sentence: _____

> [1]Many of us are annoyed by telephone solicitors who call us day and night, trying to sell us everything from magazine subscriptions to vacation homes. [2]These electronic intruders don't seem to care how much they are inconveniencing us and refuse to take "no" for an answer. [3]However, these nuisance callers can be stopped if we take charge of the conversation. [4]As soon as one of them asks if we are Mr. or Ms. X, we should respond, "Yes, and are you a telephone solicitor?" [5]This technique puts them on the defensive. [6]We then have an opening to say that we don't accept solicitations over the phone, only through the mail. [7]This puts a quick end to the conversation.

If you thought the third sentence gives the main idea, you were correct. The two sentences before the topic sentence introduce the problem; the topic sentence then gives the writer's main idea, which is that we can stop nuisance callers from going on by taking charge of the conversation. The rest of the paragraph develops that idea.

End of a Paragraph

```
Supporting Detail
Supporting Detail
Supporting Detail
Supporting Detail
Topic Sentence
```

When the topic sentence is at the end of a paragraph, the previous sentences build up to the main idea. Here is an example of a paragraph in which the topic sentence comes last.

A study at one prison showed that owning a pet can change a hardened prison inmate into a more caring person. Another study discovered that senior citizens, both those living alone and those in nursing homes, became more interested in life when they were given pets to care for. Even emotionally disturbed children have been observed to smile and react with interest if there is a cuddly kitten or puppy to hold. **Animals, then, can be a means of therapy for many kinds of individuals.**

Beginning and End of a Paragraph

```
Topic Sentence
Supporting Detail
Supporting Detail
Supporting Detail
Topic Sentence
```

Even though paragraphs have only one main idea, they may include two topic sentences, with each providing the main idea in different words. In such cases, the topic sentences are usually at the beginning and the end. In these cases, the author has chosen to introduce the main idea at the start of the paragraph and then emphasize it by restating it in other words at the end. Such is the case in the following paragraph.

We are on our way to becoming a cashless, checkless society, a trend that began with the credit card. Now some banks are offering "debit cards" instead of credit cards. The costs of purchases made with these cards are deducted from the holder's bank account instead of being added to a monthly bill. And checking accounts, which are mainly used for paying bills, are going electronic. Now some people can make computer transactions over their pushbutton phones to pay bills by transferring money from their account to the account of whomever they owe. **Soon we may be able to conduct most of our business without signing a check or actually seeing the money we earn and spend.**

Note that the main idea of the first sentence of this paragraph—that "we are on our way to becoming a cashless, checkless society"—is restated in other words in the final sentence.

➤ Practice 3

The topic sentences of the following paragraphs appear at different locations. Identify each topic sentence by filling in its sentence number in the space provided. In the one case where the paragraph has a topic sentence at both the beginning and the end, write in both sentence numbers.

A.   ¹Serious depression, as opposed to the fleeting kind we all feel at times, has several warning signs. ²One symptom of depression is a change in sleep patterns—either sleeplessness or sleeping too much. ³Another sign is abnormal eating patterns; a person either may begin to eat a great deal or may almost stop eating. ⁴Finally, a general feeling of hopelessness may signal depression. ⁵People feel indifferent to their families and jobs and may begin to think that life is not worth living.

Topic sentence(s): __1__

B.   ¹School officials complain about vandalism that leaves classrooms wrecked and damages expensive equipment. ²Teachers complain about the low salaries they get for their difficult and important jobs. ³And parents complain that their children's test scores are dropping, that their children can't read or do math. ⁴The problems within our school systems are varied and affect almost everyone involved.

Topic sentence(s): __4__

C.   ¹Every thirty-seven seconds, a car is stolen somewhere in the United States. ²Although this statistic is frightening, it is possible for drivers to prevent car theft if they take a few simple precautions. ³When they leave their cars, they should lock all valuables in the trunk or glove compartment to avoid tempting a thief to break in. ⁴Parking in the middle of the block on a busy, well-lighted street will deter would-be thieves. ⁵The most obvious precaution, of course, is always to lock the car and take the keys—even if the driver is stopping for just a minute. ⁶One out of every five stolen cars was left unlocked with the keys in the ignition.

Topic sentence(s): __2__

D.   ¹One of the most significant factors in selling a product is how it is packaged. ²When Stuart Hall Company, which manufactures notebooks and paper products for students, realized its sales were declining because fewer children were being born, it decided to change its products' appearance. ³So, beginning in 1968, the company replaced its plain tablets with colored paper and decorated the covers of its notebooks with the Pink Panther and other cartoon characters. ⁴Students loved the new designs, and sales soared. ⁵Packaging, therefore, can be a method of solving marketing problems.

Topic sentence(s): ___⋀___

Topic Sentences That Cover More Than One Paragraph

At times you will find that a topic sentence does double duty—it provides the main idea for more than one paragraph. This occurs when an author considers the development of the main idea to be too lengthy for one paragraph. He or she then breaks up the material into one or more added paragraphs to make it easier to read.

See if you can find and write down the number of the topic sentence for the paragraphs below. They are taken from an essay on factors involved in highway accidents. Then read the explanation that follows.

Topic sentence: _____

¹In addition to poor highway and automobile design, people's attitudes about driving also contribute to the high rate of traffic accidents. ²Some people persist in believing that they can drink and be alert drivers. ³Yet alcohol is estimated to be a factor in at least half of all fatal highway accidents. ⁴Refusing or forgetting to wear safety belts also increases fatalities. ⁵A negative attitude about wearing seat belts is inconsistent with statistics showing that the chances of being seriously hurt or dying in a car accident are greater when a seat belt is not worn.

⁶Another potentially deadly attitude is the point of view that the best driving is fast driving. ⁷Again, statistics contradict this attitude—fast driving is more likely to be deadly driving. ⁸After the speed limit was lowered in 1973 to fifty-five miles per hour, traffic fatalities fell significantly. ⁹Evidence on speed limits in other countries is just as telling. ¹⁰Where high-speed driving is permitted, a higher rate of accidents occurs.

After you read the first paragraph, it becomes clear that sentence 1 includes the main idea: "people's attitudes about driving also contribute to the high rate of traffic accidents." Sentences 2 and 3 deal with the attitude of those who feel that drinking does not interfere with driving. Sentences 4 and 5 deal with not wearing seat belts.

By beginning with the words "another potentially deadly attitude," the first sentence of the next paragraph tells us that it will continue to develop the topic sentence of the previous paragraph. The author has simply chosen to break the subject down into two smaller paragraphs rather than include all the information in one long paragraph. This relationship between the two paragraphs can be seen clearly in the following outline:

Main Idea: Some attitudes about driving contribute to traffic accidents.

1. Drinking does not interfere with driving.
2. Seat belts are not important.
3. Good driving is fast driving.

IMPLIED MAIN IDEAS

Sometimes a selection lacks a topic sentence, but that does not mean it lacks a main idea. The author has simply decided to let the details of the selection suggest the main idea. You must figure out what that implied main idea is by deciding upon the point of all the details. For example, read the following paragraph.

> In ancient times, irrational behavior was considered the result of demons and evil spirits taking possession of a person. Later, the Greeks looked upon irrational behavior as a physical problem—caused by an imbalance of body fluids called "humors"—or by displacement of an organ. In the highly superstitious Middle Ages, the theory of possession by demons was revived. It reached a high point again in the witch hunts of eighteenth-century Europe and America. Only in the last one hundred years did true medical explanations of mental illness gain wide acceptance.

You can see that no sentence in the paragraph is a good "umbrella" statement that covers all the others. We can decide on the main idea by considering all the details and asking, "What is the topic of this paragraph?" (in other words, "Who or what is this paragraph about?"). Once we have the topic in mind, we can ask, "What is the primary point the author is trying to make about that topic?" When we think we know the main point, we can test it out by asking, "Does all or most of the material in the paragraph support this idea?"

In the paragraph above, all of the details are about mental illness, so that must be the topic. And what is the general idea all the details are making about mental illness? The details show that people have explained mental illness in many different ways over the years. Although this idea is not stated, you can see that it is a broad enough summary to include all the other material in the paragraph—it is the main idea.

Now read the paragraph below, and see if you can pick out which of the four statements that follow it expresses the main idea. Circle the letter of the statement you choose, and then read the explanation that follows.

More and more commuters are forming car-pools to save money in gas, tolls, and wear and tear on their cars. Also, the special (and often faster) lanes many expressways provide for cars with three or more passengers during the rush hours can make the commute shorter and more hassle-free. Finally, car-pooling can reduce the boredom of the daily drive back and forth to work. Members who are not driving can talk, eat breakfast, read the paper, or get a head start on the day's work.

a. Car-pooling saves commuters money.
b. Car-pooling can mean shorter, easier commuter rides.
c. Everyone should join a car-pool.
d. There are several reasons that more commuters are forming car-pools.

As we begin to read this paragraph, we might think the first sentence is the topic sentence. If that were the main idea, however, then the details in the paragraph would have to be about the savings in money. Such details might focus on how much money can be saved by buying less gas, sharing tolls, and saving on the wear and tear of cars. But as we continue to read, we find that the paragraph, instead, goes on to give more reasons for people car-pooling, and so answer *a* is incorrect—it is too narrow to be the main idea.

Answer *b* is also too narrow to be the main idea—it also covers only a single reason for forming car-pools.

Answer *c* is incorrect because the details of the paragraph do not include any judgment about what people should do.

Answer *d* is a correct statement of the main idea. The phrase "several reasons that more commuters are forming car-pools" is a general reference to the three specific reasons listed in the paragraph: 1) Car-pooling saves money, 2) Car-pooling can make for a shorter, easier ride, and 3) Car-pool members who aren't driving can use the time riding to work to do something else.

➤ *Practice 4*

The following paragraphs have unstated main ideas, and each is followed by four sentences. In each case, circle the letter of the sentence that best expresses the unstated main idea.

Remember to consider carefully all of the details and ask yourself, "Who or what is the paragraph about?" Once you discover the topic of the paragraph, ask, "What is the author's main point about the topic?" Then test your answer by asking, "Does all or most of the material in the paragraph support this idea?"

1. One misconception about exercise is that if women lift weights, they will develop large muscles. Without male hormones, however, women cannot increase their muscle bulk as much as a man's. Another myth about exercise is that it increases the appetite. Actually, regular exercise stabilizes the blood sugar level and prevents hunger pains. Some people also think that a few minutes of exercise a day or one session a week is enough, but at least three solid workouts a week are needed for muscular and cardiovascular fitness.

    a. Women who lift weights cannot become as muscular as men.
    b. There are several myths about exercise.
    c. Exercise is beneficial to everyone.
    d. People use many different excuses to avoid exercising.

2. Since anti-smoking campaigns made teens aware of the risks of smoking, the percentage of teens smoking has dropped from 28 to 20 percent over the last ten years. Additionally, in schools where students have access to health clinics which provide birth control information and devices, pregnancy rates have declined by 30 percent. Furthermore, another study demonstrated that students in schools with comprehensive health education were less likely to use alcohol, to try drugs, or to attempt suicide.

    a. If more schools would conduct anti-smoking campaigns, the number of teens smoking would greatly decline.
    b. Evidence suggests that health education programs have a favorable effect on teen behavior.
    c. Health education clinics are a positive influence on how people of all ages take care of themselves.
    d. One study found that students in schools with comprehensive health education were less likely to use drugs or to attempt suicide.

3. The work homemakers do is essential to the economy. The estimated value of the cleaning, cooking, nursing, shopping, child care, home maintenance, money management, errands, entertaining, and other services homemakers perform has been estimated at equal to roughly one-fourth of the gross national product. In fact, the Commerce Department's Bureau of Economic Analysis has proposed a revision of the gross national product that would take into account the value of the homemaker's services. But homemaking is not formal employment that brings money or prestige. No financial compensation is associated with this position, and the *Dictionary of Occupational Titles* places mothering and homemaking skills in the lowest category of skills, lower than the occupation of "dog trainer."

    a. We no longer value the work done by homemakers.

    b. Housewives should receive salaries for their work.

    (c) Because homemaking is unpaid labor, its true value is often ignored.

    d. It's better to be a dog trainer than a homemaker.

Putting Implied Main Ideas Into Words

When you read, you often have to *infer*—figure out on your own—an author's unstated main idea, and no one will give you a list of statements to choose from. So you must be able to decide on implied main ideas on your own. The implied main idea that you come up with must not be too narrow to cover all the details in the paragraph, and it also must not be too broad. See if you can find the unstated main idea in the following paragraph. Then read the explanation below.

Some actors and rock stars are paid more than 100 times as much per year as school teachers are. We enjoy such performers, but certainly they do not do work that is many times more important than those who teach and guide our nation's students. Indeed, the reverse is true. As another example, professional athletes earn vastly more than firefighters. The first group may bring enjoyable diversion to our lives, but the latter literally saves lives. Again, there can be little doubt that the lower-paid group, firefighters, make the more important, indeed essential, contribution to society. As a last example, most high-fashion designers, who can make up to $50,000 for a single gown, far out-earn police officers. Now, we can easily live without sophisticated clothes (and probably about 99.9 percent of us do), but a society without law-enforcement officers would be unlivable for all of us.

What is the implied main idea of this paragraph? _____

_____

To find an implied main idea, consider all of the supporting details. In this case, the supporting details are three comparisons between highly paid occupations in our society and lesser paid, but more important occupations. The pairs of occupations are 1) rock stars and teachers, 2) professional athletes and firefighters, and 3) high-fashion designers and police officers. Thus the main idea is a general idea about these examples. One way of wording that general idea is: Workers in our society are not necessarily paid according to how important their work is.

➤ *Practice 5*

Write the implied main ideas of the following paragraphs in your own words.

1.   Many people think sleepwalkers drift about in a ghost-like way, with arms extended. The fact is most sleepwalkers walk around quite normally, though their eyes are usually closed or glazed. It is also commonly believed that one should never wake a sleepwalker. But it is advisable to do so if the walker seems in imminent danger—for example, going toward an open window or handling sharp objects. Another popular misconception is that sleepwalkers are not "really" sleeping or are only half-asleep. In fact, they are in a very deep state of sleep. A last commonly held belief is that sleepwalkers are easy to spot because they're in nighties or pajamas. Often this isn't true, because sleepwalkers can do routine tasks, including getting completely dressed.

Implied main idea: Common misconceptions about sleep walking

2.   Many people think that only children are lucky because of the material goods and attention they receive. But consider that only children have no privacy. Parents always feel entitled to know everything that's going on in an only child's life. Another drawback of only children is they lack the advantages that children with brothers and sisters have. They can never blame a sibling for something that goes wrong, or ask for a privilege that an older brother or sister was given earlier. In addition, only children miss the companionship of siblings. Not only can they be lonely, but they may have trouble making friends later in life because they never learned to get along with a brother or sister.

Implied main idea: the cons of being an only child

3.   After a stressful day it's restful to just put your feet up and enjoy a favorite program. And, of course, TV is entertaining for all ages. Videotaped movies, video games and special cable offerings, as well as regular network programming, provide a choice of amusements for the whole family. TV is deservedly famous for being our best source of up-to-the-minute news. When history is being made, we are often there, thanks to TV. Most importantly, television is a real educational tool. From *Sesame Street* to public television's nature programs, it teaches in a colorful and interesting fashion.

Implied main idea: pros of TV

➤ *Review Test 1*

Each of the following groups of items includes one topic, one main idea (topic sentence), and two supporting ideas. In the space provided, label each item with one of the following:

> T   (for *Topic*)
>
> MI   (for *Main Idea, expressed in a topic sentence*)
>
> SD   (for *Supporting Detail*)]

Group 1

SD a. Rubbing one's nose and eyes transfers viruses to the hands, which then contaminate whatever they touch, such as a table top or telephone.

SD b. Because the dried cold virus can live as long as three hours, you can pick it up long after the person with a cold is gone.

T c. The most likely way of catching a cold.

MI d. The most likely way to catch a cold is by touching an object that someone suffering from a cold has handled.

Group 2

MI a. Beethoven continued to compose even when he was completely deaf.

SD b. Sometimes he tried out passages at the piano to make sure they could be played, but his playing was agonizing to hear.

SD c. Every day at dawn, Beethoven began working at his desk, writing down the music he heard in his head.

T d. Beethoven.

Group 3

T a. Stretching exercises.

SD b. Limbering up after strenuous exertion reduces the risk of stiffness, soreness, and injury.

SD c. Slow, simple stretching before exercising make muscles more pliable so that vigorous activity becomes easier.

MI d. Stretching is important both before and after strenuous exercise.

Group 4

T____ a.   Love at first sight.

SP____ b.   Couples who knew each other only slightly but fell instantly in love found that their feelings for each other grew weaker instead of stronger.

MI____ c.   Love at first sight is a poor basis for a happy marriage, according to a study of one thousand married and divorced couples.

SD____ d.   The couples who considered themselves happily married reported that they were not powerfully attracted to their partners when they first met, but that they gradually found each other more attractive as they grew to know and understand each other.

➤ Review Test 2

A. The main idea (topic sentence) appears at various places in the following paragraphs. In one case, the main idea appears at both the beginning and the end of the paragraph. Identify the topic sentence of each paragraph by writing the correct sentence number in the space provided. Fill in two numbers for the paragraph in which the main idea appears twice.

1.   ¹People who are interested in physical fitness need not spend hundreds of dollars on fancy exercise equipment or health club memberships. ²Instead, they can get into good shape simply by climbing stairs. ³Stair-climbing helps in weight loss; just walking up and down two flights of stairs a day instead of riding an elevator will take off six pounds a year. ⁴Climbing stairs is also good for the heart and can prevent heart attacks. ⁵And frequent stair-climbing strengthens the muscles of the legs and buttocks.

Topic sentence(s): ____1____

2.   ¹For many couples, the first vacation they take together can either make or break their relationship. ²If they both have careers, the daily pressures of work and home responsibilities may have covered up sources of disagreement. ³However, without these distractions, the disagreements can surface. ⁴In addition, if one wants to splurge and the other prefers a no-frills camping trip, or if one is a neat packer and the other is disorganized, conflicts will certainly result. ⁵Unless both partners communicate, are willing to compromise, and remain flexible during the vacation, their first trip together may be their last.

Topic sentence(s): ____1, 5____

3.   ¹A series of crises punctuated the decade of the 1960's. ²At the beginning of the 1960's, the Cuban missile crisis brought America and the Soviet Union to the brink of nuclear war. ³Only after a nerve-racking week of uncertainty, when the Soviets backed down and agreed to remove their missiles from a base in Cuba, was the crisis resolved. ⁴The assassinations of political leaders also rocked the country; President Kennedy, Robert F. Kennedy, and Martin Luther King were all murdered within a few short years. ⁵Other crises that simmered and eventually boiled over in this decade were the civil-rights movement and the protest against the Vietnam War. ⁶The Watts riots, the underground terrorism of groups such as the Weathermen, and violent demonstrations at the 1968 political conventions were a few of the examples of the general sense of unrest.

Topic sentence(s): __1__

B. Circle the letter of the sentence that best expresses the implied main idea of paragraph 4 below. Then write out the implied main idea of paragraph 5.

4.   If you fear growing older, remember that Sigmund Freud published his first important work, on dream interpretation, at age 44; Henry Kissinger was appointed Secretary of State at 50; and Rachel Carson completed her classic book on environmental damage, *Silent Spring*, at 55. "If you continue reading, thinking and creating all of your life, your intelligence increases," says one medical researcher. The mental health of many people also tends to improve as they grow older. Young people often protect their feelings with such defenses as denial and impulsive actions. By middle age, we are more likely to use such constructive defenses as humor, altruism and creativity. Finally, age will make you more "yourself," as new or previously unexplored aspects of your personality emerge. As the actress Candice Bergen wrote in her autobiography, "It takes a long time to become a person."

   a. To keep your intelligence growing, continue reading, thinking and creating all of your life.
   b. Most people get better in all ways as they age.
   c. In several important ways, people get better as they get older.
   d. By middle age, people are less likely to protect their feelings with such defenses as denial and impulsive actions.

5.   People who wish to reduce the salt in their diets should read labels carefully, looking for telltale ingredients like sodium and monosodium glutamate (MSG). Also, they should avoid salt-coated snacks such as potato chips, pretzels, and corn chips. Canned fish should be drained to removed the salted liquid it is packed in. Finally, the salt shaker should be removed from the table and replaced with onion powder, garlic powder, herbs, or lemon juice to give food added taste.

Implied main idea: <u>Various ways to reduce salt in diet.</u>

➤ Review Test 3

A. To review what you've learned in this chapter, complete each of the following sentences about main ideas.

1. The umbrella statement that covers all of the material in a paragraph is its (*topic,* topic sentence, supporting detail) <u>topic</u>

2. The main idea of a longer selection is often called its (*topic, central point, implied main idea*) _____

3. To locate the main idea of a selection, you may find it helpful to first decide on its (*topic,* central point, implied main idea) _____

    _____

4. When a paragraph has no topic sentence, we say that its main idea is <u>implied</u>

5. To help you decide if a certain sentence is the topic sentence, ask yourself, "Is this statement supported by all or most of the <u>sentences</u>

    _____?"

B. Here is a chance to apply your understanding of main ideas to a full-length selection. Read the article below, and then answer the questions that follow on the central point and main ideas. There are also vocabulary questions to help you continue practicing the skill of understanding vocabulary in context.

Words to Watch

Following are some words in the reading that do not have strong context support. Each word is followed by the number of the paragraph in which it appears and its meaning there.

> *tequila* (1): a strong liquor made from a Mexican plant
> *peer pressure* (2): social pressure from people in the same general age and social position
> *readily* (2): quickly and easily
> *myth* (3): a false belief
> *illusion* (7): false impression
> *alter* (8): change
> *unifies* (9): brings together
> *irony* (11): a meaning that is the opposite of what is actually said

HERE'S TO YOUR HEALTH

Joan Dunayer

As the only freshman on his high school's varsity wrestling team, Tod was   1
anxious to fit in with his older teammates. One night after a match, he was offered a
tequila° bottle on the ride home. Tod felt he had to accept, or he would seem like a
sissy. He took a swallow, and every time the bottle was passed back to him, he took
another swallow. After seven swallows, he passed out. His terrified teammates
carried him into his home, and his mother then rushed him to the hospital. After his
stomach was pumped, Tod learned that his blood alcohol level had been so high that
he was lucky not to be in a coma or dead.

Although alcohol sometimes causes rapid poisoning, frequently leads to long-   2
term addiction, and always threatens self-control, our society encourages drinking.
Many parents, by their example, give children the impression that alcohol is an
essential ingredient of social gatherings. Peer pressure° turns bachelor parties,
fraternity initiations, and spring-semester beach vacations into competitions in
"getting trashed." In soap operas, glamorous characters pour Scotch whiskey from
crystal decanters as readily° as most people turn on the faucet for tap water. In films
and rock videos, trend-setters party in nightclubs and bars. And who can recall a
televised baseball or basketball game without a beer commercial? By the age of 21,
the average American has seen drinking on TV about 75,000 times. Alcohol ads
appear with pounding frequency—in magazines, on billboards, in college
newspapers—promoting a harmful myth about drinking.

Part of the myth° is that liquor signals professional success. In a slick men's   3
magazine, one full-page ad for Scotch whiskey shows two men seated in an elegant
restaurant. Both are in their thirties, perfectly groomed, and wearing expensive-
looking gray suits. The windows are draped with velvet, the table with spotless white
linen. Each place-setting consists of a long-stemmed water goblet, silver utensils, and
thick silver plates. On each plate is a half-empty cocktail glass. The two men are
grinning and shaking hands, as if they've just concluded a business deal. The caption
reads, "The taste of success."

Contrary to what the liquor company would have us believe, drinking is more   4
closely related to lack of success than to achievement. Among students, the heaviest
drinkers have the lowest grades. In the work force, alcoholics are frequently late or
absent, tend to perform poorly, and often get fired. Although alcohol abuse occurs in
all economic classes, it remains most severe among the poor.

Another part of the alcohol myth is that drinking makes you more attractive to   5
the opposite sex. "Hot, hot, hot," one commercial's soundtrack begins, as the camera
scans a crowd of college-age beachgoers. Next it follows the curve of a woman's leg
up to her bare hip and lingers there. She is young, beautiful, wearing a bikini. A
young guy, carrying an ice chest, positions himself near to where she sits. He is tan,
muscular. She doesn't show much interest—until he opens the chest and takes out a
beer. Now she smiles over at him. He raises his eyebrows and, invitingly, holds up
another can. She joins him. This beer, the song concludes, "attracts like no other."

Beer doesn't make anyone sexier. Like all alcohol, it lowers the levels of male   6
hormones in men and of female hormones in women—even when taken in small

amounts. In substantial amounts, alcohol can cause infertility in women and impotence in men. Some alcoholic men even develop enlarged breasts, from their increased female hormones.

The alcohol myth also creates the illusion° that beer and athletics are a perfect combination. One billboard features three high-action images: a basketball player running at top speed, a surfer riding a wave, and a basketball player leaping to make a dunk shot. A particular light beer, the billboard promises, "won't slow you down."   7

"Slow you down" is exactly what alcohol does. Drinking plays a role in over six million injuries each year—not counting automobile accidents. Even in small amounts, alcohol dulls the brain, reducing muscle coordination and slowing reaction time. It also interferes with the ability to focus the eyes and adjust to a sudden change in brightness—such as the flash of a car's headlights. Drinking and driving, responsible for over half of all automobile deaths, is the leading cause of death among teenagers. Continued alcohol abuse can physically alter° the brain, permanently impairing learning and memory. Long-term drinking is related to malnutrition, weakening of the bones, and ulcers. It increases the risk of liver failure, heart disease, and stomach cancer.   8

Finally, according to the myth, alcohol generates a warm glow of happiness that unifies° the family. In one popular film, the only food visible at a wedding reception is an untouched wedding cake, but beer, whiskey, and vodka flow freely. Most of the guests are drunk. After shouting into the microphone to get everyone's attention the band leader asks the bride and groom to come forward. They are presented with two wine-filled silver drinking cups branching out from a single stem. "If you can drink your cups without spilling any wine," the band leader tells them, "you will have good luck for the rest of your lives." The couple drain their cups without taking a breath, and the crowd cheers.   9

A marriage, however, is unlikely to be "lucky" if alcohol plays a major role in it. Nearly two-thirds of domestic violence involves drinking. Alcohol abuse by parents is strongly tied to child neglect and juvenile delinquency. Drinking during pregnancy can lead to miscarriage and is a major cause of such birth defects as deformed limbs and mental retardation. Those who depend on alcohol are far from happy: over a fourth of the patients in state and county mental institutions have alcohol problems; more than half of all violent crimes are alcohol-related; the rate of suicide among alcoholics is fifteen times higher than among the general population.   10

Alcohol, some would have us believe, is part of being successful, sexy, healthy, and happy. But those who have suffered from it—directly or indirectly—know otherwise. For alcohol's victims, "Here's to your health" rings with a terrible irony° when it is accompanied by the clink of liquor glasses.   11

Reading Comprehension Questions

Vocabulary in Context

1. The word *decanters* in "In soap operas, glamorous characters pour Scotch whiskey from crystal decanters as readily as most people turn on the faucet for tap water" (paragraph 2) means
   a. plain jugs.
   b. decorative bottles.
   c. barrels.
   d. glass jars.

2. The word *pounding* in "Alcohol ads appear with pounding frequency—in magazines, on billboards, in college newspapers—promoting a harmful myth about drinking" (paragraph 2) means
   a. professional
   b. forceful and great
   c. quiet but meaningful
   d. inspiring

3. The word *caption* in "In a slick men's magazine, one full-page ad for Scotch whiskey shows two mean seated in an elegant restaurant. . . . The caption reads 'the taste of success'" (paragraph 3) means
   a. man.
   b. menu.
   c. contract that seals the business deal.
   d. words accompanying the picture.

4. The word *substantial* in "Beer . . . lowers the levels of male hormones in men and of female hormones in women—even when taken in small amounts. In substantial amounts, alcohol can cause infertility . . . and impotence" (paragraph 6) means
   a. large.
   b. usual.
   c. weak.
   d. pleasing.

   (*Hint:* Look for the antonym clue.)

5. The word *impairing* in "Continued alcohol abuse can physically alter the brain, permanently impairing learning and memory" (paragraph 8) means
   a. damaging.
   b. doubling.
   c. postponing.
   d. teaching.

Central Point

6. Which sentence best expresses the author's central point?
   a. Advertising promotes false beliefs about life.
   b. Sports and alcohol don't mix.
   c. Advertising aggressively promotes harmful false beliefs about alcohol.
   d. Alcohol should finally be outlawed in this country.

Main Ideas

7. The topic sentence of paragraph 3 is its
   a. first sentence.
   b. second sentence.
   c. third sentence.
   d. last sentence.

8. Which sentence best expresses the main idea of paragraph 5?
   a. Attractive young people are often used in alcohol advertisements.
   b. College-age people drink beer at the beach.
   c. Ads promote the myth that alcohol makes one attractive to the opposite sex.
   d. In one ad, a beautiful woman has no interest in a young man until he offers her a beer.

9. Which sentence best expresses the implied main idea of paragraph 8?
   a. Drinking can make us move more slowly.
   b. Drinking can physically harm or kill people.
   c. Drinking is the main cause of death among teenagers.
   d. Long-term alcohol use can lead to permanent damage.

10. Which sentence best expresses the main idea of paragraph 10?
    a. Alcohol abuse often leads to domestic violence.
    b. Miscarriages and birth defects are caused by alcohol abuse.
    c. Alcohol can harm family life and contribute to mental problems, violent crime, and suicide.
    d. People who never drink have happy family lives.

3

Supporting Details

You know from the previous chapter that the main idea is the umbrella statement covering all of the other material in a paragraph—examples, reasons, facts, and other specific details. All of those specific details are also called *supporting details*—they are the necessary information that backs up and explains the main idea.

MAJOR AND MINOR DETAILS

There are two kinds of supporting details—major and minor. Taken together, the main idea and its major supporting details form the basic framework of paragraphs. The major details are the primary points that support the main idea. Paragraphs usually contain minor details as well. While the major details explain and develop the main idea, they, in turn, are expanded upon by the minor supporting details.

You've already learned that a paragraph's main idea is more general than its supporting details. Similarly, major supporting details are more general than minor supporting details. An important reading skill is the ability to distinguish the major details from the minor ones.

To get a better idea of the role of major and minor supporting details, consider the following main idea from a popular science article:

Main Idea

The sex lives of insects are full of horrible events.

This sentence immediately brings to mind such a question as, "Just what is meant by horrible events?" This is where supporting details come in: they clarify and explain. Turn to the next page to see the same main idea with a major supporting detail:

Main Idea and Major Detail

The sex lives of insects are full of horrible events. In many cases, only the female partner leaves a sexual encounter alive.

Now we have a better idea of what the main idea really means. Often, however, the major details themselves are further explained, and that's where the minor support comes in. A major detail introduces a new point, and minor details develop that point. Here is the same paragraph with several minor details that provide more information about the major detail:

Main Idea and Major and Minor Details

The sex lives of insects are full of horrible events. In many cases, only the female partner leaves a sexual encounter alive. The female praying mantis, for example, occasionally bites her mate's head off during sex. In the case of a certain species of fly, the female follows mating by sucking the body content of the male out through his mouth. Yet another example is seen in the queen ant and her mate, both of whom have wings. When they have finished their encounter high in the air, the male's wings fall off and he drops dead.

See if you can separate major from minor support in the following paragraph. It begins with the main idea and continues with several major and minor details. (To round off the paragraph, the main idea is restated at the end.) Try to locate and put a check in front of the *three* details that give major supporting information about the main idea.

As you read, keep an eye out for certain words that show the writer is adding a new point. Examples of such addition words are *first, next, another, in addition,* and *finally.*

Service Stations No More

Gas stations still provide gas, but often they no longer provide service. For one thing, attendants at many stations no longer pump gas. Motorists pull up to a combination convenience store and gas island where the attendant with clean hands is comfortably enclosed in a glass booth with a trap for taking money. Drivers must get out of their cars to pay for and pump their own gas, which has the bonus of perfuming their hands and clothes with a hint of gas. In addition, even at stations with "pump jockeys," workers have completely forgotten other services that once went hand in hand with pumping gas. They no longer know how to ask, "Check your oil or water?" Drivers must plead with attendants to wash windshields. And the last attendant who checked tire pressure must have died at least ten years ago. Finally, many gas stations no longer have mechanics on the premises. Limping down the highway in a backfiring car for emergency help at the friendly service station is a thing of the past. Car owners cannot even assume that their neighborhood station offers simple maintenance services. The skillful mechanic who can replace a belt or fix a tire in a few minutes has been replaced by a bored teenager in a jumpsuit who doesn't know a carburetor from a charge card. Today's gas stations are fuel stops, but too often that is all they are.

Now see if you checked correctly the three major supporting details. You'll find them after the main idea in the following outline of the paragraph:

Main idea: Many gas stations no longer provide service.

Major supporting details:
1. Attendants at many stations no longer pump gas.
2. Even at stations with "pump jockeys," workers have forgotten other services.
3. Many gas stations no longer have mechanics on the premises.

A more complete outline, showing minor details as well, would be as follows:

Main idea: Many gas stations no longer provide service.

Major and minor supporting details:

1. Attendants at many stations no longer pump gas.
   a. Stations are often combined with convenience stores, at which attendants only take money.
   b. Drivers must get out of their cars to pay for and pump gas.
2. Even at stations with "pump jockeys," workers have forgotten other services.
   a. Attendants do not ask to check oil and water.
   b. Attendants do not wash windshields.
   c. Attendants do not check tire pressure.
3. Many gas stations no longer have mechanics on the premises.
   a. The neighborhood station can no longer be counted on to help in emergencies.
   b. Stations may not even offer simple maintenance services.
   c. Skillful mechanics have been replaced by attendants who are ignorant about cars.

Notice how the complete outline about gas stations goes from the general to the specific. The more general statements are clarified and developed by the points beneath them. At a glance, you can see that the major supporting details introduce new points and that the minor details expand on those points. The outline, by its very nature, divides the paragraph into main idea, major supporting details, and minor supporting details.

One excellent way, then, to gain experience in identifying major supporting details is to outline a selection. In doing so, you make clear the relationships between the basic parts of a piece. Recognizing such relationships is an important part of effective study.

HOW TO LOCATE MAJOR DETAILS

By now you may see that to locate major details, you must (1) find the main idea and (2) decide on the points that are *primary support* for that main idea. Practice these steps by reading the paragraph below. Identify and underline the main idea. Then ask yourself, "What are the chief points the author uses to back up the main idea?" Finally, fill in the main idea and major details in the outline that follows. The rest of the details in the passage will be minor details.

[1]Two influences in particular help create teenage underachievers in school. [2]Many such underachievers have experienced poor relationships with their parents. [3]For example, parents may be poor role models, may reject their children, interact inconsistently with them, or neglect to urge them to be independent. [4]Not surprisingly, the parents of underachievers often are anxious and unhappy with themselves as parents. [5]Another influence on underachieving teens is the school itself, which may simply be too boring for the interests and needs of students. [6]The fault may lie with teachers, curriculum, or both.

Main idea: _____

_____

1. _____

_____

2. _____

_____

ˑhed the paragraph, you probably realized that the first
idea: "Two influences in particular help create
ˑl." The rest of the paragraph then develops that
ˑg the two influences. Those influences are
ˑonships with parents) and 5 (the school).
ˑor supporting details—both essential to

ˑo) go on to develop those major points—
details. Minor supporting details may be
ˑrstanding, but they can be eliminated without
ˑary points. Note how the following version of the
ˑinor details—still makes sense.

ˑuences in particular help create teenage underachievers in
ˑny such underachievers have experienced poor relationships
ˑr parents. 5Another influence on underachieving teens is the
ˑ itself, which may simply be too boring for the interests and needs
ˑstudents.

ˑe that an addition word *(Another)* introduces the second major detail.

on Maps

Many students find it helpful to organize material in a very visual way. They
create a *map*, or diagram, to show the relationship between the main parts of a
selection. A map of the above paragraph might look like this:

Influences that lead to
teenage underachievers

ˑr detail

Second major detail

ˑnship
ˑnts

Boring school
work

➤ *Practice 1*

Major and minor supporting details are mixed together in th
follow. The details in each group support a given main idea. Se
more general details from the minor ones by filling in the outline
details have been filled in for you.

Group 1

Note: Check (✓) each item after you use it. Doing so will help you
items you have left.

Main idea: There are several reasons for the failure of the neighb
clothing store.

- Two competitors within two blocks ✓
- Relied on word of mouth
- High expenses ✓
- Poor advertising
- Faced a side street ✓
- Unexpected rise in wholesale prices ✓
- No display ad in Yellow Pages ✓
- Bad location ✓
- High salaries for workers ✓

Major detail: 1.   _Bad Location_

Minor details: a.   *Two competitors within two blocks*

                    b.   *Faced a side street*

Major detail: 2.   _Poor Advertising_

Minor details: a.   _relied on word of mouth_

                    b.   _no display ad in Yellow Pages_

Major detail: 3.   *High expenses*

Minor details: a.   _Unexpected rise in wholesale prices_

                    b.   _high salaries for workers_

Group 2

Note: Check (✓) each item after you use it. Doing so will help you see which items you have left.

Main idea: Certain substitutions can lower the amount of fat in your diet .

- Ground turkey breast instead of ground beef ✓
- Substitutes for high-fat dairy products ✓
- Boiled ham instead of bacon ✓
- Reduced-calorie margarine instead of butter ✓
- Skim milk instead of whole milk ✓
- Substitutes for fats ✓
- Broth or wine instead of oil for light "frying" ✓
- Yogurt instead of sour cream ✓
- Substitutes for high-fat meats ✓

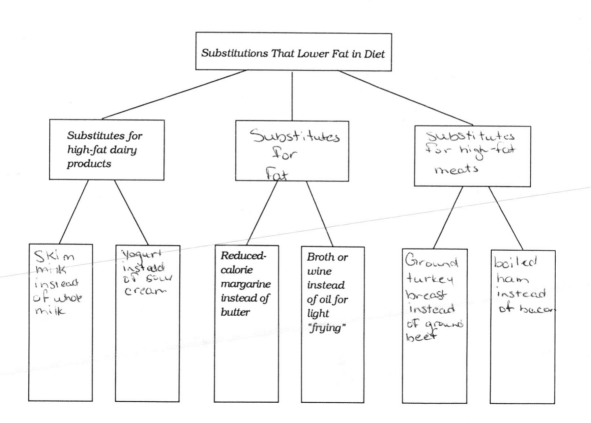

➤ *Practice 2*

Both major and minor details are used to support the main idea in each of the paragraphs that follow. Separate the major, more general details from the minor ones by filling in the outline or map in each case.

1.   Not all addictions are to drugs or alcohol. Some people are addicted to sports. Their lives in winter are spent watching, playing, and talking about football and hockey. In the summer their lives revolve around baseball, golf, and tennis. Other people are television addicts. As soon as they walk in the door of their home or apartment, they flip on the television to start getting their "fix." They seem to schedule much of their lives around their favorite shows, of which there are many. Love addicts are perhaps the most obsessive of all. Such people cannot function in their everyday lives if they don't have a boyfriend or a girlfriend, and their moods are only as good as the status of their relationship. Such people are unable to break off damaging personal relationships, and they will return again and again to a partner who misuses and abuses them.

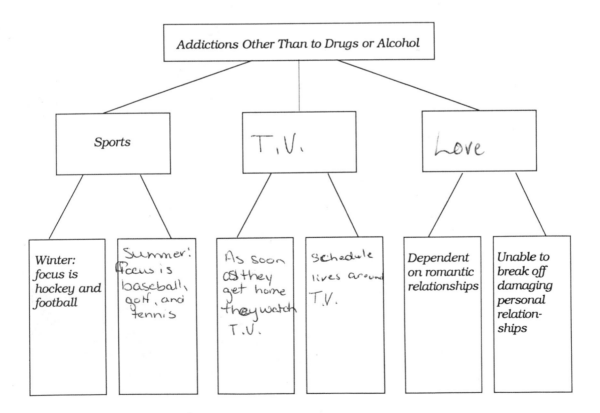

2. Animals open up their mouths for several important reasons besides
    hunger. One is to warn an intruder away from the animal's territory.
    Lizards and fish threaten other animals by opening their mouths, and bears
    and wolves show their teeth before attacking. Another reason animals
    "open wide" is to quiet aggression. The lion, for example, yawns to
    distract other lions that might be ready for a fight. Other animals,
    including the crocodile, open their mouths when they need their teeth
    cleaned. Little birds will come in and eat leftover food off the crocodile's
    teeth—acting like live toothbrushes. Finally, an open mouth may be used
    to signal an interest in the opposite sex. Wide-open beaks are an important
    part of the penguin's courtship dance.

Main idea: _Animals open their mouths for_
other reasons besides hunger

1. _Warn intruder away from their territory_
   Examples: _Lizards - fish_
   bears - wolves

2. _To quit aggression_
   Example: _lion- yawning_

3. _teeth cleaning_
   Example: _crocodiles, birds clean their teeth_

4. _Signal interest in opposite sex_
   Example: _penguin's dance_

Asking Questions

We have seen that one way to identify major details is to find the main idea and
ask, "What are the chief points the author uses to back up the main idea?"
Another way to locate major details is to turn the main idea into a question that
begins with a question word: *who, what, where, when, why,* or *how.* For the
passage earlier in this chapter on underachievers, we could have asked, "*What
are the two influences that help create teenage underachievers?*"

See if you can turn the main idea of the paragraph on the next page into a
basic question about the passage. Then try to answer that question by finding the
major supporting details of the paragraph. After filling in the blank spaces, read
the comments that follow the paragraph.

Sexual abuse of the young—a tragedy that victimizes one in every four girls and one in every ten boys under age 18—can often be prevented. When children are very young, they should be taught that they have a right to the privacy of their own bodies. In addition, parents should teach children to recognize potential abusers and how to say *no* to adults. Having been trained to be obedient, children often hesitate to expose people who tell them to "keep our special secret," especially if those persons are friends or relatives. (As many as 85 percent of sexually abused children are victims of someone they know and trust.) Similarly, parents should encourage children to trust their instincts to run away from elders that make them feel uneasy.

Question formed out of the main idea: _____

_____

Supporting details that answer the question:

1. _____
2. _____
3. _____

The first sentence of this passage states that sexual abuse of the young can often be prevented. That probably made you think of the question: "How can sexual abuse of the young be prevented?" As you read on, you see that the passage describes three ways that sexual abuse can be prevented. The fact that the paragraph answers your question confirms that you have found the main idea (stated in the first sentence). And by converting the main idea into a question, you have made yourself alert to the major supporting details of a passage. Those major details are: 1) Young children should be taught they have a right to the privacy of their own bodies, 2) parents should teach children to recognize potential abusers and how to say *no* to adults, and 3) parents should encourage children to run away from from elders that make them feel uneasy.

➢ *Practice 3*

To find the major details in the following paragraphs, you will ask and answer questions about the main idea. Note that both paragraphs have been taken from the previous chapter.

1.   Complete and then answer the question formed from the main idea of the following paragraph.

Serious depression, as opposed to the fleeting kind we all feel at times, has several warning signs. Some or all may be present within the affected individual. One symptom of depression is a change in sleep patterns—either sleeplessness or sleeping too much. Another sign is abnormal eating patterns, either eating too much or loss of appetite. Finally, a general feeling of hopelessness may signal depression. People feel indifferent to their families and jobs and may begin to think that life is not worth living.

What are the warning signs of ___serious depression___?

a. ___chg. in sleep patterns___

b. ___abnormal eating patterns___

c. ___feeling of hopelesness___

2.   Write out and then answer a question formed from the main idea of the following paragraph.

Every thirty-seven seconds, a car is stolen somewhere in the United States. Although this statistic is frightening, it is possible for drivers to prevent car theft if they take a few simple precautions. When they leave their cars, they should lock all valuables in the trunk or glove compartment to avoid tempting a thief to break in. Parking in the middle of the block on a busy, well-lighted street will also deter would-be thieves. The most obvious precaution, of course, is always to lock the car and take the keys—even if the driver is stopping for just a minute. One out of every five stolen cars was left unlocked with the keys in the ignition.

What question does the passage answer? ___how to prevent___
___car theft___

a. ___lock valuables in trunk or glove compartment___

b. ___Park on busy, well-lighted Street___

c. ___lock the car & take keys___

READING CAREFULLY

You have seen that major details support the main idea and that minor details expand on the major ones. The minor and major details thus work together to clarify the main idea. For example, let's consider again the paragraph about incompetent bosses from the previous chapter. The main idea is underlined, and the major details are boldfaced. The rest are minor details.

Many bosses share two weaknesses. First, they are **often poor communicators**. They tell people what to do and how and when to do it, without explaining the reasons for their rules, and they do not welcome feedback or questions. In addition, many bosses are **not well-rounded people**. Their jobs tend to be their lives, and they expect everybody who works for them to think and act the way they do. These bosses frown upon hearing that a family matter will keep an employee from working late, and they come out of their office looking irritated if there is too much talk or laughter during a coffee break.

Clearly, both the major and minor details are helpful for the reader to really understand the main idea. The general ideas that many bosses are often poor communicators and are not well-rounded people are clarified by the minor details. This illustrates that a careful reading of *both* major and minor details can be important for good comprehension.

Try using your recognition of major and minor details to help you carefully read the passage below. After a close reading, answer the questions that follow.

Symbols, common to all societies, take many forms. What people wear, for one thing, often has symbolic meaning. Queens, priests, the police, and medicine men wear costumes that are symbols of their occupations. A wedding band signifies that one is married, and special buttons, ribbons, and tattoos can represent various group memberships. In fact, objects of any kind may be symbols. Flags are symbols of countries, states, ships, and organizations. Trophies stand for excellence and special achievement, whether in the acting profession or for something as familiar as a baseball or bowling championship. And on our streets, red and green lights have specific meanings. However, the most common symbols of all in human society are words, which have their meanings only because people agree on what they stand for.

1. To find the major details of the paragraph, which question would be helpful?
   a. What are examples of things people wear that have symbolic meaning?
   b. What forms do symbols take?
   c. What are the most common symbols in human society?

2. The major details of the paragraph are
   a. what people wear, objects of any kind, words.
   b. queens, priests, the police, and medicine men.
   c. countries, states, ships, and organizations.

3. *Fill in the blank*: The most common symbols are _____

4. *Fill in the blank*: An example in the paragraph of a symbol worn by people

    is _____

5. Green lights (meaning "go") are an example of which major detail?

    _____

The answer to question 1 is *b*. The answer to question 2 is *a*. The answer to 3 is *words*. Any one of the following can be the answer to question 4: costumes that are symbols of their occupations, a wedding band, special buttons, ribbons, or tattoos. The answer to 5 is *objects of any kind*.

➤ Practice 4

Answer the questions that follow the paragraphs.

A. When we call someone *pig* or *swine*, we do not mean it as a compliment. But pigs do not deserve to be used as a symbol for an insult. They are probably not as dirty as they are made out to be. According to one pig keeper, swine are very clean when allowed to live in a clean environment. He feels pigs are usually dirty simply because their keepers don't clean their pens. In any case, no one has proven that the pig that wallows in mud prefers that to a cool bath. Furthermore, pigs are smarter than most people think. Many farmers, for example, have observed that pigs frequently undo complicated bolts on gates in search of adventure or romance. So the next time you call someone a pig, perhaps he or she ought to be someone you wish to praise.

1. In general, the major details of this passage are
    a. reasons why pigs are dirty.
    b. ways in which pigs are "better" than people think.
    c. ways to insult or compliment people.

2. Specifically, the major details are
    a. Pigs are probably not as dirty as people think; pigs are smarter than most people think.
    b. Pigs may be dirty because their pens are dirty; it hasn't been proved that pigs prefer mud to a cool bath; pigs have been seen undoing complicated bolts.
    c. People use *pig* and *swine* as insults; *pig* and *swine* should be considered praise.

3. One pig keeper feels that pigs will stay clean if they are
    a. given baths.
    b. praised.
    c. kept in a clean environment.

4. What example is given to show that pigs are smarter than they are often thought to be? _they've been seen undoing difficult locks or bolts._

5. The answer to question 4 is
   a. the main idea.
   (b.) a major detail.
   c. a minor detail.

B. Persons suffering from mental illness have been treated inhumanely for much of history. Some societies simply shipped their unbalanced citizens out of the country. So-called "ships of fools" would sail to uninhabited lands where the mentally ill passengers were left to fend for themselves. In other times and places, the mentally ill were thought to be witches or possessed by the devil. They were subject to torture, exorcism and even execution. Still other societies thought the mentally ill were deliberate wrong-doers who could be punished into health. These societies followed the lead of Celsus, a first-century Roman scholar, who recommended that victims of mental illness be punished "by hunger, chains, and fetters."

6. In general, the major details of this passage are
   a. causes of mental illness.
   b. places where people were mentally ill.
   (c.) inhumane ways of treating the mentally ill.

7. *Complete the summary of the first major detail:*
   Some societies got rid of their mentally ill by _shipping them away to uninhabited land_

8. *Complete the summary of the second major detail:* The mentally ill were sometimes treated as though they were _deliberate wrong - doers_ .

9. *Fill in the blank:* People who thought the mentally ill behaved badly on purpose felt that mental illness should be treated by _punishment_

10. The information in the last sentence of the passage is
    a. the main idea.
    b. a major detail.
    (c.) a minor detail.

➤ *Review Test 1*

A. The major and minor supporting details of the outline below are mixed together in the following list. Complete the outline by filling in the missing details.

Note: Check (✓) each item after you use it. Doing so will help you see which items you have left.

Main idea: My freshman English course is demanding.

- Surprise quizzes ✓
- A great deal of writing
- Three major tests ✓
- Many tests ✓
- Term paper ✓
- Three novels ✓
- Short stories in an anthology ✓
- Extensive reading load ✓
- Frequent in-class writing assignments ✓
- A few written summaries of articles assigned ✓
- Magazine and newspaper articles ✓
- Comprehensive final exam ✓

Major detail: 1. _Frequent in-class writing assignments_

Minor details: a. _a few written summaries of articles assigned_

b. _a great deal of writing_

c. _term paper_

Major detail: 2. *Extensive reading load*

Minor details: a. *Magazine and newspaper articles*

b. _three novels_

c. _Short stories in an anthology_

Major detail: 3. _Many tests_

Minor details: a. _three major tests_

b. _surprise quizzes_

c. _Comprehensive final exam_

B. Both major and minor details are used to support the main idea in the paragraph below. Separate the major, more general details from the minor ones by completing the map.

There are three principal kinds of animal diets: carnivorous, herbivorous, and omnivorous. In a carnivorous diet animals feed on other animals. Most fish are carnivorous. So too are owls, snakes, and wolves. On a herbivorous diet animals subsist on plant food. Cattle, Japanese beetles, seed-eating birds, and plant lice are among the many herbivores. With the omnivorous diet, animals have a mixed diet. They feed on both vegetable and animal matter, dead or alive. Many kinds of worms, crabs, lobsters, insects, bears and raccoons are omnivorous. Humans are also omnivores.

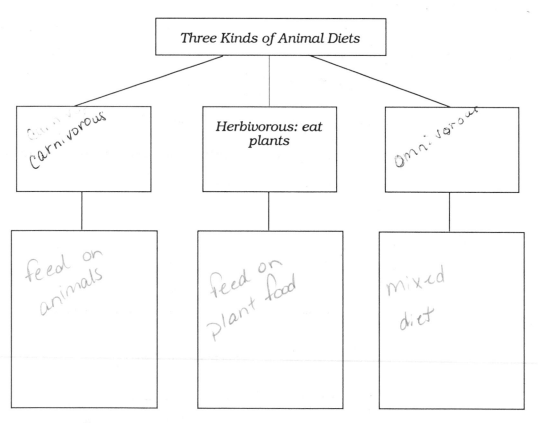

Three Kinds of Animal Diets

Carnivorous

Herbivorous: eat plants

Omnivorous

feed on animals

feed on plant food

mixed diet

➤*Review Test 2*

A. Answer the questions that follow the passage. Note that the topic sentence is boldfaced.

> Years ago, in the 1920s, thousands of people bought Florida land from smooth-talking salesmen. They were so impressed by the colorful brochures the salesmen gave them that they never visited Florida to look at the land before buying it. Later, they found out that the land they bought was at the bottom of a swamp. A swindle that is still popular today is the chain-letter or "pyramid" scheme. Everyone who gets the letter is supposed to send money to the top name on a list. Then they copy the letter, with the top name left off and their own name at the bottom, and send it to several friends. The letter promises that everyone will make money. The only sure winner, though, is the person who starts the letter in the first place. **If moneymaking offers or schemes sound too good to be true—they probably are not true.**

1. Which question would help you find the major supporting details of the paragraph?
   a. Why did so many people buy land in Florida without even seeing it?
   b. What are examples of several chain letter or "pyramid" schemes?
   c. Which moneymaking offers or schemes have sounded too good to be true?
   d. Why do some moneymaking offers or schemes sound too good to be true?

2. The major details of this paragraph are
   a. statistics.
   b. examples.
   c. steps.

3. *Fill in the blank:* The paragraph includes (*one, two, three,* or *four?*) _____ major supporting details.

4. People fooled by Florida land salesmen were influenced by
   a. their visits to Florida.
   b. the colorful brochures.
   c. the scenery at the swamp.

5. *Complete the sentence:* The person sure to benefit from the pyramid scheme is ___person who starts letter___

B. Following the passage on the next page is a question raised by the main idea of the passage. After reading the passage, answer the question by stating the major supporting details.

Dr. Elisabeth Kübler-Ross has identified five stages in the reactions of dying patients. The first stage, she says, is denial. Patients will at first deny the seriousness of their illness, claiming that some error has been made. Then patients become angry. They ask, "Why me?" Their anger may be directed against God, fate, or even their doctors. Next comes depression. During this stage, patients feel hopeless and lose interest in life. After depression comes bargaining—patients try to bargain for their lives. They may promise God or their doctors that they'll be good, stop smoking, give up alcohol or do whatever is necessary if they can only survive. The fifth stage is that of acceptance. Patients finally resign themselves to the inevitable. They are not joyful, but they gain a sense of inner peace. While there has been some criticism of Kübler-Ross's stages, her work has contributed much to making death a more comfortable and better understood subject.

What are Kübler-Ross's five stages of dying?

1. _denial_

2. _anger_

3. _depression_

4. _bargaining_

5. _acceptance_

➤ Review Test 3

A. To review what you've learned in this chapter, answer each of these questions about supporting details.

1. *Fill in the blanks:* Major supporting details are more (*general,* (*specific*)) _____ than main ideas. Minor supporting details are more (*general,* (*specific*)) _____ than major details.

2. *Circle the letter of each of the three answers that apply:* Supporting details can be

   (a.) reasons   d. main ideas
   b. topics   (e.) facts
   (c.) examples   f. central points

3. Label each part of the outline form on the next page with one of the following:

   • Main Idea
   • Major Supporting Detail
   • Minor Supporting Detail

```
_____ m i _____
1. _____ mj. Sup. det. _____
   a. ____ minor Supp. det. _____
   b. _____
2. _____ mj. Supp. det. _____
```

B. Here is a chance to apply your understanding of supporting details to a passage from a widely-used college textbook: *Psychology*, Second Edition, by Diane E. Papalia and Sally Wendkos Olds (McGraw-Hill, 1988). Read the passage and then answer the questions that follow on supporting details.

To help you continue to strengthen your work on the skills taught in previous chapters, there are also questions on vocabulary in context and central point and main ideas.

Words to Watch

Following are some words in the reading that do not have strong context support. Each word is followed by the number of the paragraph in which it appears and its meaning there.

provocation (1): annoyance
loath (1): reluctant
temperament (1): emotional makeup
competence (2): skill
exert (3): use with great energy
thrive (3): grow well
self-reliant (3): independent
assertive (3): positive and confident
detached (4): emotionally apart from others
withdrawn (4): shy
tyrants (7): cruel rulers

HOW PARENTS' CHILD-REARING STYLES AFFECT THEIR CHILDREN

Diane E. Papalia and Sally Wendkos Olds

What makes Mary burst into tears of frustration when she can't finish a jigsaw puzzle, while Gary will shrug and walk away from it, and Cary will sit with it for hours until he finishes? What makes Polly independent and Molly a clinger? What makes Tim ready to hit out at the slightest provocation° and Jim loath° to fight? One answer lies in the basic temperament° children are born with. Another very important influence on behavioral styles is the early emotional environment—how children are treated by their parents. 1

The psychologist Diana Baumrind set out to discover relationships between   2
different styles of child rearing and the social competence° of children. She reviewed
the research literature and conducted her own studies with 95 families of children in
nursery school. Using a combination of long interviews, standardized testing, and
observations at school and home, she identified three categories of parenting styles
and linked them to children's behavior.

Authoritative parents exert° firm control when necessary, but they explain why   3
they take a stand and encourage children to express their opinions. They feel
confident in their ability to guide their children, while respecting the children's
interests, opinions, and unique personalities. They combine firm control with
encouragement and love. Their children know that they are expected to perform well,
fulfill commitments, and carry out duties in the family. They know when they are
meeting expectations and when it is worth risking their parents' displeasure to pursue
some other goal. They seem to thrive° on their parents' reasonable expectations and
realistic standards, and they are most self-reliant°, self-controlled, assertive°,
exploratory, and content.

Authoritarian parents value unquestioning obedience and punish their children   4
forcibly for not conforming to set and quite absolute standards. They are somewhat
detached°, controlling, and distant. Their children tend to be discontented,
withdrawn°, and distrustful.

Permissive parents make few demands on their children, set few rules, and   5
hardly ever punish. As preschoolers, their children are immature—the least self-
reliant, self controlled, or exploratory.

On the basis of her research, Baumrind has recommended that parents who   6
want to raise competent, socially responsible, independent children should do the
following things:
- Teach by example, that is, behave the way you want your children to behave.
- Reward behaviors you want to encourage and punish behaviors you want to
  discourage, giving explanations in both cases.
- Show interest in children.
- Bestow approval only when the child has earned it.
- Demand achievement and the meeting of standards, while being open to
  hearing the child's point of view.
- Encourage original thinking.

Baumrind's work raises important issues about child-rearing practices, but   7
before we conclude that parenting is all, we have to remember what children bring to
the family. Through their own inborn temperaments, children influence their parents.
It is possible, for example, that "easy" children will elicit an authoritative attitude
from their parents, while "difficult" children may make tyrants° out of theirs.

Reading Comprehension Questions

Vocabulary in Context

1. The word *bestow* in "Bestow approval only when the child has earned it" (paragraph 6) means
   a. deny.
   b. give.
   c. accept.
   d. risk.

2. The word *elicit* in "Through their own inborn temperaments, children influence their parents. It is possible . . . that 'easy' children will elicit an authoritative attitude from their parents, while 'difficult' children may make tyrants out of theirs" (paragraph 7) means
   a. draw out.
   b. dislike.
   c. imitate.
   d. abuse.

Central Point and Main Ideas

3. Which sentence best expresses the central point of the selection?
   a. Children are greatly influenced by how they are treated by all the adults in their lives.
   b. Permissive parents make fewer demands on their children than authoritative and authoritarian parents do.
   c. Both a child's natural temperament and parents' child-rearing styles influence the child's behavior.
   d. To raise competent, socially responsible, and independent children, parents should teach by example.

4. Which sentence best expresses the main idea of paragraph 3?
   a. Authoritative parents feel confident in their ability to guide their children.
   b. Authoritative parents follow a certain pattern of child-rearing that results in well-adjusted children.
   c. Children of authoritative parents know they are expected to carry out family duties.
   d. Children should be brought up with reasonable standards and expectations.

Supporting Details

5. *Complete the sentence:* To study the 95 families of children in nursery school, Baumrind used standardized tests, observations at school and at home, and ___long interviews___

6-10. Complete the following outline of parts of the reading by filling in the blanks.

A. Two influences on how a child behaves

   1. _early emotional environment_

   2. _child's basic temperment_

B. Three parenting styles

   1. _authoritative_

   2. _authoritarian_

   3. _permissive_

4

Transitions

Consider the following sentences:

"I dislike my job. The pay is good," said Burt.

Lori enjoys working in her yard. She likes growing vegetables.

"Open your books to page 22," the teacher said. "Hand in your papers."

Does Burt dislike his job because the pay is good? Is growing vegetables all Lori does in her yard? And does the teacher expect students to open their books and hand in their papers at the same time? We're not sure because the above sentences are unclear. To clarify them, transitions are needed. *Transitions* are words and phrases that show the relationships between ideas. They are like signposts that direct travelers. To show how transitions guide us, here are those same sentences, but this time with transitional words included:

"I dislike my job, *even though* the pay is good," said Burt.

Lori enjoys working in her yard. *For example*, she likes growing vegetables.

"Open your books to page 22," the teacher said, "*after* you hand in your papers."

Now we know that Burt dislikes his job despite the good pay and that cultivating vegetables is just one of the yard projects Lori enjoys. We also now know that the teacher wants the papers handed in *before* books are opened. Transitions have smoothed the way from one idea to the other. In Latin, *trans* means "across," so transitions live up to their name—they carry the reader "across" from one thought to another.

There are a number of ways in which transitions connect ideas and show relationships. Here is a list of the major types of transitions.

1   Words that show addition
2   Words that show time
3   Words that show contrast
4   Words that show comparison
5   Words that show illustration
6   Words that show cause and effect

Each of these kinds of transitions will be explained in the pages that follow.

1   WORDS THAT SHOW ADDITION

Put a check beside the item that is easier to read and understand:

_____   People are renting more videotaped movies. Renting costs less than ever before. Videotaped movies are popular because they are now readily available everywhere.

_____   One reason people are renting more videotaped movies is that renting costs less than ever before. Videotaped movies are also popular because they are now readily available everywhere.

The words *One* and *also* in the second item make the relationship between the sentences more clear. The author is listing reasons why renting videotaped movies is so popular. The first reason is that the cost is lower than ever. A second reason is that the movies are so readily available. *One*, *also* and words like them are known as addition words.

Addition words tell you that the writer is presenting one or more ideas that continue along the same line of thought as a previous idea. They introduce ideas that *add to* a thought already mentioned. Here are some common addition words:

one	in addition	first of all	furthermore
also	moreover	second	last of all
another	next	third	finally

Examples:

My friend Ellen is so safety-conscious that she had her wooden front door replaced with a steel one. *Also*, she had iron bars inserted on all her apartment windows.

By recycling, our township has saved thousands of dollars in landfill expenses. *Furthermore*, we have made money by selling recycled glass, paper, and metal.

There are several places you can enjoy with your family without spending much money. *First*, the hands-on science museum downtown asks only for a donation. *Secondly*, there is the zoo, which is free on Sundays.

➤ *Practice 1*

Complete each sentence with a suitable transition from the box on the preceding page. Try to use a variety of transitions.

1. As soon as the weather turned warm, ants invaded our kitchen. A few _____also_____ visited the bathrooms.

2. There are several ways to use old jeans. __First of all__, you can use them for patching other jeans.

3. One million stray dogs live in the New York City metropolitan area. ____In addition____, there are more than 500,000 stray cats in the same area.

4. "____Finally____, and most important," said my adviser, "you've got to complete that term paper or you won't graduate on time."

5. Janice told me she can't go out with me on Friday night. First of all, she has to wash her hair. Second, she's expecting a phone call. And ____third____, she thinks she's going to have a headache.

2 WORDS THAT SHOW TIME

Put a check beside the sentence that is easier to read and understand:

_____ The two neighboring families got along well. They are not on speaking terms.

_____ Previously, the two neighboring families got along well. Now they are not on speaking terms.

The words *previously* and *now* in the second item clarify the relationship between the sentences. *Before* the families got along well, and *now* they don't speak to each other. *Previously* and *now* and words like them are time words.

These transitions indicate a **time relationship**. They tell us *when* something happened in relation to something else happening. Here are some common time words:

first	next	as	while
then	before	now	during
often	after	until	immediately
since	soon	previously	frequently

Examples:

First I skim the pages of the television guide to see what movies will be on. *Then* I circle the ones I want to record on the VCR.

As I got ready to go home, my boss asked me to sweep the stockroom floor.

During World War II, meat was rationed.

Helpful Points About Transitions

Here are two points to keep in mind about transitions.

1. Some transition words have the same meaning. For example, *also, moreover,* and *furthermore* all mean "in addition." Authors typically use a variety of transitions to avoid repetition.

2. In some cases the same word can serve as two different types of transition, depending on how it is used. For example, the word *first* may be used as an addition word to show that the author is continuing a train of thought, as in the following sentence:

   My mother has some strange kitchen habits. *First,* she loves to cook with the radio on full blast. Moreover, ...

   First may also may be used to signal a time sequence, as in this sentence:

   Our English class turned into a shambles this morning. *First,* the radiator began squeaking. Then, ...

➤ *Practice 2*

Complete each sentence with a suitable transition from the above box. Try to use a variety of transitions.

1. ___After___ my cousin took a long shower, there was no hot water left for anyone else in the house.

2. To make chicken stock, begin by putting a pot of water on the stove to boil. ___Next___ drop in a chicken and some diced celery and onions.

3. Dan waited impatiently all day for the Monday night football game to begin on TV, but ___during___ the first half, he fell asleep.

4. Recent advances in medicine make it possible to treat babies even ___before___ they are born.

5. Some students listen to their stereo, eat snacks, and talk on the phone ___while___ doing their homework.

3 WORDS THAT SHOW CONTRAST

Put a check beside the sentence that is easier to read and understand:

_____ Even though roller coasters scare Wanda terribly, she loves riding on them.

_____ Roller coasters scare Wanda terribly. She loves riding on them.

In the second item, the two sentences seem to contradict each other. We want to ask, "Does Wanda like roller coasters or doesn't she?" In the first item, the phrase *even though* makes clear the relationship between the two ideas: In spite of the fact that roller coasters scare her, Wanda still loves riding on them. *Even though* and words like them are contrast words.

Contrast words show that two things *differ* in one or more ways. Here are some common contrast words:

but	in contrast	conversely	on the other hand
however	instead	nevertheless	on the contrary
yet	still	even though	in spite of
although	despite		

Examples:

Some people think they have to exercise every day to stay in shape. *However*, three workouts a week are all they need to do.

Some people look upon eating as something to be done quickly, so they can get on to better things. *In contrast*, other people think eating is one of the better things.

Professional writers don't wait for inspiration. *On the contrary*, they stick to a strict schedule of writing.

➤ *Practice 3*

Complete each sentence with a suitable transition from the box on the preceding page. Try to use a variety of transitions.

1.   _Even though_ the diner was a pleasant place to eat, it still went out of business.

2.   We use seventeen muscles when we smile; _in contrast_, we have to use forty-three muscles to frown.

3.   At first we were planning on spending our vacation at a campground, _but_ now we've decided just to relax at home.

4.   Paula was not satisfied with her paper _despite_ the fact that she had already written five drafts.

5.   Keeping his independence is important to Michael. _Still_, he likes to consult his parents before he makes certain decisions.

4   WORDS THAT SHOW COMPARISON

Put a check beside the sentence that is easier to read and understand:

_____   Driving a car is a skill that we learn through practice. Writing a paper is a skill that we learn through hands-on experience.

_____   Driving a car is a skill that we learn through practice. In like manner, writing a paper is a skill that we learn through hands-on experience.

The first item makes us wonder, "What has learning to drive a car got to do with writing a paper?" The phrase *in like manner* makes it clear that the author intends to *compare* learning to write a paper with learning to drive a car. *In like manner* and words like them are comparison words.

These **comparison words** signal that the author is pointing out a similarity between two subjects. They tell us that the second idea is *like* the first one in some way. Here are some common comparison words:

like	just as	in like manner	as well
as	likewise	in a similar fashion	equally
just like	similarly	in the same way	

Examples:

When buying milk, my mother always takes a bottle from the back of the shelf. *Similarly,* when my father buys a newspaper, he usually grabs one from the middle of the pile.

If movie makers have a big hit, they tend to repeat the winning idea in their next movie, *just like* certain authors who keep writing the same type of story over and over.

When individuals communicate, they are more likely to solve their problems. *In a similar fashion*, countries can best solve their problems through communication.

➤ *Practice 4*

Complete each sentence with a suitable transition from the preceding page. Try to use a variety of transitions.

1. Lighting a cigarette in a darkened theater will not win you any friends. ___In the same way___, talking out loud with your movie partner will soon make people scowl in your direction.

2. There are so many gopher holes in our back yard that it looks ___like___ a miniature golf course.

3. Spicy foods make me very thirsty. Believe it or not, ice cream affects me ___similarly___.

4. Japanese women once blackened their teeth to improve their appearance. ___in a similar fashion___, some Indian women stained their teeth red.

5. ___Just as___ rats become hostile when they are made to live in a crowded cage, humans become more aggressive in crowded conditions.

5 WORDS THAT SHOW ILLUSTRATION

Put a check beside the sentence that is easier to read and understand:

_____ I've become very absent-minded. Last week, for instance, I went to work on my day off.

_____ I've become very absent-minded. Last week I went to work on my day off.

The second item makes us think the author's claim to be absent-minded may be totally based on what happened on his or her day off. The words *for instance* in the first item make it clear that what happened on that day off is just one *example* of the absent-mindedness. *For instance* and other words like them are illustration words.

These **illustration words** indicate that an author will provide one or more examples to develop and clarify a given idea. They tell us that the second idea is *an example* of the first. Here are some common illustration words:

for example	to illustrate	once
for instance	such as	including

Examples:

My grandmother doesn't hear well anymore. *For instance*, whenever I say, "Hi, Granny," she answers, "Fine, just fine."

There are various ways you can save money, *such as* bringing lunch to work and automatically putting aside a small portion of your check each week.

My cousin Dave will do anything on a dare. *Once* he showed up for a family dinner wearing only swimming trunks and a snorkeling mask.

➤ Practice 5

Complete each sentence with a suitable transition from the above box. Try to use a variety of transitions.

1. People have chosen to end their lives in a variety of unusual ways. For example, in ancient China people committed suicide by eating a pound of salt.

2. My mother believes in various superstitions, _Such as_ the idea that if you drop a fork, it means company's coming.

3. Ladies and gentlemen, I can spell any word in the dictionary backwards. _To illustrate_, I will now write the Pledge of Allegiance backwards on this chalkboard.

4. Animals were once tried for crimes. _Once_, in 1740 a cow convicted of witchcraft was hanged by the neck until dead.

5. There are soap opera fans that take the shows too seriously. _For instance_, some viewers actually send threats to soap opera "villains."

6 WORDS THAT SHOW CAUSE AND EFFECT

Put a check beside the sentence that is easier to read and understand:

_____ The varnish wore off our wooden patio table. Fungus has begun to grow on it.

_____ Because the varnish wore off our wooden patio table, fungus has begun to grow on it.

In the first item, it seems the author is simply listing two things that have happened to the patio table. The word *because* in the second item makes the relationship between the two ideas clear—the protective varnish wore off, *so* the fungus was able to grow. *Because* and words like it are cause-and-effect words.

These **cause-and-effect words** signal that the author is explaining why something happened or will happen. Here are some common cause-and-effect words:

thus	because	because of	if ... then
as a result	result in	consequently	since
therefore	leads to	accordingly	so

Examples:

My sister became a vegetarian *because* she doesn't want to eat anything that had a mother.

If it gets too humid out, then our wooden doors swell up and become hard to open and shut.

My boss's correspondence had built up while he was on vacation. *As a result*, I've been typing letters for the last two days.

➢ Practice 6

Complete each sentence with a suitable transition from the above box. Try to use a variety of transitions.

1. _____Since_____ property taxes in the city have gone sky high, many corporations are moving to the suburbs.

2. Lisa's résumé is impressive; _as a result_, she has already had several job interviews.

3. _____Since_____ my family is full of great Italian cooks, canned ravioli tastes like cardboard to me.

4. Some zoo animals have not learned how to be good parents. _Consequently_, baby animals are sometimes brought up in zoo nurseries and even in private homes.

5. Car dealers like to sell a certain number of cars in any given month. They are _accordingly_ more likely to hold sales near the end of a month.

➤ *Review Test 1*

A. Fill each blank with one of the words in the box. Use each word once.

because	after	as well
yet	first of all	

1. An adult elephant weighs about 12,000 pounds. __Yet__ its eyes are almost exactly the size of a human's.

2. There are three basic rules to writing headlines. __First of all__, the headline should emphasize the main point of the story.

3. __Because__ my closet is so crowded, I keep my shoes under my bed and some of my sweaters in the linen closet.

4. I can always count on meditation to relieve any stress I've built up. Exercise relaxes me after a tough day __as well__.

5. Abraham Lincoln began to grow a beard only __after__ being elected to the Presidency. An 11-year-old girl told him that with a beard he "would look a great deal better, for your face is so thin."

B. Fill in each blank with the appropriate transition from the box. Use each transition once.

such as	but	because of
then	just as	

My dentist is so funny that I never need laughing gas when he works on me. His type of humor is __just as__ deadpan as Bob Newhart's. In other words, he says the silliest things with a straight face. Once I asked him if a certain procedure was going to hurt. "Hurt?" he replied. "No, I'm sure I won't feel a thing." He __then__ looked as though a light bulb went on over his head. "Oh, you mean will it hurt *you.* Yes, it certainly will." He also likes to ask ridiculous questions, __such as__, "Do you think I could be the next great rap star?" He does sing rap lyrics (about teeth and gums), __but__ very badly. __Because of__ his silly sense of humor, I almost never dread dental visits. It's hard to laugh—well, as much as you can laugh when your mouth's being worked on—and feel pain at the same time.

➤ Review Test 2

A. First, write in the transition that correctly completes each sentence. Secondly, underline the kind of transition you chose.

1. a. The average square inch of human skin includes 19 million cells. It ____also____ includes 625 sweat glands and 60 hairs.

   therefore
   also
   however

   b. The relationship between the two sentences is one of
   1) addition.
   2) contrast.
   3) comparison.

2. a. My car keeps breaking down. ____Therefore____, I am often late for class.

   Nevertheless
   Also
   Therefore

   b. The relationship between the two sentences is one of
   1) addition.
   2) cause and effect.
   3) illustration.

3. a. There are several steps to take in getting ready for a test. ____First____, read through all of your class notes carefully and make sure you understand the main ideas and major details.

   However
   In addition
   First

   b. The relationship between the two sentences is one of
   1) time.
   2) comparison.
   3) contrast.

4. a. Many people do not know how to respond when someone they know is dying. Hospice workers, ____on the other hand,____ are experienced in giving comfort to dying people.

   first
   on the other hand
   in the same way

   b. The relationship between the two sentences is one of
   1) contrast.
   2) time.
   3) comparison.

5. a. My sister is late for everything. ___Once___ she arrived at a friend's wedding just as the bride said, "I do."

In addition
Once
In contrast

   b. The relationship of the second part of the sentence to the first part is one of
   1) addition.
   2) contrast.
   ③ illustration.

B. In the spaces provided, write the major transitions used in the following passage. You will find one example transition, one addition transition, and one comparison transition.

> According to historians, some young leaders-to-be were being trained to rule their countries' armies at the same time that they played. For instance, the young king of Rome "played" war on a chessboard full of pure gold soldiers. The soldiers were a gift from the emperor Napoleon. Another young leader, Czar Peter III of Russia, watched as his toy soldiers, dressed in full military uniforms, "changed the guard" in front of a miniature castle. In a similar fashion, Great Britain's famous wartime leader Sir Winston Churchill remembers using his model British soldiers to conduct ceremonies and to beat his brother's toy "enemy" soldiers.

Example Transition	*Addition Transition*	*Comparison Transition*
6. For istance	7. Another	8. In a similar fashion

➤ Review Test 3

A. To review what you've learned in this chapter, complete each of the following sentences about transitions.

1. Transitions are words that signal the (*main ideas in, relationships between, importance of*) _____ ideas.

2. A(n) ___addition___ transition means that the writer is adding to an idea or ideas already mentioned.

3. A(n) ___comparison___ transition signals that two things are alike in some way.

4. The transition *after* signals a ___time___ relationship.

5. The transition *therefore* signals a ___cause + effect___ relationship.

B. Here is a chance to apply your understanding of transitions to a full-length reading—an article about stress in college.

Following the reading are questions on transitions and the relationships they signal. To help you continue reinforcing the skills taught in previous chapters, there are also questions on:
- vocabulary in context
- central point and main ideas
- supporting details.

Words to Watch

Following are some words in the reading that do not have strong context support. Each word is followed by the number of the paragraph in which it appears and its meaning there.

aptitude (4): natural ability
anorexia (6): an abnormal lack of appetite which can result in serious
            illness or death
bulimia (6): an abnormal craving for food that leads to heavy eating and
            then intentional vomiting
stability (9): steadiness
bombarded (9): attacked
devastating (9): very destructive
magnitude (11): great importance
meditation (13): a relaxation technique involving mental concentration
relevant (14): related to and important to the issue at hand

STUDENTS IN SHOCK

John Kellmayer

If you feel overwhelmed by your college experiences, you are not 1
alone—many of today's college students are suffering from a form of shock. Going to college has always had its ups and downs, but today the "downs" of the college experience are more numerous and difficult, a fact that the schools are responding to with increased support services.

Lisa is a good example of a student in shock. She is an attractive, intelligent 2
twenty-year-old college junior at a state university. Having been a straight-A student in high school and a member of the basketball and softball teams there, she remembers her high school days with fondness. Lisa was popular then and had a steady boyfriend for the last two years of school.

Now, only three years later, Lisa is miserable. She has changed her major four 3
times already and is forced to hold down two part-time jobs in order to pay her tuition. She suffers from sleeping and eating disorders and believes she has no close friends. Sometimes she bursts out crying for no apparent reason. On more than one occasion, she has considered taking her own life.

Dan, too, suffers from student shock. He is nineteen and a freshman at a local   4
community college. He began college as an accounting major but hated that field. So
he switched to computer programming because he heard the job prospects were
excellent in that area. Unfortunately, he discovered that he had little aptitude° for
programming and changed majors again, this time to psychology. He likes
psychology but has heard horror stories about the difficulty of finding a job in that
field without a graduate degree. Now he's considering switching majors again. To
help pay for school, Dan works nights and weekends as a sales clerk at K-Mart. He
doesn't get along with his boss, but since he needs the money, Dan feels he has no
choice except to stay on the job. A few months ago, his girlfriend of a year and a half
broke up with him.

Not surprisingly, Dan has started to suffer from depression and migraine   5
headaches. He believes that in spite of all his hard work, he just isn't getting
anywhere. He can't remember ever being this unhappy. A few times he considered
talking to somebody in the college psychological counseling center. He rejected that
idea, though, because he doesn't want people to think there's something wrong with
him.

What is happening to Lisa and Dan happens to millions of college students   6
each year. That means roughly one-quarter of the student population at any time will
suffer from symptoms of student shock. Of that group, almost half will experience
depression intense enough to warrant professional help. At schools across the
country, psychological counselors are booked up months in advance. Stress-related
problems such as anxiety, migraine headaches, insomnia, anorexia°, and bulimia° are
epidemic on college campuses.

Suicide rates and self-inflicted injuries among college students are higher now   7
than at any other time in history. The suicide rate among college youth is fifty
percent higher than among nonstudents of the same age. It is estimated that each year
more than 500 college students take their own lives.

College health officials believe that these reported problems represent only the   8
tip of the iceberg. They fear that most students, like Lisa and Dan, suffer in silence.

There are three reasons today's college students are suffering more than in   9
earlier generations. First is a weakening family support structure. The transition from
high school to college has always been difficult, but in the past there was more
family support to help get through it. Today, with divorce rates at a historical high
and many parents experiencing their own psychological difficulties, the traditional
family is not always available for guidance and support. And when students who do
not find stability° at home are bombarded° with numerous new and stressful
experiences, the results can be devastating°.

Another problem college students face is financial pressure. In the last decade   10
tuition costs have skyrocketed—up about sixty-six percent at public colleges and
ninety percent at private schools. For students living away from home, costs range
from eight thousand dollars to as much as twenty thousand a year and more. And at
the same time that tuition costs have been rising dramatically, there has been a
cutback in federal aid to students. College loans are now much harder to obtain and
are available only at near-market interest rates. Consequently, most college students
must work at least part-time. And for some students, the pressure to do well in school
while holding down a job is too much to handle.

A final cause of student shock is the large selection of majors available. 11
Because of the magnitude° and difficulty of choosing a major, college can prove a
time of great indecision. Many students switch majors, some a number of times. As a
result, it is becoming commonplace to take five or six years to get a degree. It can be
depressing to students not only to have taken courses that don't count towards a
degree but also to be faced with the added tuition costs. In some cases these costs
become so high that they force students to drop out of college.

While there is no magic cure-all for student shock, colleges have begun to 12
recognize the problem and are trying in a number of ways to help students cope with
the pressures they face. For one thing, many colleges are upgrading their
psychological counseling centers to handle the greater demand for services.
Additional staff is being hired, and experts are doing research to learn more about the
psychological problems of college students. Some schools even advertise these
services in student newspapers and on campus radio stations. Also, upperclassmen
are being trained as peer counselors. These peer counselors may be able to act as a
first line of defense in the battle for students' well-being by spotting and helping to
solve problems before they become too big for students to handle.

In addition, stress-management workshops have become common on college 13
campuses. At these workshops, instructors teach students various techniques for
dealing with stress, including biofeedback, meditation°, and exercise.

Finally, many schools are improving their vocational counseling services. By 14
giving students more relevant° information about possible majors and career choices,
colleges can lessen the anxiety and indecision often associated with choosing a
major.

If you ever feel that you're "in shock," remember that your experience is not 15
unique. Try to put things in perspective. Certainly, the end of a romance or failing an
exam is not an event to look forward to. But realize that rejection and failure happen
to everyone sooner or later. And don't be reluctant to talk to somebody about your
problems. The useful services available on campus won't help you if you don't take
advantage of them.

Reading Comprehension Questions

Vocabulary in Context

1. The word *prospects* in "he switched to computer programming because he
   heard the job prospects were excellent" (paragraph 4) means
   a. failures.
   b. possibilities.
   c. candidates.
   d. limitations.

2. The word *warrant* in "Of that group, almost half will experience depressions intense enough to warrant professional help. At schools across the country, psychological counselors are booked up months in advance" (paragraph 6) means
   a. fight.
   b. have no need for.
   c. get degrees in.
   d. justify.

Central Point and Main Ideas

3. Which sentence best expresses the central point of the selection?
   a. Going to college is a depressing experience for many students.
   b. College life has become more stressful, so schools are increasing support services.
   c. Lisa and Dan have experienced too much stress at school to enjoy college life.
   d. Colleges should increase their counseling services.

4. The main idea of paragraphs 2 and 3 is stated in
   a. the first sentence of paragraph 2.
   b. the second sentence of paragraph 2.
   c. the first sentence of paragraph 3.
   d. the last sentence of paragraph 3.

5. The topic sentence for paragraphs 9, 10, and 11 is
   a. the first sentence of paragraph 9.
   b. the first sentence of paragraph 10.
   c. the first sentence of paragraph 11.
   d unstated.

Supporting Details

6. Following is a brief outline of "Students in Shock." Fill in the missing major supporting point.

   A. Introduction and central point
   B. Two examples of students in shock
   C. Symptoms of students in shock
   D. _3 reasons students are in shock_
   E. Ways colleges are trying to help students in shock
   F. Conclusion

Transitions

7. The first sentence of paragraph 9 states, "There are three reasons today's college students are suffering more than in earlier generations." The reasons are then introduced in paragraphs 9, 10, and 11 by what three transitions?

Transition introducing first reason for student shock: _first_

Transition introducing the second reason for student shock: _another_

Transition introducing the third reason for student shock: _final cause_

8. The transitions that introduce the major details of paragraphs 9, 10, and 11 signal
   a. time.
   b. addition.
   c. comparison.
   d. illustration.

9. The relationship between the two parts of the sentence below is one of
   a. time.
   b. addition.
   c. contrast.
   d. cause-effect.

   Because of the magnitude and difficulty of choosing a major, college can prove a time of great indecision. (Paragraph 11)

10. The relationship between the two parts of the sentence below is one of
    a. time.
    b. addition.
    c. contrast.
    d. cause-effect.

    Certainly, the end of a romance or failing an exam is not an event to look forward to. But realize that rejection and failure happen to everyone sooner or later. (Paragraph 15)

5

Patterns of Organization

To help readers understand their main points, authors try to present supporting details in a clearly organized way. Details might be arranged in any of several common patterns. Sometimes authors may build a paragraph or longer passage exclusively on one pattern; often, the patterns are mixed. By recognizing the patterns, you will be better able to understand and remember what you read.

THE FIVE BASIC PATTERNS OF ORGANIZATION

Here are the most commonly used patterns of organization:

1 Time Order
2 List of Items
3 Comparison and/or Contrast
4 Cause and Effect
5 Definition and Example

All five of the patterns are based on relationships you learned about in the last chapter. All five, then, involve transition words that you should now recognize. The time order pattern, for example, is marked by transitions that show time (*first, then, next, after,* and so on). The list on the next page shows some of the transitions used with each pattern:

Pattern	*Transitions Used*
Time order	Words that show time (*first, then, next, after . . .*)
List of Items	Words that show addition (*also, another, moreover, finally. . .*)
Comparison/Contrast	Words that show comparison or contrast (*like, just as, however, in contrast . . .*)
Cause and Effect	Words that show cause and effect (*because, as a result, since, leads to . . .*)
Definition and Example	Words that show illustration (*for example, to illustrate, such as . . .*)

The following pages provide explanations and examples of each pattern.

1   TIME ORDER

Arrange the following group of sentences into an order that makes sense. Put a *1* in front of the sentence that should come first, a *2* in front of the sentence that comes next, and a *3* in front of the sentence that should be last. The result will be a short paragraph.

_____ By 1959, the number of TV sets in the country had risen to 50 million.

_____ After eight years, there were a million TV sets in the U.S.

_____ Interest in television grew rapidly after the major radio networks, NBC and CBS, began broadcasting television programs in July of 1941.

Authors usually present events in the order in which they happen, resulting in a pattern of organization known as *time order*. Clues to the pattern of the above sentences are dates and a transition (*after*) that shows time. The sentences should read as follows:

> Interest in television grew rapidly after the major radio networks, NBC and CBS, began broadcasting television programs in July of 1941. After eight years, there were a million TV sets in the U.S. By 1959, the number of TV sets in the country had risen to 50 million.

As a student, you will see time order used frequently. Textbooks in all fields describe events and processes, such as the events leading to the Boston Tea Party, the important incidents in Abraham Lincoln's life, the steps involved as for a bill to travel through Congress, or the process of photosynthesis.

The following transition words often signal that a paragraph or selection is organized according to *time order*:

Time Transitions

first	next	as	while
second	before	now	during
then	after	until	when
since	soon	later	finally

Other signals for this pattern are dates, times, and such words as *stages, series, steps,* and *process.*

The two most common kinds of time order involve a *series of events or stages* and a *series of steps (directions).* Each is discussed below.

Series of Events or Stages

Following is a paragraph that is organized according to time order. Complete the outline of the paragraph by listing the missing stages in the order in which they happen.

Children master language in predictable stages. At about six months, babies start to babble, which means they repeat simple sounds, such as "ma-ma-me-me." About three or four months later, they can repeat sounds that others make. During this stage, parents and babies often babble alternately almost as if they are carrying on little conversations. These interchanges are rich in emotional meaning, although the sounds themselves are meaningless. At the next stage, toddlers learn the meanings of many words, but they are not yet able to talk themselves. A toddler might understand a sentence such as "Bring me your sock" but be unable to say any of the words. Eventually, the child begins to talk in single words and in two-word sentences.

Main idea: _Children master language in predictable stages._

1. _____

_____

2. _Three or four months later, babies can repeat sounds and carry_

on little "conversations."

3. _____

_____

4. _____

_____

You should have added these points to the outline: (1) At about six months, babies begin to repeat simple sounds. (3) Toddlers understand many words, but cannot talk. (4) Eventually a child talks in single words and two-word sentences.

➤ Practice 1a

The following passage describes a sequence of events. Outline the paragraph by filling in the main idea and major details.

The 1960s were a time of profound turmoil and change in America. The first thunderclap occurred in 1964, with the bullets that assassinated President John Kennedy and depressed the spirit of the country. Then in 1965, urban riots brought to the foreground the simmering issue of racial equality. A minor summer incident involving police in Watts, a black section of Los Angeles, set off five days of looting and rioting that left thirty-four people dead. Over a hundred major urban riots, all centered in black ghettos in cities like Newark and Detroit, were to follow. And by 1968, anti-war protests against the increasing American presence in Vietnam began to spread across the country. They centered on college campuses, and soon almost every major campus in the United States was torn by rallies, teach-ins, and riots.

Main idea: _The 1960's were a time of turmoil_
1. _1964 - President Kennedy was shot_
2. _1965 - riots in Watts, Newark + Detroit_
3. _1968 - anti-war protests concerning Vietnam_

Series of Steps (Directions)

Below is an example of a paragraph in which steps in a process are organized according to time order. Complete the outline of the paragraph that follows by listing the missing steps in the correct sequence.

Here is a way to relax that is easy and can even be done in just a few minutes. First, lie down with your arms at your sides and your fingers open. When you are comfortable, close your eyes and put all distracting thoughts out of your mind. Next, tighten all the muscles of your body at once. Push your toes together, tighten your buttocks and abdomen, clench your fists, and squeeze your eyes shut. Hold this position for about seven seconds. Then, let everything relax, and feel the tension flow out of your body. After that, take a deep breath through your mouth and hold it for twenty seconds; then let it out slowly, and breathe slowly and easily, as you do when you are sleeping. Finally, think of a pleasant scene. Concentrate on this scene as you feel your whole body becoming calm and relaxed.

Main idea: _To relax quickly, follow an easy five-step relaxation_
              technique.

1. _____

   _____

2. _____

   _____

3. _Tighten all muscles, and then relax._

4. _____

   _____

5. _____

   _____

You should have added these steps: (1) Lie down, arms at your sides and fingers open. (2) When comfortable, close your eyes and clear your mind. (4) Take a deep breath through your mouth, hold it for twenty seconds, let it out, and breathe slowly and easily. (5) Concentrate on a pleasant scene as you feel yourself relax.

➤ Practice 1b

The following passage gives directions that involve several steps that must be done in order. Complete the outline below the paragraph.

> There are several steps to remembering your dreams. To begin with, you must make up your mind to do so, for consciously deciding that you want to remember increases the likelihood that it will happen. Then put a pen and a notebook near your bed, so that you can write down what you remember as soon as you wake up. When possible, turn off your alarm before you go to sleep so that you can wake up gradually, which will increase the likelihood of remembering your dreams. Finally, when you wake up in the morning and remember a dream, write it down immediately, even before getting out of bed.

Main idea: There are several steps to remembering your dreams.

1. _Make up your mind to remember your dreams._

2. Put a pen and a notebook near your bed.

3. Turn off your alarm before you go to bed

4. Write down your dream as soon as you wake up.

2   LIST OF ITEMS

Arrange the following group of sentences into an order that makes sense. Put a *1* in front of the sentence that should come first, a *2* in front of the sentence that comes next, and a *3* in front of the sentence that should be last. The result will be a short paragraph.

_____ Also check a puppy's personality by watching how it plays with other puppies.

_____ There are some important points to keep in mind when choosing a puppy.

_____ First of all, look for signs of good health, including clear and bright eyes and firm pink gums.

This paragraph begins with the main idea: "There are some important points to keep in mind when choosing a puppy." The next two sentences go on to list two of those points, resulting in the pattern of organization known as a *list of items*. The transitions *first of all* and *also* introduce the points being listed and indicate their order: "First of all, look for signs of good health, including clear and bright eyes and firm pink gums. Also, check a puppy's personality by watching how it plays with other puppies."

A *list of items* refers to a series of details (such as examples, reasons, or facts) that support a point. The items have no time order, so they are listed in the order the author prefers. The transitions used in lists of items tell us that another supporting detail is being added to one or more already mentioned. Following are some transitions that show addition and that often signal a listing pattern of organization:

Addition Transitions

and	in addition	first of all	furthermore
also	moreover	first	last of all
another	next	second	finally

A List of Items Paragraph

In the passage below, the main point has been italicized. See if you can count the number of items in the author's list and also identify the type of item being listed. Note that transitions will help you find the items. After doing this exercise, read the explanation that follows.

Poverty has changed in significant ways in the last thirty years. For one thing, poverty today is increasingly an urban phenomenon. At one time, most of America's poor lived in small towns and rural areas. Today, poverty has risen in urban areas, as many industries have moved out of central cities. Second, poverty has been increasingly feminized. Over half of the poor families in the country are headed by women. Single, deserted, or divorced mothers (and their children) are five times as likely to be poor as two-parent families. Last, although the great majority of the poor are white, racial minorities are overrepresented in the ranks of poverty. Blacks are three times as likely as white to be poor, and Hispanics twice as likely.

Number of items listed: _____

What type of item is listed? _____

_____

This paragraph consists of a main idea, stated in the topic sentence (the first sentence), followed by a list of three items, all supporting the main idea. The type of item listed in the paragraph is *changes in poverty* (urban, feminized, overrepresentation of racial minorities). Notice that the items might have been listed in any order without affecting the main idea of the paragraph.

> ## Practice 2

The following passages use a listing pattern. Underline each main idea. Then count the number of items used to support the main idea. Finally, answer the questions that follow each passage.

1.   Parents should seriously consider their children's requests for a pet, for there are definite advantages to owning a pet. First, if parents set down rules and stick to them, a child can learn responsibility by taking charge of feeding and, in the case of dogs, walking a pet. Also, while caring for any pets, such as tropical fish or hamsters, children learn about the animals' characteristics and habits. And finally, the unconditional love most pets express for their owners is another advantage; children benefit from the warmth and love their pets provide.

How many items are listed? ___3___

What type of item is listed? _reasons for allowing your child to own a pet._

2.   There are several ways to be an active listener. A common way to show that you are listening and interested is to ask questions about what the other person is saying. You can also rephrase what the other person has said to be sure you have understood. For example, you might say something like, "So what you're saying is . . . ." Yet another way to show your interest is to watch for clues to feelings in the other person's tone of voice or posture. That allows you to comment on or ask about the emotional reactions you notice, which shows that you care about that person's feelings.

How many items are listed? ___3___

What type of item is listed? __ways to be an active__ __listener__

3 COMPARISON AND/OR CONTRAST

Arrange the following group of sentences into an order that makes sense. Put a *1* in front of the sentence that should come first, a *2* in front of the sentence that comes next, and a *3* in front of the sentence that should be last. The result will be a short paragraph.

_____ Buffalo and Monte Carlo are about the same distance from the equator.

_____ Buffalo, New York, and the European resort town of Monte Carlo, Monaco, are strangely alike and different, geographically speaking.

_____ Yet Buffalo is known for its long brutal winters and very hot summers, and Monte Carlo is famous for its mild climate.

The first sentence of this paragraph is the general one, the one with the main idea: "Buffalo, New York, and the European resort town of Monte Carlo, Monaco, are strangely alike and different, geographically speaking." The words *alike* and *different* suggest a comparison and/or contrast pattern of organization. The comparison word *same* and the contrast word *yet* in the other two sentences show that the cities are indeed being compared *and* contrasted: "Buffalo and Monte Carlo are about the same distance from the equator. Yet Buffalo is known for its long brutal winters and very hot summers, and Monte Carlo is famous for its mild climate."

The *comparison-contrast* pattern shows how two things are alike or how they are different, or both. When things are *compared*, their similarities are pointed out; when they are *contrasted*, their differences are discussed. (Buffalo and Monte Carlo are similar in their distance from the equator; they are different in their climates.)

In our daily lives we compare and contrast things all the time, whether we are aware of it or not. For example, a simple decision such as whether to make a hamburger or a Swiss cheese sandwich for lunch requires us to compare and contrast the two choices. We may consider them both because of their similarities—they both taste good and are filling. We may, however, choose one over the other because of how they differ—a hamburger requires cooking while a cheese sandwich can be slapped together in about thirty seconds. If we are in a rush, we will probably choose the sandwich. If not, we may decide to have a hot meal and cook a hamburger instead.

Here are some common transitions showing comparison and contrast:

Comparison Transitions

like	just like	just as	alike
likewise	equally	resembles	also
similarly	similarities	same	similar

Contrast Transitions

however	on the other hand	different
in contrast	as opposed to	differently
instead	unlike	differs from

A Comparison/Contrast Paragraph

In the following paragraph, the main idea is stated in the first sentence. As is often the case, the main idea indicates a paragraph's pattern of organization. In this case, the transition *differently* is a hint that the paragraph may be organized in a comparison-contrast pattern. Read the paragraph, and answer the questions below. Then read the explanation that follows.

> In middle age, men and women often view life very differently, especially among couples who have led traditional lives. By middle age, the husband is often comfortable in his position at work and has given up any dreams of advancing further. He may then become more family oriented. In contrast, once the children are grown, the wife may find herself free to explore interests and develop abilities she has had no time for in the previous fifteen or twenty years. Unlike her husband, she may be more interested in non-family activities than ever.

1. Is this paragraph comparing, contrasting, or both?

    _____

2. What two things are being compared and/or contrasted? _____

    _____

3. Which three comparison or contrast transition words are used in the paragraph?

    _____

This paragraph is only contrasting, not comparing—it discusses only differences, not similarities. The two things being contrasted are the views of traditional middle-aged men and women. The transition words that show contrast are *differently, in contrast,* and *unlike.*

➤ *Practice 3*

The following passages use the pattern of *comparison* or *contrast*. Read each passage and answer the questions which follow.

A.   Although mysteries and science fiction may seem like very different kinds of writing, the two forms share some basic similarities. First of all, both are action-oriented, emphasizing plot at the expense of character development. Possibly for this reason, both types of literature have been scorned by critics as being "mere entertainment" rather than "literature." But this attack is unjustified, for both mysteries and science fiction share a concern with moral issues. Science fiction often raises the question of whether or not scientific advances are beneficial to humanity. And a mystery story rarely ends without the guilty person being brought to justice.

Check the pattern which is used in this paragraph:

___X___ Comparison

_____ Contrast

What two things are being compared or contrasted?

1. _mysteries_____   2. _science fiction_____

B.   The conflict over secrecy between the federal government and journalists arises from the different roles they play in society. The government has the job of conducting foreign policy. To do so effectively, government officials sometimes prefer to distort or withhold information. Journalists, however, see their role as digging up and giving information to the public. If they always sought government permission before publishing information, they would be able to print or broadcast only what the government wanted to appear in the media.

Check the pattern which is used in this paragraph:

_____ Comparison

___X___ Contrast

What two things are being compared or contrasted?

1. _secrecy of federal gov't._   2. _journalists freedom to give info._

4   CAUSE AND EFFECT

Arrange the following group of sentences into an order that makes sense. Put a *1* in front of the sentence that should come first, a *2* in front of the sentence that comes next, and a *3* in front of the sentence that should be last. The result will be a short paragraph.

_____ The need for the specialized knowledge of industry leads to a system of formal education.

_____ A society's change from an agricultural base to an industrial one results in the growth of formal education and a weaker family.

_____ And because formal education replaces the instruction of older family members, the family's authority is weakened.

As the words *leads to, results in,* and *because* suggest, this paragraph is organized in a *cause and effect* pattern. The paragraph begins with the general idea: "A society's change from an agricultural base to an industrial one results in the growth of formal education and a weaker family." Next comes a more detailed explanation: "The need for the specialized knowledge of industry leads to a system of formal education. And because formal education replaces the instruction of older family members, the family's authority is weakened."

Information that falls into a *cause-effect* pattern addresses itself to the questions "Why does an event happen?" and "What are the results of an event?" In other words, this pattern answers the question "What are the *causes* and/or *effects* of an event?"

Authors usually don't just tell what happened; they try to tell about events in a way that explains both *what* happened and *why.* A textbook section on the sinking of the ship the *Titanic,* for example, would be incomplete if it did not include the cause of the disaster—going at a high speed, the ship collided with an iceberg. Or if the banks of the Mississippi River are flooded, a newspaper will not simply report about the flooding. An article on this event would also tell why the flooding happened—heavy rains caused the river to overflow. An important part of any effort to understand events and processes includes learning about cause-effect relationships.

Explanations of causes and effects very often use transitions such as the following:

Cause-and-Effect Transitions

thus	because	because of	causes
as a result	result in	result	effects
therefore	since	consequently	leads to

A Cause and Effect Paragraph

Read the paragraph on the next page and see if you can answer the questions about cause and effect. Then read the explanation to see how you did.

Drinking alcohol can lead to different states of consciousness. Although the changes vary from person to person, some broad generalizations are possible. One or two drinks usually result in feelings of warmth, relaxation, and decreased inhibitions. Such limited drinking can be enjoyed by many people without serious drawbacks. Slightly heavier drinking often causes people to believe they can do things better than they really can. For example, after a few drinks a person may believe he is speaking eloquently when, in fact, his speech is slurred or even unintelligible. Or someone may believe she can drive perfectly well when her reactions and judgment have actually been weakened by alcohol.

1. What are the two *causes* described in this paragraph?

    a. _____

    b. _____

2. What are the two kinds of *effects*?

    a. _____

    b. _____

3. What three cause-effect signal words or phrases are used?

    _____

While this paragraph discusses drinking alcohol as a cause in general, it divides drinking into two categories—"one or two drinks" and "slightly heavier drinking." The first cause, then, is "one or two drinks"; its effect can be "feelings of warmth, relaxation, and decreased inhibitions." The second cause is "slightly heavier drinking"; its effect can be to make drinkers "believe they can do things better than they really can." The cause-effect signals here are *lead to, result in,* and *causes.*

➤ Practice 4

The three activities that follow (A, B, and C) will give you a sharper sense of cause-and-effect relationships.

A. The following sentences describe a cause-and-effect relationship. For each sentence, identify both the cause and the effect.

    1. The orange crop in Florida is poor this year because of a late spring freeze.

       Cause: _late spring freeze_

       Effect: _orange crop in Florida is poor_

2. Mr. Coleman's bankruptcy was the result of his compulsive gambling.

Cause: _his compulsive gambling_

Effect: _Mr. Coleman's bankruptcy_

3. Last winter I twisted my ankle by slipping and falling on a patch of ice.

Cause: _slipping and falling on ice_

Effect: _twisted ankle_

4. Linda's new boss did not appreciate her excellent work habits, so Linda began to do her work carelessly.

Cause: _Linda began to work carelessly_

Effect: _her boss didn't appreciate her good work_

B. The following sentences all list either two causes leading to the same effect or two effects resulting from a single cause. Identify causes and effects in each sentence. Here is an example of how to do this activity.

Example

High winds and hailstones as big as golf balls resulted in $10,000 worth of property damage.

High winds: *cause*
Hailstones: *cause*
Property damage: *effect*

5. Uncontrolled high blood pressure can lead to a stroke or a heart attack.

Uncontrolled high blood pressure: _cause_

Stroke: _effect_

Heart attack: _effect_

6. Because the defense lawyer's objection was valid, the judge threw out the evidence and dismissed the case.

Valid objection: _cause_

Thrown-out evidence: _effect_

Dismissed case: _effect_

7. After ammunition and food supplies had run low, the general surrendered.

Ammunition was low: _cause_

Food supplies were low: _cause_

The general surrendered: _effect_

8. Tonia's grades have improved since she put herself on a study schedule and stopped going out on weeknights.

A study schedule: ___*cause*___

Tonia's better grades: ___*effect*___

Not going out on weeknights: ___*cause*___

C. Each of the following passages lists either several causes leading to the same effect or several effects resulting from a single cause. In the spaces provided, identify the causes and effects in each paragraph.

9. Even the best listeners cannot possibly listen carefully to everything that they hear. Among the reasons for this is the overload of messages most of us encounter each day. Besides the numerous hours we spend hearing other people speak, we may spend several more hours listening to the radio or television. It isn't possible to avoid having our attention wander at least part of all this time. Preoccupation with our personal concerns is another reason we don't always listen carefully. A romance gone sour or a good grade on a test may take prominence in our mind even as someone is speaking to us. In addition, the simple fact that we are at times surrounded by noise interferes with listening. For example, many voices at a noisy party or the sound of traffic may simply make it difficult for us to hear everything that is being said.

Inability to listen carefully all the time: _____

Message overload: _____

Preoccupation with personal concerns: _____

Surrounding noise: _____

10. Research over the last decade or so has shown that meditation can have positive effects on drug users and people with certain health problems. Studies have demonstrated that when people who take drugs become meditators, they either cut back on drug use or stop using drugs altogether. In one study of a group that practiced meditation, for example, the number of marijuana users fell from 78 percent to 12 percent after twenty-one months of meditation. Meditation has also been shown to lower blood pressure and regulate the heartbeat, both of which may be of considerable help to those with cardiovascular problems. And because meditation is a highly effective relaxation technique, it can also prove useful to those with stress-related diseases.

Meditation: _____

Decrease or elimination of drug use: _____

Cardiovascular improvements: _____

Stress relief: _____

5   DEFINITION AND EXAMPLE

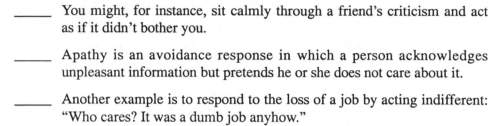

Arrange the following group of sentences into an order that makes sense. Put a *1* in front of the sentence that should come first, a *2* in front of the sentence that comes next, and a *3* in front of the sentence that should be last. The result will be a short paragraph.

_____   You might, for instance, sit calmly through a friend's criticism and act as if it didn't bother you.

_____   Apathy is an avoidance response in which a person acknowledges unpleasant information but pretends he or she does not care about it.

_____   Another example is to respond to the loss of a job by acting indifferent: "Who cares? It was a dumb job anyhow."

This paragraph begins with a definition: "Apathy is an avoidance response in which a person acknowledges unpleasant information but pretends he or she does not care about it." The second sentence clarifies the special meaning of apathy here with an example: "You might, for instance, sit calmly through a friend's criticism and act as if it didn't bother you." The third sentence then provides a second example: "Another example is to respond to the loss of a job by acting indifferent: 'Who cares? It was a dumb job anyhow.'" The second and third sentences include the illustration transitions *for instance* and *example*. As you can see, the *definition and example* pattern of organization includes just what its name suggests: a definition and one or more examples.

To communicate successfully, an author must help readers understand the words and ideas that are being expressed. If a word is likely to be new to readers, the author may take time to include a *definition* before going on. Then, to clarify the definition, which might be too general to be easily understood, the author may present explanatory details, including one or more *examples*. Examples help readers better understand what is meant and strengthen support for the ideas they illustrate.

Textbooks often contain definitions and examples. They introduce students to new words and provide examples of how those words are used to make them clearer and more familiar. Typically, the definition appears first, followed by one or more examples. But sometimes the examples are given first and then the definition. And note that definitions may be given without examples, and examples are frequently used to illustrate general statements other than definitions.

Examples are often introduced by transitions like the following:

Example Transitions

for example	to illustrate	one
for instance	such as	specifically
as an illustration	to be specific	including

A Definition and Example Paragraph

The following paragraph defines a word, explains it a bit, and then gives an example of it. After reading the paragraph, see if you can answer the questions that follow.

[1]Acrophobia is an intense, unreasonable fear of high places. [2]People with acrophobia exhibit physical symptoms in response to being at great heights. [3]One sufferer from extreme acrophobia, Sally Maxwell, is unable to go above the third floor of any building without feeling enormous anxiety. [4]Her acrophobia began one evening when she was working alone in her office on the eighth floor of a large building. [5]Suddenly she was struck with terror by the idea that she might jump or fall out the open window. [6]She crouched behind a steel filing cabinet, trembling, unable to move. [7]When she finally gathered her belongings and left the building, she was sweating, her breathing was rapid, and her heart was pounding. [8]Yet she had no rational explanation for her fears.

What word is being defined? _____

What is the definition? _____

_____

Which sentence explains more about the word? _____

In which sentence does the example begin? _____

The word "acrophobia" is defined in the first sentence—"an intense, unreasonable fear of high places." The second sentence explains a bit more about acrophobia. The story about Sally Maxwell, which begins in the third sentence, provides an example of how acrophobia affects one sufferer; by including it, the author makes the new term more clear by helping readers better visualize what it means.

➤ *Practice 5*

The following passages include a definition and one or more specific examples, each marked by a transition. In the spaces provided, write the number of the definition sentence and the number of the sentence where each example begins.

A. [1]A boycott is an organized refusal by a group of people to deal with another person or group to achieve a specific goal. [2]An illustration is the famous boycott that began in 1955 when Mrs. Rosa Parks of Montgomery, Alabama, refused to obey a local ordinance requiring black people to sit at the back of city busses. [3]Mrs. Parks was arrested, and that sparked off a boycott of the Montgomery bus system by blacks. [4]The boycott was organized and led by Dr. Martin Luther King, Jr. [5]Rather than continue to lose revenue needed to run the bus system, the city repealed the ordinance.

Definition _____   Example _____

B. [1]Although most people would agree that lying to gain unfair advantage over an unknowing victim is wrong, another kind of mistruth—the "white lie"—isn't so easy to dismiss as completely unethical. [2]White lies are untruths that are unmalicious, or even helpful, to the person to whom they are told. [3]Over half of all white lies are justified as a way to prevent embarrassment. [4]Such lying is often given the approving label "tact." [5]Sometimes a face-saving lie saves face for the recipient, such as when you pretend to remember someone at a party in order to save them from the embarrassment of being forgotten. [6]Other white lies are told to prevent a large conflict. [7]You might, for instance, say you're not upset at a friend's teasing in order to prevent the hassle that would result if you expressed your annoyance.

Definition _____   Example 1 _____   Example 2 _____

Topic Sentences and Patterns of Organization

A paragraph's topic sentence often indicates its pattern of organization. For example, the topic sentence of a paragraph you worked on earlier is: *There are several steps to remembering your dreams.* This sentence probably made you suspect that the paragraph goes on to list those steps. If so, the paragraph would be organized according to time order (a series of steps). When a paragraph turns out to include the information you expect (as it does in that case), then you know you have found the correct pattern.

Another good example is the paragraph you read earlier on drinking alcohol. The topic sentence of that paragraph is: *Drinking alcohol can lead to different states of consciousness.* The words *lead to* suggest that this paragraph may be about causes and effects. And, in fact, the paragraph *is* about two causes ("one or two drinks" and "slightly heavier drinking") and their effects.

So if you are having trouble recognizing a paragraph's pattern of organization, you may find it helpful to think about its topic sentence. Try, for instance, to guess the pattern of the paragraph with this topic sentence:

While there are thousands of self-help groups, they all fall into three basic classifications.

The statement that self-help groups "fall into three basic classifications" is a strong indication that the paragraph will list those classifications. The topic sentence helps us guess that the paragraph may be a list of three items—that is, the three classifications.

➤ Practice 6

Circle the letter of the pattern of organization that each topic sentence suggests.

1. Cleaning up a playground can have surprising results.

    a. Definition and example   b. Cause and effect   c. Comparison/contrast

2. Although Abby and Susan are twins, you could not find two more different girls.

    a. Time order   b. Cause and effect   c. Comparison/contrast

3. Once upon a time, there was an evil princess.

    a. Time order   b. List of items   c. Definition and example

4. Bicycles can be equipped with many extra safety features.

    a. Definition and example   b. Cause and effect   c. List of items

5. An *antonym* is a word that means the opposite of another word.

    a. Time order   b. Cause and effect   c. Definition and example

➤ Review Test 1

Label each item with the letter of its main pattern of organization. Each pattern is used twice.

a Time order
b Items in a list
c Comparison and/or contrast
d Cause and effect
e Definition and example

_____ 1. The construction of federally subsidized highways and the shortage of housing in central cities led to the movement to the suburbs.

_____ 2. While some birds meet only to mate, others stay together and share in the child-rearing.

_____ 3. Propaganda is information, whether true or false, that is methodically spread in order to advance a cause or point of view. Advertising is an obvious form of propaganda.

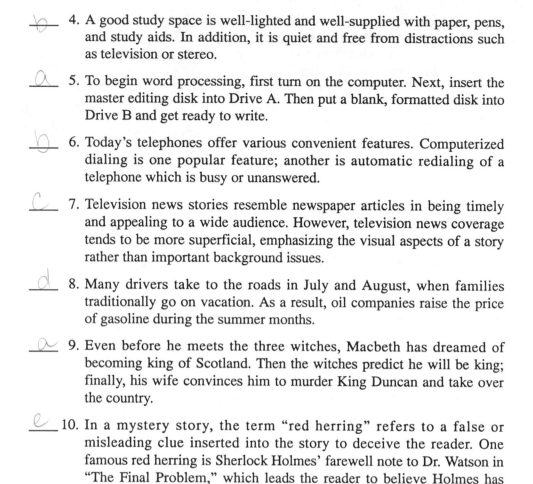

___b___ 4. A good study space is well-lighted and well-supplied with paper, pens, and study aids. In addition, it is quiet and free from distractions such as television or stereo.

___a___ 5. To begin word processing, first turn on the computer. Next, insert the master editing disk into Drive A. Then put a blank, formatted disk into Drive B and get ready to write.

___b___ 6. Today's telephones offer various convenient features. Computerized dialing is one popular feature; another is automatic redialing of a telephone which is busy or unanswered.

___c___ 7. Television news stories resemble newspaper articles in being timely and appealing to a wide audience. However, television news coverage tends to be more superficial, emphasizing the visual aspects of a story rather than important background issues.

___d___ 8. Many drivers take to the roads in July and August, when families traditionally go on vacation. As a result, oil companies raise the price of gasoline during the summer months.

___a___ 9. Even before he meets the three witches, Macbeth has dreamed of becoming king of Scotland. Then the witches predict he will be king; finally, his wife convinces him to murder King Duncan and take over the country.

___e___ 10. In a mystery story, the term "red herring" refers to a false or misleading clue inserted into the story to deceive the reader. One famous red herring is Sherlock Holmes' farewell note to Dr. Watson in "The Final Problem," which leads the reader to believe Holmes has fallen to his death.

➤ Review Test 2

Read each paragraph; then answer the question and complete the outline or map that follows .

A. Successful garage sales are planned well in advance. About a month before the sale, find out whether the town or city you live in requires you to get a permit to hold your sale. Next, gather and prepare all the items you want to sell, sprucing them up whenever possible by washing or repairing them. Then print and post notices of your sale. Last of all, arrange your merchandise on card or picnic tables, along with price labels for each item, and get ready to collect your well-earned profits.

1. The main pattern of organization of the paragraph is
   a. time order   b. comparison/contrast   c. list of items

2. Complete the map of the paragraph. (You'll recall from page 53 that a map, or diagram, is a very visual way of showing the relationship between the main parts of a selection.)

Steps in a Garage Sale

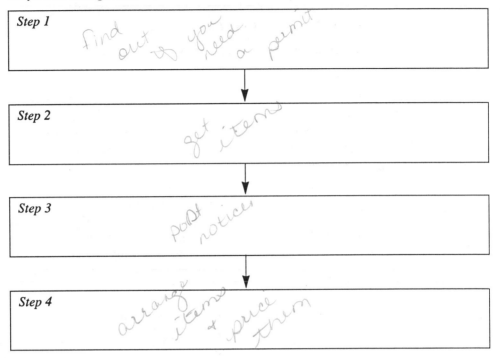

Step 1 — find out if you need a permit

Step 2 — get items

Step 3 — post notices

Step 4 — arrange items & price them

B. Middle-aged adults are returning to school in increasing numbers. Some want to learn to do their jobs better. College courses can help them improve their job skills and keep up in their fields. Others return to school because more credits may mean a raise or promotion. Teachers, for instance, get raises for reaching certain levels of education. Also, some adults return to the classroom because of interest in a new field, such as telecommunication or computer programming. Finally, others, simply for the sake of learning, want to study subjects such as foreign languages, history, or literature. Such classes help adults spend their time in more productive and interesting ways and deepen their understanding of themselves and their world.

1. The main pattern of organization of the paragraph is

   a. time order   b. definition and example   c. cause and effect

2. Complete the outline of the paragraph.

Main idea: There are several reasons why middle-aged adults are returning to school.

1. *To learn to do their jobs better.*
2. _to get paid_
3. _learn @ new fields_
4. _just to learn_

C.   The process by which children learn their sex roles contains three main elements. One is conditioning through rewards and punishments. For example, boys who play with model airplanes and girls who play with dolls will usually be encouraged by their parents. On the other hand, boys who prefer dolls and girls who prefer airplanes will often be criticized or even punished. Another element is imitation. Young children will usually imitate adults who they think are like themselves. This means that boys will usually imitate their fathers and girls their mothers. The third and perhaps the most important element is self-definition. Children quickly learn that all people are either male or female and define themselves as belonging to one sex rather than the other. They then use this self-definition to choose their future interests and to develop their personalities and social roles.

1. The main pattern of organization of the paragraph is

   a. time order   b. list of items   c. comparison/contrast

2. Complete the diagram of the paragraph.

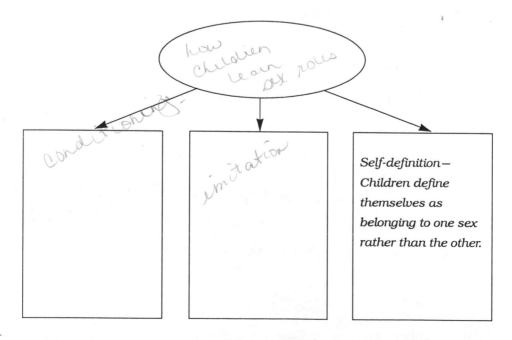

D.   Cable television represents a clear improvement over network television. For one thing, cable TV offers better movie-watching. Cable viewers get to see the latest box-office hits only months after they play the theaters. And the movies are not edited by network censors. In addition, no commercials interrupt the flow of the action or the mood of the film. In contrast, movies on network TV are often years old. Some of the dialogue may be dubbed to eliminate offensive language. Often, scenes are left out or clumsily edited to tone down violence or sex. And ads constantly interrupt the flow of network movies. Cable TV also shows better specials than the networks do. Cable viewers get to see current pop stars such as Carly Simon or Randy Travis in concert. They also see quality dramas, such as Broadway plays, and popular comedians doing hour-long shows. The best musicians on the networks, on the other hand, are on the ads. There are very few network musical specials. The network comedy specials are on the level of Bob Hope's tired variety shows, and its dramas are pilots of shows that weren't good enough to become weekly series. Finally, on cable TV, programs are conveniently repeated at various times over the month. A person who works at night can see a movie at one o'clock in the afternoon, and a person who missed the first twenty minutes of a program can catch up at a later time. To catch up on a network show, on the other hand, you have to wait for reruns.

1. The main pattern of organization of the paragraph is

    a. time order   b. comparison/contrast   c. definition and example

2. Complete the outline of the paragraph by filling in the missing major and minor details.

Main idea: Cable TV is an improvement over network television.

	Cable	*Network TV*
Better movie watching	*Latest movies*	*Movies often years old*
	no commercials	dialogue dubbed
	no dubbing	scenes left out
Better specials	*Current pop stars*	*Best musicians are on ads*
Convenient times		

➤ *Review Test 3*

A. To review what you've learned in this chapter, complete each of the following sentences about patterns of organization.

1. A paragraph's pattern of organization is the pattern in which its (supporting details, *main idea, causes and effects*) _____ _____ is or are organized.

2. The pattern in which a series of details are presented in any order the author considers best is called a ___list of item___.

3. The pattern in which the details discuss how two or more things are alike or different is a pattern of ___comp. contrast___.

4. When a passage provides a series of directions, it uses a ___time order___ order.

5. When textbook authors provide a definition of a term, they are likely to also provide one or more ___list of order___ to help make that definition clear.

B. Here is a chance to apply your understanding of patterns of organization to a passage from a widely-used college textbook: *Sociology*, Fifth Edition, by Donald Light, Suzanne Keller, and Craig Calhoun (Alfred E. Knopf, 1989). Whether you live in a small country town or a large city, you will probably find something familiar in this textbook passage about rural and urban areas.

To help you continue to strengthen your work on the skills taught in previous chapters, there are also questions on
  • vocabulary in context
  • central point and main ideas
  • supporting details
  • transitions.

Words to Watch

Following are some words in the reading that do not have strong context support. Each word is followed by the number of the paragraph in which it appears and its meaning there.

pseudonym (2): a fictitious name
decidedly (2): definitely
aloof (3): distant in personal relations
oriented (3): related
scrutiny (3): examination
indiscretions (3): unwise acts

spectrum (4): range
vestiges (4): traces; remaining bits
revitalization (5): a bringing back to life

COMMUNITIES AND CITIES

Donald Light
Suzanne Keller
Craig Calhoun

Main Street in Mineville starts to awaken at about 5 a.m. The cook at the   1
restaurant arrives at this hour to start heating the stove and brewing the coffee. The
postmaster makes an appearance at 5:30 to empty the one mailbox in this town of
1,400 people. All the out-of-town letters must be sorted and stamped in time to leave
on the 6:30 train. Shortly before 6:30 the quiet is broken by the rumblings of the
large dump truck that carries ore from the mine to the train station. Next, Reavley's
cab pulls up at the depot to let off the few passengers who are taking the early train to
Gold for shopping or business. By 7:00 the street is filled with miners on their way to
work. They walk in groups, carrying their lunches; most of them have known each
other since boyhood. At 8:30 a wave of children floods Main Street. Laughing,
talking, running to catch up with friends, they head for the local school. The next big
event is the arrival of the bus from Smelters, which delivers the daily papers. By
11:00 everyone is asking, "Is Julius [the bus driver] here yet?" With the papers in,
attention turns to the arrival of the noontime mail train. For the rest of the day the
post office is the busiest place in town. The people of Mineville go there not just to
pick up their mail, but to chat with friends and neighbors and to catch up on town
gossip.

New York City is 2,000 miles away from Mineville (a pseudonym° for a town   2
in Montana), but considering its life style the distance seems more like 200,000. On
Manhattan's Upper West Side, for example, Columbus Avenue is the center of
conspicuous consumption. Young urban professionals stroll through its stores on
weekends, buying $400 sports jackets and $200 slacks, perfect for sitting in a
fashionable cafe sipping Perrier at $5 a glass. On a typical Sunday thousands of
people are part of this yuppie scene. One store owner reports that his new hardwood
floor wore out from foot traffic in just two years! Some of these shoppers come from
the suburbs, some from other sections of New York City, but a great many are Upper
West Siders. They live in the same small area (five blocks wide by roughly twenty-
seven blocks long), and yet while browsing through a new shop, dining in a
restaurant, or drinking at a bar, they usually do not know any of the people around
them. The Upper West Side is decidedly° a "community" of strangers. Each resident
is acquainted with only a tiny fraction of its 100,000 population.

Comparisons between Mineville and the Upper West Side of Manhattan could   3
fill many pages. In Mineville the residents are involved in a continual round of
community-centered activities, such as dances, club meetings, church programs, and
projects sponsored by civic organizations. People are expected to participate, at least
to some extent, in these activities. Those who do not are considered aloof° and

antisocial. In contrast, on the Upper West Side most people's social lives are not at all neighborhood oriented°. In fact, to be extremely neighborly tends to invite suspicion. Most Upper West Siders know almost nothing about the people who share their apartment building. It is common not even to know the tenant next door except as a name beneath a doorbell. Such anonymity is unheard of in Mineville. There, people know countless details about one another's lives. Sharing gossip about fellow residents is a favorite town pastime. Such close scrutiny° of everyone's activities helps to keep the people of Mineville from stepping very far out of line. Of course, sexual indiscretions°, incidents of drunkenness, and occasional teenage vandalism take place. But serious crime is so rare that the town council declared the office of police chief indefinitely vacant. Upper West Side residents would be horrified at the prospect of dismissing their police force. Muggings, robberies, rapes, and murders are a daily occurrence in New York City. Fear of crime drives many residents to install two, three, even four locks on their apartment door.

How can we sum up the differences between Mineville and the Upper West   4 Side of Manhattan? What is the essence of the contrasts between them? Those contrasts are essentially differences of place, differences between a small town and a large city. Granted, Albert Blumenthal wrote his sociological description of Mineville in the early 1930s, a time when the United States was in many ways different than it is today. But small towns like Mineville still exist in our society. There are still places where, despite modern technology and mass communication, the basic features of small town life remain. According to sociologist Ernest Burgress, these features include "close acquaintanceship of everyone with everyone else, the dominance of personal relations, and subjection of the individual to continuous observation and control by the community." None of these features are found on the Upper West Side of Manhattan. In fact, the Upper West Side seems to present the opposite of the spectrum° in all three respects. Can we therefore conclude that the Upper West Side is nothing at all like Mineville? Probably not, because as you will see later in this chapter, some sociologists argue that vestiges° of traditional communities—and sometimes entirely new kinds of communities—thrive in even the most urbanized settings.

This chapter takes a sociological look at life in towns and cities. First, we   5 examine the question of whether urbanization has destroyed community or simply given new form to the close, enduring relationships found in places like Mineville. Second, we consider the historical process of urbanization. Where and when did cities first appear and why did they develop? Has the basic form and function of cities changed much over the centuries? What are the differences between, say, Venice, Italy, during the Renaissance and the sprawling metropolis of Los Angeles today? Third, we look more closely at the contemporary urban environment and evaluate several theories that attempt to explain its spatial organization. We conclude the chapter by returning to the relationship between community and urbanization and by considering two recent trends: revitalization° of inner-city neighborhoods and commercial districts, and the rapid growth of small towns where huge new industrial plants have been built.

Reading Comprehension Questions

Vocabulary in Context

1. The term *conspicuous consumption* in "Columbus Avenue is the center of conspicuous consumption. Young urban professionals stroll through its stores on weekends, buying $400 sports jackets and $200 slacks, perfect for sitting in a fashionable cafe sipping Perrier at $5 a glass" (paragraph 2) means
   a. modest behavior.
   b. eating at expensive places.
   c. showy overspending.
   d. ordinary shopping.

2. The word *anonymity* in "Most Upper West Siders know almost nothing about the people who share their apartment building. . . . Such anonymity is unheard of in Mineville" (paragraph 3) means a condition of
   a. not being personally known.
   b. fear and shame.
   c. real estate.
   d. wastefulness.

Central Point and Main Ideas

3. Which sentence best expresses the central point of the first four paragraphs of the selection? (Note that the last paragraph is a more general introduction to the chapter.)
   a. People are more neighborly in small towns than in big cities.
   b. While small towns and large cities may share some characteristics, they are very different in important ways.
   c. Although the residents of the Upper West Side of New York live in a small area, they are strangers to each other.
   d. Mineville is the fictitious name of a real Montana town that was studied by a sociological researcher in the early 1930s.

4. Which sentence best expresses the main idea of paragraph 3?
   a. Sentence 1
   b. Sentence 2
   c. Next to the last sentence
   d. Last sentence

Supporting Details

5. In general, the supporting details of paragraph 1 are
   a. events.
   b. reasons.
   c. statistics.
   d. quotations.

Transitions

6. In the final paragraph, what is the primary kind of transition that the authors use to organize their details?
   a. Time
   b. Addition
   c. Cause and effect
   d. Illustration

7. The relationship of the second sentence below to the first is one of
   a. addition.
   b. contrast.
   c. cause and effect.
   d. illustration.

   > Of course, sexual indiscretions, incidents of drunkenness, and occasional teenage vandalism take place. But serious crime is so rare that the town council declared the office of police chief indefinitely vacant. (Paragraph 3)

Patterns of Organization

8. The pattern of organization of paragraph 1 is
   a. time order.
   b. list of items.
   c. cause and effect.
   d. definition and example.

9. Paragraph 3
   a. lists various events of Mineville and the Upper West Side of Manhattan in a time order.
   b. contrasts the community relationships and crime in Mineville to those in the Upper West Side.
   c. explains the causes and effects of social life and crime in Mineville and in the Upper West Side.
   d. defines and illustrates small town life and big city life.

10. Like paragraphs, longer selections have patterns of organization. Overall, "Communities and Cities" is organized according to a
    a. list of items pattern.
    b. time order pattern.
    c. comparison and contrast pattern.
    d. cause and effect pattern.

6

Fact and Opinion

On the television police drama *Dragnet*, whenever witnesses began to speak emotionally or to give their own theories, the hero, Sgt. Joe Friday, would ask for "just the facts." He wanted neutral, unbiased information—the kind that can be proven true or false—rather than a witness's interpretation of what happened.

The kind of information Sgt. Friday preferred, however, isn't easy to come by. When most speakers and writers communicate, they include their opinions of a subject. What they say is therefore at least partly biased.

While bias is often unavoidable, many writers do try to remain as objective as possible. News articles and scientific reports are examples of writing in which authors try to be as factual as they can. However, opinions are central to other types of materials, such as editorials, political speeches, and advertisements. Writers of these materials try to convince readers who have different viewpoints to change their minds.

Both facts and opinions can be valuable to readers, but knowing the difference between the two is important in evaluating what is read. Thus, like Sgt. Friday, skilled readers must be able to distinguish *fact* from *opinion*.

Sorting out facts from opinions is something you do already, perhaps without even realizing it. For example, imagine a friend saying, "I saw a science-fiction movie last night about aliens invading Earth. The special effects were great; the aliens looked like reptiles—they had green skin and forked tongues. The acting was terrible, though." Hearing this description, you would probably realize your friend's comments are a mixture of fact and opinion.

FACT

A *fact* is a statement that can be proven true through objective evidence. This evidence may be physical proof or the spoken or written testimony of witnesses. In the friend's comments about the movie, the facts are that it was about aliens invading Earth and that the aliens had green skin and forked tongues. If you wanted to, you could check the truth of these statements by questioning other witnesses or watching the movie yourself.

Following are some more facts—they can be checked for accuracy and thus proven true.

> *Fact:* The Quad Tower is the tallest building in this city.
> (A researcher could go out and, through inspection, confirm that the building is the tallest.)

> *Fact:* Albert Einstein willed his violin to his grandson.
> (This statement can be checked in historical publications or with Einstein's estate.)

> *Fact:* The 1990 Cincinnati Reds won the World Series in four games.
> (Anyone can check sports records to confirm this.)

OPINION

An *opinion* is a statement that cannot be objectively proven true or false. Opinions usually express the beliefs, feelings, or judgments that a person has about a subject. Your friend, for instance, said that the movie's special effects were great and that the acting was terrible. These statements may be reasonable ones with which other people would agree, but they cannot be objectively proven. They are opinions. You might see the movie and reach very different conclusions.

Here are some more opinions:

> *Opinion:* The Quad Tower is the ugliest building in the city.
> (There's no way to prove this statement because two people can look at the same building and come to different conclusions about its beauty. "Ugly" is a *value word*, a word we use to express a value judgment. Value words are signals that an opinion is being expressed. By their very nature, these words represent opinions, not facts.)

> *Opinion:* Einstein should have willed his violin to a museum.
> (Who says? Not his grandson. This is an opinion.)

Opinion: The 1990 Cincinnati Reds were the best team in the history of baseball.

(Whether something is "best" is always debatable. "Best" is another value word.)

Writing Facts and Opinions

To get a better sense of fact and opinion, take a few minutes to write three facts about yourself and then to write three of your opinions. Here, for example, are three facts about me and three of my opinions.

Facts about me:

- I am six feet tall.
- I do my writing on a Macintosh computer.
- I have two sisters and one wife.

Three of my opinions:

- Schools, including colleges, should require students to do a great deal of reading.
- Macintosh computers are superior to IBM computers.
- In its first five seasons, *L. A. Law* was the best dramatic series ever shown on television.

Now write your facts and opinions in the space below:

Facts about you:

- _____
  _____
- _____
  _____
- _____
  _____

Three of your opinions:

- _____
  _____
- _____
  _____
- _____
  _____

More About Fact and Opinion

To sharpen your understanding of fact and opinion, read the following statements and decide whether each is fact or opinion. Put an **F** (for "fact") or an **O** (for "opinion") beside each statement.

_____ 1. My brother Gary is very handsome.

_____ 2. Last night, a tree outside our house was struck by lightning.

_____ 3. Installing a new sink is an easy job for the do-it-yourselfer.

_____ 4. Richard Nixon was the worst president our country ever had.

_____ 5. Certain birds bury their eggs on the slopes of a dying volcano, where heat from volcanic steam incubates the eggs.

_____ 6. Ellen believes in astrology.

_____ 7. Ostriches do not hide their heads in the sand.

_____ 8. The economy, in fact, is in the worst shape it's been in for years.

_____ 9. The Grimm brothers collected their fairy tales from other collections and from storytellers.

_____ 10. The pop star Madonna is a bad influence on our son.

Now read carefully the following explanations of the ten items.

1. This is an opinion. You may like the way your brother looks (maybe because he looks so much like you), but other people might not find him so attractive. The word *handsome* is another value word.

2. This is a statement of fact. You and your family might have seen or heard the lightning strike, or you could go outside later and see the type of damage done to the tree.

3. This is an opinion. The word *easy* suggests a judgment is being made and can mean quite different things to different people.

4. This is an opinion. Not everyone would evaluate Richard Nixon's performance in this way. Here the value word *worst* shows us that a judgment is being expressed.

5. This is a statement of fact. People have observed and recorded this aspect of the life of these birds; it's not a matter of opinion.

6. This is a fact. Ellen's belief is an opinion, but the fact that she has that belief can be confirmed—we can ask her.

7. This is a fact (contrary to popular opinion) which can be checked through observation and reports of observations.

8. This is an opinion. Just because someone says something is a fact doesn't make it so. Different people will judge economic factors differently.

9. This is a fact. It can be confirmed through the Grimms' writings and through research on the background of their stories.

10. This is an opinion—it all depends on what someone considers "bad."

➤ *Practice 1*

Here are short reviews taken from a newspaper movie guide. Some reviews present only factual reports; others contain opinions about the movie as well. Identify the factual reviews with an **F** and the reviews that include both a factual report and an opinion with an **F + O**.

F+O   1. **Room Service '38.** The Marx Brothers, Lucille Ball. A penniless theatrical producer and his aides fake the measles to keep from being kicked out of a hotel.

F+O   2. **Born Free '66.** Virginia McKenna, Bill Travers. Touching story of a pet lioness who must be trained to live in the wilds of Kenya. Good family viewing.

F   3. **Pretty Woman '90.** Richard Gere, Julia Roberts. A corporate raider pays a hooker to be his escort for a business week in Beverly Hills.

F+O   4. **Chinatown '74.** Jack Nicholson, Faye Dunaway. One of the few undisputed classics of the '70s, a near-perfect thriller. Nicholson is great as the half-boiled private eye, Dunaway is suitably mysterious as "The Woman," and the score is hypnotic.

F   5. **Killer Klowns From Outer Space '88.** Grant Cramer, Suzanne Snyder. Teens flee from large clowns who shoot people with popcorn.

F   6. **Cocoon '85.** Don Ameche, Wilford Brimley. Residents of a Florida retirement home find a fountain of youth in an abandoned swimming pool supercharged with an alien life force.

F   7. **The Little Mermaid '88.** A mermaid princess falls in love with an earthly prince. From the Hans Christian Anderson tale. Animated.

F+O   8. **9 to 5 '80.** Jane Fonda, Lily Tomlin, Dolly Parton. Some inspired early scenes in this satire about oppressed secretaries, but it comes apart about halfway through. You'll know when.

F   9. **Crazy People '90.** Dudley Moore, Daryl Hannah. An adman lands in a mental asylum and turns the inmates into copywriters.

___F_O___ 10. **Whose Life Is It Anyway? '81.** Richard Dreyfuss, John Cassavetes. Dreyfuss is superb as a paralyzed sculptor who wants to die. His comic gifts keep this adaptation of Brian Clark's Broadway play from being unrelievedly sad.

Other Points About Fact and Opinion

There are several added points to keep in mind when separating fact from opinion.

1   Statements of fact may be found to be untrue.

Suppose you went to the science-fiction movie your friend spoke of and discovered the aliens actually had blue rather than green skin. (Perhaps your friend is color-blind.) His statement would then be an error, not a fact. It is not unusual for evidence to show that a "fact" is not really true. It was once considered to be a fact that the world was flat, for example, but that "fact" turned out to be an error.

2   Opinions may be masked as facts.

People sometimes present their opinions as facts, as shown in practice sentence 8 on page 118. Here are two more examples:

In point of fact, neither candidate for the mayor's office is well-qualified.

The truth of the matter is that frozen foods taste as good as fresh foods.

Despite the words to the contrary, the above are not statements of fact but statements of opinion.

3   Remember that value words often represent opinions. Here are examples of value words:

Value Words

best	great	beautiful
worst	terrible	bad
better	lovely	good
worse	disgusting	wonderful

Value words often express judgments—they are generally subjective, not objective. While factual statements report on observed reality, subjective statements interpret reality. For example, the observation that it is raining outside is an objective one. The statement that the weather is bad, however, is subjective, an interpretation of reality. (Some people consider rain to be good weather.)

4   Finally, remember that much of what we read and hear is a mixture of fact and opinion.

Recognizing facts and opinions is important because much information that sounds factual is really opinion. A political candidate, for example, may say, "My record is outstanding." Voters would be wise to wonder what the value word *outstanding* means to this candidate. Or an advertisement may claim that a particular automobile is "the most economical car on the road today," a statement that at first seems factual. But what is meant by *economical*? If the car offers the most miles per gallon but the worst record for expensive repairs, you might not agree that it's economical.

➤ *Practice 2*

Some of the statements below are facts, and some are opinions. Label facts with an **F** and opinions with an **O**. Remember that facts can be proven, but opinions give personal views.

___F___ 1. Novels by Dean R. Koontz include *Cold Fire, Watchers,* and *The Bad Place.*

___O___ 2. *Watchers,* by Dean R. Koontz, is a terrifying story that is bound to keep you awake at night.

___F___ 3. A Colorado farmer wrote the car maker Henry Ford asking to exchange six mounted moose heads for a new car.

___O___ 4. Henry Ford was wrong when he claimed that laziness and idleness cause most of the world's troubles.

___O___ 5. Letting a faucet drip continually is the best way to prevent frozen water pipes.

___F___ 6. Permanent precautions against frozen pipes include wrapping them in fiberglass insulation or heat tape.

___O___ 7. Too many drugs are prescribed for people suffering from depression.

___F___ 8. Depression is most common among persons between the ages of twenty-five and forty-four.

___F___ 9. More Bibles have been printed than any other book in history.

___O___ 10. The Roman Catholic concept of God is more correct than the Protestant or the Jewish view.

➤ *Practice 3*

Some of the statements below are facts, and some are opinions; in addition, three include fact and opinion. Label facts with an **F**, opinions with an **O**, and statements of fact *and* opinion with an **F + O**.

___O___ 1. German shepherds are the scariest dogs alive.

_____ 2. The dog that bites people the most often, according to one twenty-seven-year study, is the German shepherd.

_____ 3. German shepherds, which always make poor pets, are used in police work and as guide dogs for the blind.

_____ 4. Because many studies have concluded that smoking is a health hazard, cigarettes should be banned.

_____ 5. Smokers have no regard for other people's health.

_____ 6. Smoking is a major cause of lung cancer.

_____ 7. Executives of corporations that pollute the environment should be jailed.

_____ 8. Waste chemicals from some companies have gotten into community water supplies.

_____ 9. Canada and the United States negotiated on how to control acid rain, the biggest pollution problem of all.

_____ 10. In point of fact, pollution is the greatest danger humankind faces today.

Facts and Opinions in Passages

People tend to accept what they read as fact, but much of what we read is actually opinion. Keeping an eye out for opinion will help you to think for yourself and to question what you read.

Two sentences in the following passage are facts, two are opinions, and one combines fact and opinion. Read the passage, and identify facts with an **F**, opinions with an **O**, and the statement of fact *and* opinion with an **F + O**.

> [1]There were several queens of Egypt by the name of Cleopatra, including the one who ruled in the days of Antony and Caesar. [2]She is one of the most interesting figures in Egyptian history. [3]History records that she was born in 69 B.C. and killed herself almost forty years later. [4]The story of how she killed herself is very easy to believe. [5]Reports say she killed herself with an asp, the Egyptian cobra— a symbol of Egyptian royalty, so there could have been no better way for the queen to end her life.

1. _____   2. _____   3. _____   4. _____   5. _____

Sentence 1 contains facts set down in historical records. Sentence 2 expresses an opinion—some may feel Cleopatra is not one of the most interesting figures in Egyptian history. Sentence 3 contains more facts of history. Sentence 4 contains an opinion—how easy something is to believe will differ from person to person. The last sentence is a mixture of fact and opinion: The beginning parts of the sentence are facts, but what the best way would have been for Cleopatra to end her life is certainly a matter of opinion.

➤ Practice 4

The following passage contains five sentences. Two sentences are facts, two are opinions, and one combines fact and opinion. Identify the facts with an **F**, the opinions with an **O**, and the statement of fact *and* opinion with an **F + O**.

[1]Plants that people call weeds are often undeserving of such a negative name. [2]Ralph Waldo Emerson had the right idea—he once described a weed as "a plant whose virtues have not yet been discovered." [3]Clearly, weeds aren't always so bad. [4]For example, they can replenish depleted top soil with minerals. [5]Also, some plants that are called weeds are edible and contain vitamins.

1. _O_   2. _F+O_   3. _O_   4. _F_   5. _F_

➤ Review Test 1

A. Three of the statements below are facts, and three are opinions. Identify facts with an **F** and opinions with an **O**.

_____ 1. A bouquet of red roses is the best possible Mother's Day gift.

_____ 2. Roses have been found in dry bouquets in ancient Egyptian tombs.

_____ 3. The voting age in America is eighteen.

_____ 4. If eighteen-year-olds are old enough to serve in the military, they're old enough to vote.

_____ 5. At the turn of the century, only one of ten married women held a paying job.

_O_ 6. For self-fulfillment, any mother in today's world should hold down an outside job as well as care for her children.

B. Here are short reviews taken from a newspaper movie guide. Some reviews present only factual reports; others contain opinions about the movie as well. Identify the factual reviews with an **F** and the reviews that include both a factual report and an opinion with an **F + O**.

___F___ 7. **My Mom's a Werewolf '89.** Susan Blakely, John Saxon. Bitten on the toe by a pet-shop owner, a woman turns into a werewolf.

___F+O___ 8. **Witness for the Prosecution '58.** Tyrone Power, Marlene Dietrich. Agatha Christie's nail-biter about a London murder trial, directed by the matchless Billy Wilder. Superb acting by Power as the accused and Dietrich as his wife.

___F+O___ 9. **Little Darlings '80.** Tatum O'Neal, Kristy McNichol. Two sexually curious girls go to summer camp and make a bet: whoever loses her virginity first, wins. Sounds vulgar, but with affecting performances, especially McNichol's.

___F___ 10. **Hard to Kill '90.** Steven Seagal, Kelly Le Brock. Pronounced dead but not, a cop recovers years later and seeks revenge.

➤ Review Test 2

A. Some of the statements below are facts, and some are opinions; in addition, two include both fact and opinion. Identify facts with an **F**, opinions with an **O**, and statements of fact *and* opinion with an **F + O**.

___F___ 1. My son once left half a sandwich under his bed for over a week.

___O___ 2. My son is the most considerate person in our family.

___F+O___ 3. Although my son got a B in English this semester, he deserved an A.

___F___ 4. New York City is not the capital of New York State.

___F+O___ 5. New York City, where visitors can see Broadway plays, museums, and the Statue of Liberty, is the perfect place for a summer vacation.

___O___ 6. The Empire State Building is easily the most memorable of all the sights in New York.

___F___ 7. Elephants are the largest of all land animals.

___F___ 8. Researchers have found that elephants react nervously to rabbits and dachshunds, but not to mice.

___O___ 9. Maybe the lively scampering of the rabbits and dachshunds is what makes elephants nervous.

___F+O___ 10. Because they use their trunks both to clean themselves and to eat, elephants are the most fascinating animals in the zoo.

B. Each passage below contains five sentences. Two are facts, two are opinions, and one combines fact and opinion. Identify facts with an **F**, opinions with an **O**, and statements of fact *and* opinion with an **F + O**.

1.   [1]There are few more annoying problems than hiccups, which can last for hours or even days. [2]According to one doctor who has studied them, hiccups are usually caused by eating or drinking too quickly. [3]People do some pretty strange things to remedy this ridiculous problem. [4]Some common remedies include holding your breath, eating a teaspoon of sugar, and putting a paper bag over your head. [5]Undoubtedly, that last one is the strangest one of all.

    1. _F+O_   2. _F_   3. _O_   4. _F_   5. _O_

2.   [1]The Lincoln Memorial is surely America's best loved public monument. [2]Designed by Henry Beacon, it was dedicated on Memorial Day, 1922, more than fifty years after a memorial to Lincoln was first proposed. [3]Built to resemble a Greek temple, it contains a seated figure of Lincoln by sculptor Daniel Chester French. [4]Many people probably learn to admire the monument long before they visit it in person through seeing its picture, which is on the penny and the five-dollar bill. [5]All Americans must feel pride mingled with sorrow when they come to Washington in person and look up at the kindly, mournful face of Abraham Lincoln.

    1. _O_   2. _F_   3. _F_   4. _F+O_   5. _O_

➤ Review Test 3

A. To review what you've learned in this chapter, complete each of the following sentences about facts and opinions.

1.   A (*fact, opinion*) _____fact_____ can be proven true through objective evidence.

2.   (*Facts, Opinions*) _____opinions_____ often include words that express judgments.

3.   An example of a comparison that expresses a personal judgment is (*taller, more attractive*) _____more attractive_____.

4.   Readers would probably expect a(n) (*editorial, political speech, news report, film review*) _____news report_____ to be totally factual.

B. Here is a chance to apply your understanding of facts and opinions to a full article. The selection will help you think about how much other people's expectations can influence your behavior.

Following the selection are questions on facts and opinions. To help you continue reinforcing the skills taught in previous chapters, there are also questions on:
- vocabulary in context
- central point and main ideas
- supporting details
- transitions
- patterns of organization.

Words to Watch

Following are some words in the reading that do not have strong context support. Each word is followed by the number of the paragraph in which it appears and its meaning there.

randomly (7): without choosing in any particular way
incredibly (8): unbelievably
critical (12): of key importance; crucial
determinant (14): a factor that contributes to an effect

HOW PEOPLE RISE—AND FALL— TO EXPECTATIONS OF OTHERS

Darrell Sifford

I was at the seashore, listening to a radio station that plays big-band music, and I couldn't believe what I was hearing—not big-band music, but an announcement about a dance to which parents, it said, should be certain to direct their adolescents. **1**

It was a fine idea for a dance, the announcer said, because it would bring peace of mind to the parents whose children attended. When everybody arrived, shortly after 7 on a Saturday night, the doors would be locked—yes, locked—and nobody would be permitted to leave until 10, when the dance would end and parents could pick up their children. There would be no need for parents to worry about liquor, drugs, fights or undesirable people. Responsible adults would be there to supervise things, which would be safe and secure. Not to worry. Just bring your child and enjoy your Saturday night. **2**

You understand—don't you?—why I couldn't believe what I heard. Can you imagine that at this date, anybody still believes that it's prudent for parents to announce to their children that they don't trust them and that the only way they—the parents—can relax is to know that their children are locked up? Yes, safe and secure. Not to worry. **3**

I wonder what the parents will do when their children go off to college. **4**

It is so well established that it's beyond serious challenge, that people tend to   5
rise—or drop—to the expectations of others who are important in their lives.

Psychologist Kevin Leman has told me all about learning tracks. Children who   6
are in the so-called Eagle reading class know that they're expected to do better, that
they're considered brighter than everybody else—and, as a result, they consistently
perform better. They're merely equaling what is expected of them. On the other hand,
those in the Crow reading class know that they're expected to fumble and bumble,
that they're considered somewhat slow in the head. And they don't disappoint those
who have communicated their lack of high expectation.

There was an experiment that has become a legend in education—about a   7
teacher who randomly° placed some students on a fast track and told them that they
belonged there, and some students on a slow track and told them that they belonged
there. The stated expectation carried more weight than the students' intelligence,
because nearly all of them performed as they had been told they would—and should.

Psychiatrist Spurgeon English once told me during an interview that children   8
tend to equal expectations in just about everything—not just educationally, but
behaviorally. A child who constantly is told by parents that he is good and
worthwhile acts that way. A child who constantly is told that he's no good acts that
way, too. After that, things rapidly go downhill, and parents, incredibly°, scratch their
heads and wonder what's wrong with the child.

To a great extent, it works the same way with adults, too. We tend to equal   9
expectations, good or bad, high or low. During the 1989 football season, you may
recall, Mike Ditka, coach of the Chicago Bears, announced at a news conference
after a disappointing loss that his team was so inept, that it probably wouldn't win
another game all year. It would surprise him, said Ditka, if the players had enough
inside them to win again.

True to Ditka's expectation, the rest of the season was a disaster. The Bears   10
unquestionably were the most disappointing team in the National Football League.
What happened? During an interview after the season had ended, the Bears' all-pro
line-backer, Mike Singletary, explained it this way:

"We have a lot of young kids on this team, and if they're told often enough that   11
they're not any good, they begin to believe it—and that's how they play."

Of course, it can work the other way, too. One of the many things I admired   12
about Whitey Herzog, former manager of the St. Louis Cardinals baseball team, was
how he handled many of his young players who had just been called up from the
minor leagues. Time and time again he would throw them into critical° games—an
inexperienced kid would be assigned to pitch in the heat of a pennant race—and time
and time again, the inexperienced kid would deliver. Why? I like to think that it was
because they wanted to equal Herzog's expectation that they were good enough to be
Cardinals, that they belonged there.

Within marriage, expectations tend to be fulfilled, too. If you expect your   13
spouse to treat you fairly—and if this is conveyed to the spouse—there is greater
likelihood of your getting fair treatment. If you expect your spouse to cheat—and
communicate this expectation through your actions—there is greater likelihood that
your spouse will cheat.

At work, the boss who expects the people in his department to perform well 14
consistently outshines the boss who expects his people to perform poorly. A few
years ago, psychologist Alan Loy McGinnis, in his book *Bringing Out the Best in
People*, listed expectation, clearly communicated to employees, as a key
determinant° in how they performed.

Professional athletes, married people, workers—all of us, I am convinced—are 15
captives of expectation. That's just the way people are.

I found myself thinking for days about the announcement of the lockup dance. 16
Who—what youngster—would go to a lockup dance? I suspect that only those whose
parents forced them to go—so they, the parents, could have a night off, free of worry.
My guess is that someday, the parents might find that they had paid a high price for
their nights off.

What do you think? 17

Reading Comprehension Questions

Vocabulary in Context

1. The word *inept* in "Mike Ditka . . . announced . . . that his team was so
   inept, that it probably wouldn't win another game all year" (paragraph 9)
   means
   a. quiet.
   b. unskilled.
   c. underweight.
   d. unpopular.

Central Point and Main Ideas

2. The central point of the article is stated in paragraph
   a. 1.
   b. 3.
   c. 5.
   d. 6.

3. Which sentence best expresses the main idea of paragraph 13?
   a. Sentence 1
   b. Sentence 2
   c. Sentence 3

Supporting Details

4. People are influenced by what is expected of them by
   a. spouses.
   b. bosses.
   c. both of the above.
   d. neither of the above.

Transitions

5. *Complete the sentence:* The contrast transition in paragraph 6 is

   <u>on the other hand</u>

6. The relationship expressed in the sentence below is one of
   a. addition.
   b. illustration.
   c. contrast.
   d. cause and effect.

   If you expect your spouse to treat you fairly—and if this is conveyed to the spouse—there is greater likelihood of your getting fair treatment. (Paragraph 13)

Patterns of Organization

7. The article
   a. narrates a series of events in a time order.
   b. discusses a certain type of cause and effect.
   c. presents a definition with examples.

Fact and Opinion

8. Paragraph 1 expresses
   a. fact.
   b. opinion.
   c. a mixture of fact and opinion.

9. Paragraph 7 is primarily
   a. fact.
   b. opinion.

10. In the last two sentences of paragraph 16, the author expresses
    a. facts about parents.
    b. his opinions.

7

Inferences

You have probably heard the expression "to read between the lines." When you "read between the lines," you pick up ideas that are not directly stated in what you are reading. These implied ideas are often important for a full understanding of what an author means. Discovering the ideas in writing that are not stated directly is called *making inferences*, or *drawing conclusions*.

INFERENCES IN EVERYDAY LIFE

Consider first how often you make inferences in everyday life. For example, suppose you are sitting in a coffee shop at lunchtime. A woman sits down at the next table. Here is what you observe:

- She is wearing an expensive-looking suit, a silk blouse, gold jewelry, and a gold band on the third finger of her left hand.
- The woman opens a brief case and takes out some manila folders; she begins to study them.
- You notice that she also has a child's crayon drawing in the briefcase.

As you sit in the coffee shop, you may make several inferences about this woman:

- She's on her lunch break.
- She works in an office, perhaps as a lawyer or an executive.
- She is married and has a young child.

How did you arrive at these inferences? First of all, you used your experience and general knowledge of people. Secondly, you made informed guesses based on the facts you observed. Of course, not all your inferences might prove true. For example, the woman could own her own business, or the child's drawing might have been done by her nephew or niece. You cannot prove or disprove your guesses without asking the woman directly, but your inferences may well be correct.

Take a moment now and jot down what you might infer if you saw each of the following:

1. A high school has uniformed security guards patrolling the halls.

    Your inference: _____

2. A dog cringes when someone tries to pet him.

    Your inference: _____

The inferences you probably made are that, in the first situation, the high school has had some very disturbing discipline and/or crime problems and, in the second situation, the dog has previously been mishandled.

Take a moment now to look at the following *New Yorker* cartoon.

"Dad, can you read?"

Drawing by Peter Steiner; © 1990 The New Yorker Magazine, Inc.

Now put a check by the two inferences that are most logically based on the information given in the cartoon.

＿＿ 1. The father has a problem with his vision.

＿＿ 2. The little boy is doing his homework.

＿＿ 3. The man must watch a great deal of television.

＿＿ 4. The father cannot read.

＿＿ 5. The father prefers a good novel to watching TV.

Here is an explanation of each item:

1.   This inference is well supported by the cartoon. The father is wearing glasses, and he is sitting very close to the TV set.

2.   This is not a logical inference. The cartoonist would have given us more clues if he wanted us to think that the boy was reading a school book.

3.   This is a logical inference. The boy's question and the father's activity in the picture lead us to believe that the boy never sees his father reading, only watching TV.

4.   This inference is not well supported. The father doesn't seem to read much, but that doesn't mean he cannot; in fact, the magazine on the television suggests that he can read.

5.   This is not a logical inference. The boy's question tells us that he never sees his father reading.

➤ Practice 1

Put a check by the inference *most logically based* on the information provided. Look first at the example.

Example

A student always sits in the back of the classroom.

____ a. The student dislikes the course.

____ b. The student is unprepared for class.

✓ c. The student feels uncomfortable in the front of the room.

____ d. The student is farsighted.

The correct answer is *c*. Based on the information we are given, we can conclude only that the student—for some reason—does not like sitting in the front. We are not given enough information to know why the student feels this way.

1.   A pencil has teeth marks on it.

____ a. The person who used the pencil was nervous.

____ b. The pencil was chewed up by a toddler or pet.

____ c. Someone or something chewed the pencil.

____ d. The pencil belongs to someone who is trying to quit smoking.

2.   A person is in the lobby of a hospital in a wheelchair.

____ a. The person is paralyzed.

____ b. The person would like someone to push him or her.

____ c. The person is disabled in some way.

____ d. The person is about to be admitted to the hospital.

3. A car has bumper stickers that read, "I Brake for Animals," "Save the Whales," and "Have You Thanked a Green Plant Today?"

____ a. A driver of the car supports environmental issues.

____ b. A driver of the car is an environmental scientist.

____ c. A driver of the car has pets.

____ d. The owner of the car is a college student.

4. The street is wet, but the sidewalks are dry.

____ a. An unusual rain fell only on the street.

____ b. It rained everywhere, but someone dried the sidewalks.

____ c. A street-cleaning vehicle sprayed the street.

____ d. Children with water guns must have played on the street.

5. Inside of a car with an out-of-town license are several maps, suitcases, and bags of snacks.

____ a. The driver of the car is on vacation.

____ b. The driver of the car is on a business trip.

____ c. The driver of the car has children.

____ d. The driver of the car is on a trip of some kind.

INFERENCES IN READING

In reading, too, we make logical leaps from the information given in a straightforward way to ideas that are not stated directly. As the scholar S. I. Hayakawa has said, inferences are "statements about the unknown made on the basis of the known." To draw inferences, we use all the clues provided by the writer, our own experience, and logic.

In this book, you have already practiced making inferences in the chapter on vocabulary. There you had to use context clues within sentences to infer the meanings of words. Also, in the chapter on main ideas, you had to "read between the lines" in order to find implied main ideas. The intent of this chapter is to broaden your ability to make inferences about what you read.

Read the following passage and then check the three inferences that can logically be drawn from it.

A famous psychology experiment conducted by Dr. John B. Watson demonstrates that people, like animals, can be conditioned—trained to respond in a particular way to certain stimulations. Watson gave an eleven-month-old baby named Albert a soft, furry white rat. Each time Albert tried to stroke the rat, Dr. Watson hit a metal bar with a hammer. Before long, Albert was not only afraid of white rats but also of white rabbits, white dogs, and white fur coats. He even screamed at the sight of a Santa Claus mask.

___ 1. Dr. Watson did not like small children.

___ 2. Before the experiment, Albert was not afraid of white rats.

___ 3. Albert had been familiar with rats before the experiment.

___ 4. If he had seen a black fur coat, Albert would have screamed.

___ 5. Albert connected the loud noise of the hammer striking the metal bar with the white rat.

___ 6. Albert was afraid of loud noises from the beginning.

Here is an explanation of each item:

1. This is not a logical inference. While the passage may make us wonder about Watson's attitude toward babies, it doesn't give enough information for us logically to infer that he did not like small children.

2. This is a logical inference. Because Albert tried to pet the rat, it is fair to assume that he wasn't frightened of the animal.

3. This is not a logical inference. The passage gives no clues about Albert having previous experience with rats.

4. This is not a logical inference. The passage makes no mention of Albert's response to any color but white.

5. This is a logical inference. Because the loud noise appears to have changed Albert's attitude toward the rat, we can assume he associated the noise with the rat.

6. This is a logical inference. Since the noise is what made Albert afraid of the rat, we have to infer that he was afraid of the noise. In addition, experience tells us that babies are likely to be frightened of unexpected loud noises.

The following activities will improve your ability to make inferences as you read.

➤ Practice 2

Read the following passage. Then circle the letter of the most logical answer to each question, based on the facts given in the passage.

A corporate president recently made a visit to a nearby Indian reservation as part of his firm's public relations program. "We realize that we have not hired any Indians in the five years our company has been located in this area," he told the assembled tribesmen, "but we are looking into the matter very carefully." "Hora, hora," said some of the Indians. "We would like to eventually hire 5 percent of our total work force from this reservation," he said. "Hora, hora," shouted more of the Indians. Encouraged by their enthusiasm, the president closed his short address by telling them that he hoped his firm would be able to take some hiring action within the next couple of years. "Hora, hora, hora," cried the total group. With a feeling of satisfaction the president left the hall and was taken on a tour of the reservation. Stopping in a field to admire some of the horses grazing there, the president asked if he could walk up closer to the animals. "Certainly," said his Indian driver, "but be careful not to step in the hora."

1. To get the main point of this passage, the reader must infer
   a. the location of the reservation.
   b. what kind of company the president headed.
   c. the meaning of the word "hora."

2. From the president's speech, we can infer that
   a. his firm had a great interest in hiring the Indians.
   b. his firm had little interest in hiring the Indians.
   c. his firm had a stated policy never to hire Indians.

3. From the passage, we can infer that
   a. the Indians believed the president's speech.
   b. the Indians did not believe the president's speech.
   c. the Indians were confused by the president's speech.

4. From the passage, we can infer that the president
   a. thought the Indians deserved to be hired.
   b. thought his company should not hire the Indians.
   c. misinterpreted the Indians' reaction to his speech.

5. From the passage, we can infer that the main reason the president spoke to the Indians about jobs was that
   a. they needed the jobs.
   b. he thought promising jobs to the Indians would make his company look good.
   c. he thought hiring the Indians would be good for his company.

➤ *Practice 3*

Read the following passage and check the three inferences that are most logically based on the given facts.

The *Chicago Tribune* once wrote that Henry Ford was an ignoramus. Ford sued, challenging the paper to "prove it." During the trial, Ford was asked dozens of simple, general information questions: "When was the Civil War?" "Name the presidents of the United States." And so on. Ford, who had little formal education, could answer very few. Finally, exasperated, he said, "I don't know the answers to those questions, but I could find a man in five minutes who does. I use my brain to think, not store up a lot of useless facts."

___ 1. Henry Ford was probably angered by the article in the *Chicago Tribune*.

___ 2. Ford frequently sued people.

___ 3. Ford won the case in court.

___ 4. The *Tribune* won the case in court.

___ 5. Ford would have been more successful had he had a formal education.

___ 6. Ford believed that knowing where to find a fact is good enough.

___ 7. Ford regretted not having a more formal education.

___ 8. Ford believed that knowing how to think is more important than knowing facts.

INFERENCES IN LITERATURE

Inference is very important in reading literature. While writers of factual material usually state directly what they mean, creative writers often *show* what they mean. It is up to the reader to infer the point of what the creative writer has to say. For instance, a non-fiction writer might write the following:

Marian was angry at her father.

But the novelist might write:

Marian's eyes narrowed when her father spoke to her. She cut him off in mid-sentence with the words, "I don't have time to argue with you."

The author has *shown* us the anger with specific detail rather than simply stating the fact of the anger. To understand imaginative writing, then, you must often use your inference skills—just as you do in everyday life.

Applying inferences skills can increase your appreciation of such literary forms as novels, short stories, plays, essays, autobiographies, and poetry. Poetry, especially, by its nature implies much of its meaning. Implications are often made through comparisons. For example, Emily Dickinson begins one of her poems:

Hope is the thing with feathers
That perches in the soul
And sings the tune without the words,
And never stops at all.

Dickinson compares hope here with a singing bird. This implies, among other things, that hope is a sweet and welcome thing.

On the next page is the passage that starts the autobiography *Growing Up* by the *New York Times'* columnist Russell Baker. Read it, and then do the activity that follows.

At the age of eighty my mother had her last bad fall, and after that her mind wandered free through time. Some days she went to weddings and funerals that had taken place half a century earlier. On others she presided over family dinners cooked on Sunday afternoons for children who were now gray with age. Through all this she lay in bed but moved across time, traveling among the dead decades with a speed and ease beyond the gift of physical science.

"Where's Russell?" she asked one day when I came to visit at the nursing home.

"I'm Russell," I said.

She gazed at this improbably overgrown figure out of an inconceivable future and promptly dismissed it.

"Russell's only this big," she said, holding her hand, palm down, two feet from the floor. That day she was a young country wife with chickens in the backyard and a view of hazy blue Virginia mountains behind the apple orchard, and I was a stranger old enough to be her father.

Early one morning she phoned me in New York. "Are you coming to my funeral today?" she asked.

It was an awkward question with which to be awakened. "What are you talking about, for God's sake?" was the best reply I could manage.

"I'm being buried today," she declared briskly, as though announcing an important social event.

"I'll phone you back," I said and hung up, and when I did phone back she was all right, although she wasn't all right, of course, and we all knew she wasn't.

She had always been a small woman—short, light-boned, delicately structured—but now, under the white hospital sheet, she was becoming tiny. I thought of a doll with huge, fierce eyes. There had always been a fierceness in her. It showed in that angry, challenging thrust of the chin when she issued an opinion, and a great one she had always been for issuing opinions.

"I tell people exactly what's on my mind," she has been fond of boasting. "I tell them what I think, whether they like it or not." Often they had not liked it. She could be sarcastic to people in whom she detected evidence of the ignoramus or the fool.

"It's not always good policy to tell people exactly what's on your mind," I used to caution her.

"If they don't like it, that's too bad," was her customary reply, "because that's the way I am."

And so she was. A formidable woman. Determined to speak her mind, determined to have her way, determined to bend those who opposed her. In that time when I had known her best, my mother had hurled herself at life with chin thrust forward, eyes blazing, and an energy that made her seem always on the run.

She ran after squawking chickens, an axe in her hand, determined on a beheading that would put dinner in the pot. She ran when she made the beds, ran when she set the table. One Thanksgiving she burned herself badly when, running up from the cellar oven with the ceremonial turkey, she tripped on the stairs and tumbled back down, ending at the bottom in the debris of giblets, hot gravy and battered turkey. Life was combat, and victory was not to the lazy, the timid the slugabed, the drugstore cowboy, the libertine, the mushmouth afraid to tell people exactly what was on his mind whether people liked it or not. She ran.

Now put a check by the six inferences most solidly based on the words and images in the passage. Refer to the passage as needed when making your choices.

____ 1. Baker's mother knew she was remembering past events.

____ 2. Baker's mother thought she was actually living at the time of some memories.

____ 3. The author's mother's last bad fall must have affected her mind.

____ 4. Baker's mother predicted the day of her own funeral.

____ 5. Once she imagined that her funeral would take place that day.

____ 6. In describing the incident in which his mother said, "I'm being buried today," Baker uses the term "all right" with two different meanings.

____ 7. Baker's mother had been a calm woman with a patient, encouraging manner.

____ 8. She was an energetic, blunt person.

____ 9. Baker chose to describe his mother more sentimentally than realistically.

____ 10. His mother's travels "among the dead decades" caused Baker himself to remember earlier days.

Here are explanations for each of the ten inferences.

1-2. Because Baker's mother expected the real Russell to be only two feet high, we know that she was unaware of where she was and that she was mentally experiencing earlier times in her life. Thus inference 1 is not well supported, but inference 2 is solidly based on the given details.

3. The first sentence of the passage connects Baker's mother's fall with her mind wandering "free through time." Therefore the details of the passage also support inference 3.

4-5. Baker doesn't state that his mother's funeral took place on the day she said it would. This tells us that she did not predict the day of her funeral, but that she only imagined it was about to happen. You thus should have checked 5, but not 4.

6. Since the two uses of the term "all right" seem contradictory ("she was all right, although she wasn't all right"), we can assume that Baker intends them to have different meanings. Thus the statement is a well-supported inference.

In writing "when I did phone back she was all right," Baker refers to his mother having overcome the false belief that she was being buried that day. But when he states "she wasn't all right, of course, and we all knew she wasn't," Baker refers to his mother's general poor physical and mental condition, which she had not overcome.

7-8. The author's description of his mother as someone who had been "always on the run" tells us she was more energetic than calm. And because he describes her as someone with "fierceness in her" who "always told people exactly what was on her mind," sometimes sarcastically, we can conclude that she was more blunt than patient and encouraging. Thus inference 7 is not well supported, but inference 8 is.

9. This inference is not supported by the passage. In discussing a senile parent, some writers might be tempted to dwell on their warmest, sweetest memories. Since Baker describes his mother as a blunt and impatient person who was often disliked, we can conclude that he has avoided sentimentality.

10. This inference is strongly based on the details of the passage. Baker remembers, for instance, how determined and energetic a person his mother was, running after chickens with an axe and once tumbling down the basement stairs after running up with the Thanksgiving turkey.

➤ *Practice 4*

Below is the beginning of Philip Roth's novel *Goodbye, Columbus*. Read the passage, and then circle the letter of the most logical answer to each question, based on the facts given in the passage.

myopic: better able to see things near at hand than things far away

The first time I saw Brenda she asked me to hold her glasses. Then she stepped out to the edge of the diving board and looked foggily into the pool; it could have been drained, myopic° Brenda would never have known it. She dove beautifully, and a moment later she was swimming back to the side of the pool, her head of short-clipped auburn hair held up, straight ahead of her, as though it were a rose on a long stem. She glided to the edge and then was beside me. "Thank you," she said, her eyes watery though not from the water. She extended a hand for her glasses but did not put them on until she turned and headed away. I watched her move off. Her hands suddenly appeared behind her. She caught the bottom of her suit between thumb and index finger and flicked what flesh had been showing back where it belonged. My blood jumped.

That night, before dinner, I called her.

"Who are you calling?" my Aunt Gladys asked.

"Some girl I met today."

"Doris introduced you?"

"Doris wouldn't introduce me to the guy who drains the pool, Aunt Gladys."

"Don't criticize all the time. A cousin's a cousin. How did you meet her?"

"I didn't really meet her. I saw her."

"Who is she?"

"Her last name is Patimkin."

"Patimkin I don't know," Aunt Gladys said, as if she knew anybody who belonged to the Green Lane Country Club. "You're going to call her you don't know her?"

"Yes," I explained. "I'll introduce myself."

"Casanova," she said, and went back to preparing my uncle's dinner. None of us ate together; my Aunt Gladys ate a five o'clock, my cousin Susan at five-thirty, me at six, and my uncle at six-thirty. There is nothing to explain this beyond the fact that my aunt is crazy.

"Where's the suburban phone book?" I asked after pulling out all the books tucked under the telephone table.

"What?"

"The suburban phone book. I want to call Short Hills."

"That skinny book? What, I gotta clutter my house with that, I never use it?"

"Where is it?"

"Under the dresser where the leg came off."

"For God's sake," I said.

"Call information better. You'll go yanking around there, you'll mess up my drawers. Don't bother me, you see your uncle'll be home soon. I haven't even fed you yet."

"Aunt Gladys, suppose tonight we all eat together. It's hot, it'll be easier for you."

"Sure, I should serve four different meals at once. You eat pot roast, Susan with the cottage cheese, Max has steak. Friday night is his steak night, I wouldn't deny him. And I'm having a little cold chicken. I should jump up and down twenty different times? What am I, a work-horse?"

"Why don't we all have steak, or cold chicken—"

"Twenty years I'm running a house. Go call your girl friend."

1. Brenda may not have put on her glasses until she turned away because she was
   a. confused.
   b. forgetful.
   c. vain.

2. When the narrator says his blood jumped, he is referring to his
   a. distaste for Brenda's behavior.
   b. surprise.
   c. sexual interest.

3. From the comparison of Brenda's head to "a rose on a long stem," we can infer that
   a. the narrator is interested in flowers.
   b. the narrator admires Brenda.
   c. Brenda is a florist.

4. We can conclude that Doris
   a. is related to the narrator.
   b. is a good friend of the narrator.
   c. once dated the narrator.

5. Aunt Gladys's nephew probably wants to call Brenda
   a. to arrange to introduce her to Doris.
   b. to watch her swim again.
   c. to ask her out on a date.

6. Aunt Gladys thinks
   a. her nephew should only call girls he has been formally introduced to.
   b. her nephew is being overly forward by calling Brenda Patimkin.
   c. both of the above.

7. Aunt Gladys appears to be
   a. a quiet, easygoing woman.
   b. a blunt, stubborn, and unreasonable woman.
   c. a mean, revengeful, and insane woman.

8. Brenda lives
   a. in the city.
   b. in the suburbs.
   c. at the country club.

9. We can conclude that the members of Aunt Gladys's family
   a. dislike each other.
   b. have different tastes in foods.
   c. have different working hours and so cannot eat together.

10. The narrator's attitude toward his "crazy" aunt is one of
    a. anger and hate.
    b. disappointment and shame.
    c. tolerance and affection.

➤ Review Test 1

A. After reading each passage, put a check by the *two* inferences that are most firmly based on the given facts.

1. Pulling the collar of his ragged jacket up against the rain, the unshaven man headed for the shelter of a store doorway. He bit his lip as he thought about how wet everything would be tonight and wondered if he would need to pay for a dry bed.

   ____ a. The man is homeless.

   ____ b. He's thinking of stealing some money.

   ____ c. He sometimes sleeps outside at night.

2. The freak weather transformed the outdoors into a rigid fairyland. Young leaves hung stiffly, and the daffodils seemed buried alive under a glass-like coating.

_____ a. The daffodils were encased in ice.

_____ b. Such weather had never happened before.

_____ c. Rain had turned to ice in spring.

3.   Shortly after the young woman sat down in the bus, she lit a cigarette. The man next to her waved some smoke away, nudged her, and pointed to the sign at the front of the bus.

_____ a. The man had never smoked.

_____ b. The smoke was bothering the man.

_____ c. The man pointed to a no-smoking sign.

B. After reading each passage, put a check by the *two* inferences that are most firmly based on the given facts.

4.   A restaurant by the name of Broiler Inn was very successful. There was another restaurant by the same name in a town a hundred miles away. One day, the second Broiler Inn was temporarily shut down by the health department because several customers had suffered food poisoning. The case received a lot of publicity in the newspapers. Before long, that Broiler Inn went out of business. And, although the first one hadn't changed in any way, it suffered a great loss of customers. Within a few months, it too had to close.

_____ a. Both restaurants were run by the same people.

_____ b. The customers with food poisoning sued the restaurant.

_____ c. The health department must have tried to find the cause of the food poisoning.

_____ d. The publicity about the second Broiler Inn affected the first one.

_____ e. There was an excellent chance of getting food poisoning at the first Broiler Inn.

5.   "I would suggest you concentrate your studying on the last chapter of the text," said Professor Moore. "And it would be a good idea to review the grammar rules we've discussed because errors will count against your grade. Finally, I'm going to pass out copies of a short story by Edgar Allan Poe, which will be the basis of an essay question. Study it well. Good luck to you all, and have a nice summer."

_____ a. Professor Moore is teaching an English class.

_____ b. He is a tough grader.

_____ c. The test will be all essay questions.

_____ d. The class has read other short stories by Poe.

_____ e. The test marks the end of the spring session.

➤ *Review Test 2*

A. Following is a passage from *A Hole In the World*, an autobiographical account by the Pulitzer Prize-winning author Richard Rhodes. Read the passage, and then check the *five* statements that can be logically inferred from the information given.

> We played dodgeball at recess. Dodgeball was my sport. I was light and quick and often managed to escape being picked off until I was the last of my team inside the circle, the winner of the round. My friend was usually my competition. One day I kidded him too sharply when he lost and I won. He gathered a knot of classmates afterward, the girl I dreamed about among them. They strolled over and surrounded me. They were smiling and I thought they were friendly; it didn't occur to me to dodge. The boys grabbed me. My friend led them. "You stink," he told me happily. "We think you're dirty. We want to see." They jerked down the straps on my bib overalls, held my arms high, peeled off my ragged shirt. They exposed my filth, my black armpits, my dirty neck for everyone to see. The faces of those children, the girl well forward among them, filled with horror perverted with glee. I went the only way I could go, down, dropping to the asphalt of the playground. They formed a circle around me, laughing and pointing. I couldn't get away. I covered my head and drew up my knees. I knew how to make myself invisible. I'd learned to make myself invisible when my stepmother attacked. It worked because I couldn't see her even if she could still see me. I made myself invisible. They couldn't hear me crying.

   ____ 1. The event took place when the author was a schoolboy.

   ____ 2. The event took place in the middle of winter.

   ____ 3. The author was usually clean, but just happened to be dirty that day.

   ____ 4. The author's friend meant to embarrass him.

   ____ 5. The author probably wasn't very well cared for at home.

   ____ 6. The author's stepmother abused him.

   ____ 7. Most stepmothers are cruel.

   ____ 8. Despite his stepmother's attacks, the author was very fond of her.

   ____ 9. When the author made himself "invisible," he was really putting others out of sight.

   ____ 10. The author never won at dodgeball again.

B. On the next page is a poem by Matthew Prior (who lived in England from 1664–1721). Read the poem, and then check the *five* inferences most solidly based on it.

A Reasonable Affliction°

On his death-bed poor Lubin lies
   His spouse is in despair;
With frequent cries, and mutual sighs,
   They both express their care.

"A different cause," says Parson Sly,
   "The same effect may give:
Poor Lubin fears that he may die;
   His wife, that he may live."

°*affliction:* a condition of pain, suffering, or anxiety

____ 1. Lubin is deathly ill.

____ 2. His wife is also deathly ill.

____ 3. Lubin and his wife are very religious.

____ 4. The poet recognizes that most marriages are bad ones.

____ 5. The poet recognizes that spouses aren't always devoted to each other.

____ 6. The reader's view of Lubin and his wife changes greatly in the second stanza.

____ 7. Lubin is a poor man.

____ 8. Lubin's wife hopes to inherit his great wealth.

____ 9. When Parson Sly speaks of "a different cause," he refers to the different reasons why Lubin is crying and his wife is crying.

____ 10. The word *affliction* (in the title) refers to two different problems, Lubin's and his wife's.

➤ Review Test 3

A. To review what you've learned in this chapter, complete each of the following sentences about inferences.

1. An inference is a conclusion that is (*directly stated, suggested*) _____ by the author.

2. When making inferences, it is (*a mistake, useful*) _____ to use our own experience as well as the author's clues.

3. When making inferences, it is (*a mistake, useful*) _____ to use our sense of logic as well as the author's clues.

4. Drawing inferences is a key skill in reading literature because writers of fiction do not so much (*tell, show*) _____ us what they mean as (*tell, show*) _____ us with specific details.

B. Here is a chance to apply your understanding of inferences to a full-length article. The reading, from *Newsday Magazine,* is a firsthand account of what it was like for one boy to be the first black student in a midwestern school.

Following the reading are questions on inferences. To help you continue reinforcing the skills taught in previous chapters, there are also questions on:
- vocabulary in context
- central point and main ideas
- supporting details
- transitions
- patterns of organization
- fact and opinion.

Words to Watch

Following are some words in the reading that do not have strong context support. Each word is followed by the number of the paragraph in which it appears and its meaning there.

pristine (2): still pure
prevailing (2): common
deplored (4): disapproved of
incipient (6): in the first stage of existence
derivative (7): not original
tentatively (9): with uncertainty
groused (10): complained
ventured (10): dared
mortified (11): humiliated

I BECAME HER TARGET

Roger Wilkins

My favorite teacher's name was "Deadeye" Bean. Her real name was Dorothy. 1 She taught American history to eighth graders in the junior high section of Creston, the high school that served the north end of Grand Rapids, Michigan. It was the fall of 1944. Franklin D. Roosevelt was president; American troops were battling their way across France; Joe DiMaggio was still in the service; the Montgomery bus boycott was more than a decade away, and I was a 12-year-old black newcomer in a school that was otherwise all white.

My mother, who had been a widow in New York, had married my stepfather, a 2 Grand Rapids physician, the year before, and he had bought the best house he could afford for his new family. The problem for our new neighbors was that their neighborhood had previously been pristine° (in their terms) and that they were ignorant about black people. The prevailing° wisdom in the neighborhood was that we were spoiling it and that we ought to go back where we belonged (or alternatively, ought not intrude where we were not wanted). There was a lot of angry talk among the adults, but nothing much came of it.

But some of the kids, those first few weeks, were quite nasty. They threw   3
stones at me, chased me home when I was on foot and spat on my bike seat when I
was in class. For a time, I was a pretty lonely, friendless and sometimes frightened
kid. I was just transplanted from Harlem, and here in Grand Rapids, the dominant
culture was speaking to me insistently. I can see now that those youngsters were
bullying and culturally disadvantaged. I knew then that they were bigoted, but the
culture spoke to me more powerfully than my mind and I felt ashamed for being
different—a nonstandard person.

I now know that Dorothy Bean understood most of that and deplored° it. So   4
things began to change when I walked into her classroom. She was a pleasant-
looking single woman, who looked old and wrinkled to me at the time, but who was
probably about 40. Whereas my other teachers approached the problem of easing in
their new black pupil by ignoring him for the first few weeks, Miss Bean went right
at me. On the morning after having read our first assignment, she asked me the first
question. I later came to know that in Grand Rapids, she was viewed as a very liberal
person who believed, among other things, that Negroes were equal.

I gulped and answered her question and the follow-up. They weren't brilliant   5
answers, but they did establish the facts that I had read the assignment and that I
could speak English. Later in the hour, when one of my classmates had bungled an
answer, Miss Bean came back to me with a question that required me to clean up the
girl's mess and established me as a smart person.

Thus, the teacher began to give me human dimensions, though not perfect ones   6
for an eighth grader. It was somewhat better to be an incipient° teacher's pet than
merely a dark presence in the back of the room onto whose silent form my classmates
could fit all the stereotypes they carried in their heads.

A few days later, Miss Bean became the first teacher ever to require me to   7
think. She asked my opinion about something Jefferson had done. In those days, all
my opinions were derivative°. I was for Roosevelt because my parents were and I
was for the Yankees because my older buddy from Harlem was a Yankee fan.
Besides, we didn't have opinions about historical figures like Jefferson. Like our high
school building or old Mayor Welch, he just was.

After I had stared at her for a few seconds, she said: "Well, should he have   8
bought Louisiana or not?"

"I guess so," I replied tentatively°.   9

Why! What kind of question was that, I groused° silently. But I ventured° an   10
answer. Day after day, she kept doing that to me, and my answers became stronger
and more confident. She was the first teacher to give me the sense that thinking was
part of education and that I could form opinions that had some value.

Her final service to me came on a day when my mind was wandering and I was   11
idly digging my pencil into the writing surface on the arm of my chair. Miss Bean
impulsively threw a hunk of gum eraser at me. By amazing chance, it hit my hand
and sent the pencil flying. She gasped, and I crept mortified° after my pencil as the
class roared. That was the ice breaker. Afterward, kids came up to me to laugh about
"Old Deadeye Bean." The incident became a legend, and I, a part of that story,
became a person to talk to. So that's how I became just another kid in school and
Dorothy Bean became "Old Dead-Eye."

Reading Comprehension Questions

Vocabulary in Context

1. The word *bungled* in "when one of my classmates bungled an answer, Miss Bean came back to me with a question that required me to clean up the girl's mess and established me as a smart person" (paragraph 5) means
   a. improved.
   b. handled poorly.
   c. whispered.
   d. corrected.

Central Point and Main Ideas

2. Which sentence best expresses the central point of the article?
   a. A boy used to Harlem schools had to go to a previously all-white school in Grand Rapids.
   b. The author was a lot smarter than the other kids thought he would be.
   c. A teacher helped the first black student in school to grow intellectually and to be welcomed as an individual.
   d. Teachers are the most important influences in a person's life.

3. Which sentence best expresses the main idea of paragraph 7?
   a. Miss Bean asked the author for his opinion about something Thomas Jefferson had done.
   b. Miss Bean was the first teacher to ask the author to have his own opinion about something.
   c. The author had been in favor of Franklin D. Roosevelt and the Yankees because his parents had been in favor of them.
   d. It seemed odd to the author to have opinions about historical figures like Thomas Jefferson.

Supporting Details

4. At first, the teachers at the school other than Miss Bean
   a. ignored the author.
   b. challenged the author.
   c. praised the author.
   d. protected the author.

Transitions

5. The first word of the *last* sentence of paragraph 11 signals a relationship of
   a. time.
   b. addition.
   c. illustration.
   d. cause and effect.

Patterns of Organization

  6. The pattern of paragraph 11 is a combination of
      a. a list of items and comparison/contrast.
      b. time order and cause/effect.
      c. time order and definition/example.
      d. contrast and definition/example.

Fact and Opinion

  7. The first paragraph is made up of
      a. facts.
      b. opinions.
      c. facts and opinions.

Inferences

  8. From the reading, we suspect that the author
      a. had been a poor student in Harlem.
      b. had never before attended a primarily white school.
      c. had begged not to move to Grand Rapids.
      d. moved away from Grand Rapids as soon as possible.

  9. In stating "the teacher began to give me human dimensions" (paragraph 6),
     the author means
      a. she made him physically stronger.
      b. she helped the other students see him as a person, not a stereotype.
      c. she described his size.
      d. she helped him to become a better student and the teacher's pet.

  10. Wilkins must have considered Miss Bean's throwing the eraser at him to
      be a "service" to him because
      a. it helped him to return his thoughts to the learning activity going on in
         class.
      b. it showed him that she really cared about him.
      c. it made other students see his human side and gave them something to
         laugh about with him.
      d. it made Miss Bean gasp in front of all of the other students.

8

Purpose
and Tone

An important part of reading critically is realizing that behind everything you read is an author. This author is a person who has a reason for writing a given piece and who works from a personal point of view. To fully understand and evaluate what you read, you must recognize *purpose*—the reason why the author writes. You must also be aware of *tone*—the expression of the author's attitude and feeling. Both purpose and tone are discussed in this chapter.

PURPOSE

Authors write with a reason in mind, and you can better evaluate what is being said by determining what that reason is. The author's reason for writing is also called the *purpose* of a selection. Three common purposes are:

- **To inform**—to give information about a subject. Authors with this purpose wish to give their readers facts.

- **To persuade**—to convince the reader to agree with the author's point of view on a subject. Authors with this purpose may give facts, but their main goal is to promote an opinion.

- **To entertain**—to amuse and delight; to appeal to the reader's senses and imagination. Authors with this purpose entertain in various ways, through fiction and nonfiction.

Read each of the three paragraphs below and decide whether the author's purpose is to inform, to persuade, or to entertain. Write in your answers, and then read the explanations that follow.

1. Using the present measurement system is as inefficient and old-fashioned as using Roman numerals. If more Americans realized how easy it is to convert milliliters to liters as opposed to converting tablespoons to quarts, the metric system would be adopted immediately.

   Purpose: _____

2. About 113 billion people have lived and died in the history of our planet, according to scientific estimates. Of all these people, the names of about seven billion, or approximately 6 percent, are recorded in some way—on monuments or in books, manuscripts, and public records. The other 106 billion people are gone without a trace.

   Purpose: _____

3. Because of the contrast between his medium-size wardrobe and his extra-large-size body, my brother has made a commitment to only three meals a day. His definition of a meal, however, is as broad as his belly. If we spot a pretzel salesman or a hot-dog stand on our way to an Italian restaurant, for example, he is not beyond suggesting that we stop. "It'll make a good appetizer," he says.

   Purpose: _____

In the first paragraph, the writer's purpose is to *persuade* the audience that Americans should change over to the metric system. That is clear because the author claims that our present system is "inefficient and old-fashioned," that conversions in the metric system are "easy," and that people would prefer the metric system. These are statements that are used to convince us rather than to inform us. The purpose of the second paragraph is to *inform*. The author is simply providing readers with information about the people who have lived and died on Earth. In paragraph three, the playful and exaggerated details tell us the author's main goal is to *entertain* with humor.

At times, writing may seem to blend two purposes. An informative article on losing weight, for example, may include comic touches, or a persuasive letter to the editor may contain factual information. Remember in such cases to focus on the author's primary purpose. Ask yourself, "What is the author's main idea?" That will help you determine his or her principal intention.

➤ *Practice 1*

Label each item according to its main purpose: to inform (**I**), to persuade (**P**), or to entertain (**E**).

_I_ 1. In the 1886 baseball World Series, sixty-three errors were committed.

_P_ 2. Nurses assigned to intensive care units should be given shorter shifts and higher pay because the work is unusually demanding and stressful.

_P_ 3. It's easy to quit smoking; I've done it hundreds of times.

_P_ 4. Shoparama has low, low prices, an outstanding selection of health and beauty products, and a convenient location near you.

_I_ 5. The career of a professional athlete is usually quite short.

_I_ 6. An artificial odor is added to natural gas so that people can tell whether or not gas is leaking.

_E_ 7. Fred believes in a seafood diet: when he sees food, he eats it.

_P_ 8. More women should get involved in local politics and support the growing number of female candidates for public office.

_E_ 9. The best approach to take when you feel the urge to exercise is to lie down quickly in a darkened room until the feeling goes away.

_I_ 10. In ancient Egypt, priests plucked all the hair from their bodies, including their eyebrows and eyelashes.

➤ *Practice 2*

Following are three passages: from a textbook, a humor book, and a collection of essays. Label each item according to its main purpose: to inform (**I**), to persuade (**P**), or to entertain (**E**).

_P_ 1. We have all heard the story of how the young, impoverished Abraham Lincoln trekked miles to borrow books from a neighbor and then read them by firelight. We know that nineteenth-century readers would rush to the wharf to greet the ship carrying the latest chapters of a Dickens novel. Today, reading seems less urgent and less exciting to many of us. Worse, few people impart a passion for books to their children. Instead, they leave the children in front of the television and hope, weakly, that too much watching won't be bad for them. But we cannot afford to stop reading. Books shed a light that illuminates our problems and crises. They are also mirrors that reflect the truest image of ourselves.

____ 2. Most of what I know about carpentry, which is almost nothing, I learned in Shop. You should know that I took Shop during the Eisenhower administration, when boys took Shop and girls took Home Economics—a code name for "cooking." Schools are not allowed to separate boys and girls like that anymore. They're also not allowed to put students' heads in vises and tighten them, which is what our Shop teacher, Mr Schmidt, did to Ronnie Miller in the fifth grade when Ronnie used a chisel when he should have used a screwdriver. (Mr. Schmidt had strong feelings abut how to use tools properly.) I guess he shouldn't have put Ronnie's head in the vise, but it (Ronnie's head) was no great prize to begin with, and you can bet Ronnie never confused chisels and screwdrivers in later life—assuming he made it to later life.

____ 3. Studies of job satisfaction indicate that the vast majority of workers are at least somewhat satisfied with their jobs and would continue to work even if they didn't have to. The meaning of work varies from person to person. To some, it is a course of self-respect and life purpose. For others, work is a means of passing time. To still others, it is primarily a source of financial independence. Among women, available work is often less satisfying than home management. Yet, most women report increases in self-esteem when employed, especially if they experience support from their families.

TONE

A writer's tone reveals the attitude he or she has toward a subject. Tone is expressed through the words and details the writer selects. Just as a speaker's voice can project a range of feelings, a writer's voice can project one or more tones, or feelings: anger, sympathy, hopefulness, sadness, respect, dislike, and so on. Understanding tone is, then, an important part of understanding what an author has written.

To appreciate the differences in tone that writers can employ, read the following versions of a murder confession:

"I just shot my husband five times in the chest with this .357 Magnum." (*Tone:* matter-of-fact, objective.)

"How could I ever have killed him? I just can't believe I did that!" (*Tone:* shocked, disbelieving.)

"Oh, my God. I've murdered my husband. How can I ever be forgiven for this dreadful deed?" (*Tone:* remorseful, regretful)

"That dirty rat. He's had it coming for years. I'm glad I finally had the nerve to do it." (*Tone:* revengeful, triumphant)

Below is a list of words commonly used to describe tone. Note that two different words may refer to the same tone or similar tones—for example, matter-of-fact and objective, or comic and humorous. Brief meanings are given in parentheses for some of the words.

A List of Words That Describe Tone

straightforward	cheerful
matter-of-fact	joyous
objective	light-hearted
serious	amused
formal	humorous
informal	comic
solemn	playful
bitter	outspoken (*spoken boldly and freely*)
sorrowful	impassioned (*filled with passion and strong feeling*)
depressed	tolerant (*respecting of other views and behavior*)
distressed	remorseful (*filled with guilt over a wrong one has done*)
angry	outraged (*very angered*)
critical	sarcastic (*making sharp or wounding remarks; ironic*)
cruel	mocking (*ridiculing; sneering; holding up for scorn*)
hesitant	scornful (*looking down on someone or something*)
fearful	ironic (*meaning the opposite of what is expressed*)
anxious	arrogant (*conceited*)
alarmed	irreverent (*lacking respect*)
tragic	cynical (*believing the worst of others*)
self-pitying	indignant (*angry about something unfair or mean*)
disbelieving	revengeful (*wanting to hurt someone in return for an injury*)
surprised	vindictive (*very revengeful*)
regretful	malicious (*spiteful; intentionally harmful*)
sympathetic	contemptuous (*expressing great scorn and disgust*)
compassionate	ambivalent (*uncertain about a choice*)
loving	optimistic (*looking on the bright side of things*)
sentimental	pessimistic (*looking on the gloomy side of things*)
forgiving	desperate (*having a great desire or need for something*)
excited	grim (*harsh; dealing with unpleasant subjects*)

More About Tone

Below are five statements expressing different attitudes about a shabby apartment. Five different tones are used:

optimistic	tolerant	humorous
bitter	sentimental	

Label each statement according to which of these five tones you think is present. Then read the explanation that follows.

_____ 1. This place may be shabby, but since both of my children were born while we lived here, it has a special place in my heart.

_____ 2. This isn't the greatest apartment in the world, but it's not really that bad.

_____ 3. If only there were some decent jobs out there, I wouldn't be reduced to living in this miserable dump.

_____ 4. This place does need some repairs, but I expect the landlord to get around to them any day now.

_____ 5. When we move away, we're planning to release three hundred cockroaches and two mice so we can leave the place exactly as we found it.

The tone of item 1 is *sentimental*. "It has a special place in my heart" expresses tender emotions. In item 2, the words "not really that bad" show that the writer is *tolerant*, accepting the situation while recognizing that it could be better. We could describe the tone of item 3 as *bitter*. The writer resents a situation that he blames for forcing him to live in a "miserable dump." Item 4 is *optimistic* since the writer is expecting the apartment to be improved soon. Finally, the tone of item 5 is *humorous*. Its writer claims to be planning a comic revenge on the landlord by returning the apartment to the intolerable condition it was in when the tenants moved in.

A Note on Irony

One commonly used tone is that of *irony*. When writing has an ironic tone, it says one thing but means the opposite. Irony is found in everyday conversation as well as in writing. Following are a few examples; notice that the quotation in each says the opposite of what is meant.

If at the beginning of a semester you discover that one of your teachers is particularly demanding, you might comment, "This class is sure going to be a barrel of laughs!"

After seeing a terrible performance in a movie, someone might say about the actor involved, "Now there's a person with a great chance for an Oscar."

If a person is a klutz, someone might remark, "There goes an Olympic champion."

Irony also refers to situations in which what happens is the opposite of what we might expect. We could call it ironic, for example, if a man bites a dog. So another way for a writer to be ironic is to describe such situations. Here are a few more examples of this type of irony:

Helen won a lifetime supply of Marlboros a week after she quit smoking.

To get some quick extra cash, Elliot sold his stereo. For his birthday the next day, his girlfriend bought him the new Whitney Houston album.

Lenny, who adores basketball, is five feet five inches tall. His brother Frank, who plans on being a cartoonist and has no interest at all in sports, is six feet three.

➤ Practice 3

A. Below are five statements expressing different attitudes about a boss. Five different tones are used:

admiring	sympathetic	objective
ironic	critical	

For each statement, write the tone that you think is present.

admiring 1. Tony is an excellent manager—the best one I've ever had.

sympathetic 2. I know Tony's boy has been sick. Naturally it's hard for him to concentrate on work right now.

critical 3. Tony's too ambitious for his own good. That ambition may yet destroy him and the company.

objective 4. Under Tony Robertson's leadership, sales in the appliance division have increased 30 per cent in the last six months.

ironic 5. Tony's wonderful, all right. He's gotten as far as he has without the slightest idea of how to manage a division.

B. The following conversation between a mother and son involves five of the tones shown in the box below. For each statement, write the tone that you think is present.

threatening	joyful	solemn	straightforward
sympathetic	pessimistic	self-pitying	ironic
nostalgic	disbelieving		

Straightforward 6. "Please take the garbage out on your way to school this morning."

pessimistic 7. "Sure, Mom. I've been looking forward to that chore all morning."

threatening 8. "Listen, young man, if you don't start fulfilling your responsibilities around this house, your father and I will start asking you for rent or to find your own place."

self-pitying 9. "Okay, I'll take the garbage out. But you know it's not easy going to school full-time, working twenty hours a week, and just getting over a bad case of the flu."

sympathetic 10. "I know, honey, this semester has been an especially difficult one for you."

➤ Practice 4

Each passage illustrates one of the tones in the box below. In each space, put the letter of the tone that best applies. Don't use any letter more than once.

Remember that the tone of a selection reflects the author's attitude. To find the tone of a paragraph, ask yourself what attitude is revealed by its words and phrases.

a. arrogant	b. forgiving	c. worried	d. sorrowful
e. revengeful	f. affectionate	g. hypocritical	h. scornful

_h_ 1. Spam—that slimy canned pork product—is surprisingly still around after more than fifty years. Despite its high fat content (more than three and a half teaspoons per two-ounce serving) and high calorie count (171 calories per serving), more than four billion cans have been sold since 1937. Spam's greasy, rubbery consistency and salty flavor have made it the butt of many jokes—such as David Letterman's suggestion of Spam-on-a-rope for people who want to eat and shower at the same time. Shareholders in George Hormel and

Company must be laughing all the way to the bank. More than three cans of Spam are consumed every second, despite its high cost—pound for pound it costs about the same as strip steak.

f 2. My grandfather lived with my family as I grew up, and some of my warmest early memories revolve around him. He was a sweet man with simple tastes. He liked Western movies, and when I was a preschooler, he often took me along to see them. After the movies, we would go to a nearby Bridgeman's ice-cream shop. He would order a hot chocolate. It always came with a couple of sugar cookies, which he would give to me to eat with my scoop of ice cream. Once I began school, he would go to the Westerns alone. But it wasn't unusual for me to come home from school and find those same sugar cookies waiting for me in a Bridgeman's napkin.

c 3. By the year 2000 there will be nearly ten million Americans over the age of eighty. Can we expect these people to be cared for by their relatives, who are themselves in their sixties? If the caregivers are retired, they may have more time to take care of older family members, but the costs of such care (especially in terms of retirement income) are high. As the retirees grow older, the task of caring for older people becomes harder. This is made more difficult by the fact that old age can be distressing because it is a time of continual loss. Too often adults take in ailing, elderly relatives without being aware that they are taking on an immense full-time job. Such caregivers should have somewhere to turn for help.

4. Are you on my list? If you know me, you may well be. See, I keep a record of everyone who's ever crossed me. Whether it's for making fun of my new dress, or stealing my boyfriend, I believe in getting mad and getting even. It may take a while, but I settle the score with everyone on my list—the girl who made fun of my dress, for example. It took me a whole year to get back at her. Finally, one night a date took me to a party she gave. I took advantage of the opportunity and spilled red nail polish on the white rug in her powder room. That night, I took great satisfaction in crossing her name off my list.

5. My mother died a week after I had given birth to my first child. Mother and I had both wanted desperately for her to see little Emily. And Mom had managed to hang on for months, despite the cancer that was ravaging her body. I had just spoken to her the night before, and my plans were to bring Emily the fifty miles to see Mom that weekend. "I'm going to do it," Mom had said. "I'm going to hold my granddaughter before I die." But it was not to be.

➤ *Review Test 1: Purpose*

In the space provided, indicate whether the primary purpose of each passage is to inform (**I**), to persuade (**P**), or to entertain (**E**).

P   1. Americans love parks and wildlife refuges, but the crowding they find there is a national disgrace. Parking lots are packed, and roadways through parks and refuges are often so jammed that they might as well be the parking lots. Playing fields and barbecue grills are claimed early in the day, and even on remote trails voices can be heard from every direction. Americans badly need more land devoted to open space where nature walks, picnics, and camping can take place in uncrowded tranquility. Communities across the nation should establish parks and trails that provide free access to open space for everyone.

I   2. Sediment will sometimes accumulate in shower heads, causing the water to flow unevenly or completely clogging the shower head. Sometimes briskly opening and closing the adjustment mechanism a few times is enough to solve the problem. If this does not work, remove the shower head from the wall, holding onto the pipe while you unscrew the shower head so that you do not loosen the pipe inside the wall. Once you have removed the shower head, try cleaning it with a toothpick or wire. If necessary, take the shower head apart and soak it in water overnight to soften the mineral deposits.

E   3. One afternoon a man entered a bar with his dog and ordered two martinis. He drank one martini, and his dog drank the other. The same thing happened for the next three days. On the fifth afternoon, the dog came in alone, and the bartender served him a drink without even asking. The next day the man came in carrying a box. "You were so nice to my dog yesterday that I brought you a present," he said. "It's a king crab." "Oh, thanks," said the bartender. "I'll take him home for dinner." "Oh no," said the man. "He's already had dinner. Why not take him out to a movie instead?"

I   4. During the fifties and sixties, researchers discovered that monosodium glutamate (MSG), commonly used to flavor foods, caused brain damage in baby rats, mice, and monkeys. In 1970, a National Academy of Sciences committee concluded that MSG in food is unlikely to harm human infants, but the committee nevertheless recommended that MSG not be used in baby food. By then, however, the baby-food industry had already stopped using MSG because of public pressure.

5. The practice of tipping goes back thousands of years, at least to the times of the ancient Romans. You would think that by now the public would have refused to cooperate with such an unfair and bothersome habit. Who else besides restaurant owners can get away with underpaying their employees and expect their customers to make up the difference? It has gotten so that waiters no longer look at a tip as a reward for superior service. Instead, it is an expected part of their day's pay, to the point that even a waiter who has provided lousy service will demand a tip if a customer does not offer one. Restaurant customers should band together and demand the elimination of this ridiculous custom.

➤ Review Test 2: Tone

Each of the following passages illustrates one of the tones in the box below. In the space provided, put the letter of the tone that best applies to each passage. Don't use any letter more than once.

Remember that the tone of a selection reflects the author's attitude. To find the tone of a paragraph, ask yourself what attitude is revealed by its words and phrases.

a. joyous	b. pessimistic	c. mocking	d. indignant
e. objective	f. sentimental	g. forgiving	h. pleading

     1. Emperor penguins are among the most adorable animals in the world. Like all penguins, they look like cute little people dressed in tuxedos. They flap their wings and waddle into the water in an utterly charming way. The most enchanting thing they do is care for their sweet little babies. The newborn chick squats on its father's feet, where it is warmed by his body and cared for affectionately until its mother returns from a trip to find food. Emperor penguins love their babies so much that they have been known to try to hatch blocks of ice if their own little ones die. This is a delightful testimony to the power of parental affection.

     2. During my last physical, the doctor found a little lump in my throat. I'm going into the hospital tomorrow so they can check out what it is. The doctor said it was most likely a harmless cyst, but of course he would say that. What's he going to say: "Sorry—looks like cancer to me?" He also said that if it is cancer, it's probably of a kind that is easily treated. Right, I thought. He's trying to be nice, I know, but I

also know how these things go. First he'll say it's nothing; then he'll say it's cancer but no big deal; and finally he'll tell me the truth. I'm done for.

_e/_   3. The first radio advertisement was broadcast on August 28, 1922, on New York station WEAF. A real estate firm, Queensboro Corporation, bought a ten-minute segment for one hundred dollars in order to advertise its apartments. According to the advertisement, the apartment complex, Hawthorne Court, was named after the American author Nathaniel Hawthorne. The apartments were described as conveniently near the subway but also "right at the boundaries of God's great outdoors" near golf and tennis courts and other "pleasure-giving, health-giving activities." As a result of the advertisements, two apartments were sold, and commercial radio was born.

    4. Recently I shared a book with a little girl from a home where no one reads. When I finished the book, the girl urged, "Read it again." I was reading one of my own books, *Barbie and the Bandits*, so her request was one of the most satisfying I could receive. Yet what I felt was not pleasure, but dismay. This little girl's family, like many families, is indifferent to books. What will happen to children from homes like these? Will they ever learn to love books? It is unlikely, unless you do something. I know you believe in the joy and power of reading. Don't let the burdens you face—cataloging books, preparing budgets, and meeting with the library board—keep you from a more important purpose: bringing the joy of reading to children who might otherwise never know it.

_d_   5. Relentless greed and horrifying dishonesty characterized the treatment of Indians in the 1860's and 1870's, when massacres of native Americans were commonplace. The massacre at Sand Creek in Colorado in 1864 was sadly typical. The territorial governor had persuaded the Indians to gather there and had promised them protection. Despite this pledge, Colonel J. M. Chivington's militia attacked the defenseless Indian camp. They disregarded that sacred symbol, the American flag, and the white flag of truce that the Indians were flying at Sand Creek. Four hundred fifty peaceful Indians—men, women, and children—were slaughtered in what has been called "the foulest and most unjustified crime in the annals of America." This was only one of the heartless massacres that history records.

➤ *Review Test 3*

A. To review what you've learned in this chapter, complete each of the following sentences about purpose and tone.

1. What is the purpose of each of the types of writing below? Label each according to their usual main purpose: to inform, to persuade, or to entertain.

    A news report: _to inform_

    A mystery novel: _to entertain_

    An editorial: _to persuade_

2. *Complete the sentence:* The tone of a selection reveals the author's

    attitude toward his or her subject.

3. An ironic comment is one that means the _opposite_ of what is said. For example, if everything goes wrong after a person gets up in the morning (there is no hot water for the shower, milk for the cereal is sour, a pool of oil is under the car, and so on) a person might ironically make which of the following statements: *(circle one letter)*
    a. "What a lousy start to the day."
    (b) "What a great day this is going to be."
    c. "Good grief. What did I do to deserve this?"

B. Here is a chance to apply your understanding of purpose and tone to a full-length selection. This reading is about one family's struggle over when to tell a child the truth about Santa Claus.

   Following the reading are questions on purpose and tone. To help you continue to strengthen your work on the skills taught in previous chapters, there are also questions on:

   - vocabulary in context
   - central point and main ideas
   - supporting details
   - transitions
   - patterns of organization
   - fact and opinion
   - inferences.

Words to Watch

On the next page are some words in the reading that do not have strong context support. Each word is followed by the number of the paragraph in which it appears and its meaning there.

hedgy (2): avoiding a direct answer
pretentious (2): overly dignified
deceit (8): dishonesty
squiggliest (8): waviest
modicum (10): small amount
diplomatically (18): in a tactful way
reproachfully (32): in a disapproving way

COPING WITH SANTA CLAUS

Delia Ephron

Julie had turned 8 in October and as Christmas approached, Santa Claus was more and more on her mind. During the week before Christmas, every night she announced to her father, "I know who really brings the presents. You do!" Then, waiting a moment, she added, "Right?"   1

Jerry didn't answer. Neither he nor I, her stepmother, was sure she really wanted the truth. We suspected she did, but couldn't bring ourselves to admit it to her. And we both felt uncomfortable saying something hedgy°. Something pretentious°. Something like, "But Santa does exist dear, he exists in spirit—in the spirit of giving in all of us." That sounded like some other parents in some other house with some other child.   2

I actually resented Julie for putting us on the spot. Wasn't the truth about Santa something one learned from a classmate? The same classmate who knows a screwed-up version of the facts of life. Or else from a know-it-all older sister—as I did. Mine sneaked into my room on Christmas Eve, woke me and said, "Go into the hall and look. You'll see who really puts out the presents."   3

There was another problem. Jerry and I were reluctant to give up Santa Claus ourselves. We got to tell Julie and her younger brother, Adam, to put out the cookies in case Santa was hungry. We made a fuss about the fire being out in the fireplace so he wouldn't get burned. We issued a few threats about his list of good children and bad. It was all part of the tension and thrill of Christmas Eve—the night the fantasy comes true. And that fantasy of a fat jolly man who flies through the sky in a sleigh drawn by reindeer and arrives via chimney with presents—that single belief says everything about the innocence of children. How unbearable to lose it. For them and for us. So Jerry and I said nothing. And the next night Julie announced it again.   4

Christmas Eve Julie appeared with a sheet of yellow, lined paper. At the top she had written, "If you are real, sign here." It was, she said, a letter to Santa. She insisted that on this letter each of us—her father, Adam and I—write the words "Santa Claus," so if Santa were to sign it, she could compare our handwriting with his. Then she would know she had not been tricked.   5

Jerry signed. I signed. Adam, who was 5 and couldn't write, gave up after the letter "S." Julie folded the paper into quarters, wrote "Santa Claus" on the outside and stuck it on a ledge inside the chimney along with two Christmas cookies.   6

After much fuss, Julie and Adam were tucked into bed. Jerry and I put out the presents. We were not sure what to do about the letter.   7

After a short discussion, and mostly because we couldn't resist, we opted for   8
deceit°. Jerry took the note and, in the squiggliest° printing imaginable, wrote "Merry
Christmas, Santa Claus." He put the note back in the fireplace and ate the cookies.

The next morning, very early, about 6, we heard Julie and Adam tear down the   9
hall. Jerry and I, in bed, listened for the first ecstatic reactions to the presents.
Suddenly, we heard a shriek. "He's real! He's real! He's really real!!!!" The door to
our room flew open. "He's REAL!!!" she shouted. Julie showed us the paper with the
squiggly writing.

Somehow, this was not what we had bargained for. I had expected some   10
modicum° of disbelief—at least a "Dad, is this for real?"

Julie clasped the note to her chest. Then she dashed back to the presents.   11

That afternoon, our friend Deena came over to exchange gifts. "Santa Claus is   12
real," said Julie.

"Oh," said Deena.   13

"I know for sure, for really, really sure. Look!" And Julie produced the proof.   14

Just then the phone rang. Knowing it was a relative calling with Christmas   15
greetings, Julie rushed to answer it. "Santa Claus is real," I heard her say to my sister
Nora, the same sister who had broken the bad news about Santa Claus to me 30 years
ago. Julie handed me the phone.

"What is this about?" asked Nora.   16

I told her the story, trying to make it as funny as possible, hoping she wouldn't   17
notice how badly Jerry and I had handled what I was beginning to think of as "the
Santa issue." It didn't work.

"We may have made a mistake here," said Nora, diplomatically° including   18
herself in the mess.

"You're telling me!" I said. "Do you think there's any chance Julie will forget   19
all this?" That was what I really wanted, of course—for the whole thing to go away.

"I doubt it," said Nora.   20

We had a wonderful day—good food, good presents, lots of visitors. Then it   21
was bedtime.

"Dad?" said Julie, as he tucked her in.   22

"What?"   23

"If Santa's real, then Rudolph must be real, too."   24

"What!"   25

"If Santa's real—"   26

"I heard," said Jerry. He sat down on her bed and took a deep breath. "You   27
know, Julie," and then he stopped. I could see he was trying to think of a way, any
way, to explain our behavior so it wouldn't sound quite as deceptive, wrong and
stupid as it was. But he was stumped.

"Yeah," said Julie.   28

"I wrote the note," said Jerry.   29

She burst into tears.   30

Jerry apologized. He apologized over and over while Julie sobbed into her   31
pillow. He said he was wrong, that he shouldn't have tricked her, that he should have
answered her questions about Santa Claus the week before.

Julie sat up in bed. "I thought he was real," she said reproachfully°. Then   32
suddenly she leaned over the bed, pulled out a comic from underneath and sat up
again. "Can I read for five minutes?" she said.

"Sure," said Jerry.   33

And that was it. One minute of grief at Santa's death, and life went on.   34

Jerry and I left Julie's room terribly relieved. I immediately got a craving for 35
leftover turkey and headed for the kitchen. I was putting the bird back in the
refrigerator when I heard Adam crying. I went down the hall. The door to his room
was open and I heard Julie, very disgusted, say: "Oh, Adam, you don't have to cry!
Only babies believe in Santa Claus."

READING COMPREHENSION QUESTIONS

Vocabulary in Context

1. The words *opted for* in "because we couldn't resist, we opted for deceit.
   Jerry took the note and, in the squiggliest printing imaginable, wrote
   'Merry Christmas, Santa Claus'" (paragraph 8) mean
   a. questioned.
   b. chose.
   c. decided against.
   d. admired.

Central Point and Main Ideas

2. Which sentence best expresses the central point of this selection?
   a. Children will eventually learn that Santa Claus does not exist.
   b. When children seriously ask who brings the Christmas presents, it's
      time to tell them the truth.
   c. Jerry made a mistake in eventually telling Julie the truth.
   d. Parents should always tell their children the truth.

3. Which sentence best expresses the main idea of paragraph 4?
   a. The fantasy of Santa says everything about the innocence of children.
   b. Delia and Jerry were reluctant to tell Julie the truth not only so she
      could hold on to the fantasy of Santa, but so that they could too.
   c. Delia and Jerry loved to tell the children to put out cookies on
      Christmas Eve in case Santa was hungry.
   d. The fantasy of Santa allowed Delia and Jerry to threaten the children
      using Santa's list of good and bad children.

Supporting Details

4. Delia and Jerry
   a. felt Julie reacted in an immature way.
   b. never told Julie that the signature was a fake.
   c. realized that they had handled the problem poorly.
   d. thought it was best that Adam also know the truth.

Transitions

5. The relationship of the last sentence below to the sentences before it is one of
   a. time.
   b. comparison.
   c. contrast.
   d. cause and effect.

   > And that fantasy of a fat jolly man who flies through the sky in a sleigh drawn by reindeer and arrives via chimney with presents—that single belief says everything about the innocence of children. How unbearable to lose it. For them and for us. So Jerry and I said nothing. (Paragraph 4)

Patterns of Organization

6. The main pattern of organization of paragraphs 5 through 35 is
   a. time order.
   b. list of items.
   c. cause and effect.
   d. contrast.

Fact and Opinion

7. Which of the following is mainly a statement of opinion?
   a. "We made a fuss about the fire being out in the fireplace so he wouldn't get burned."
   b. "We issued a few threats about his list of good children and bad."
   c. "And that fantasy of a fat jolly man who flies through the sky in a sleigh drawn by reindeer and arrives via chimney with presents—that single belief says everything about the innocence of children."
   d. "Christmas Eve Julie appeared with a sheet of yellow, lined paper."

Inferences

8. In paragraph 27, the author implies that Jerry
   a. finally knew he had to tell Julie the truth.
   b. is not a caring father.
   c. never realized they had misjudged how to deal with Julie.
   d. felt Julie had reacted badly to the truth about Santa Claus.

Purpose and Tone

9. _____ TRUE OR FALSE? The author's primary purpose in this narration is to persuade, through her own family's experiences, that it's better to tell children the truth about Santa when they seriously ask.

10. The author writes about her and her husband's mistakes in a tone of
    a. great shame.
    b. pride.
    c. bitterness.
    d. straightforwardness.

9

Propaganda

What do you think is the main difference between the following two evaluations of a city?

> The weather isn't bad in Philadelphia, if you don't mind a few months of winter. And the city has wonderful museums and restaurants. But the streets are often dirty there, and state and city taxes keep going up.

> Philadelphia is the place to live! Once you experience its pleasant climate, its museums, and restaurants, you'll agree with Phillies baseball star Ken Greyson when he says, "Home base for me is Philadelphia. Living here is a ball!"

Did you notice that the first evaluation is an attempt to be objective about Philadelphia? It mentions both positive and negative points so the reader will get a balanced picture of the city. The second approach, however, includes only positive points. It was not meant to provide a balanced, objective view of the city. Instead, it was designed to influence people to come live in Philadelphia. When such biased information is methodically spread in order to promote or oppose a cause—whether the cause is a city, a political view, a product, or an organization—it is *propaganda*.

PROPAGANDA TECHNIQUES

Propaganda may use one or more common techniques for convincing people by appealing to their emotions. Recognizing these techniques will help you separate the substance of a message (if there is any) from its purely emotional appeal. If you are not aware of the propaganda devices, you may make decisions as a result of emotional manipulation. This chapter will introduce you to seven of the more common propaganda techniques:

- Bandwagon
- Testimonial
- Transfer
- Plain Folks
- Name Calling
- Glittering Generalities
- Card Stacking

Once you have learned these techniques, you will recognize one or more of them in just about every advertisement you encounter.

1 Bandwagon

Old-fashioned parades usually began with a large wagon carrying a brass band. To "jump on the bandwagon," therefore, means to join a parade. For example, we are often told to buy a product or vote for a political candidate because, in effect, "everybody else is doing it." An ad for a cereal may claim that "Sugar-O's is Everybody's Favorite Breakfast." A political commercial may show people from all walks of life all saying they will vote for Candidate Harry Hogwash. The ads imply that if you don't jump on the bandwagon, the parade will pass you by.

Here are two examples of real TV ads that have used the *bandwagon* appeal:

To a background of appealing music, shots of many people wearing the sponsor's jeans appear on the screen.

On a beautiful day, almost everyone on the beach leaves in a hurry in order to attend the sponsor's sale.

➤ *Practice 1*

Circle the numbers of the two descriptions of ads that use the bandwagon appeal.

1. Famous actress Margo Lane explains that she loves to use a certain hair coloring.

2. Most of the people in a crowd at the ballgame are drinking the sponsor's cola beverage.

3. A very well-built man and woman in very tight exercise clothes demonstrate the sponsor's exercise equipment.

4. The tune of "God Bless America" is being played in the background as an announcer says to support the home baseball team by coming out to games.

5. An ad for a new movie shows people waiting to buy tickets in a line that extends halfway around the block.

2 Testimonial

Famous athletes often appear on television as spokespersons for all sorts of products, from soft drinks to automobiles. Movie stars make commercials endorsing products and political issues. The idea behind this approach is that the testimony of famous people influences the television viewers that admire these people.

What viewers must remember is that famous people get paid to endorse products. In addition, these people are not necessarily experts about the products or political issues they promote. This does not in itself mean that what they say is untrue. But realizing that celebrities receive money to recommend products that they may know little about should help consumers think twice about such messages.

Here are two examples of real ads that have used the appeal of *testimonials*:

A famous comedienne, now a senior citizen, promotes a cleaner for false teeth.

A popular singer with a wholesome image is spokesperson for a breakfast cereal.

➤ *Practice 2*

Circle the numbers of the two descriptions of ads that use a testimonial.

1. Numerous people crowd around the department store door, waiting for the store to open.

2. Famous actress Margo Lane explains that she loves to use a certain hair coloring.

3. A grandmother, serving a canned vegetable soup to her grandson, says, "This has all the simple, healthy, and delicious ingredients I use in my own vegetable soup."

4. A sports star talks about and laces on a particular brand of basketball sneakers.

5. A cheerful mother announces that a day without a certain orange juice is like a day without sunshine.

3 Transfer

Ads that use the transfer technique associate a product with a symbol or image that people admire or love. The advertiser hopes that people's positive feelings for the symbol or image will *transfer* to the product. For example, calling an automobile "The All-American Car" appeals to would-be buyers' patriotism; the "All-American" image calls to mind all that is best in America. Or consider a recent real-life ad in which several nuns are surprised and impressed that the fresh-brewed coffee they think they are drinking is actually Folger's instant coffee. The qualities people associate with nuns—seeing them as honest, trustworthy, and highly selective in their worldly pleasures—are then associated with the product as well.

There is also a good deal of transfer value in good looks. Consumers *transfer* the positive feelings they have towards a sexy-looking person to the product being advertised. Many ads today use handsome men and beautiful women to pitch their products; more than ever, Madison Avenue seems convinced that "sex sells."

To summarize, the transfer technique depends upon the appeal value of two special categories:

1) admired and/or beloved symbols and images
2) sex appeal

Here are two examples of real ads that have used transfer:

An American eagle symbolizes the United States Post Office's Express Mail service.

A tanned blonde in a bikini is stretched out on the beach, holding in her hand a can of light beer.

➤ *Practice 3*

Circle the numbers of the two descriptions of ads that use the transfer approach.

1. An announcer claims that a competitor's tires don't last as long as the sponsor's tires do.

2. The tune of "God Bless America" is being played in the background as an announcer says to support the home baseball team by coming out to games.

3. A very well-built man and woman in very tight exercise clothes demonstrate the sponsor's exercise equipment.

4. Several ordinary, friendly-looking young men in jeans buy the sponsor's beer.

5. "My opponent hasn't made up his mind about state taxes," says a candidate for mayor. "He's too wishy-washy to be mayor."

4   Plain Folks

Some people distrust political candidates who are rich or well-educated. They feel that these candidates, if elected, will not be able to understand the problems of the average working person. Therefore, candidates often try to show they are just "plain folks" by referring in their speeches to how poor they were when they were growing up or how they had to work their way through school. They also pose for photographs wearing overalls or buying a hot dog from a curbside vendor.

Likewise, the presidents of some companies appear in their own ads, trying to show that their giant enterprises are just family businesses. If a corporation can convince potential customers that it is run by people just like them, the customers are more likely to buy the corporation's product than if they felt it was run by ruthless millionaire executives. In other words, people using the *plain-folks* approach tell their audience, "We are ordinary folks, just like you."

Yet another plain-folks approach is for a company to show us a product being used and enjoyed by everyday types of people—persons just like ourselves. (In contrast, the propaganda technique of testimonial features famous people.)

Here are two examples of real ads that have used the appeal of plain folks:

A president of a fast-food hamburger chain, dressed in shirt sleeves, carries a food tray to a small table in one of his restaurants, all the while pitching his burgers to the viewer.

Average-looking American kids are shown trying and enjoying a cereal.

➤ *Practice 4*

Circle the numbers of the two descriptions of ads that use the plain folks approach.

1.   Two ordinary, friendly-looking young men in jeans buy the sponsor's beer.

2.   A famous baseball player wears the sponsor's jeans.

3.   A man leaves a theater after seeing a play with a big smile on his face. Then his chauffeur pulls up in a Cadillac to take him home.

4.   "Drink our soda," says the announcer. "It's the real thing."

5.   A grandmother, serving a canned vegetable soup to her grandson, says, "This has all the simple, healthy, and delicious ingredients I use in my own vegetable soup."

5   Name Calling

Name calling is the use of emotionally loaded language or negative comments to turn people against a rival product, candidate, or movement. An example of name calling would be a political candidate's labeling an opponent "uncaring," "radical," or "wimpy." Or a manufacturer may say or imply that a competing product is "full of chemicals," though in reality everything is made up of chemicals of one kind or another. Or one group may call another group's beliefs "un-American" when all they mean is that they disapprove of them.

Here are two examples of name calling taken from real life:

In the early days of the "cold war" with the Soviet Union, in the 1950s, an exaggerated concern about communism in this country brought charges of un-Americanism against many.

A fast-food chain accuses a competitor of selling a seaweed burger simply because the competitor used a seaweed extract to keep its burger moist.

➤ *Practice 5*

Circle the numbers of the two descriptions of ads that use name calling.

1.   "Drink our soda," says the announcer. "It's the real thing."

2.   "Brand X's spaghetti sauce tastes like Mom used to make," says a man to his wife. "And you know what a lousy cook she was." Then he suggests trying the sponsor's brand.

3.   A cheerful mother announces that a day without a certain orange juice is like a day without sunshine.

4.   "My opponent has lived in our state for only two years," says a candidate for state senator. "Let's not put an outsider into state office."

5.   An ad for cigarettes shows a beautiful woman in a strapless gown smoking the sponsor's product and being admired by several handsome men.

6 Glittering Generalities

A *glittering generality* is an important-sounding but unspecific claim about some product, candidate, or cause. It cannot be proved true or false because no evidence is offered to support the claim. Such claims use general words that different people would define differently, such as "progress," "great," and "freedom."

"Simply the best," an ad might say about a certain television set. But no specific evidence of any kind is offered to support such a generality. "Janet Mayer has the Right Stuff! Vote Mayer for Congress," a campaign slogan might claim. But what seems like "the right stuff" to her campaign manager might seem very wrong to you. The point is that the phrase sounds good but says nothing definite.

Here are two examples of ads that use glittering generalities:

A car ad claims, "It just feels right."

A canned-food ad boasts of "nutrition that works."

➤ *Practice 6*

Circle the numbers of the two descriptions of ads that use glittering generalities.

1. "For a forward-looking government," says the announcer, "vote for Ed Dalton for governor."

2. A well-known astronaut says that he uses the sponsor's aspirins.

3. "Millions of satisfied customers can't be all wrong," says the announcer of an ad for grass seed.

4. "My opponent attends Alcoholics Anonymous meetings," says a candidate for city council. "Do you want him to represent you on the council?"

5. A cheerful mother announces that a day without a certain orange juice is like a day without sunshine.

7   Card Stacking

Card stacking refers to stacking the cards in your favor and presenting only the facts and figures that are favorable to your particular side of the issue. It could also be called the "Too-Good-to-Be-True Technique" or the "Omitted Details Technique."

Part of every writer's job is to choose what information to include and what to omit. This right to choose also carries a responsibility. When making a case, writers are occasionally tempted to omit facts that oppose their arguments. Writers should face those facts and either explain why they do not apply, or, if that proves impossible, modify their original arguments. But the temptation to take a short cut and ignore unpleasant facts is sometimes too strong to resist.

In legal language, deliberately leaving out inconvenient facts is called "concealing evidence." In advertising, such evidence may be concealed in the interests of selling a product. For example, advertisements for the drug Tylenol call it "the pain reliever hospitals use most," and this statement is perfectly true. What these advertisements fail to mention is that the manufacturer of Tylenol offers hospitals large discounts. Since other drug companies may not offer similar discounts, or did not in the past, most hospital administrators have chosen to buy Tylenol. The advertising campaign depends on people jumping to the conclusion, "Hospitals use more Tylenol than any other pain reliever. They must consider it the best drug of its kind available." In fact, other drugs with the same pain reliever as Tylenol might work just as well.

Read the following passage and then the list of omitted details below it. Then decide which of the missing details you think Credit Information Services deliberately left out of its ad.

> For only forty dollars, Credit Information Services will provide a copy of your credit report. Haven't you been wondering what information a potential lender gets when you apply for a loan? Now you will have all the information you need for a single low yearly fee.

Missing details:

a.   Each additional use of this service will cost only thirty-five dollars.
b.   Credit Information Services already has 300,000 customers nationwide.
c.   Federal law gives you the right to find out what is in your credit report—free.

Answer: _____

If you chose *c*, you are right. If you know this detail, you are not likely to send forty dollars to Credit Information Services.

➤ *Practice 7*

Which missing details does the reader need to know in order to avoid being tricked? Circle the letter of the important detail that has been purposely omitted from each paragraph.

1. Congratulations! You have just won an all-expenses-paid three-night vacation to Atlantic City, New Jersey. You will dine at glamorous restaurants, enjoy stage shows, and swim in the beautiful Atlantic Ocean—all free. This free trip has been awarded to only a handful of selected winners in your area.

   a. The voucher for your free trip will arrive by registered mail within two weeks of your acceptance of this offer.
   b. You may stay at your choice of two casino hotels: Trump's Castle or Resorts International.
   c. You must pay $399 to join a travel club before you become eligible for your free trip.

2. For a set fee you can make as many long-distance calls as you wish at special times. This is your chance to get back in touch with all the family members and friends you've been meaning to call. Now you can afford the pleasure of talking regularly with the people who mean the most to you. Talk as long as you wish to anyone in the continental United States for only one hundred dollars a month.

   a. Merely dial the number you want. You need not dial extra access numbers.
   b. The service is available now in your area.
   c. Calls can be made only between 10 P.M. and 6 A.M.

3. Sunnyside College offers a wide choice of majors, ranging from liberal studies to high technology. On its beautiful campus students can take advantage of up-to-date laboratory equipment, an Olympic-sized swimming pool, and a new four-story library. The faculty are well-known for their commitment to students.

   a. More than eighty percent of the students are from the northeastern part of the country.
   b. Only five percent of the graduates that apply to graduate school are accepted.
   c. More people major in high technology than in liberal studies.

➤ *Review Test 1*

In each pair of sentences below, the first sentence does *not* illustrate a propaganda technique, but the second one does. On the line, write the letter of the propaganda technique used in the second sentence.

_____ 1. • Kiddy Kare is the largest day-care center in town.

• Kiddy Kare's competitor's day-care center is more concerned about profits than children.

    a. bandwagon   c. testimonial
    b. transfer   d. name calling

_____ 2. • Sureguard sunglasses filter out harmful ultraviolet rays.

• "I'm proud to wear Sureguard sunglasses," says actress Judy Winsor. "You'll love them too."

    a. testimonial   c. plain folks
    b. transfer   d. name calling

_____ 3. • As a young man, Candidate Alan Wilson had a variety of jobs working in a department store and in his family's TV station.

• As a young man, Candidate Alan Wilson learned what it means to work hard by spending long hours lifting boxes and sweeping floors.

    a. name calling   c. plain folks
    b. bandwagon   d. glittering generalities

_____ 4. • Two recent polls suggest that Dick Levy may win next week's election.

• Add your vote to the landslide victory Dick Levy will win in next week's election.

    a. bandwagon   c. transfer
    b. testimonial   d. name calling

_____ 5. • Starn pianos are available in every major city in the United States.

• Starn pianos are used in the finest concert halls in America and around the world.

    a. plain folks   c. bandwagon
    b. name calling   d. testimonial

_____ 6. • A college degree opens up job doors.

• Comedian Bill Groff says, "A college degree opens up job doors."

    a. glittering generalities   c. testimonial
    b. plain folks   d. name calling

_d_____ 7. • Twin Oaks is a residential development near Des Moines, Iowa.

• There's nothing else quite like Twin Oaks, an exclusive residential community where you will be proud to live.

    a. bandwagon   c. transfer

    b. testimonial   d. glittering generalities

_b_____ 8. • Olson's pizzas are lower in fat and calories.

• Other pizza-makers don't care about your health.

    a. plain folks   c. glittering generalities

    b. name calling   d. transfer

_a_____ 9. • Our Presidential candidate supports our country's farmers.

• The Presidential candidate has her own small farm, so she knows the farmers' concerns.

    a. plain folks   c. glittering generalities

    b. testimonial   d. transfer

_c_____ 10. • Linda Byrne will make an impressive mayor; her record as deputy mayor and state senator shows that she is an excellent speaker, a hard worker, and a capable administrator.

• Linda Byrne will make an impressive mayor; she's a natural wonder.

    a. bandwagon   c. glittering generalities

    b. testimonial   d. transfer

➤ Review Test 2

A. Each of the passages below illustrates a particular propaganda technique. On the line next to the passage, write the letter of the technique being used.

_b_____ 1. The most beautiful hair this season has shape, style, and a luxuriant, natural feel. Leslie Langtree, the television actress whose lovely hair is her trademark, reveals that her secret is Flirt. "Flirt softens my hair and gives it great body," Leslie says. "Thanks to Flirt, my hair has never looked better."

    a. plain folks   c. name calling

    (b.)testimonial   d. bandwagon

_d_____ 2. Senator Bernita Walters does not know the most elementary facts about how to represent her state. To call her a legislator is laughable. She is dishonest, lazy, and stupid—the last person you should consider supporting in next fall's election.

    a. glittering generalities   c. testimonial

    b. transfer   (d.)name calling

_C_   3. Liberty Bell Airlines flies anywhere in this great land, from sea to shining sea. We proudly hail America's finest: Liberty Bell.

a. plain folks
c. transfer
b. testimonial
d. name calling

_c_   4. Monroe Archer is a millionaire and the president of a large corporation, yet he has never lost touch with his small-town roots. Despite his power and fame, he still likes returning to his hometown to enjoy a summer band concert and a simple supper at Charley's Diner.

a. name calling
c. plain folks
b. bandwagon
d. testimonial

_a_   5. Feel like a princess on your wedding day! The Royal Bridal Shop features stunning brides' dresses as beautiful as those worn by Great Britain's royal brides, Lady Di and Fergie.

a. transfer
c. plain folks
b. testimonial
d. name calling

_b_   6. Come one! Come all! Everybody's going to Linwood Furniture for the big eighth annual sale, a sale so big we rented a tent to hold it all!

a. name calling
c. transfer
b. bandwagon
d. testimonial

_a_   7. Cast your vote next Tuesday for Larry Lewis. This fine man has much to offer his community and his nation. As your representative, he pledges to do his best to better conditions and to bring you closer to the fulfillment of your highest dreams.

a. glittering generalities
c. bandwagon
b. transfer
d. name calling

_d_   8. One of the hottest trends this season is shorter skirts. In the office, on the street, in restaurants—everywhere you look, increasing numbers of women are switching to this new look.

a. name calling
c. transfer
b. testimonial
d. bandwagon

B. The following ads are too good to be true in some way. Circle the letter of the important detail that the advertiser has intentionally omitted.

9. Our new line of light cakes is made without any fats at all.
   a. The cakes come in six flavors.
   b. The cakes have the same number of calories as the cakes that aren't called "light."
   c. The cakes cost a little less than cakes that aren't called "light."

10. "As President," says a candidate, "I will do everything in my power to keep income taxes from rising."
    a. The candidate was governor of a large state for two terms.
    b. The candidate played basketball in college.
    c. The candidate is in favor of raising sales taxes.

➤ *Review Test 3*

A. To review what you've learned in this chapter, complete each of the following sentences about propaganda.

1. Propaganda is usually intended to appeal to our (*logic, emotions*) emotions .

2. An important difference between a testimonial and a plain folks appeal is that testimonials feature (*famous, ordinary*) famous people.

3. The (*transfer, plain folks*) transfer technique associates a product with symbols and images that people respect.

4. (*Glittering generalities, Card stacking*) Glittering generalities is the technique of making dramatic but unspecific and unsupported claims.

B. Here is a chance to apply your understanding of propaganda after reading a full-length article. Its author wishes to replace the words "till death do us part" with a more temporary agreement. Read the selection, and see if you agree.

Following the reading are questions on propaganda. To help you continue to strengthen your work on the skills taught in previous chapters, there are also questions on

- vocabulary in context
- central point and main ideas
- supporting details
- transitions
- patterns of organization
- fact and opinion
- inferences
- purpose and tone.

Words to Watch

Following are some words in the reading that do not have strong context support. Each word is followed by the number of the paragraph in which it appears and its meaning there.

valid (5): in effect
concrete (6): specific

ON BEHALF OF MARRIAGE CONTRACTS

Kerrie Brady

After five years of rocky marriage, Paul and Michelle were considering 1
divorce. Both complained that life together just wasn't what they had expected. For
instance, Michelle wanted to save every extra penny for a house, while Paul wanted
to spend money freely. Michelle wanted to have friends over often. Paul preferred
spending evenings alone. Paul was a regular churchgoer. Michelle wanted to sleep in
on Sundays. Michelle wasn't sure she wanted children. Paul wanted four.

"It's incredible that Paul and I got married in the first place," Michelle told 2
their marriage counselor. "We disagree on practically everything. And yet we seemed
to get along so well when we were dating!"

Every year, thousands of couples like Paul and Michelle marry unwisely. Their 3
decision to wed is based on the great rush of emotion that comes along with falling in
love. "We love each other!" they proclaim. "Of course our marriage will work!"
Unfortunately, the rosy glow that accompanies romantic love doesn't last forever.
Couples who promise "Till death do us part" often regret that vow a few months or
years later. They may feel that their decision was made hastily, that they didn't know
each other well enough, that their ideas about marriage are too different. And then
they are faced with two unhappy options. They can continue on in a disappointing
marriage, or they can start proceedings for an unpleasant, expensive, time-consuming
divorce.

A third option is what is needed here. People who want to marry should not 4
merely participate in a ceremony. They should also sign renewable marriage
contracts.

A marriage contract could be valid° for three years, at which time the partners 5
would decide whether or not to renew the agreement. If they did not choose to stay
together, no divorce would be necessary. They would simply file a paper stating that
they would not be renewing their contract.

There are definite advantages to the marriage contract system. First of all, the 6
system would force couples to think in concrete° terms about their
marriages—something that people wildly in love do not often do. They would have
to talk ahead of time about some essential questions. Examples might be: How will
our money be handled? How will work around the house be divided? Will we have
children? How will they be raised? Will we have a religious life? How often will our
in-laws visit?

It would not be surprising if many couples in the process of working on a 7
contract decided that they shouldn't get married after all. And that would be a good
thing. They are the couples whose marriages probably wouldn't survive the first
clash with reality.

If Paul and Michelle, for instance, had talked seriously about finances earlier, 8
they might well never have gotten married. "Buying our own house was very
important to me," said Michelle. "I hate the feeling of throwing rental money away. I
just assumed that Paul felt the same way. But we never really talked about buying a
house or saving money when we were dating. Heck, we never talked about anything
very seriously. We just had fun. Now I know that just because you have fun with
someone isn't reason enough to marry them."

In addition, a contract would encourage couples to work harder at their   9
marriages. They couldn't afford to let problems simmer under the surface, assuming
that they had unlimited years to fix them. If they knew that their contract was coming
up for renewal every few years, people would give as much attention to their
marriages as they do to their careers or relationships with friends.

When Paul looks back at the five years he and Michelle have spent together, he   10
wishes they had faced the pressure of a contract. "Now things have probably gone
too far with Michelle and me," he admitted. "Our problems seem so complicated that
it'd just be a lot easier to split up. But when we first got married, we really did want
it to work. If we'd had a marriage contract, maybe we would have tried harder to fix
problems early on. For instance, it was probably six months into our marriage that I
realized it really bugged me that Michelle wouldn't go to church. At that point, it
would have been good if I could have said, 'Look, this is really a problem for me.
Let's try to work out some kind of compromise so that it isn't an issue when our
contract comes up for renewal.' Instead, we've both spent five years being mad about
it."

Finally, a renewable marriage contract would make ending a marriage far   11
easier than it is today. No longer would both partners have to hire expensive lawyers
and endure long waits in the divorce courts. Their marriage contract would spell out
the terms of a split. It would say how property would be divided and how custody of
children would be handled. Ending a marriage would require the simple filing of a
paper in the courthouse. The man and woman would then go their own ways, sadder
perhaps, but wiser about what it takes to make a marriage work.

For Paul and Michelle, it may be too late. Their marriage seems headed for the   12
divorce courts. "I dread the whole thing, and I wish it was over," said Michelle. "It's
hard to believe that people who think they are so right for each other can turn out to
be so wrong," said Paul.

"A marriage contract might have saved us, either before our wedding or after   13
it," Paul said. He added, "If there's a next time, I'm going to insist that we sit down
and draw one up."

Michelle agreed. "You wouldn't buy a car or take a job without a contract," she   14
pointed out. "A marriage is important enough to deserve one, too."

Basic Skill Questions

Vocabulary in Context

1. The word *incredible* in "'It's incredible that Paul and I got married in the
   first place,' Michelle told their marriage counselor. 'We disagree on
   practically everything'" (paragraph 2) means
   a. well-known.
   b. expensive.
   c. doubtful.
   d. unbelievable.

2. The word *options* in "they are faced with two unhappy options. They can
   continue on in a disappointing marriage, or they can start proceedings for
   an unpleasant . . . divorce" (paragraph 3) means

    a. questions.
    b. places.
    c. choices.
    d. ways to divorce.

Central Point and Main Ideas

3. Which sentence best expresses the central point of the selection?
    a. Many couples should not marry.
    b. Paul and Michelle may be unable to save their marriage.
    c. Couples could head off problems with renewable marriage contracts.
    d. Some couples never discuss serious issues.

4. The first sentence of paragraph 6 provides the main idea for
    a. paragraphs 6-7.
    b. paragraphs 6-8.
    c. paragraphs 6-11.
    d. paragraphs 6-12.

Supporting Details

5. Paul and Michelle are used as an example of a couple with disagreements about
    a. money.
    b. religion.
    c. having children.
    d. all of the above.

6. According to the author, marriage contracts would
    a. discourage some marriages.
    b. make marriages too complicated.
    c. guarantee successful marriages.
    d. take all the pressure off of marriages.

Transitions

7. *Fill in the blank:* The three major details supporting the first sentence of paragraph 6 are introduced with the transitions "first of all," "in addition,"

    and "Finally_____."

8. The relationship between the two sentences below is one of
    a. time.
    b. addition.
    c. contrast.
    d. illustration.

    We disagree on practically everything. And yet we seemed to get along so well when we were dating! (Paragraph 2)

9. The relationship between the two sentences below is one of
   a. time.
   b. addition.
   c. comparison.
   d. cause and effect.

   If they knew that their contract was coming up for renewal every few years, people would give as much attention to their marriages as they do to their careers or relationships with friends. (Paragraph 9)

Patterns of Organization

10. The major details supporting the first sentence of paragraph 6 are
    a. items in a list.
    b. steps in a process.
    c. comparisons or contrasts.
    d. a definition and examples.

Advanced Skill Questions

Fact and Opinion

11. Which sentence expresses an opinion?
    a. "Michelle wanted to sleep in on Sundays."
    b. "There are definite advantages to the marriage contract system."
    c. "When Paul looks back at the five years he and Michelle have spent together, he wishes they had faced the pressure of a contract."

12. Paragraph 4 of the reading expresses
    a. facts.
    b. opinions.

Inferences

13. We can conclude that the author feels being "wildly in love"
    a. is a bad idea.
    b. can interfere with clear thinking.
    c. is not important for marriage.
    d. should come after people decide to get married.

14. The author implies that
    a. Michelle and Paul should not divorce.
    b. Michelle was wrong not to want children.
    c. divorces are too easy to get.
    d. having a good marriage requires hard work from both partners.

Purpose and Tone

15. The main purpose of the selection is
    a. to inform.

b. to persuade.

c. to entertain.

16. The author's tone when discussing the idea of renewable marriage is one of
    a. discouragement.
    b. optimism.
    c. secrecy.
    d. joy.

17. Paul and Michelle's comments in paragraphs 13-14 have a tone of
    a. fear.
    b. delight.
    c. doubt.
    d. conviction.

Propaganda

18. If an ad for renewable marriage contracts stated only the sentence below, which propaganda technique would the ad be using?
    a. Bandwagon
    b. Testimonial
    c. Plain folks
    d. Glittering generality

    Renewable marriage contracts are the marriage solution!

19. Which of the following fictional ads for renewable marriage contracts uses the transfer technique?
    a. Actors Marie Lane and Charles Bowman credit their long and happy marriage to a renewable marriage contract.
    b. Norma Ashe and Billy Silver, small-town residents, say a renewable marriage contract helped them end their marriage relatively painlessly.
    c. Renewable marriage contracts are in the great American tradition of the individual's right to freedom and the pursuit of happiness.
    d. Millions of Americans—both married and divorced—have enjoyed the benefits of a renewable marriage contract.

20. Which of the following fictional ads for renewable marriage contracts uses a testimonial?
    a. Actors Marie Lane and Charles Bowman credit their long and happy marriage to a renewable marriage contract.
    b. Norma Ashe and Billy Silver, small-town residents, say a renewable marriage contract helped them end their marriage relatively painlessly.
    c. Renewable marriage contracts are in the great American tradition of the individual's right to freedom and the pursuit of happiness.
    d. Millions of Americans—both married and divorced—have enjoyed the benefits of a renewable marriage contract.

10

Argument

Many of us enjoy a good argument. A good argument is not an emotional experience where people's feelings get out of control, leaving them ready to start throwing things. Instead, it is a rational discussion where each person advances and supports a point of view about some matter. We might argue with a friend, for example, about where to eat or what movie to go to. We might argue about whether a boss or a parent or a teacher is acting in a fair or unfair manner. We might argue about whether certain performers or sports stars deserve to get paid as much as they do. In a good argument, the other person listens carefully as we state our case, waiting to see if we really have solid evidence to support our point of view.

Argumentation is, then, a part of our everyday dealings with other people. It is also central to many of the papers that we write, and it is a basic structure in much of the material that we read. Very often the two most important things we must do as *writers* are to:

1 Make a point.
2 Support the point.

Very often the two most important things we must do as *readers* are to:

1 Recognize the point.
2 Recognize the support for the point.

The essence of a good argument is this: a clear point and evidence that truly backs up that point. Clear and logical thinkers are persons who can advance a point and provide valid evidence to support that point.

This chapter will be divided into two parts. In the first part, you will practice the basics of a good argument: making a clear point and solidly supporting that point. In the second part, you will learn to recognize common errors in reasoning that prevent clear and logical thinking.

THE BASICS OF ARGUMENT: POINT AND SUPPORT

A good argument is one in which you make a point and then provide persuasive and logical evidence to back it up. Here is a point:

Point: The Beef and Burger Shop is a poor fast-food restaurant.

This statement hardly discourages us from visiting the Beef and Burger Shop. "Why do you say that?" we might legitimately ask. "Give your reasons." Support is needed so we can decide for ourselves whether a valid point has been made. Suppose the point is followed by these three reasons:

1. The burgers are full of gristle.
2. The roast beef sandwiches have a chemical taste.
3. The fries are lukewarm and soggy.

Clearly, the details provide solid support for the point. They give us a basis for understanding and agreeing with the point. In light of these details, our mouths are not watering for lunch at the Beef and Burger Shop.

We see here, then, a small example of what clear thinking in an argument is about: making a point and providing support that truly backs up that point. (Another way to describe a valid argument is: stating a conclusion and providing logical reasons to support the conclusion.)

Let's look at another example:

Point: My neighbors are inconsiderate.

We don't really yet know if the neighbors are inconsiderate. We might trust the opinion of the person who made the statement, but we don't know for sure until supporting details enable us to see and judge for ourselves. Here are details:

1. They play their stereo very loud late at night.
2. They let their children play on my front lawn.
3. They don't stop their dog from running into my back yard.

Again, the solid support convinces us that a logical point has been made.

In everyday life, of course, people don't simply say, "Here is my point" and "Here is my support." Nor do writers of material that you read state their basic ideas so directly. Even so, the basic structure of point and support is still at work beneath the surface, and you will benefit enormously from developing the ability to discover it. In particular, to become a more skilled reader and thinker, you should learn to analyze what you read. You want to be able to determine whether a given selection really does have a logical foundation, based on a clear point and logical support for that point.

To help you distinguish, first of all, between point and support for that point—or a conclusion and reasons for that conclusion—do the following activity.

➤ *Practice*

In each group of statements, one statement is the point, and the other statement or statements are support for the point. Identify each point with a **P**, and identify each statement of support with an **S**.

Hint: If you can insert the word *because* in front of a sentence, you probably have a statement of support.

1. _____ I can't keep my eyes open any longer.
   _____ I'd better take a nap.

2. _____ That traffic light has stayed red for at least five minutes.
   _____ That traffic light must be broken.

3. _____ His face looks tight and he seldom smiles.
   _____ He's smoking more than usual.
   _____ When asked how he is, he quickly changes the subject.
   _____ Something must really be bothering Craig.

4. _____ The library should be kept open on Sundays and holidays.
   _____ Many students save their studying for days when they do not have classes.
   _____ Library facilities are already overcrowded on weekdays.
   _____ It's difficult to find research materials during the week; other students are often using the books.

5. _____ The dialogue sounded like junior high school jokes.
   _____ The monsters belonged in a salad, not a laboratory.
   _____ *Invasion of the Asparagus People* is a terrible science fiction movie.
   _____ The ending just didn't make sense. Who's ever heard of bacteria that like to eat asparagus?

Using Informal Outlines to Evaluate Arguments

An excellent way to develop your skill at thinking clearly is to do informal outlines. In an informal outline, you identify the basic point and the basic support of a selection. Such outlines are invaluable, whether for a paper you plan to write, a speech you plan to give, or a reading selection you want to understand and study. The outline helps you think about the point that is being made and about whether the point has been adequately and logically supported.

Consider the following point. It is followed by six items of support, only three of which logically back up the point. See if you can circle the three items.

Point: My dog Otis does not appear to be very bright.

1. He's five years old and doesn't respond to his name yet.
2. He cries when I leave for work every day.
3. He always gets excited when visitors arrive.
4. He often attacks the back yard hedge as if it's a hostile animal.
5. He gets along very well with my neighbor's cat.
6. I often have to put food in front of him because he can't find it by himself.

Now read the following comments on the six items to see which ones you should have circled and why.

1. Most dogs know their names, so Otis's unfamiliarity with his own name reveals a weak memory, one aspect of intelligence. You should have circled the number to this item.
2. Even an intelligent dog might be sad when its companions leave the house.
3. Both bright and not-so-bright dogs are happy to see old and new human friends.
4. The inability to distinguish between a bush and an animal—friendly or hostile—suggests a lack of analytical skills. *Four* is the second number you should have circled.
5. Contrary to the comic book stereotype, dogs of all degrees of intelligence have been known to be friendly with cats.
6. Since most dogs recognize food much more often than their owners would like them to, Otis's inability to find food clearly indicates poor problem-solving skills. You should also have circled the number of this item.

➤ *Practice*

Each point below is followed by six items, three of which logically support the point, and three of which do not. In the spaces provided, write the letters of the three items that logically support each point.

1.   **Point:**   My neighbors are weird folks.
   a. Each family member, including the males, has purple fingernails.
   b. They call me if their dog gets loose.
   c. They have lived in the house for the past two years.
   d. They keep cows and goats inside the house.
   e. On nights with a full moon, they sit on lawn chairs placed on their roof.
   f. Each member of the family has his or her own car.

   Items that logically support the point: _____   _____   _____

2. **Point:** Alcohol and tobacco are among the most dangerous drugs that Americans use.

   a. Cancer from cigarette smoking kills a number of Americans every year.

   b. During Prohibition, liquor bootleggers fought one another as drug dealers do today.

   c. About half of all fatal traffic accidents are due to drunk driving.

   d. Nothing is more annoying than trying to enjoy a restaurant meal when the people at nearby tables are smoking and drinking heavily.

   e. We often don't think of alcohol and tobacco as "drugs," because they are legal.

   f. Alcohol abuse causes many people to become more aggressive and violent.

   Items that logically support the point: _____ _____ _____

3. **Point:** Halloween should be abolished.

   a. The holiday encourages vandalism in older children.

   b. Summer would have been a better time for Halloween because it stays light longer then.

   c. Children who wear vision-obstructing masks and dark, hard-to-see costumes are in danger of being struck by cars.

   d. Thanksgiving is a lot more meaningful than Halloween.

   e. Some local business people overcharge for Halloween costumes and candy.

   f. More and more incidents of poisoned treats are occurring.

   Items that logically support the point: _____ _____ _____

4. **Point:** There should be a limit on how much can be spent for political campaigns.

   a. The television networks profit greatly from the ads for local and national elections.

   b. Elected officials could spend more time on their jobs and less on raising money.

   c. Once and for all, candidates should stop using personal attacks in their campaigns.

   d. Candidates with less money would have a more fair chance of competing.

   e. Citizens must learn to evaluate political campaigns in a logical manner.

   f. Elected officials would be less likely to be influenced by rich contributors to their campaigns.

   Items that logically support the point: _____ _____ _____

MORE ABOUT ARGUMENTS: ERRORS IN REASONING

Learning about some common errors in reasoning will help you to spot weak points in arguments. The rest of this chapter will familiarize you with some of those errors, also known as *fallacies*. Specifically, you'll look at these unsound reasoning patterns:

Four Fallacies That Ignore the Issue:

- Changing the Subject
- Circular Reasoning
- Personal Attack
- Straw man

Four Fallacies that Overgeneralize or Oversimplify Issues:

- Hasty Generalization
- False Cause
- False Comparison
- Either-Or Fallacy

Following are explanations of these eight common types of fallacies. Exercises throughout give you practice in spotting them.

Fallacies That Ignore the Issue

Fallacy 1. Changing the Subject

This method of arguing tries to divert the audience's attention from the true issue by presenting evidence that actually has nothing to do with the argument. You have already had experience with this method in the activity on pages 188-189, where you had to separate relevant support from support that was beside the point. Here are two more examples:

> I think you should buy a bird, not a dog. Many dogs shed all over the house.
> (Saying that many dogs shed is beside the point; it is possible to buy a dog that does not shed.)

> The congressman is clearly an able leader. He has a warm family life and attends church every Sunday.
> (Mention of the congressman's family and church life sidesteps the issue of just how able a leader he is.)

This fallacy is also called a *red herring*. In a fox hunt, drawing a red herring across the dogs' path causes them to lose the scent, allowing the fox to escape. Someone who changes the subject when arguing may hope the audience will lose track of the real point of the argument.

Now read the following paragraph and try to find the sentence that does *not* support the point, which is in the first sentence.

Sigmund Freud was one of the most important scientists of the twentieth century. He was among the first to study mental disorders, such as hysteria and neurosis, in a systematic way. He developed the theory of the unconscious and showed how people's behavior is greatly affected by forgotten childhood events. His discoveries are the basis of psychoanalysis, a method of treating mental illness that is still important today. He was highly regarded by scientists of his time.

The point of this argument is that Freud "was one of the most important scientists of the twentieth century." Any statement that doesn't help prove this point is irrelevant. The manner in which the scientists of his day viewed Freud isn't a logical reason for his being one of the most important scientists of this century. Many scientists have been highly regarded in their time without being very important. Thus the last sentence is irrelevant to the argument.

➤ Practice 1

One sentence in each paragraph below does not support the point of the argument. Read the paragraph, and then decide which sentence is not relevant to the argument. To help you decide if a sentence is irrelevant or not, ask yourself, "Does this have anything to do with the point that is being proved?"

1. ¹Soon, the personal computer will be as necessary to every American home as the telephone is today. ²Every family member will be able to use the computer in some way. ³Parents will find a computer of value for keeping family information such as tax records and recipe collections. ⁴Software programs now exist even for such annoying chores as balancing the family checkbook. ⁵Of course, banks are already beginning to offer a computer service that balances customers' checkbooks for them. ⁶In addition, children's grades will improve when they use a computer to master a subject or write an English paper. ⁷And everyone will enjoy taking a break with one of the popular computer games.

Which of the following statements does not contribute to the author's conclusion that soon every American home will have a personal computer?

a. Sentence 3   c. Sentence 5
b. Sentence 4   d. Sentence 6

2. ¹The proposed new highway linking Interstate 95 with the turnpike is a disaster. ²The plans for this highway were drawn over thirty years ago, when the affected area was lightly settled. ³Now, a generation later, the area has become developed, and hundreds of families would lose their homes if the highway were built. ⁴There are already too many forces weakening the American family structure these days. ⁵The environment will also be negatively affected by the construction of a new superhighway. ⁶Hundreds of thousands of birds and small animals, including several endangered species, will lose their natural habitats and may die out.

Which of the following is not a sound argument in support of the author's conclusion that the proposed highway is a disaster?

a. Sentence 2   c. Sentence 4
b. Sentence 3   d. Sentence 6

Fallacy 2. Circular Reasoning

Part of a point cannot reasonably be used as evidence to support it. That type of argument is called *circular reasoning*, also known as *begging the question*. A simple and obvious example of such reasoning is: "Mr. Green is a great teacher because he is so wonderful at teaching." The supporting reason given in this point itself ("he is so wonderful at teaching") is really the same as the conclusion ("Mr. Green is a great teacher"). We still do not know why he is a great teacher. No real reasons have been given—the statement merely has repeated itself.

Can you spot the circular reasoning in the following arguments?

1. Vitamins are healthy, for they improve your well-being.
2. Since people under 21 are too young to vote, the voting age shouldn't be lowered below age 21.
3. Abortion is an evil practice because it is so wrong.

Let's look more closely now at these arguments:

1. The word *healthy*, which is used in the conclusion, conveys the same idea as *well-being*.
2. The author uses the idea that people under 21 are too young to vote as both the conclusion *and* the reason of the argument. No real reason is given for *why* people under 21 are too young to vote.
3. The claim that abortion is wrong is simply a restatement of the idea that it is an *evil practice*.

In all these cases, the reasons merely repeat an important part of the conclusion. The careful reader wants to say, "Tell me something new. You are reasoning in circles. Give me supporting evidence, not a repetition."

➤ *Practice 2*

Circle the number of the one item that contains an example of circular reasoning.

1. Why support Ray O'Donnell's highway safety proposal? He's got the biggest collection of speeding tickets in the district.
2. The government should lower our taxes because taxes are entirely too high.
3. Our football team is going to be number one this year. We have a new stadium to play in, and the half-time show is better than ever.
4. The people who are in favor of gun control are obviously not concerned about criminals taking control of this fine country.

Fallacy 3. Personal Attack

This fallacy often occurs in political debate. Here's an example:

> Senator Snerd's opinions on public housing are worthless. He can't even manage to hold his own household together, having married and divorced three times already.

Senator Snerd's family life may or may not reflect a weakness in his character, but it has nothing to do with the value of his opinions on public housing. This kind of fallacy ignores the issue under discussion and concentrates instead on the character of the opponent.

Sometimes personal attacks take the form of accusing people of taking a stand only because it will benefit them personally. For instance, here's a personal attack on a Congressman who supports the Equal Rights Amendment (ERA): "He doesn't care about the ERA. He only supports it in order to get more women to vote for him." This argument ignores the Congressman's detailed defense of the ERA as a way to insure equal rights for both men and women. The key to recognizing personal attack is that it always involves an opponent's personal life or character, rather than simply his or her public ideas.

➤ *Practice 3*

Circle the number of the one item that contains an example of personal attack.

1. Why support Ray O'Donnell's highway safety proposal? He's got the biggest collection of speeding tickets in the district.
2. The government should lower our taxes because taxes are entirely too high.
3. Our football team is going to be number one this year. We have a new stadium to play in, and the half-time show is better than ever.
4. The people who are in favor of gun control are obviously not concerned about criminals taking control of this fine country.

Fallacy 4. Straw Man

An opponent made of straw can be defeated very easily. Sometimes, if one's real opponent is putting up too good a fight, it can be tempting to build a scarecrow and battle it instead. For example, take the following passage from a debate on the death penalty.

> Ms. Collins opposes capital punishment. But letting murderers out on the street to kill again is a crazy idea. If we did that, no one would be safe.

Ms. Collins, however, never advocated "letting murderers out on the street to kill again." In fact, she wants to keep them in jail for life rather than execute them. This fallacy suggests that the opponent favors an obviously unpopular cause—when the opponent really doesn't support anything of the kind.

➤ Practice 4

Circle the number of the one item that contains an example of straw man.

1. Why support Ray O'Donnell's highway safety proposal? He's got the biggest collection of speeding tickets in the district.
2. The government should lower our taxes because taxes are entirely too high.
3. Our football team is going to be number one this year. We have a new stadium to play in, and the half-time show is better than ever.
4. The people who are in favor of gun control are obviously not concerned about criminals taking control of this fine country.

Fallacies That Overgeneralize or Oversimplify

Fallacy 5. Hasty Generalization

To be valid, a point must be based on an adequate amount of evidence. Someone who draws a point or conclusion on the basis of insufficient evidence is making a *hasty generalization*. This is a very common fallacy. It is not unusual, for instance, to hear an argument like this one:

> The Chinese people have a natural talent for art. Two Chinese girls took an art course with me last semester, and they were the best students in the class.

Forming a conclusion about the quarter of a billion Chinese people in the world based on two examples is an illogical jump.

In the argument on the next page, three supporting reasons are given, followed by four possible points. Three of the points are hasty generalizations which cannot logically be drawn from the small amount of evidence given. The fourth is a valid conclusion. Choose the one point you think is valid and put a check mark beside it. Then read the explanation that follows.

1. The first time I went to that beach, I got a bad case of sunburn.
2. The second time I went to that beach, I couldn't go in the water because of the pollution.
3. The third time I went to that beach, I stepped on a starfish and had to go to the emergency room to have the spikes removed from my foot.

Which of the following is a valid conclusion that can be drawn from the evidence above?

____ a. That beach is unsafe and should be closed.

____ b. I've had a string of bad experiences at that beach.

____ c. Beaches are not safe places.

____ d. We're never going to get this planet cleaned up.

The correct answer is *b*. Answer *a* is simply not supported by three isolated instances; we'd need many more reports of dangerous conditions before considering having the beach closed. Answer *c* is even more poorly supported. We'd need many, many reports of dangerous conditions at beaches worldwide to come to the conclusion stated in *c*. Answer *d* is supported in part by the reference to pollution in statement 2, but the other two statements (about sunburn and starfish) are not examples of pollution.

➤ *Practice 5*

Check the sentence that states a valid point based on the supporting evidence in each group below. Remember that the point, or conclusion, should follow logically from the evidence. Do not jump to a conclusion that is not well-supported.

Group 1

- My grandmother's cottage is in the country.
- The only sounds we hear are bird calls and the wind rustling in the pine trees.
- On Grandmother's front porch, we often enjoy watching the sunset over the lake.

Check the one valid conclusion that can be drawn from the evidence above:

____ a. The speaker would rather be at his grandmother's cottage than anywhere else.

____ b. His grandmother often invites him to her cottage.

____ c. His grandmother's cottage is the most peaceful place he's ever been.

____ d. His grandmother's cottage at the lake is very peaceful.

Group 2

- Some people put off writing or calling a friend because they feel they did not have time to do it right, but a quick note or call is often better than nothing.
- Sometimes it makes sense to do a routine chore quickly rather than perfectly in order to save time for something more important.
- Even a desk and office need not be perfectly neat; sometimes cleaning them up is just an excuse for putting off more important work.

Check the one valid conclusion that can be drawn from the evidence above:

___ a. Perfection is not always a worthwhile goal.

___ b. People who aim for perfection never get around to important tasks.

___ c. You can be better organized if you plan each day more carefully.

___ d. Getting things done haphazardly is always better than not getting them done at all.

Fallacy 6. False Cause

You have probably heard someone say as a joke, "I know it's going to rain today because I just washed the car." The idea that someone can make it rain by washing a car is funny because the two events obviously have nothing to do with each other. However, with more complicated issues, it is easy to make the mistake known as the fallacy of *false cause*. The mistake is to assume that because Event B follows Event A, Event A has *caused* Event B.

Cause-and-effect situations can be difficult to analyze, and people are often tempted to oversimplify them by ignoring other possible causes. To identify an argument using a false cause, look for alternative causes. Consider this argument:

The Macklin Company was more prosperous before Ms. Williams became president. Clearly, she is the cause of the decline.

(*Event A:* Ms. Williams became president.
Event B: The Macklin Company's earnings declined.)

What other possible causes could have been responsible for the decline? Perhaps the policies of the previous president are just now affecting the company. Perhaps the market for the company's product has changed. In any case, it's easy but dangerous to assume that just because A *came before* B, A *caused* B.

➤ *Practice 6*

Circle the number of the one item that contains an example of false cause.

1. You'll either have to get a good job soon or face the fact that you'll never be successful.
2. Cincinnati has terrible weather. I visited there for a week last summer, and the sun didn't shine even once.
3. After visiting Hal today, I came home with a headache. I must be allergic to his dog.
4. Of course the legalization of prostitution will work in America. It's worked in European countries, hasn't it?

Fallacy 7. False Comparison

When the poet Robert Burns wrote, "My love is like a red, red rose," he meant that both the woman he loved and a rose are beautiful. In other ways—such as having green leaves and thorns, for example—his love did not resemble a rose at all. Comparisons are often a good way to clarify a point. But because two things are not alike in all respects, comparisons (sometimes called *analogies*) often make poor evidence for arguments. In the error in reasoning known as *false comparison*, the assumption is that two things are more alike than they really are. For example, read the following argument.

> It didn't hurt your grandfather in the old country to get to work without a car, and it won't hurt you either.

To judge whether or not this is a false comparison, consider how the two situations are alike and how they differ. They are similar in that both involve a young person's need to get to work. But the situations are different in that the grandfather didn't have to be at work an hour after his last class. In fact, he didn't go to school at all. In addition, his family didn't own a car he could use. The differences in this case are more important than the similarities, making it a false comparison.

➤ *Practice 7*

Circle the number of the one item that contains an example of false comparison.

1. You'll either have to get a good job soon or face the fact that you'll never be successful.
2. Cincinnati has terrible weather. I visited there for a week last summer, and the sun didn't shine even once.
3. After visiting Hal today, I came home with a headache. I must be allergic to his dog.
4. Of course the legalization of prostitution will work in America. It's worked in European countries, hasn't it?

Fallacy 8. Either-Or

It is often wrong to assume that there are only two sides to a question. Offering only two choices when more actually exist is an *either-or fallacy*. For example, the statement "You are either with us or against us" assumes that there is no middle ground. Or consider the following:

People opposed to unrestricted free speech are really in favor of censorship.

This argument ignores the fact that a person could believe in free speech as well as in laws that prohibit slander or that punish someone for yelling "Fire!" in a crowded theater. Some issues have only two sides (Will you pass the course, or won't you?), but most have several.

➤ Practice 8

Circle the number of the item that contains an example of the either-or fallacy.

1. You'll either have to get a good job soon or face the fact that you'll never be successful.
2. Cincinnati has terrible weather. I visited there for a week last summer, and the sun didn't shine even once.
3. After visiting Hal today, I came home with a headache. I must be allergic to his dog.
4. Of course the legalization of prostitution will work in America. It's worked in European countries, hasn't it?

➤ Review Test 1

A. In each group of statements, one statement is the point, and the other statement or statements are support for the point. Identify each point with a **P**, and identify each statement of support with an **S**.

Hint: If you can insert the word *because* in front of a sentence, you probably have a statement of support.

1. _____ I'd better look for another pre-school for my son.

    _____ He says he hates his pre-school teacher.

    _____ Yesterday he hid under his bed when it was time to go to pre-school.

2. _____ The math tutors at school have helped many students raise their math grades.

    _____ I'm having trouble with math this quarter.

    _____ I think I'll make an appointment to see a tutor.

3. _____ Scientists have proven that acid rain harms trees and bodies of water.

_____ Laws should be passed to reduce acid rain.

_____ The damage done by acid rain is hard or impossible to undo.

4. _____ The roaches seem to be taking over this apartment.

_____ I'd better look for another apartment.

_____ The landlord refuses to fix the leaky faucet.

_____ The people upstairs make a lot of noise.

B. Each point below is followed by six items, three of which logically support the point, and three of which do not. In the spaces provided, write the letters of the three items that logically support each point.

5. **Point:** Drinking coffee can have unpleasant effects.

a. Some people don't like the taste of decaffeinated coffees.
b. Coffee in the evening can interfere with sleep at night.
c. As addictions go, coffee is less dangerous than tobacco.
d. Too much coffee can cause the hands to shake.
e. Drinking too much coffee can lead to a faster heartbeat and lightheadedness.
f. Most coffees cost under five dollars a pound.

Items that logically support the point: _____ _____ _____

6. **Point:** Some people have very poor telephone manners.

a. They never identify themselves, but just begin the conversation.
b. They often make their calls on cordless phones.
c. They have an unlisted telephone number.
d. They conduct conversations with people around them at the same time they're talking on the phone.
e. Some people don't like to talk on the phone.
f. They often call around 6 p.m., which is most people's dinner hour.

Items that logically support the point: _____ _____ _____

➤ *Review Test 2*

A. Circle the letter of the *irrelevant* sentence in each paragraph—the sentence that changes the subject.

1.   ¹If the township would put street lights along Holly Drive, it would make life safer and easier for those of us who live along that street and our guests. ²This township never seems to take the needs of the citizens into account. ³It is so dark on Holly Drive that people have trouble seeing where they are going. ⁴A few months ago, an elderly woman visiting a neighbor's home couldn't see a step and fell, breaking her hip bone. ⁵And people who visit my home frequently complain about not being able to see our address, even though we have a light outside our front door.

   Which of the following is not relevant to the author's conclusion that it would be safer and more convenient if the township put in street lights?

   a. Sentence 2   c. Sentence 4
   b. Sentence 3   d. Sentence 5

2.   ¹Children should be given an allowance as soon as they are old enough to want it. ²Having to make decisions about what to do with their money is good training for the future. ³They eventually learn to use their money on what they really want, instead of spending impulsively. ⁴Furthermore, an allowance is one good way of telling a child that he or she is a responsible member of the family and that membership brings benefits as well as obligations. ⁵That will make the expectation that they also have to do chores more reasonable. ⁶Unfortunately, some people are reluctant to give young children an allowance.

   Which of the following does not support the author's conclusion that children benefit from being given an allowance?

   a. Sentence 2   c. Sentence 5
   b. Sentence 3   d. Sentence 6

B. Circle the letter of the fallacy contained in each argument below.

3.   Supporters of state lotteries apparently don't think that anyone should work hard for what he gets. They believe it's better to get something for nothing.
   a. Circular reasoning *(a statement repeats itself rather than providing a real supporting reason to back up an argument)*
   b. Personal attack *(the argument shifts to irrelevant personal criticism)*
   c. Straw man *(an argument is made by claiming an opponent holds an extreme position and then opposing that extreme position)*

4. Councilman Hawkins is wholly unqualified to be elected mayor. He is a
    well-known homosexual.
    a. Circular reasoning *(a statement repeats itself rather than providing a real
       supporting reason to back up an argument)*
    b. Personal attack *(the argument shifts to irrelevant personal criticism)*
    c. Straw man *(an argument is made by claiming an opponent holds an extreme
       position and then opposing that extreme position)*

C. Check the sentence that states a valid point based on the supporting evidence in
    each group below. Remember that the point, or conclusion, should follow
    logically from the evidence. Do not jump to a conclusion that is not well-
    supported.

Group 1

- There's been a Shrimp Boat seafood restaurant on Thayer Street for
  about five years.
- Last week, two new Shrimp Boats opened in local shopping malls.
- A display ad in the classified section reads, "Shrimp Boat: Franchises
  Available in Top Money-Making Locations."

5. Check the one valid conclusion that can be drawn from the evidence
    above:

    ___ a. Shrimp Boat serves the best seafood in town.

    ___ b. The Shrimp Boat restaurant chain is expanding.

    ___ c. People who work at a Shrimp Boat restaurant can expect to make a
    lot of money.

    ___ d. Anyone who wants to can open a Shrimp Boat restaurant.

Group 2

- Last week, when I tried to take a copy of *Readings for Managers* out of
  the library, it wasn't on the shelf.
- Yesterday, I tried again, and it still wasn't there.
- Today, I asked the librarian, who said there was no record of anyone
  borrowing that book.

6. Check the one valid conclusion that can be drawn from the evidence
    above:

    ___ a. *Readings for Managers* has been stolen.

    ___ b. The librarian is careless.

    ___ c. The book has been misfiled.

    ___ d. The book is not where it is supposed to be.

D. Circle the letter of the fallacy contained in each argument below.

7.   I knew I shouldn't have taken the baby to the park today. Now he's got a cold.
   a. False cause *(the argument assumes that the order of events alone shows cause and effect)*
   b. False comparison *(the argument assumes that two things being compared are more alike than they really are)*
   c. Either-or *(the argument assumes that there are only two sides to a question)*

8.   I don't know why you're so worried about my grades. Albert Einstein had lousy grades in high school, and he did all right.
   a. False cause *(the argument assumes that the order of events alone shows cause and effect)*
   b. False comparison *(the argument assumes that two things being compared are more alike than they really are)*
   c. Either-or *(the argument assumes that there are only two sides to a question)*

➤ Review Test 3

A. To review what you've learned in this chapter, complete each of the following sentences about evaluating arguments.

1.   Often the two most important things we must do when we read are to identify the _____ of a selection and also the _____ that backs it up.

2.   A valuable step in reading, writing, or speaking clearly is to first prepare a(n) _____.

3.   A fallacy is an error in (*reading, reasoning, changing the subject*) _____ that makes an argument illogical.

4.   The fallacies of personal attack and straw man are specific versions of (*circular reasoning, changing the subject, hasty generalization*) _____ because they present evidence that is beside the point.

5.   Assuming that there are only two sides to a question is called the (*false cause, false comparison, either-or*) _____ fallacy.

B. Can flunking be good for students? Here is a chance to apply your understanding of arguments to an essay that addresses that question.

Following the reading are questions on arguments. To help you continue to strengthen your work on the skills taught in previous chapters, there are also questions on

- vocabulary in context
- central point and main ideas
- supporting details
- transitions
- patterns of organization

- fact and opinion
- inferences
- purpose and tone
- propaganda.

Words to Watch

Following are some words in the reading that do not have strong context support. Each word is followed by the number of the paragraph in which it appears and its meaning there.

trump card (4): a tactic that gives one an advantage (like a trump suit in card games)
flustered (6): nervously confused
composure (6): calmness and self-control
radical (6): extreme
conspiracy (11): plot

IN PRAISE OF THE F WORD

Mary Sherry

Tens of thousands of 18-year-olds will graduate this year and be handed meaningless diplomas. These diplomas won't look any different from those awarded their luckier classmates. Their validity will be questioned only when their employers discover that these graduates are semiliterate. 1

Eventually a fortunate few will find their way into educational-repair shops—adult-literacy programs, such as the one where I teach basic grammar and writing. There, high-school graduates and high-school dropouts pursuing graduate-equivalency certificates will learn the skills they should have learned in school. They will also discover they have been cheated by our educational system. 2

As I teach, I learn a lot about our schools. Early in each session I ask my students to write about an unpleasant experience they had in school. No writers' block here! "I wish someone would have had made me stop doing drugs and made me study." "I liked to party and no one seemed to care." "I was a good kid and didn't cause any trouble, so they just passed me along even though I didn't read well and couldn't write." And so on. 3

I am your basic do-gooder, and prior to teaching this class I blamed the poor academic skills our kids have today on drugs, divorce and other impediments to concentration necessary for doing well in school. But, as I rediscover each time I 4 walk into the classroom, before a teacher can expect students to concentrate, he has to get their attention, no matter what distractions may be at hand. There are many ways to do this, and they have much to do with teaching style. However, if style alone won't do it, there is another way to show who holds the winning hand in the classroom. That is to reveal the trump card° of failure.

I will never forget a teacher who played that card to get the attention of one of   5 my children. Our youngest, a world-class charmer, did little to develop his intellectual talents but always got by. Until Mrs. Stifter.

Our son was a high-school senior when he had her for English. "He sits in the   6 back of the room talking to his friends," she told me. "Why don't you move him to the front row?" I urged, believing the embarrassment would get him to settle down. Mrs. Stifter looked at me steely-eyed over her glasses. "I don't move seniors," she said. "I flunk them." I was flustered°. Our son's academic life flashed before my eyes. No teacher had ever threatened him with that before. I regained my composure° and managed to say that I thought she was right. By the time I got home I was feeling pretty good about this. It was a radical° approach for these times, but, well, why not? "She's going to flunk you," I told my son. I did not discuss it any further. Suddenly English became a priority in his life. He finished out the semester with an A.

I know one example doesn't make a case, but at night I see a parade of students   7 who are angry and resentful for having been passed along until they could no longer even pretend to keep up. Of average intelligence or better, they eventually quit school, concluding they were too dumb to finish. "I should have been held back," is a comment I hear frequently. Even sadder are those students who are high-school graduates who say to me after a few weeks of class, "I don't know how I ever got a high-school diploma."

Passing students who have not mastered the work cheats them and the   8 employers who expect graduates to have basic skills. We excuse this dishonest behavior by saying kids can't learn if they come from terrible environments. No one seems to stop to think that—no matter what environments they come from—most kids don't put school first on their list unless they perceive something is at stake. They'd rather be sailing.

Many students I see at night could give expert testimony on unemployment,   9 chemical dependency, abusive relationships. In spite of these difficulties, they have decided to make education a priority. They are motivated by the desire for a better job or the need to hang on to the one they've got. They have a healthy fear of failure.

People of all ages can rise above their problems, but they need to have a reason   10 to do so. Young people generally don't have the maturity to value education in the same way my adult students value it. But fear of failure, whether economic or academic, can motivate both.

Flunking as a regular policy has just as much merit today as it did two   11 generations ago. We must review the threat of flunking and see it as it really is—a positive teaching tool. It is an expression of confidence by both teachers and parents that the students have the ability to learn the material presented to them. However, making it work again would take a dedicated, caring conspiracy° between teachers and parents. It would mean facing the tough reality that passing kids who haven't learned the material—while it might save them grief for the short term—dooms them to long-term illiteracy. It would mean that teachers would have to follow through on their threats, and parents would have to stand behind them, knowing their children's

best interests are indeed at stake. This means no more doing Scott's assignments for
him because he might fail. No more passing Jodi because she's such a nice kid.

This is a policy that worked in the past and can work today. A wise teacher,   12
with the support of his parents, gave our son the opportunity to succeed—or fail. It's
time we return this choice to all students.

Basic Skill Questions

Vocabulary in Context

1. The word *validity* in "[the diplomas'] validity will be questioned . . . when
   . . . employers discover that these graduates are semiliterate" (paragraph 1)
   means
   a. wording.
   b. soundness.
   c. dates.
   d. supply.

2. The word *impediments* in "I blamed the poor academic skills our kids have
   today on drugs, divorce and other impediments to concentration"
   (paragraph 4) means
   a. questions.
   b. skills.
   c. obstacles.
   d. paths.

Central Point and Main Ideas

3. Which sentence best expresses the central point of the selection?
   a. Before students will concentrate, the teacher must get their attention.
   b. Many adults cannot read or write well.
   c. English skills can be learned through adult literacy programs.
   d. The threat of failure can be a positive teaching tool.

4. Which sentence best expresses the main idea of paragraph 6?
   a. According to his teacher, Sherry's son sat at the back of the room,
      talking to his friends.
   b. Mrs. Stifter said that she didn't move seniors, she flunked them.
   c. The fear of flunking motivated Sherry's son to do well in English.
   d. Sherry was at first nervous and confused to learn that her son might be
      flunked by Mrs. Stifter.

Supporting Details

5. Sherry's night students are
   a. motivated to learn.
   b. usually unemployed.
   c. doing drugs.
   d. poor students.

6. The supporting details of paragraph 3 are
   a. events.
   b. student regrets.
   c. quotations from students who had flunked.
   d. reasons for flunking.

7. According to the author, many students who get "passed along"
   a. are lucky.
   b. don't get into trouble.
   c. eventually feel angry and resentful.
   d. never find a job.

Transitions

8. The relationship between the two sentences below is one of
   a. time.
   b. addition.
   c. cause and effect.
   d. illustration.

   [In adult-literacy programs] high-school graduates and high-school dropouts pursuing graduate-equivalency certificates will learn the skills they should have learned in school. They will also discover they have been cheated by our educational system. (Paragraph 2)

9. The relationship between the two sentences below is one of
   a. time.
   b. addition.
   c. comparison.
   d. contrast.

   Many students I see at night could give expert testimony on unemployment, chemical dependency, abusive relationships. In spite of these difficulties, they have decided to make education a priority. (Paragraph 9)

Patterns of Organization

10. The main pattern of organization of paragraph 6 is
    a. time order.
    b. list of items.
    c. definition and example.
    d. comparison.

Advanced Skill Questions

Fact and Opinion

11. Paragraph 6 of the selection is primarily
    a. fact.
    b. opinion.

12. Paragraph 11 of the selection is primarily
    a. fact.
    b. opinion.

Inferences

13. The author implies that our present educational system is
    a. doing the best that it can.
    b. the best in the world.
    c. not demanding enough of students.
    d. very short of teachers.

14. From the selection, we may assume that the author based her opinion on
    a. educational research.
    b. expert professional testimony.
    c. statistics.
    d. her personal and professional experiences.

Purpose and Tone

15. The author's primary purpose in this article is
    a. to inform.
    b. to persuade.
    c. to entertain.

16. The tone of the author's discussion about our schools can be described as
    a. bitter and cruel.
    b. sympathetic and forgiving.
    c. excited but confused.
    d. distressed and critical.

Propaganda

17. The ad below (suggested by the article) is an example of which propaganda technique?
    a. Bandwagon *(the appeal to do what many others are doing)*
    b. Testimonial *(the use of a well-known spokesperson)*
    c. Plain folks *(showing candidates, company executives, or customers as ordinary folks)*
    d. Glittering generalities *(use of an important-sounding but unsupported claim)*

    Stay in school! Join the tens of thousands of 18-year-olds who will be handed their high school diplomas over the next few years.

Argument

18. Label the point of the following argument from the reading with a **P**; label the two statements of support for the point with an **S**. Note that one statement should not be labeled—it is neither the point nor the support of the argument.

    _____ Fear of failure motivated the author's son to do well in English.

    _____ The fear of failure is a good motivator.

    _____ Some people learn skills after high school in adult literacy programs.

    _____ Even troubled students have a healthy fear of failure because they want to hold on to their jobs or get a better one.

19. In stating "one example doesn't make a case" (paragraph 7), Sherry refers to the fallacy of
    a. changing the subject *(the evidence sounds good but has nothing to do with the argument).*
    b. hasty generalization *(the argument makes a generalization based on insufficient evidence).*
    c. false cause *(assumes that the order of events alone shows cause and effect).*
    d. false comparison *(the argument assumes that two things being compared are more alike than they really are).*

20. If someone advanced the statement "Teachers who pass students without skills are out to destroy the American educational system," what fallacy would be involved?
    a. Straw man *(an argument is made by claiming an opponent holds an extreme position and then opposing that extreme position)*
    b. Circular reasoning *(a statement repeats itself rather than providing a real supporting reason to back up an argument)*
    c. False comparison *(the argument assumes that two things being compared are more alike than they really are)*
    d. False cause *(the argument assumes that the order of events alone shows cause and effect)*

Part II

MASTERY TESTS

VOCABULARY IN CONTEXT: Test 1

Figure out the meanings of the following five words by studying them in context.
Then complete the matching and fill-in test that follows.

1 **apathy**
(ap'-ə-thē)

Since voter **apathy** was high, the turnout on election day was very low.

Student **apathy** turned to intense interest when the psychology teacher discussed Freud's views on sex.

2 **ecstatic**
(ek-stat'-ik)

I wouldn't be just glad if I won the lottery; I'd be **ecstatic**.

The smallest thing, like an ice pop on a hot day or a ladybug in the grass, can make a child **ecstatic**.

3 **longevity**
(lon-jev'-i-tē)

The animal with the greatest **longevity** is the giant land tortoise, which can live several hundred years.

Volvos and Hondas, known for their **longevity**, outlast more expensive cars.

4 **prone**
(prōn)

Mr. Walker is **prone** to high blood pressure, so he limits his salt intake.

Prone to fits of laughter during class, Chris sometimes controls the impulse by biting into his pen.

5 **revert**
(ri-vûrt')

After his release from jail, Sam **reverted** to his old habit of stealing.

Helene gave up smoking while she was pregnant, but she **reverted** to smoking a pack a day after her daughter was born.

A. Match each word with its definition.

1. apathy _____ having a tendency; inclined

2. ecstatic _____ a long span of life

3. longevity _____ lack of interest and concern

4. prone (to) _____ to return to a previous habit, opinion, or condition

5. revert (to) _____ joyful

(Continues on next page)

211

B. Fill in each blank with one of the words in the box. Use each word once.

apathy	**ecstatic**	**longevity**
prone	**revert**	

6. Nan is _____ to accidents, so her car insurance rates are quite high.

7. My brother vowed to eat only one Oreo a day, but I'm afraid he'll _____ to his old habit of eating the entire bag of cookies at one sitting.

8. Research suggests that our parents' _____ doesn't necessarily affect how long we will live.

9. Sidewalk litter is a sign of _____ , showing that people don't care about a clean environment.

10. "I'm _____ ," said Dinah on the day of her divorce. "I wasn't even this happy on my wedding day."

VOCABULARY IN CONTEXT: Test 2

Figure out the meanings of the following five words by studying them in context. Then complete the matching and fill-in test that follows.

1	**dwindle** (dwin'-dəl)	As the number of leaves on the tree **dwindled**, the number on the ground increased.
		The nicotine gum helped Jane's craving for cigarettes to **dwindle** until she was down to two cigarettes a day.
2	**extrovert** (ek'-strō'-vûrt)	Surprisingly, not all performers are **extroverts**. When offstage, many are quiet and shy.
		My boss was looking for someone to greet and chat with her clients, so I recommended Robert for the job because he's such an **extrovert**.
3	**frugal** (froo'-gəl)	You can really stretch your dollars by being **frugal**. For example, using store coupons and waiting for expensive items to be on sale can save a lot of money.
		"Gowns are so expensive," Mimi said, "that I've decided to be **frugal** and rent a wedding dress instead of buying one."
4	**incentive** (in-sen'-tiv)	The thought of myself in a bathing suit next summer provides me with adequate **incentive** to exercise.
		Airlines offer "frequent flyer credits" toward free trips as an **incentive** to people who fly often.
5	**vital** (vī'-təl)	Water is **vital** to the survival of all living things.
		For Teresa to pass her math course, it is **vital** that she pass the final exam.

A. Match each word with its definition.

1. dwindle _____ thrifty

2. extrovert _____ something that moves one to take action or work harder

3. frugal _____ to gradually lessen or shrink

4. incentive _____ necessary; very important

5. vital _____ an outgoing, expressive person

(Continues on next page)

B. Fill in each blank with one of the words in the box. Use each word once.

dwindle	extrovert	frugal
incentive	vital	

6. The insurance company offers the _____ of a free vacation to salespeople who reach a certain sales figure.

7. "I wish I were more of a(n) _____," Miko told her counselor. "I'm so shy that sometimes I can barely talk to people."

8. Diane usually buys designer jeans, but because I need to be more _____, I buy store-brand jeans.

9. Because Carrie left out a(n) _____ ingredient, the apple cake came out looking like a pancake.

10. If you study too long at one sitting, your concentration begins to _____.

VOCABULARY IN CONTEXT: Test 3

Figure out the meanings of the following five words by studying them in context. Then complete the matching and fill-in test that follows.

1 **elicit**
(i-lis'-it)

Elizabeth Taylor's violet eyes always **elicit** admiration and wonder.

Peter's jokes are in such bad taste that they **elicit** looks of disgust instead of laughter.

2 **fortify**
(fôr'-tə'-fī')

Babies need milk to **fortify** their bones.

The builders plan to **fortify** the old tower with steel beams.

3 **indolent**
(in'-də-lənt)

Sue is so **indolent** that she thinks if she works five minutes, she deserves a coffee break.

My uncle has been fired from three jobs for being **indolent**. He shows up on time, but he does little work and leaves early.

4 **persistent**
(pər-sis'-tənt)

At first Tony wouldn't go out with Lola, but she was **persistent** in asking him. Now they're engaged.

I am a very **persistent** salesman. I work with customers for as long as it takes for them to buy something.

5 **skeptical**
(skep'-ti-kəl)

Jessica's family is so rich that she is **skeptical** about any man who asks her out. She wonders if he's interested in her or in her money.

I am **skeptical** about the articles on movie stars and space aliens in supermarket newspapers. My brother, however, believes every word he reads in those papers.

A. Match each word with its definition.

1. elicit _____ refusing to quit; stubbornly continuing

2. fortify _____ to draw forth

3. indolent _____ to strengthen

4. persistent _____ doubting; questioning

5. skeptical _____ lazy; avoiding or disliking work

(Continues on next page)

B. Fill in each blank with one of the words in the box. Use each word once.

elicit	fortify	indolent
persistent	skeptical	

6. The night before running the marathon, Elsa will probably _____ herself by eating a large plate of pasta.

7. My mother's rose garden is so gorgeous that it _____s compliments from strangers who pass by.

8. When the roofer gave us an estimate that was much lower than what others charged, we became _____ about the quality of his work.

9. My sister is so _____ that the most work she ever does is pushing the remote control to switch the TV channel.

10. Abby was _____ in her efforts to change the Little League's boys-only rule. After seven months of trying, she was finally allowed to join the team.

VOCABULARY IN CONTEXT: Test 4

Figure out the meanings of the following five words by studying them in context. Then complete the matching and fill-in test that follows.

1 blunt
(blunt)

"I'll be **blunt**," Phil said, as plainspoken as ever. "You're a jerk."

Kay can be **blunt** to the point of cruelty. She once told a guy that she'd never date him because he's so short.

2 deplore
(di-plōr')

Martin Luther King, Jr., **deplored** all bigotry.

Some people who **deplore** child pornography are working for stricter laws against the practice.

3 provoke
(prə-vōk')

"Mr. Jackson **provoked** me by saying nasty things about my mother, so I hit him," Terry told the judge.

My father is slow to anger, but this morning my sister's wisecracks began to **provoke** him.

4 revitalize
(rē-vīt'-ə-līz')

If Dwight is tired after work, he finds a brief nap will **revitalize** him for a night on the town with friends.

The City Council hopes to **revitalize** the currently lifeless shopping district by offering tax breaks for new businesses.

5 scrutiny
(scrōōt'-ə-nē)

Store security guards keep people with large bags under careful **scrutiny**, since the bags may be used to shoplift.

Before being published, a book comes under the **scrutiny** of a proofreader, who examines it for grammar and spelling errors.

A. Match each word with its definition.

1. blunt   _____ to feel or express disapproval of

2. deplore   _____ close inspection; careful examination

3. provoke   _____ to renew the strength and energy of; to restore to a vigorous, active condition

4. revitalize _____ rudely brief and straightforward

5. scrutiny   _____ to stir up anger or resentment in someone

(Continues on next page)

B. Fill in each blank with one of the words in the box. Use each word once.

blunt	**deplore**	**provoke**
revitalize	**scrutiny**	

6. If the teacher had been _____, she would have told Kevin his essay was terrible. Instead, she politely said, "It could use much more work."

7. Dusty usually doesn't let his older sister's teasing _____ him, but he gets angry whenever she calls him "baby."

8. Federal agents kept the house of the suspected terrorists under _____ for weeks, but no unusual behavior was seen.

9. No one _____s drinking and driving more than Elena, whose son was killed by a drunk driver.

10. The African violets in my kitchen aren't doing well. Do you think some fertilizer would _____ them?

MAIN IDEAS: Test 1

Circle the letter of the correct topic of each paragraph. (To find the topic, remember to ask yourself, "Who or what is the paragraph about?") Then circle the letter of the main idea—-the author's main point about the topic.

1. A llama—a South American animal with large brown eyes—can climb a mountain trail at a two- or three-mile-per-hour pace, about the same as a hiker can. In addition, a llama can carry about eighty pounds of gear, yet require only a fraction of the food that a mule or horse would need. For these reasons, the llama makes an ideal pack animal.

   Topic: a. South America   c. Climbing mountain trails
               b The llama   d. Mules and horses

   Main Idea: a. The llama eats less than a mule or horse.
                b. The llama is an ideal pack animal.
                c. A pack animal is useful when climbing a mountain trail.
                d. Llamas can climb a mountain trail about as fast as a hiker can.

2. When people remain single, their friends and families often think of them as odd and wait impatiently for them to finally get married. Furthermore, unattached people are often considered threats to married couples: "Will she or he steal my spouse?" As a result, single people have been treated—and have often come to think of themselves—as "different."

   Topic: a. Marriage   c. Threats to married couples
                b. Single people   d. Being different

   Main Idea: a. Marriage is better than being single.
                b. Most people don't like to feel different than others.
                c. Single people are treated as different and often think of themselves as odd.
                d. Married people are worried about people stealing their spouses.

3. Spanking is one of the least effective ways of shaping a child's behavior. For one thing, a child's reaction to being spanked will probably be anger and frustration. He hasn't really learned anything positive from the punishment. In addition, the spanking may actually lead to more bad behavior. He wants to pass on what he's experienced, so he acts destructively or even attacks smaller children. And finally, spanking tells him that there are certain things he must not do in the presence of his parents. Once he is out of their sight, however, he feels he can get away with his bad behavior.

(Continues on next page)

Topic: a. Parents   c. Spanking
            b. Shaping a child's behavior   d. Anger and frustration

Main Idea: a. A child will react to spanking with anger and frustration.
                 b. Spanking is a poor way to shape a child's behavior.
                 c. A child who is spanked will act destructively.
                 d. There are several ways to shape a child's behavior.

4.   Swiss bank accounts are no longer the safe places they once were for Americans hoping to evade U.S. laws. The Swiss have agreed to reveal information about the accounts of Americans accused of stock swindles. And, although tax evasion is not a crime according to Swiss law, the Swiss will now release information about the bank accounts of American mobsters charged with not paying their taxes.

Topic: a. Safe places   c. U.S. laws
            b. Swiss bank accounts   d. American mobsters

Main Idea: a. American mobsters seek safe places in which to hide the money they earned illegally.
                 b. Swiss bank accounts are not the safe places they once were for Americans hoping to escape U.S. laws.
                 c. According to American law, tax evasion is a crime.
                 d. The Swiss will now reveal information about the bank accounts of Americans accused of stock swindles.

5.   If you want to improve productivity, improve quality. Think about it. If every person and machine did things right the first time, the same number of people could handle much larger volumes of work. High costs of inspection could be channeled into productive activities, and managers could take all the time they spend checking and devote it to productive tasks. Wasted materials would become a thing of the past. In fact, it's been estimated that attention to quality can reduce the total cost of operations anywhere from 10 to 50 percent. As Philip Crosby said: "Quality is free. What costs money are the unquality things—all the actions that involve not doing jobs right the first time."

Topic: a. Quality   c. High costs of inspection
            b. Business   d. Philip Crosby

Main Idea: a. Philip Crosby is an expert in quality in business.
                 b. It is wasteful to spend so much money on plant inspections.
                 c. Businesses can improve their sales in several ways.
                 d. If quality is improved, productivity improves.

MAIN IDEAS: Test 2

Each of the following groups of statements includes one topic, one main idea (topic sentence), and two supporting ideas. Identify each item in the space provided as either the topic (**T**), main idea (**MI**), or a supporting detail (**SD**).

Group 1

_____ a. Personal checking and automatic teller machines are free.

_____ b. Full-service banks can offer services unavailable at smaller financial institutions.

_____ c. Full-service banks.

_____ d. Depositors have several investment options besides the traditional savings account, such as renewable certificates and money-market accounts.

Group 2

_____ a. Owning a videocassette recorder.

_____ b. Recording programs for later viewing permits daytime soap-opera fans to see their favorites at night.

_____ c. Owning a videocassette recorder has distinct advantages.

_____ d. Owning programs on videotape allows viewers to "rerun" their favorites whenever they wish.

Group 3

_____ a. During the Middle Ages, wearing garlic was thought to protect people against werewolves and vampires.

_____ b. The Romans believed that eating garlic gave strength and courage.

_____ c. Throughout the ages, people have believed that garlic has special powers.

_____ d. Garlic.

(Continues on next page)

Group 4

_____ a. Powerwalking and jogging.

_____ b. Since powerwalkers always have one foot on the ground, they feel only half as much impact when they touch down.

_____ c. For the city dweller, powerwalking—or walking briskly—has several advantages over jogging.

_____ d. The hard surfaces in our cities are much better suited to walking than to running.

Group 5

_____ a. Driving at night is less safe than in the daytime.

_____ b. Driving after dark.

_____ c. In 1981, 62 percent of all traffic deaths took place at night.

_____ d. The chances of being in a fatal accident are nearly four times greater at night than during the day.

MAIN IDEAS: Test 4

A. The following selections have main ideas (topic sentences) that may appear at any place within the paragraph. Identify the topic sentence of each paragraph by filling in the correct sentence number in the space provided.

1. ¹Finding a good way to get rid of garbage is a problem that faces many municipalities today. ²It may be of some consolation for them to know, however, that getting rid of garbage has almost always involved problems. ³When settlements were very small, garbage was simply thrown outdoors, where it eventually decomposed. ⁴But as communities grew, pigs and other animals helped clear away garbage by eating it; of course, the animals, in turn, recycled that garbage and thus created an even less appealing garbage problem. ⁵The first municipal effort to deal with garbage was begun by Benjamin Franklin, whose solution was to have it dumped into the Delaware River. ⁶A century later, municipal incinerators, generally located in the most crowded part of town, burned garbage and produced the worst of odors as a by-product.

    Topic Sentence: _____

2. ¹An author doing research for a book asked thousands of Americans what made them happy. ²Among the popular responses she received were: eating ice-cream sandwiches and candy, being offered a football ticket, and visiting city parks. ³Other common responses included eating ravioli, feeling the cool underside of a pillow, and rereading old love letters. ⁴Almost no one gave the answer of owning flashy jewelry, showy cars or other fancy things. ⁵The author concluded that most of the things that put a smile on our face are simple, free or inexpensive.

    Topic Sentence: _____

3. ¹It is estimated that 80 percent of Americans suffer from some degree of shyness. ²That figure may seem high. ³However, consider that many forms of behavior are really coverups for shyness. ⁴For example, the person who chatters constantly may not really have that much to say—he or she may simply dread a pause in conversation. ⁵Shy people especially dislike lulls, because they fear appearing as socially awkward as they feel. ⁶Another example of behavior used as a coverup for shyness may be a defiant "I don't care" attitude. ⁷Actually, the shy person cares very much about what others think—but he or she fears appearing too vulnerable or weak. ⁸This fake defiance is used as "armor." ⁹Last, people who are overly generous

(Continues on next page)

with gift-giving or picking up the tab may feel too unsure of themselves to try to win friends through normal social interaction; therefore, they attempt to "buy" approval. [10]If they felt more confident about themselves—and less shy—they would have less of a need for overly grand gestures.

Topic Sentence: _____

B. The following paragraphs have unstated main ideas. Each paragraph is followed by four sentences. After reading each paragraph, circle the letter of the sentence that best expresses the implied main idea.

4.   You don't have to scare your family with statistics about heart attacks. To get them to exercise more often, emphasize instead how good they'll feel and how much better they'll look if they do daily calisthenics. Another method that works is to set an example. If they see you walking to the convenience store instead of driving, they might be encouraged to do likewise the next time they have errands in the neighborhood. Finally, make exercise a family activity. Suggest that the whole family go swimming together, take up early morning jogging, or join the Y at the group rate.

   a. Statistics on heart attacks may scare your family into exercising.
   b. Exercise is good for the whole family.
   c. There are several ways to get your family to exercise.
   d. Most American families are in poor physical condition.

5.   Salespeople who want to increase their sales may make promises which the company's production and accounting departments find difficult to support. Production, for example, may not be able to meet the sales department's schedule because purchasing didn't get raw materials in time. While salespeople might like to have large inventories available, production and finance are likely to resist building up stocks because of the high cost of storing and/or owning unsold goods. Also, if production is in the middle of union negotiations, it is likely to feel they are more important than anything else. At the same time, however, salespeople may feel that nothing is more urgent than increasing sales.

   a. The demands of the sales department should be given priority in an organization.
   b. Union demands can slow up production.
   c. Businesses tend to be disorganized due to lack of communication.
   d. Different parts of an organization may have competing needs.

MAIN IDEAS: Test 6

A. The following selections taken from college textbooks have main ideas (topic sentences) that may appear at any place within the paragraph. Identify the topic sentence of each paragraph by filing in the correct sentence number in the space provided.

1.   [1]With so many young, single people having babies, the question arises as to how happy they are being young parents. [2]A national survey of young, single mothers and fathers reveals that most were happier before they became parents. [3]Sixty-seven percent of the 9,000 new parents, aged 16 to 22, who responded to the survey said having a baby presented more problems than they envisioned. [4]Fifty-six percent of the respondents said they had to drop out of school, despite their hopes that they could manage schoolwork plus rearing a baby. [5]A majority (73 percent) said they were forced to seek financial help from family, friends and/or government agencies, and 37 percent said they accepted low-paying, unsatisfying jobs out of necessity. [6]Also, 70 percent said they missed the "good times" with friends that they enjoyed before their babies were born.

Topic Sentence: _____

2.   [1]Criticism is a valuable means of helping ourselves and others achieve personal growth. [2]But because it is often done carelessly or cruelly, criticism has a bad reputation. [3]Here are some guidelines for offering criticism constructively. [4]First, wait until the person asks for feedback on his performance or actions. [5]Unasked-for criticism is not usually valuable. [6]Second, describe the person's behavior as specifically as possible before you criticize it. [7]Instead of just saying, "You were awful," tell the person exactly what you observed. [8]And finally, try to balance your criticism with positive statements. [9]Look for significant points in the other person's performance that you can honestly praise.

Topic Sentence: _____

3.   [1]A young girl looks at a fashion magazine and sees clothes modeled by women carrying 115 pounds on their 5'10" frames. [2]She receives a "teen doll" as a present and studies its proportions: legs nearly two-thirds the length of its body, tiny waist, non-existent hips and thighs. [3]She goes to the movies and observes screen heroines who in their leanness resemble adolescent boys more than mature women. [4]Her favorite television shows are filled with commercials for weight-loss programs that equate slenderness with desirability. [5]By the time the girl reaches her teens, she

(Continues on next page)

has been thoroughly bombarded with society's message that to be thin is the only acceptable option.

Topic Sentence: _____

B. The following paragraphs, taken from college textbooks, have unstated main ideas. Each paragraph is followed by four sentences. After reading each paragraph, circle the letter of the sentence that best expresses the implied main idea.

4.   A clinical psychologist normally holds a Ph.D. or M.A. degree, while a psychiatrist is an M.D. The Ph.D. clinical psychologist has taken four or five years of postgraduate work; the M.A. clinical psychologist has had about two years of postgraduate work and works under the supervision of a Ph.D. psychologist. The psychiatrist, on the other hand, has gone to medical school and has then completed three or four years of residency training in psychiatry. This difference in training means that the clinical psychologist, who has no medical training, cannot prescribe drugs. It also means that whenever there is a possibility of a medical disorder, a patient should be examined by a psychiatrist. Further, only a psychiatrist can commit a patient to a hospital for care and treatment.

    a. Patients should be under the care of psychiatrists, not psychologists.
    b. Psychologists and psychiatrists must undergo a great deal of training.
    c. Psychologists and psychiatrists differ in training and capabilities.
    d. Medical disorders should be treated by psychiatrists.

5.   Much of what falls to earth from outer space is made up of tiny fragments of comets so light that they do not burn up as they float through the air. Sometimes pieces of comets are large enough to survive their passage through the air as shooting stars. These large meteorites can weigh as much as several tons. Also, at least one rock seems to have fallen to earth from the moon. It is a greenish-brown stone the size of a golfball which was found in Antarctica in 1982. It is identical in makeup to rocks brought back from the moon by the Apollo 15 astronauts. Other rocks have been found that are probably from Mars, although no positive identification can be made until astronauts bring rock samples back from Mars.

    a. Matter from various places in outer space has landed on Earth.
    b. A stone found in Antarctica is thought to have come from the moon.
    c. Some pieces of comets that land on earth weigh as much as several tons.
    d. Earth contains a wide variety of rocks of various kinds.

SUPPORTING DETAILS: Test 1

A. The major and minor supporting details of the outline are mixed together in the following list. Complete the outline by filling in the missing details.

Note: Check (✓) each item after you use it. Doing so will help you see which items you have left.

Main idea: Several factors have been found to influence the justice system's treatment of criminals.

- Race of offenders affects their treatment
- Women less likely to receive death penalty than men ✓
- Nonwhites awarded parole and probation less often
- More lenient sentences for the elderly ✓
- Sex of offenders influences severity of sentences
- Blacks executed more often for capital crimes
- Young offenders given special treatment
- More reluctant to send a mother to prison than a father
- Age of offenders considered in sentencing ✓

Major detail: 1. _____

Minor details: a. *Women less likely to receive death penalty than men*

          b. _____

Major detail: 2. _____

Minor details: a. _____

          b. _____

Major detail: 3. *Age of offenders considered in sentencing*

Minor details: a. _____

          b. *More lenient sentences for the elderly*

(Continues on next page)

B. Complete a map of the following paragraph by filling in the four major supporting details. Note that the main idea of the paragraph is boldfaced.

Experts are unsure about what should be the dominant purpose for imprisonment in our country. Prior to 1800 it was widely assumed that the *punishment* of deviants is necessary if the community is to feel morally satisfied. In recent years there has been a renewed interest in punishment—not for the sake of vengeance, but to restore a sense of moral order. During the last century and a half, the concept of *rehabilitation* has dominated penal philosophy. In this view, crime resembles "disease," something foreign and abnormal to most people. It is presumed that individuals are not to blame for the disease, and that we should focus on curing them. The notion of *deterrence* rests on assumptions about human nature that are difficult to prove. Even so, studies suggest that the certainty of apprehension and punishment does tend to lower crime rates. Finally, some argue that neither rehabilitation or deterrence really works, so that it is useless to send people to prison with these goals in mind. Instead, imprisonment should be used as *selective confinement*, reducing crime rates by keeping "hard core" criminals off the streets. One study of young men in Philadelphia showed that 6 percent of the men were responsible for over the half the crimes committed by the entire group.

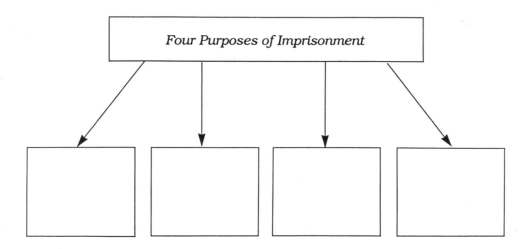

SUPPORTING DETAILS: Test 2

A. The major and minor supporting details of the outline are mixed together in the following list. Complete the outline by filling in the missing details.

Note: Check (✓) each item after you use it. Doing so will help you see which items you have left.

Main idea: Divorce has serious negative consequences.

- Social adjustment is troublesome.
- Feelings of guilt and resentment may persist between the former husband and wife.
- Starting to date again can be nerve-wracking. ✓
- Emotional difficulties among the original family members are common. ✓
- Married friends may exclude singles from social plans.
- Financial adjustments are necessary.
- Children may be confused, hurt, and even blame themselves.
- Alimony, child support, and property dispersal must be dealt with. ✓
- High lawyers' fees can be a burden.

Major detail: 1. _____

Minor details: a. *Starting to date again can be nerve-wracking.*

              b. _____

_____

Major detail: 2. *Emotional difficulties among the original family members are common.*

Minor details: a. _____

_____

              b. _____

_____

Major detail: 3. _____

Minor details: a. *Alimony, child support, and property dispersal must be dealt with.*

              b. _____

_____

(Continues on next page)

B. Prepare a map of the paragraph by finishing the main heading and filling in the three major details. Use brief phrases, not full sentences.

Everyone is familiar with steam heat, gas heat, and solar heat. But how about corn heat? Inventor Carroll Buckner has devised a stove that runs on raw kernels of corn. Buckner claims the stove has several advantages. First, it's economical. He claims his invention can heat a house in the winter for about thirty dollars a month, assuming that corn is two dollars a bushel. Also, whereas the emissions from wood-burning stoves can harm the environment, a corn-burning stove, says Buckner, doesn't pollute the air. Finally, the stove would help the economy. Specifically, by creating a demand for corn, the stove would provide a new market for America's troubled farmers.

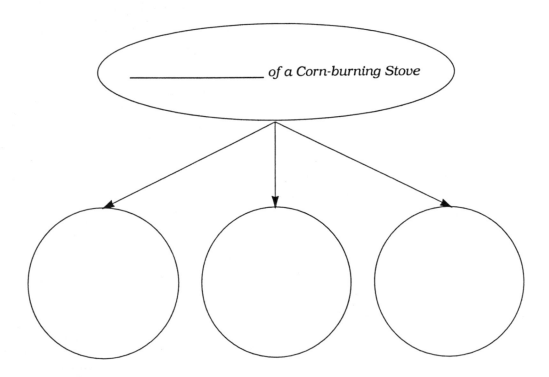

_____ *of a Corn-burning Stove*

SUPPORTING DETAILS: Test 3

A. Below each of the following passages is a question raised by the main idea of the passage. After reading each passage, answer the question by stating the major supporting details. You may use either the words of the passage or your own words.

> Most teenagers who smoke are familiar with the health hazards of smoking, yet for various reasons they drift into the habit anyway. A teenager with one parent who smokes is twice as likely to smoke as one with nonsmoking parents. Also, young people are more likely to smoke if their friends do. The chances are nine out of ten that a teenager whose best friend smokes will also start to smoke. In addition, teens who mature late are more likely to smoke than others, apparently because they hope that smoking will make them look more adult.

What are three factors that increase the likelihood that teenagers will smoke?

1. _____

2. _____

3. _____

> You are part of a network of family and friends that can always be available to give you advice, emotional support, and practical help. However, this network works most effectively when you use it well. First, be sure you are willing to help others at least as much as they help you. People are going to be much more ready to give of themselves if you have built up a history of giving to them as well. When you do need advice or help, try to ask for only one thing at a time rather than overwhelming someone with too many requests. Most people are ready to lend a hand, but they may understandably balk if too much is expected. After all, they need time to deal with the daily needs and conflicts of their own life. Finally, you should be willing to accept the advice and offers of help you do get. There is little benefit to brushing them off and giving excuses for not doing anything about the problems in your life.

What are ways to make sure your personal support network works well?

4. _____

5. _____

6. _____

(Continues on next page)

B. Carefully read the paragraph, and then answer the questions that follow.

> The climate becomes colder when the amount of dust at high altitudes in the atmosphere increases. There are several ways that dust can get into the atmosphere. Volcanic eruptions can add so much dust that sunlight is scattered back to outer space. Chimneys, especially industrial smokestacks, also throw large amounts of dust into the atmosphere. The burning of tropical forests to clear land for farming is another way the amount of airborne dust is increased. Finally, should a nuclear war ever occur, it might add so much dust to the atmosphere that it could cause a new ice age—a nuclear winter in which the climate becomes so cold that no new crops can be grown.

7. The major details of this paragraph are
   a. reasons why dust in the atmosphere makes the climate colder.
   b. ways that dust can get into the atmosphere.
   c. natural causes of dust getting into the atmosphere.
   d. ways that industry puts dust into the atmosphere.

8. *Fill in the blank:* The paragraph includes (*one, two, three, or four?*) _____ major supporting details.

9. One source of dust in the atmosphere is
   a. sunlight.
   b. farming.
   c. chimneys.
   d. cold weather.

10. An enormous amount of dust in the atmosphere could lead to
    a. cool summers.
    b. burning of tropical forests.
    c. volcanic eruptions.
    d. a new ice age.

SUPPORTING DETAILS: Test 4

A. Carefully read the paragraph, and then answer the questions that follow.

[1]Vietnamese and American cultures are sharply different. [2]New immigrants coming from Vietnam to this country may have a difficult time adjusting. [3]One major area of difference between the cultures relates to the showing of affection. [4]In Vietnam, two men or two women often show affection in public, but affection between the sexes is not considered acceptable. [5]Vietnamese are often surprised by American family relations. [6]Three or four generations generally live together in one Vietnamese household, with elderly people cared for by their children and grandchildren. [7]And many Vietnamese are not accustomed to conveniences that Americans take for granted. [8]In Vietnam, many people do not use a telephone, drive an automobile or make use of a bank.

1. In general, the major supporting details of this paragraph are
   a. two cultures.
   b. ways in which all new immigrants to America must adjust.
   c. areas of difference between the Vietnamese and the American cultures.
   d. American family relations and Vietnamese family relations.

2. Specifically, the major supporting details are
   a. the Vietnamese culture and the American culture.
   b. number of generations in a Vietnamese household and in an American household.
   c. the telephone, the automobile, and banks.
   d. how affection is shown, family relations, use of certain conveniences.

3. Which question would help you find the major supporting details of this paragraph?
   a. From which country do immigrants have difficulty adjusting to American life?
   b. How do the Vietnamese and the Americans differ in how they show affection?
   c. Which conveniences do Americans take for granted that are strange to the Vietnamese?
   d. What are some cultural differences that account for the trouble Vietnamese immigrants have adjusting to American life?

(Continues on next page)

4. In Vietnam, the showing of affection in public
   a. between men is acceptable.
   b. between a man and a woman is not acceptable.
   c. both of the above.
   d. neither *a* nor *b*.

5. *Fill in the blank:* The answer to question 4 can be found in sentence number _____ .

6. The statement that many Vietnamese do not use a telephone is a (*major or minor?*) _____ detail in the paragraph.

B. Carefully read the paragraph, and then answer the questions that follow.

> The dance of death, which was performed in the fourteenth century in response to the Black Death, had several interesting characteristics. First, it often took place in a graveyard, an appropriate place for a plague which killed one-fifth to one-half of the population of Europe, Africa, and Asia. Moreover, to show that the plague struck rich and poor alike, the dancers dressed to represent people from all walks of life. Finally, perhaps the most significant aspect of this dance was the part when one dancer fell down during the performance as if he or she were dead. Members of the opposite sex then kissed the "victim," who rose up as if returned to life. Unfortunately, this kissing often brought not life, but death, because it helped to spread the plague.

7. The major details of this paragraph are
   a. characteristics of the dance of death.
   b. countries where the plague struck.
   c. ways that the plague struck rich and poor alike.
   d. ways that the plague was passed from one person to the next.

8. *Fill in the blank:* The paragraph includes (*one, two, three, or four?*) _____ major supporting details.

9. *Fill in the blank:* The second major detail is introduced with the addition word (*first, moreover,* or *finally*) _____

10. According to the passage, those who performed the dance of death
    a. all soon died themselves.
    b. had relatives who died of the plague.
    c. dressed like people in various walks of life.
    d. lived in Europe or Africa.

SUPPORTING DETAILS: Test 5

A. Carefully read the textbook paragraph below, and then answer the questions that follow.

> Everything that we notice—see, smell, hear or touch—forms a brief mental impression called a "sensory memory." Information is stored in this sensory memory for only a few tenths of a second before it disappears forever. Information that is retained for slightly longer must enter what's called the "short-term memory." This form of memory can store about seven items for about 30 seconds—about enough information to dial a telephone number. In order to be remembered for a long period, information must pass into the "long-term memory." No one knows just how much information can be stored in a person's long-term memory, but the capacity seems enormous. The three types of human memory allow a person to discard unnecessary information and retain more important information for as long as it is valuable.

1. In general, the major supporting details of this paragraph are
   a. everything that we notice.
   b. information that we remember.
   c. the types of human memory.
   d. problems of human memory.

2. Specifically, the major supporting details of this paragraph are
   a. seeing, smelling, hearing, and touching.
   b. sensory memory, short-term memory, long-term memory.
   c. what is remembered and what is forgotten.
   d. keeping information and discarding information.

3. The last sentence of the paragraph provides
   a. the main idea.
   b. a major supporting detail.
   c. minor supporting detail.

4. A sensory memory
   a. is a brief mental impression.
   b. lasts for about 30 seconds.
   c. lasts for a long period.
   d. usually makes its way into the long-term memory.

(Continues on next page)

5. The answer to question 4 can be found in
   a. the first sentence.
   b. the second sentence.
   c. the last sentence.
   d. the next-to-the-last sentence.

6. *Fill in the blank:* To be available for more than seconds, a memory must pass into a person's _____

7. The storage available for long-term memories
   a. seems very limited.
   b. seems the same as that for short-term memories.
   c. seems very large.
   d. is just enough for about seven items.

B. Complete the map of the following textbook passage by filling in the major details. You may use brief phases. Note that the main idea is boldfaced.

> **Many people pass through three stages in reacting to their unemployment.** At first they undergo a sequence of shock, relief, and relaxation. In many cases they had anticipated that they were about to lose their jobs, so when the dismissal comes, they may feel a sense of relief that at last the suspense is over. On the whole they remain confident and hopeful that they will find a new job when they are ready. During this time, they maintain normal relationships with their family and friends. The first stage lasts for about a month or two. The second stage centers on a concerted effort to find a new job. If workers have been upset or angry about losing their jobs, the feeling tends to evaporate as they marshal their resources and concentrate on finding a new job. This stage may last for up to four months. But if another job is not found during this time, people move into the third stage, which lasts about six weeks. Their self-esteem begins to crumble, and they experience high levels of self-doubt and anxiety.

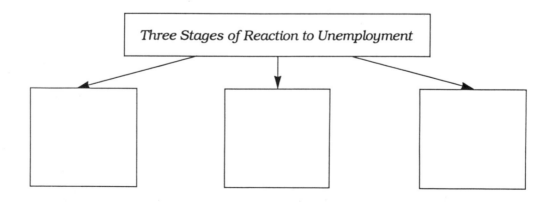

SUPPORTING DETAILS: Test 6

A. Carefully read the textbook paragraph below, and then answer the questions that follow.

Stereotyping consists of assigning characteristics to people solely on the basis of their class or category. P.F. Second, C.W. Backman, and D.R. Slavitt suggest that stereotyping has four distinct phases. First, a person distinguishes some category or class of people, for example, economists. Second, the person observes that one or more of the individuals in this category exhibit certain traits, for example, dullness. Third, the person generalizes from this perception that everyone in this category possesses these characteristics, for example, that all economists are dull. Finally, when confronted with an individual the person is not acquainted with but knows to be, for example, an economist, the person stereotypes this individual as dull.

1. The major supporting details of this paragraph are
    a. characteristics given to people solely on the basis of their class or category.
    b. people who have studied stereotypes.
    c. examples of stereotyping.
    d. the stages people go through when they stereotype.

2. *Fill in the blank:* This paragraph lists (*one, two, three,* or *four*) _____ major supporting details.

3. *Complete the sentence:* The major supporting details are introduced with these addition words: _____

4. The second sentence of the paragraph provides
    a. the main idea.
    b. a major detail.
    c. a minor detail.

5. According to Second, Backman, and Slavitt, the process of stereotyping always begins with distinguishing
    a. people in a profession.
    b. a category or class of people.
    c. mainly economists.
    d. phases.

(Continues on next page)

6. According to Second, Backman, and Slavitt, people who stereotype end up by judging
   a. phases.
   b. friends.
   c. acquaintances.
   d. individuals they are not acquainted with.

7. Economists are used in the paragraph as part of
   a. the main idea.
   b. major details.
   c. minor details.

B. Complete the outline of the following paragraph by filling in the three major supporting details.

Although the debate over the relative importance of heredity versus environment continues, scientists have determined that a number of human characteristics clearly have hereditary factors. Physical traits are most strongly determined by heredity. For example, height, obesity, pulse and breathing rates, patterns of tooth decay, and age of first menstruation are just a few of the traits that have been found to be genetically determined. Intellectual traits are also strongly influenced by hereditary factors. To illustrate, research indicates that scores on intelligence tests, word fluency, and memory have a strong hereditary basis. In addition, personality and emotional disorders are significantly influenced by heredity. Shyness, anxiety, special aptitudes and interests, emotionality, and schizophrenia are all influenced by genetic transmission. Though the influence of environment cannot be underestimated, science is finding that genes have a great influence on physical, intellectual, and emotional makeup.

Main Idea: Three types of traits are influenced by heredity.

8. _____

9. _____

10. _____

TRANSITIONS: Test 1

A. Fill in each blank with the appropriate transition from the box. Use each transition once.

also	because	but
for instance	until	

1. _____ there are no clocks in gambling casinos, gamblers can easily lose all sense of time. That is clearly what the casino management wants to happen. The longer people stay at the tables or in front of the slot machines, the better.

2. Tina's father is an overly cautious parent. He wants to know where she is every minute, and he won't let her drive his car _____ she is 20.

3. At first, fast-food restaurants only sold relatively high-fat, high-calorie foods. In recent years, however, most fast-food restaurants have gradually increased their menus. _____, many of them now have salad bars. McDonald's now even sells low-fat burgers.

4. My little brother is an odd kid. Other boys like to collect normal things, like baseball cards or stamps, but Dwayne collects dead bugs. He _____ collects bars of soap from motels and loose chunks of sidewalk (which he insists on calling moon rocks).

5. My problem with the history final was not that I hadn't studied. I really knew the material well, _____ I had stayed up so late studying that I was too tired to think clearly during the test.

(Continues on next page)

B. Fill in each blank with the appropriate transition from the box. Use each transition once.

after	also	as a result
despite	in addition	

My grandfather was a remarkable man. Shortly (6) _____ coming to this country from Russia as a young man, he began a vest-making business. (7) _____ the fact that he spoke almost no English, he was able to quickly build his business, hiring many local people. (8) _____ to being a successful businessman, he was a kind and generous man. Grandfather always honored his employees' requests for advances on their salaries, and he often loaned or gave money to needy friends and relatives. He (9) _____ threw Sunday ice-cream-and-cake parties and games for the neighborhood children. (10) _____, he earned the loyalty and affection of all who knew him.

TRANSITIONS: Test 2

A. In the spaces provided, write the major transitions used in the following passage. You should look for the following types of transitions:

2 addition transitions	1 contrast transition
1 cause and effect transition	1 time transition

I really hate shopping for clothing. First of all, my small budget doesn't allow me to buy anything expensive. Consequently, it takes me a lot of walking around just to find something I like that is both moderately priced and that I really want to wear. Another thing I dislike about shopping is having to try on so many clothes, most of which make me look resemble a misshapen pear (except, of course, for the clothes that I can't even get into). "There have to be better things we are meant to do with our lives," I mutter, "than shop for clothes." In spite of my annoyance at the process, I persist; I want to get it over with and not have to think about it again for a long time. After an afternoon of walking in and out of stores in the mall, scrubbing the kitchen floor and cleaning the oven begin to sound good to me.

Addition Transitions

    1. _____

    2. _____

Cause and Effect Transition

    3. _____

Contrast Transition

    4. _____

Time Transition

    5. _____

(Continues on next page)

B. Fill in each blank with the appropriate transition from the box. Use each transition once. Be sure to read the passage carefully to see which transition logically fits in each answer space.

also	for example	however
such as	while	

An altruistic person helps other people without expecting to get something in return. (6)_____, an altruistic person who walks by a parked car with its lights on may try to turn them off. Many ordinary people have been known to watch (7)_____ someone else is being harmed without trying to help at all. Altruism can (8)_____ motivate people to give money and time to worthy causes. Extreme altruists—(9)_____ the person who leaps in front of a train to save a child's life—will give their lives for others. In short, altruistic actions can range from the trivial to the heroic. (10)_____, some people feel there is really no such thing as altruism; they feel that a so-called altruistic action is basically motivated by discomfort at seeing someone else's suffering. Help is given, they say, in order for the giver to become comfortable.

TRANSITIONS: Test 4

This test will check your ability to recognize the relationships (signaled by transitions) within and between sentences. Read each passage and answer the questions that follow.

A. [1]Many of today's children learn that Cinderella wore glass slippers, but the popular heroine didn't always have breakable shoes. [2]Her old and international story was accidentally slightly changed in that regard by the French writer Charles Perrault, who popularized it with his version, published in 1697. [3]Perrault referred to Cinderella's slippers as being made of "verre," the French word for glass. [4]However, the old French versions which were his sources used the word "vair"—white squirrel fur. [5]In other words, generations of children have had the pleasure of the dramatic image of glass shoes because of a mistranslation.

1. The relationship between the two parts of sentence 1 is one of
   a. contrast.
   b. comparison.
   c. cause and effect.
   d. addition.

2. The relationship of sentence 4 to sentence 3 is one of
   a. addition.
   b. illustration.
   c. comparison.
   d. contrast.

B. [1]Have you ever had the experience of recognizing someone's face but not being able to recall his or her name? [2]This happens because that information is split up and stored in the two different sides of your brain, and each side has its own way of thinking and remembering. [3]Remembering someone's face is the task of the right side of your brain, which understands whole things at once and is responsible for visualizing, recognizing similarities, and supplying intuitions. [4]This side of your brain provides insights that are hard to put into words. [5]On the other hand, the words themselves—including the name that you have forgotten—are stored in the left side of your brain. [6]This is the side responsible for speaking, reading, writing and reasoning.

3. The relationship of sentence 2 to sentence 1 is one of
   a. addition.
   b. contrast.
   c. comparison.
   d. cause and effect.

4. The relationship of sentence 5 to sentence 4 is one of
   a. addition.
   b. contrast.
   c. cause and effect.
   d. summary.

(Continues on next page)

C.   [1]Leaders of totalitarian movements usually have been men of great charisma who are able to motivate the masses. [2]Such leaders often seemed to be solely driven by their cause, without a care for the material things that motivate others, which undoubtedly added to their ability to gain people's confidence. [3]Fidel Castro, for example, was a superb speaker and got the backing of the majority of Cubans with his Christlike appearance, dedication to his cause, and long, eloquent television speeches. [4]Those speeches included attacks against his opponents, who often fled the country as a consequence of one of his assaults.

5. The relationship of sentence 3 to the first two sentences is one of
   a. comparison.
   b. illustration.
   c. cause and effect.
   d. addition.

6. The second half of sentence 4 gives a(n)
   a. contrast.
   b. illustration.
   c. cause and effect.
   d. comparison.

D.   [1]A calorie is the amount of heat required to raise the temperature of a kilogram (about a quart) of water one degree Celsius. [2]To determine the number of calories in a portion of food, a technician uses a device called a bomb calorimeter. [3]This device has a chamber that rests in a container of water. [4]The food is placed in this chamber, which is then filled with oxygen under high pressure. [5]Next, the food is set on fire. [6]As it burns, it gives off heat; the result is that the temperature of the water in the container rises. [7]Finally, the total rise in temperature is measured, giving the calorie content of the food.

7. The relationship between sentences 4 and 5 is one of
   a. time.
   b. illustration.
   c. contrast.
   d. cause and effect.

8. Sentence 6 shows a relationship of
   a. addition.
   b. time.
   c. comparison.
   d. cause and effect.

TRANSITIONS: Test 5

A. This part of the test will check your ability to recognize the relationships (signaled by transitions) within and between sentences. Read each passage and answer the questions that follow.

Passage 1

¹The use of fire by prehistoric people probably affected wildlife both intentionally and unintentionally. ²In all likelihood, early people used fire to drive game toward waiting hunters. ³Later, new plant growth in the burned areas would attract more wild animals. ⁴In addition, accidental fires must have also occurred frequently. 5Because prehistoric people had trouble starting fires, they kept burning embers on hand. ⁶The result must have been widespread accidental fires, especially in dry areas. ⁷Certainly, these fires also would have greatly altered the habitat for wildlife.

1. The relationship of sentence 4 to sentences 2 and 3 is one of
   a. addition.   c. contrast.
   b. comparison.   d. illustration.

2. The relationship between the two parts of sentence 5 is one of
   a. contrast.   c. illustration.
   b. cause and effect.   d. addition.

Passage 2

¹In spite of the stereotype of the hardworking Asian immigrant who achieves the American dream against all odds, many refugees from Cambodia, Laos, and Vietnam are suffering from the same kind of postwar trauma as Vietnam veterans. ²Like the returned vets, they are haunted by memories of the horrors of war and feel alienated from those who did not share that experience. ³But unlike the vets, they must deal with being culturally uprooted and torn apart from their families as well as learning to function in a language and a society foreign to them. ⁴Both groups, however, share symptoms common to war survivors, including recurring night terrors, inability to eat or sleep, and chronic depression.

3. The relationship between the first phrase of sentence 2 and the rest of the sentence is one of
   a. addition.   c. contrast.
   b. comparison.   d. illustration.

(Continues on next page)

4. The word *including* in sentence 4
   a. signals that one symptom is being added to symptoms named earlier.
   b. introduces a list of the causes of symptoms that are common to war survivors.
   c. introduces a list of examples of symptoms that are common to war survivors.
   d. signals a comparison between Asian immigrants and Vietnam vets.

B. The following six transitions have been removed from the textbook passage below. Read the passage carefully to see which transition logically fits in each answer space. Then write in each transition.

Note: You may find it helpful to check (✓) each transition after you insert it into the passage.

also	because	during
for example	in contrast	similarly

   (5)_____ with preindustrial societies, modern societies make it much easier for people to get divorced. Today, geographic mobility allows people who get divorced to do so in relative privacy. (6)_____ or following a divorce, many couples do not have to face all of their relatives and old friends or even one another. . . .

   Female employment and small families (7)_____ make divorce more likely in modern societies. A major impact of the massive entry of women into the labor force has been to decrease the dependence of wives on their husbands for economic support. This change has had many beneficial effects. (8)_____, a woman need no longer cling to a brutal or drunken husband merely because she has nowhere else to turn. But it also encourages some women to give up on a relationship more quickly. (9)_____, husbands have greater economic freedom to divorce wives who work,

   (10) _____ working wives are seldom granted a great deal of alimony. The conditions that have enabled people to seek marriages based on romance have also enabled them to continue that search if a marriage fails to satisfy.

TRANSITIONS: Test 6

A. This part of the test will check your ability to recognize the relationships (signaled by transitions) within and between sentences. Read each passage and answer the questions that follow.

Passage 1

¹High school seniors are expected to make crucial decisions about their future careers, yet many of them are still unrealistic about what they plan to do. ²They seem to have little knowledge of what their chosen careers involve or how much training they require. ³For instance, a study of more than 6,000 high school seniors in Texas showed that only about half were planning to get the appropriate amount of education for the careers they had chosen. ⁴The rest were planning too many or too few years of training. ⁵A more disturbing finding is that most of the students did not seem to be choosing careers that matched their interests.

1. The relationship between the two parts of sentence 1 is one of
   a. addition.
   b. contrast.
   c. illustration.
   d. cause and effect.

2. The relationship of sentence 3 to sentence 2 is one of
   a. addition.
   b. contrast.
   c. illustration.
   d. time.

Passage 2

¹In 1850 an old pear tree stood at the corner of Third Avenue and East Thirteenth Street in New York City. ²It still bore fruit although it had been planted more than two hundred years before by Peter Stuyvesant when he came from Holland to what was then New Amsterdam. ³The tree was finally removed after it was destroyed in a carriage accident in 1867. 4Then the streets were made of cobblestones, which were hard to walk on, but pathways made of smooth, flat stones were provided for pedestrians at street corners. ⁵Today one of the buildings that stood near the corner in the 1860s remains, but most of the buildings, like the old tree, are gone. 6Likewise, the cobblestones have been replaced by smooth asphalt streets, and an electric traffic light stands today where the pear tree once stood.

3. The relationship of sentence 4 to sentence 3 is signaled by the word
   a. *Then.*
   b. *of.*
   c. *which.*
   d. *on.*

(Continues on next page)

4. The transition at the beginning of sentence 6 shows a relationship between sentence 6 and sentence 5 of

   a. illustration.   c. contrast.

   b. cause and effect.   d. comparison.

B. The following six transitions have been removed from the textbook passage below. Read the passage carefully to see which transition logically fits in each answer space. Then write in each transition.

Note: You may find it helpful to check (✓) each transition after you insert it into the passage.

finally	however	just as
leads to	first of all	third

     The use of tobacco is interesting to any student of psychoactive drug use for a number of reasons. (5)_____, very few people—whether they are smokers or not—think of ordinary cigarettes as containing a potent drug, and practically no one thinks of smokers as drug users. (6)_____, in sufficient doses, nicotine is (7)_____ psychoactive as any current illegal drug. Second, as we'll see, tobacco creates a powerful dependence, and making cigarettes unavailable to committed smokers (8)_____ a powerful craving not unlike the one that truly addicting drugs foster. (9)_____, as we saw earlier, cigarette smoking is connected to illegal drug use, in that adolescent smokers are more likely to go on to use marijuana, cocaine, and heroin than are non-smokers. And (10)_____, governments have attempted to control or eliminate the use of tobacco in the past—with dismally unsuccessful results.

PATTERNS OF ORGANIZATION: Test 1

A. 1-5. Arrange the scrambled sentences below into a logical paragraph by numbering them *1, 2, 3, 4,* and *5* in an order that makes sense. Then circle the letter of the primary pattern of organization used.

Note that transitions will help you by clarifying the relationships between sentences.

_____ A third reaction to danger used by opossums is to bluff their way out of a tight spot by hissing and baring their teeth.

_____ The opossum reacts to danger in one of several ways.

_____ First, some varieties of opossum can spray an unpleasant odor.

_____ Opossums are also very likely to run away from danger.

_____ Finally, the best-known of possum defenses is to "play dead" by entering into a coma-like state brought on by fear.

6. The passage's primary pattern of organization is:
    a. time order.   c. comparison.
    b. list of items.   d. definition and example.

B. For each passage, put the number of the topic sentence in the space provided. Then circle the letter of the answer that identifies the primary pattern of organization of the passage.

7-8. [1]According to the National Institute on Drug Abuse, 30 million Americans—one out of eight people—suffer from a drug or alcohol dependency. [2]The development of an addiction typically unfolds in four stages. [3]First, some stimulus—drugs, alcohol, sex, chocolate—holds out the promise of short-lived pleasure or excitement. [4]Next, an individual discovers that indulging in one of these activities temporarily satisfies some psychological need, makes the person feel good, if only for a short time. [5]Third, certain recurring situations start to trigger the addictive behavior and the pattern repeats itself. [6]Finally, the habit takes control and the individual loses self-control. [7]Often by this stage a physical dependency will have been added to a psychological one, thereby making the addictive behavior pattern even more difficult to break.

Topic sentence: _____

Passage's main pattern of organization:
a. List of items
b. Comparison
c. Time order

(Continues on next page)

9-10.   ¹Cities in developing countries are noticeably different from those in wealthier nations. ²Visitors often comment on the number of younger people in the less developed countries. ³Almost half of all city residents in these countries are children and young people as compared to less than one quarter of the population of cities in developed countries. ⁴Also, many unskilled workers found jobs in European and North American cities when the economies there became industrialized. ⁵In contrast, one quarter of the work force is unemployed in a typical city in a developing country. ⁶Although homeless people are found in Europe and North America, many more people live on the street and in improvised shacks in the less-developed nations. ⁷In Mexico City, for instance, more than four million squatters live in improvised shelters.

Topic sentence: _____

Passage's main pattern of organization:
a. Time order
b. Contrast
c. Cause and effect

PATTERNS OF ORGANIZATION: Test 3

A. 1-5. Arrange the scrambled sentences below into a logical paragraph by numbering them *1, 2, 3, 4,* and *5* in an order that makes sense. Then circle the letter of the primary pattern of organization used.

Note that transitions will help you by clarifying the relationships between sentences.

_____ Check the classified ads and two or three real estate offices for apartments within your price range and desired locale.

_____ To find a satisfactory apartment, begin by making a list of promising openings.

_____ When you have chosen your apartment, have a lawyer or other person knowledgeable about leases examine your lease before you sign it.

_____ As you inspect each apartment, make sure that faucets, toilets, stoves, and electrical wiring and outlets are functioning efficiently and safely.

_____ After you have made a solid list, visit at least five of the most promising openings.

6. The passage's primary pattern of organization is:
   a. time order.   c. cause and effect.
   b. contrast.   d. definition and example.

B. For each passage, put the number of the topic sentence in the space provided. Then circle the letter of the answer that identifies the primary pattern of organization of the passage.

7-8. [1]While management styles vary, there are certain factors that separate the good administrator from the poor one. [2]A good manager anticipates problems and prepares for them, but a poor manager is often taken by surprise. [3]The effective administrator recognizes repeated problems and makes changes to eliminate them; the less effective boss deals with one crisis at a time, never seeing the connections between them. [4]In addition, a good boss delegates work to others, while the poor one prefers to take on one extra task after another rather than train employees to do the work right. [5]The effective administrator is also flexible enough to adapt to changing situations. [6]In contrast, the poor one often clings to the old rules whether or not they apply.

Topic sentence: _____

Passage's main pattern of organization:
a. Contrast
b. Cause and effect
c. Definition and example

(Continues on next page)

9-10. [1]In January of 1954, Ernest and Mary Hemingway left Nairobi on a vacation trip on which they flew over grazing elephants, hippos bathing in the lakes, and huge flocks of feeding flamingos. [2]As they were circling a spectacular waterfall, a flock of ibises flew in front of the plane. [3]When the pilot dived to avoid the birds, he struck an abandoned telegraph wire that crossed the gorge. [4]In the crash that followed, Ernest sprained his shoulder; Mary was only slightly injured. [5]Luckily, a boat came down the river the next morning, and its crew rescued them. [6]By that evening, they were on board a small plane bound for Entebbe. [7]The plane lifted from the plowed field that served as a runway, then crashed and burst into flames. [8]Ernest escaped by breaking through a window with his head and injured shoulder, and Mary got out through another window. [9]Twice in two days they had crashed and come out alive, but Ernest had injured his head, his backbone, and a kidney; after this, even writing a letter was difficult for him.

Sentence with the main idea: _____

Passage's pattern of organization:
a. Time order
b. List of items
c. Contrast

PATTERNS OF ORGANIZATION: Test 4

A. 1-5. Arrange the scrambled sentences below into a logical paragraph by numbering them *1, 2, 3, 4,* and *5* in an order that makes sense. Then circle the letter of the primary pattern of organization used.

Note that transitions will help you by clarifying the relationships between sentences.

_____ Artifacts are those objects made and used by a society.

_____ Americans, for example, use an enormous variety of artifacts, from paper clips to spaceships.

_____ They may have originated with the society or have been borrowed from others.

_____ On the other hand, in technologically advanced societies, there are numerous artifacts.

_____ In those societies whose technologies are relatively undeveloped, there are few artifacts—a few tools, cooking utensils, and so on.

6. The passage's primary pattern of organization is:

   a. time order.   c. cause and effect.

   b. comparison.   d. definition and example.

B. For each passage, put the number of the topic sentence in the space provided. Then circle the letter of the answer that identifies the primary pattern of organization of the passage.

7-8. [1]Mass hysteria is a type of group behavior that involves a widely held and contagious anxiety, usually as a result of a false belief. [2]The medieval witch hunts were a case of mass hysteria; they were based on the belief that witches were the cause of the many problems in late medieval society, including natural disasters and illness. [3]Those accused of being witches (mainly old women) were tortured until they confessed or they died. [4]If they confessed, they were burned to death. [5]They were also forced under torture to name accomplices, so the list of witches grew, feeding the hysteria. [6]As many as 500,000 people were burned to death by the clergy between the fifteenth and seventeenth centuries.

Topic sentence: _____

Passage's main pattern of organization:

a. Time order

b. Comparison

(Continues on next page)

9-10. [1]People who are continually exposed to too much noise can feel tired all the time, yet be unable to sleep soundly. [2]Their bodies may be plagued by digestive spasms, increased heart rates, and constricted blood vessels. [3]Studies conducted on animals show that noise pollution can eventually result in damage to the ears, heart, and brain. [4]Thus for humans, noise pollution may be one of the reasons not only for hearing loss but also for high blood pressure, ulcers, and emotional disorders.

Topic sentence: _____

Passage's main pattern of organization:
a. Time order
b. Contrast
c. Cause and effect

PATTERNS OF ORGANIZATION: Test 5

Read each textbook passage; then answer the question and complete the outline or map that follows.

A. Before appearing in a newspaper, a news item must pass to the reporter as a news release or in a news conference. He or she then decides whether the item is important enough to be covered and how much coverage should be given to it. If the reporter decides the item is important, he or she may rewrite the press release or write a story about the press conference or perhaps dictate the item over a telephone to a rewrite person at the newspaper. The rewrite person then functions as the next gate in evaluating the story's importance; he or she may rewrite the story. Next a copy editor edits the item and judges its importance. The story may also appear before additional gates—the national or international editor—before a determination is made as to if and where the story will be run in the next edition.

1. The main pattern of organization of the passage is
   a. time order.   b. cause and effect.   c. definition and example.

2-5. Complete the outline of the paragraph.

   Main idea: A news item must pass to several people before appearing in a newspaper.

   1. _____
      a. Decides if item is important and how much coverage it merits
      b. Rewrites, writes a story, or dictates story thought to be important

   2. _____
      a. Evaluates story
      b. May rewrite story
   3. Copy editor
      a. Edits an item

      b. _____

   4. _____

(Continues on next page)

267

B.   Why do people daydream? One cause of daydreaming is routine or boring jobs that are tolerable only when workers imagine themselves doing something else. Deprivation also leads to daydreaming. During World War II, conscientious objectors who volunteered to go on semistarvation diets for six months focused their daydreams on food. Some even hung enticing pictures of foods on their walls to give themselves something to daydream about. Another reason people daydream is to discharge hostile feelings. For example, if an angry student imagines dropping his instructor out of a classroom window, it might help him to laugh at and dismiss his annoyance with her. Some people also daydream as a way to plan for the future so that by the time they face the situations they imagine, they will know what to say and how to act.

6. The main pattern of organization of the paragraph is
   a. time order   b. comparison/contrast   c. cause and effect

7-10. Complete the map of the paragraph.

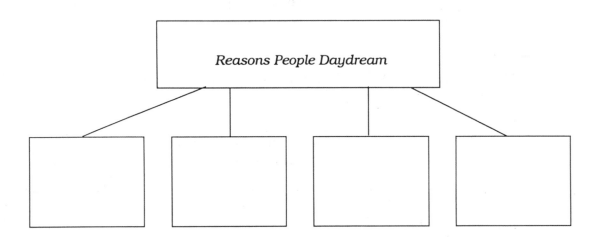

Reasons People Daydream

PATTERNS OF ORGANIZATION: Test 6

Read each textbook passage; then answer the question and complete the outline or map that follows.

A. In order to make the transition from dependence on parents to dependence on one's self, the adolescent must develop a stable sense of self. One researcher has identified four possible results of an adolescent's attempts to achieve a stable sense of identity. Identity achievers have succeeded in making personal choices about the goals that they should pursue. They are comfortable with their various roles and are confident that their values and actions meet with the approval of others. In contrast, other adolescents adopt foreclosure: they prematurely settle on an identity that is provided for them by others and become what those others want them to be. Still other adolescents declare a moratorium and set aside the problem of developing an identity while they continue to explore various alternatives and choices. In a sense, they put everything on "hold." Finally, some adolescents experience identity confusion. They are dissatisfied with their present place in society, but they are also unable to develop a new identity that "feels right." They can't "find themselves" and may resort to escapist activities in order to counter the anxiety that they feel.

1. The one pattern of organization *not* used in the paragraph is
   a. list of items.
   b. contrast.
   c. cause and effect.
   d. time order.

2-5. Complete the outline of the paragraph by filling in the four missing items:

   Four Outcomes of Attempt to Achieve Identity

   1. _____

   2. _____

   3. _____

   4. _____

(Continues on next page)

B.   Role conflict refers to the condition in which the different roles an individual is expected to play make incompatible demands. A working mother provides an example. In meeting the requirements of a full-time job, she automatically violates the expectation that a mother will put her children's needs before everything else. In meeting the cultural demands of motherhood (staying home if the child is sick, attending school plays), she automatically violates the requirements of a nine-to-five job. A priest provides another example. He is expected to treat confessions as strictly confidential. But a priest, like any other citizen, has responsibilities toward the community. What should he do if a parishioner confesses that he has committed several rapes and cannot control his behavior? In living up to one role expectation (confidentiality), the priest violates another (community responsibility). The key point here is that the difficulties the individuals in these positions experience—the feelings of conflict, inadequacy, and anguish—are not of their own making. They are built into their roles.

6. This paragraph defines and illustrates the term _____.

7. To illustrate that term, the author has used (*one, two, three,* or *four*) _____ example(s).

8-10. Complete the map of the passage.

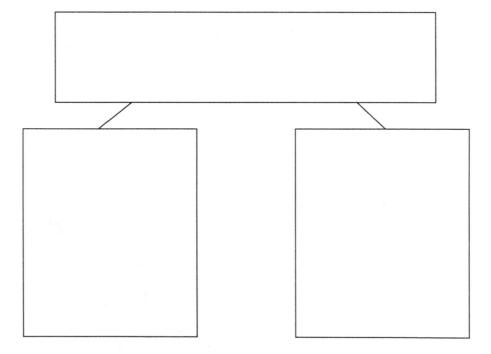

FACT AND OPINION: Test 1

A. Five of the statements below are facts, and five are opinions. Identify statements of fact with an **F** and statements of opinion with an **O**.

_____ 1. The equator is 24,901.55 miles long.

_____ 2. In 1924, the Model T Ford could be purchased for $290.

_____ 3. The Model T was the most significant invention of the first half of this century.

_____ 4. By the end of this century, electric cars and small family helicopters will be in common use.

_____ 5. The core of a pencil is made out of graphite and clay, not lead.

_____ 6. It's never too early to teach children to have good manners and to share in some small way in the household chores.

_____ 7. Masses of flowers all in one color are more attractive than plantings of two or more colors.

_____ 8. Marujuana affects the heart, raising the blood pressure and heart rate as much as 50% after only one joint.

_____ 9. Baltimore's traffic lights were designed with the color-blind in mind—green lights have a vertical shape, and red ones are horizontal.

_____ 10. The most important fact about any job is whether you like the people you work with.

B. Here are short reviews taken from a newspaper movie guide. Some reviews provide only factual reports; others contain opinions about the movie as well. Identify the factual reviews with an **F**; identify reviews that also contain an opinion with an **F + O**.

_____ 11. **Glory, '89.** Matthew Broderick, Denzel Washington. White Col. Robert Gould Shaw trains and leads the Civil War's first black regiment. Washington's performance won him an Oscar.

_____ 12. **Treasure Island, '50.** Bobby Driscoll, Robert Newton. Walt Disney changes the ending of Stevenson's novel, and everything is prettier, of course. Great fun, nonetheless, and Driscoll is terrific as young Jim Hawkins.

(Continues on next page)

_____ 13. **Streets, '90.** Christina Applegate, David Mendenhall. A teenage prostitute and a runaway rich kid flee a motorcycle patrol officer who is a murderer.

_____ 14. **Stagecoach, '66.** Lifeless remake of the John Ford western classic about misfits making a trip through hostile Indian country is hampered by the fact that not one of the performers matches up to the originals (John Wayne, Clair Trevor, etc.).

_____ 15. **Friday the 13th, Part VIII: Jason Takes Manhattan, '89.** Jensen Daggett, Scott Reeves. Hockey-masked slasher Jason follows a Crystal Lake teen and her friends on a cruise to New York.

_____ 16. **Divorce, American Style, '67.** Dick Van Dyke, Debbie Reynolds. Some funny, funny moments in this satire of the American institution of divorce with a hilarious supporting performance from Jason Robards as a divorced man scheming to get his ex remarried.

_____ 17. **Tango & Cash '89.** Sylvester Stallone, Kurt Russell. Framed and sent to prison, two rival Los Angeles police officers must work together to clear themselves.

_____ 18. **The Morning After, '86.** Jane Fonda, Jeff Bridges. A boozing actress wakes up next to a stabbed man and drives around Los Angeles with a stranger trying to figure out what happened.

_____ 19. **Boston Strangler, The '68.** Tony Curtis, Henry Fonda. Curtis is really quite good as Beantown's most famous mass-murderer, a psychotic woman-killer who makes murderous house-calls. A psychological drama, not a slasher movie.

_____ 20. **Good Guys Wear Black, '79.** Chuck Norris, Anne Archer. Norris is a U.S. secret agent. Includes the stunt where he crashes feet-first through the windshield of a speeding car.

FACT AND OPINION: Test 2

A. Four of the statements below are facts, and four are opinions; in addition, two include both fact and opinion. Identify facts with an **F**, opinions with an **O**, and statements of fact *and* opinion with an **F + O**.

_____ 1. The first television commercial, for a Bulova wristwatch, was broadcast in 1941.

_____ 2. Children should not be allowed to watch more than one hour of television a day.

_____ 3. Johnny Carson, the greatest talk-show host of them all, became host of *The Tonight Show* in 1962.

_____ 4. Watching sports events in person is better than watching them on TV.

_____ 5. Nothing is better for a stomachache than peppermint tea.

_____ 6. Every cook needs to become familiar with basil, which is a member of the mint family.

_____ 7. In laboratory experiments, peppermint extracts have counteracted some viruses in test tubes.

_____ 8. Bessie Smith, known as the "Empress of the Blues," was killed in a car accident in 1937.

_____ 9. A week after the stock-market crash, Columbia released Smith's recording of "Nobody Knows You When You're Down and Out."

_____ 10. Nobody, not even Anita Baker, can sing that song better than Smith did.

B. Each paragraph below includes five sentences. Three sentences express facts, and two express opinions. In the spaces provided, identify facts with an **F** and opinions with an **O**.

1. [1]There is no food that delights Americans more than the hot dog. [2]They eat frankfurters at the rate of eighty per person each year, enough to reach the moon and back to Earth two and a half times. [3]In fact, hot dogs have already been in space, as part of the diet of the Apollo astronauts who went to the moon. [4]The frankfurter dates back to 1852, when some German butchers in Frankfurt created and named it. [5]They would be astonished to know that their creation has ended up as an essential part of the American baseball scene.

    1. _____   2. _____   3. _____   4. _____   5. _____

(Continues on next page)

2.   [1]While in the minds of many, Mickey Mouse is associated with Walt Disney, the cartoon rodent was originally drawn by Disney's old friend Ubbe Iwerks. [2]Without Iwerks, Mickey Mouse would have remained a minor, forgotten character, and Disney would never have come into his own. [3]Iwerks worked for the Disney studio from 1924 to 1930 and then again from 1940 until his death in 1971. [4]During these years he worked on various animated films, including *Song of the South* (1946) and *Mary Poppins* (1964). [5]The teamwork of Disney and Iwerks was the single most important step in the success of the Disney studio.

1. _____   2. _____   3. _____   4. _____   5. _____

FACT AND OPINION: Test 4

A. Some of the statements below are facts, some are opinions, and some include both fact and opinion. Identify facts with an **F**, opinions with an **O**, and statements of fact *and* opinion with an **F + O**.

_____ 1. Couples should know each other for at least a year before getting married.

_____ 2. Some spouses take separate vacations, which reflects their unfortunate lack of commitment to each other.

_____ 3. In point of fact, it is always better for spouses to vacation together.

_____ 4. The weather report in this morning's newspaper says that rain is likely today.

_____ 5. Here's a disgusting fact: By the time the average person is 70, he or she will have shed about 40 pounds of dead skin.

_____ 6. There is simply no excuse for being late.

_____ 7. Any student who walked into our biology class after the bell rang was marked late.

_____ 8. Science has done more to improve humanity than all the world's philosophers combined.

_____ 9. Rubber is a wonderful elastic substance at first made only from the sap of certain tropical plants and now often made synthetically.

_____ 10. Joseph Priestley, an eighteenth-century scientist, named the substance *rubber* because it could rub away pencil marks.

B. Each paragraph below contains five sentences. Some sentences express facts, and some express opinions. In addition, each paragraph includes one statement of fact and opinion. Identify facts with an **F**, opinions with an **O**, and statements of fact *and* opinion with an **F + O**.

1. [1]A common definition of retirement includes the idea of leaving the labor force, but that notion of retirement is too narrow. [2]After retiring, it is much better to remain involved in the work world part-time. [3]Some companies have recently supported this type of involvement for the retired by hiring two or three older part-timers in place of one full-time employee. [4]The Travelers Corporation, for example, has employed six hundred retired employees for three hundred shared jobs. [5]Other retirees have continued to work part-time by volunteering for organizations such as hospitals and museums.

   1. _____   2. _____   3. _____   4. _____   5. _____

(Continues on next page)

2.   [1]School administrators should either improve our children's unhealthy lunch menus or be replaced. [2]There is little value in teaching academics to children only to hurt their minds and bodies with junk food at lunch time. [3]A survey of schools throughout the country shows that school lunch menus include high-sodium, high-fat, and low-fiber foods. [4]In addition, some school districts allow sugary and high-fat foods to be sold in vending machines, which proves that school administrators really care too little about our children. [5]The first step towards improving our children's health should be to abolish vending machines from the schools.

1. _____   2. _____   3. _____   4. _____   5. _____

FACT AND OPINION: Test 5

A. Four of the following textbook excerpts are facts, three are opinions, and three include both fact and opinion. Identify facts with an **F**, opinions with an **O**, and statements of fact *and* opinion with an **F + O**.

_____ 1. Alcohol was discovered and drunk during the Stone Age; its use precedes the fashioning of metal instruments.

_____ 2. Most of all, a successful marriage requires tolerance and understanding between partners.

_____ 3. Many years ago, J. P. Foley defined abnormal as "a deviation from the statistical norms of a particular cultural group." There are good points and bad points about Foley's definition .

_____ 4. Beethoven came on the scene at a favorable moment in history.

_____ 5. Studies have repeatedly shown that age is no barrier to the benefits of exercise.

_____ 6. Galen was one of the greatest medical doctors the world has known. Although he was born and educated in Greece a century or so after the death of Christ, Galen spent much of his adult life practicing medicine in Rome.

_____ 7. All seed-producing plants have roots which grow downward in the young seedling even as the stem grows upward.

_____ 8. Perhaps the best resource guide is the Magazine Index, a microfilm machine index of more than 350 magazines with articles from the previous five years.

_____ 9. All too often, the social policy in America has seemed to imply that the poor are not interested in working for a living.

_____ 10. In the United States the amount of touching usually decreases with age. Sixth graders touch each other less than do first graders. Parents touch their older children less often than their younger ones.

B. The textbook paragraph below contains five sentences. Some express facts, and some express opinions. Identify facts with an **F** and opinions with an **O**.

[11]Jimmy Carter shone brightly in comparison with Nixon, and he seemed more forward-looking and imaginative than Ford. [12]After delivering his inaugural address, he walked with his wife Rosalynn and their small daughter Amy in the parade from the Capitol to the White House instead of riding in a limousine. [13]For his first talk on television he wore a sweater instead of a coat and tie, in order to dramatize the need to

(Continues on next page)

conserve energy by turning down thermostats. [14]Soon after taking office he held a "call-in"; for two hours he answered questions phoned in by people from all over the country. [15]But Carter's actual administration of his office did not go nearly so well.

11. _____   12. _____   13. _____   14. _____   15. _____

C. Read the following passages from newspaper columns—the first is Ann Landers' syndicated column and the second is Darrell Sifford's column in *The Philadelphia Inquirer*. Identify each of the listed statements from the passages as either a fact (**F**) or an opinion (**O**).

• *From Ann Landers:*

Dear Loomis: I have long supported the use of marijuana for medicinal purposes. It has indeed proven helpful to asthmatics, as well as cancer and glaucoma patients. Marijuana can and should be made available to physicians for these purposes. But legalize it? No. We do not need any more stoned, zonked-out people on our streets and highways or anywhere else, for that matter.

16._____   It has indeed proven helpful to asthmatics, as well as cancer and glaucoma patients.

17._____   We do not need any more stoned, zonked-out people on our streets and highways or anywhere else, for that matter.

• *From Darrell Sifford:*

I think it's important to acknowledge our fears—to ourselves if to nobody else. It's part of understanding ourselves. I also think that it's important to understand that we don't necessarily have to do anything about our fears.

Some people are afraid to fly, and some of them—like John Madden, the football analyst—find other ways to travel. Other people don't think this inconvenience is practical, and they enroll in programs designed to overcome their fear of flying.

One solution is not necessarily better than the other one.

18._____   I think it's important to acknowledge our fears—to ourselves if to nobody else.

19._____   Some people are afraid to fly, and some of them—like John Madden, the football analyst—find other ways to travel.

20._____   One solution is not necessarily better than the other one.

FACT AND OPINION: Test 6

A. Read the following textbook excerpts and identify facts with an **F**, opinions with an **O**, and statements of fact *and* opinion with an **F + O**.

_____ 1. Nixon, responding to charges that he had paid almost no income taxes during his presidency, published his 1969-1972 returns. They showed that he had paid $1,600 in two years during which his income had exceeded half a million dollars.

_____ 2. Vitamin supplements are probably the most misunderstood and misused substances in the realm of health.

_____ 3. The best way to get started on a paper is to use a prewriting activity; such activities include freewriting, brainstorming, and asking questions.

_____ 4. So widespread is depression that doctors often refer to it as the "common cold of mental illness." Yet, although it is almost always treatable, with a combination of antidepressant drugs and psychotherapy, just one in five victims seeks help.

_____ 5. Low political participation by voters may, of course, only be a symptom of a deeper dissatisfaction with the policies and programs produced by elected officials.

_____ 6. Since Orville and Wilbur Wright made the first successful airplane flight in 1903, airplanes have produced many changes in modern life. The most important of these changes may be to have made the world much smaller.

B. Read the following textbook passage, and then identify each statement from the passage as either a fact (**F**) or an opinion (**O**).

The economic decline that followed the stock market crash of October 1929 was unparalleled in the nation's history. Over 4 million people were unemployed in 1930, 8 million in 1931, and almost 13 million, or close to one-quarter of the total civilian labor force, in 1933. Detroit, a city symbolic of the high-flying consumer economy of the 1920s, suffered in proportion to its earlier prosperity. Of the city's 690,000 gainful workers in October 1930, 223,000 were without jobs in March 1931. Because millions of small farmers reacted to falling prices by continuing to produce full crops, agricultural production fell little; farm income, however, was halved in the four years after 1929.

(Continues on next page)

Work for wages was the heart of the economy of the early 1930s, and when it faltered, the effects rippled through every area of American life. In one sixty-day period in Detroit, for example, some 50,000 homeowners lost the equity in their property—the banks foreclosed on their mortgages and took their homes. Black children went to school without food. Throughout that city, people of all races rummaged through garbage cans in the city's alleys, stole dog biscuits from the pound, and even tried to dig homes in the ground.

Herbert Hoover was not a do-nothing president. His attempts to persuade business to maintain wage rates were moderately successful for more than two years. Through the Agricultural Marketing Act, passed four months prior to the crash, the national government sought to maintain agricultural prices. National expenditures on public works increased. The Reconstruction Finance Corporation lent funds to banks, railroads, building and loan associations, and insurance companies. It saved a number of institutions from bankruptcy.

Perhaps Hoover's greatest failure was his firm opposition to national expenditures for relief. Private charity and city government, the primary agencies or relief, soon proved inadequate.

7. _____ Over 4 million people were unemployed in 1930, 8 million in 1931, and almost 13 million, or close to one-quarter of the total civilian labor force, in 1933.

8. _____ His attempts to persuade business to maintain wage rates were moderately successful for more than two years.

9. _____ Throughout that city, people of all races rummaged through garbage cans in the city's alleys, stole dog biscuits from the pound, and even tried to dig homes in the ground.

10. _____ Perhaps Hoover's greatest failure was his firm opposition to national expenditures for relief.

INFERENCES: Test 1

A. Read each passage below. Then check the *two* statements after each passage which are most logically supported by the information given.

1. My day has not ended. When I get home I suddenly realize that I have between thirty and forty pounds of fish to clean—rockfish yet, all full of spines and pricklers and razor-sharp teeth. When I'm finished I have so many holes in me I look like a composite of George Custer, Saint Sebastian, Bonnie and Clyde, but my family comes out to view the catch and restore my faith in the whole enterprise.

    "Yuk," says my daughter.

    "That's a lot of codfish for people who aren't all that into codfish," says my wife.

    "I wouldn't eat that on a bet," says my son.

    ___ a. The family is on vacation.

    ___ b. Rockfish are difficult to clean.

    ___ c. The author's family appreciates his hard work to feed them.

    ___ d. The family will have fish for dinner.

    ___ e. When he praises his family for restoring his faith, the author is being sarcastic.

2. I guess I did it because I hadn't studied very much. And it seemed so easy—everybody knows that Mr. Brown keeps his office door unlocked. It's just too bad things didn't work out for me. Now my classmates are mad at me because they must re-study for the new test Mr. Brown is making up. My parents have taken away my car keys. And even worse, I'll have to go to summer school for biology.

    ___ a. The speaker stole a test.

    ___ b. The speaker had been failing the course.

    ___ c. The class was a biology class.

    ___ d. The speaker regrets not studying more.

    ___ e. The speaker will never cheat again.

B. Read the passage on the next page, written by *Philadelphia Inquirer* columnist Clark DeLeon. Then check the *six* statements which are most logically supported by the information given.

(Continues on next page)

sallow: sickly pale and yellow   *lest:* for fear that
tacitly: by unspoken agreement   *defiant:* brave

There was a weird girl in my high school whom we all called the Bird. We called her that because of her nervous, birdlike movements and the way she would hunch her shoulders toward her ears as if she was hoping her head would disappear into her body. She had sallow skin that looked as if it had never felt the sun, and there was usually a blotchy red rash in the middle of her forehead. She had fine black hair on her arms long enough to comb, and she wore clothes that had been out of fashion since Shirley Temple was singing "The Good Ship Lollipop." She was also the object of such contempt and scorn, such cruel ridicule, that it shames me to this day to think I was part of it, even tacitly.

Oh, I was never one to say anything to her face, I wasn't that brave. I'd wait until she hurried by with her books held tightly to her chest and join in the chorus of birdcalls with the other guys. She was always good for a laugh. And it's important when you're a teenager to join the laughter, lest the laughter turn on you.

I remember one day when the Bird was surrounded by three or four suburban-variety greasers who had stopped her in the corridor between classes. They were flapping their arms and screeching in her ear. She was terrified. Her eyes darted in panic. A couple of her books fell to the floor. When she stopped to pick them up, they bent over her in a circle, closing in, screeching, screeching.

Then this girl came out of nowhere. I'd never seen such anger in a girl before. She went up to the leader of the tormentors and ripped into him with a hot fury. "Stop it!' she shouted. "Can't you see what you're doing?" The guys backed off, stunned. Then the girl went over to the Bird and put her arm around her shoulder and walked her to class.

I thought about the Bird when I read about Nathan Faris, the little boy who shot a classmate and killed himself after being the target of teasing by the kids in his school. I thought of how I had been a part of her misery, how more than twenty years later it still bothers me. But I also think of what I learned that day about decency and bravery, about being a human being, from a girl whose name I don't even know. And I wonder if that one act of defiant kindness may have saved another girl's life.

____ 1. The "Bird" must have been physically abused by her parents.

____ 2. Teenagers are especially sensitive about being laughed at.

____ 3. The "Bird" wore clothing very different from that worn by the author and his classmates.

____ 4. Teenage teasing is not all that harmful.

____ 5. Teenagers are sometimes mean in order to avoid having others be mean to them.

____ 6. It took bravery to laugh with the others at "the Bird" as she passed by.

____ 7. The kind girl was more concerned with how the "Bird" was being treated than with what the greasers would think of her.

____ 8. It is not always easy to be kind.

____ 9. The author feels that an act of kindness may have long-term effects.

____ 10. The author had been teased a lot himself in high school.

INFERENCES: Test 2

A. Read the two passages below. Then check the *two* statements after each passage which are most logically supported by the information given.

1. A high school once offered a course called "Home Economics for Boys." Not very many boys signed up for the course. Then someone decided to rename the course instead of dropping it. So the next time the course was offered it was called "Bachelor Living," but the course otherwise remained the same. The class then drew 120 students.

   ____ a. Most of the boys intend to remain bachelors.

   ____ b. Most of the boys did not want to sign up for a class that sounded like a class for girls.

   ____ c. Boys aren't really interested in cooking.

   ____ d. Both boys and girls signed up for the course.

   ____ e. Names can influence people.

2. Thinking his company had entirely too many rules, an office worker decided to do something about it. So he posted an official-looking notice next to the pencil sharpener. Next to that, he posted a log sheet. For each use of the sharpener, said the notice, everyone must write on the log the date, his or her name, and the number of pencils sharpened. After two weeks, seventeen people had signed the log. The worker who had thought it up had also signed it—twice. "Everyone else was doing it, so I thought I should sign it, too," he explained.

   ____ a. Workers in that office were used to obeying orders.

   ____ b. This is the first of many times the writer of the notice would try to do something about office rules.

   ____ c. The writer of the notice rarely followed office rules.

   ____ d. The writer of the notice did not want to appear different from the others.

   ____ e. The workers who did not sign the log were soon let go by the company.

B. Ten statements follow the passage on the next page, taken from the essay "How to Say Nothing in 500 Words" by the American scholar Paul Roberts. Check the *six* statements which are most logically supported by the information given.

(Continues on next page)

It's Friday afternoon, and you have almost survived another week of classes. You are just looking forward dreamily to the weekend when the English instructor says: "For Monday you will turn in a five-hundred word composition on college football."

Well, that puts a good big hole in the weekend. You don't have any strong views on college football one way or the other. You get rather excited during the season and go to all the home games and find it rather more fun than not. On the other hand, the class has been reading Robert Hutchins in the anthology and perhaps Shaw's "Eighty-Yard Run," and from the class discussion you have got the idea that the instructor thinks college football is for the birds. You are no fool, you. You can figure out what side to take.

After dinner you get out the portable typewriter that you got for high school graduation. You might as well get it over with and enjoy Saturday and Sunday. Five hundred words is about two double-spaced pages with normal margins. You put in a sheet of paper, think up a title, and you're off:

Why College Football Should Be Abolished

College football should be abolished because it's bad for the school and also bad for the players. The players are so busy practicing that they don't have any time for their studies.

This, you feel, is a mighty good start. The only trouble is that it's only thirty-two words. You still have four hundred and sixty-eight to go, and you've pretty well exhausted the subject. It comes to you that you do your best thinking in the morning, so you put away the typewriter and go to the movies. But the next morning you have to do your washing and some math problems, and in the afternoon you go to the game. The English instructor turns up too, and you wonder if you've taken the right side after all. Saturday night you have a date, and Sunday morning you have to go to church. (You shouldn't let English assignments interfere with your religion.) What with one thing and another, it's ten o'clock Sunday night before you get out the typewriter again.

_____ 1. The author is writing humorously about what he feels is a typical student.

_____ 2. The student agrees with Robert Hutchins' views on football.

_____ 3. The student believes one gets a better grade by defending a point of view the instructor will agree with.

_____ 4. At first, the student's instructor seemed to be against college football.

_____ 5. In class, the instructor has directly expressed his or her opinions on football.

_____ 6. The student would probably skip church on Sunday if there were a desirable social event.

_____ 7. Writing essays probably comes easily to the student.

_____ 8. The student is better at procrastinating than at writing compositions.

_____ 9. The student is failing his English course.

_____ 10. The student will be doing homework until late into Sunday night.

INFERENCES: Test 3

A. Read the passage below, taken from the autobiographical book *Move On* by television journalist Linda Ellerbee. Check the *five* statements which are most logically supported by the information given.

Television changed my family forever. We stopped eating dinner at the dining-room table after my mother found out about TV trays. We kept the TV trays behind the kitchen door and served ourselves from pots on the stove. Setting and clearing the dining-room table used to be my job; now, setting and clearing meant unfolding and wiping our TV trays, then, when we'd finished, wiping and folding our TV trays. Dinner was served in time for one program and finished in time for another. During dinner we used to talk to one another. Now television talked to us. If you had something you absolutely had to say, you waited until the commercial, which is, I suspect, where I learned to speak in thirty-second bursts. As a future writer, it was good practice in editing my thoughts. As a little girl, it was lonely as hell. Once in a while, I'd pass our dining-room table and stop, thinking I heard our ghosts sitting around talking to one another, saying stuff.

____ 1. Ellerbee preferred eating at the dining-room table to eating in front of the TV.

____ 2. Ellerbee must have been an only child.

____ 3. Families should never watch television together.

____ 4. Watching television during dinner can interfere with family communication.

____ 5. It's possible to feel lonely even when others are around.

____ 6. As a child, Ellerbee never enjoyed watching television.

____ 7. Watching TV became more important at dinnertime than what a member of Ellerbee's family had to say.

____ 8. As a little girl, Ellerbee had few friends.

____ 9. Ellerbee's childhood home was haunted.

____ 10. When Ellerbee imagined the ghosts, she was remembering better times.

B. Read the passage on the next page, taken from an essay in *Ms.* magazine titled "Being a Boy," by Julius Lester. Check the *five* statements which are most logically supported by the information given.

pummeling: beating   *assertion:* claim
adept: very skilled   *decathlon:* an athletic competition with ten track-and-field events

(Continues on next page)

As boys go, I wasn't much. I mean, I tried to be a boy and spent many childhood hours pummeling my hardly formed ego with failure at cowboys and Indians, baseball, football, lying, and sneaking out of the house. When our neighborhood gang raided a neighbor's pear tree, I was the only one who got sick from the stolen fruit. I also failed at setting fire to our garage, an art at which any five-year-old boy should be adept. I was, however, the neighborhood champion at getting beat up. "That Julius can take it, man," the boys used to say, almost in admiration, after I emerged from another battle, tears brimming in my eyes but refusing to fall.

My efforts at being a boy earned me a pair of scarred knees that are a record of a childhood spent falling from bicycles, trees, the tops of fences, and porch steps; of tripping as I ran (generally from a fight), walked, or simply tried to remain upright on windy days. I tried to believe my parents when they told me I was a boy, but I could find no objective proof for such an assertion. Each morning during the summer as I cuddled up in the quiet corner with a book, my mother would push me out the back door and into the yard. And throughout the day as my blood was let as if I were a patient of 17th-century medicine, I thought of the girls sitting in the shade of porches, playing with their dolls, toy refrigerators and stoves.

There was the life, I thought! No constant pressure to prove oneself. No necessity always to be competing. While I humiliated myself on football and baseball fields, the girls stood on the sidelines laughing at me, because they didn't have to do anything except be girls. The rising of each sun brought me to the starting line of yet another day's Olympic decathlon, with no hope of ever winning even a bronze medal.

Through no fault of my own I reached adolescence. While the pressure to prove myself on the athletic field lessened, the overall situation got worse—because now I had to prove myself with girls. Just how I was supposed to go about doing this was beyond me, especially because, at the age of 14, I was four foot nine and weighed seventy-eight pounds. (I think there may have been one 10-year-old girl in the neighborhood smaller than I.) Nonetheless, duty called, and off I went.

____ 1. The author was never part of the neighborhood gang.

____ 2. Being small can be a disadvantage to a boy.

____ 3. The author's mother sometimes physically abused him.

____ 4. As a boy, the author wasn't strong, but he was brave.

____ 5. The author had no brothers or sisters.

____ 6. Despite his humiliations, the author continued to try to prove himself as a male.

____ 7. Life would be easier for some people if society allowed for more individual differences.

____ 8. The author finally began to play "girls' games."

____ 9. The author eventually became more skilled on the athletic field.

____ 10. The author's athletic humiliations were replaced by dating difficulties.

INFERENCES: Test 4

A. Following is Edward Arlington Robinson's well-known poem about a wealthy man named Richard Cory. Read the poem, and then check the *five* statements which are most logically supported by the information given.

Note that the meanings of a few words in the poem are given below.

Clean favored: privileged to be clean (since he did no manual work).
imperially: in a superior way (since the rich had a superior, more healthy diet than the poor)
quietly arrayed: not dressed in a showy manner

Richard Cory

Whenever Richard Cory went down town,
We people on the pavement looked at him;
He was a gentleman from sole to crown,
Clean favored, and imperially slim.

And he was always quietly arrayed,
And he was always human when he talked;
But still he fluttered pulses when he said
"Good-morning," and he glittered when he walked.

And he was rich—yes, richer than a king,
And admirably schooled in every grace;
In fine, we thought that he was everything
To make us wish that we were in his place.

So on we worked, and waited for the light,
And went without the meat, and cursed the bread;
And Richard Cory, one calm summer night,
Went home and put a bullet through his head.

____ 1. Richard Cory treated the poor disrespectfully.

____ 2. Richard Cory had many personal friends.

____ 3. The speaker is poor.

____ 4. Richard Cory was admired.

____ 5. Richard Cory was married.

____ 6. The poor people in town thought Richard Cory was happy.

____ 7. Richard Cory had an unhappy love affair.

____ 8. Richard Cory was not as fortunate as he seemed.

____ 9. The poor preferred bread to meat.

____ 10. Money does not buy happiness.

(Continues on next page)

B. Ten statements follow the passage below, taken from a book titled *The Silver Horn* by Thomas Sancton. Check the *five* statements which are most logically supported by the information given.

> Little things that happened during these years seemed of great importance. I remember that in my first year at camp I wore an ill-fitted Boy Scout hat. One of the counselors, a boy five years my senior who seemed to me to belong already to the grown-up world of brilliance and authority, began, in a pleasant way, to tease me about the hat. Every morning for a week he led us to the abandoned logging road and clocked us as we walked and trotted a measured mile. My hat was anchored down by a heavy chin strap; it flopped and sailed about my head as I ran to the finish line. The boy began to laugh at me. He waved his arms and called out, "Come on, you rookie!" The other kids took it up and Rookie became my first nickname. I loved it. I tingled when someone called it out. I painted it on my belt, carved it on my packing case, inked it into my hatband, and began to sign it to my letters home. Years later when we were grown I knew this camp officer again. The gap between our ages had vanished and in real life now he seemed to me a rather colorless young lawyer. He did not remember about the hat.

____ 1. The author is writing about his childhood.

____ 2. He thought it was wonderful to be a grown-up.

____ 3. He resented being teased about his Boy Scout hat.

____ 4. Having a nickname made Sancton feel good.

____ 5. The author hated the ill-fitting hat with the heavy chin strap.

____ 6. Rookie was the only nickname he ever had.

____ 7. After they grew up, the author disliked his camp counselor.

____ 8. After they grew up, the author no longer admired his camp counselor.

____ 9. The author never went to camp again.

____ 10. The hat incidents were more important to the author than they had been to his counselor.

INFERENCES: Test 5

A. Following is a well-known poem, "Ozymandias" (pronounced ŏ-zĭ-măn´-dē-əs), by the English poet Percy Shelley. Read the poem, and then circle the letters of the inferences which are most logically supported by the information given.

vast: large	*pedestal:* bottom support
visage: face	*colossal:* huge
sneer: scornful smile	*boundless:* endless

Ozymandias

I met a traveler from an antique land,
Who said: Two vast and trunkless legs of stone
Stand in the desert. Near them, on the sand,
Half sunk, a shattered visage lies, whose frown,
And wrinkled lip, and sneer of cold command,
Tell that its sculptor well those passions read,
Which yet survive, stamped on these lifeless things,
The hand that mocked them, and the heart that fed:
And on the pedestal these words appear:
"My name is Ozymandias, King of Kings:
Look on my works, ye Mighty, and despair!"
Nothing beside remains. Round the decay
Of that colossal wreck, boundless and bare
The lone and level sands stretch far away.

1. The place the traveler described was
   a. an old, yet active desert city.
   b. a barren spot in the desert where a culture once thrived.
   c. a land where travelers can find numerous antiques on sale.

2. At that place was
   a. a broken statue.
   b. a painting.
   c. an imaginary person.

3. The features on the face were those of
   a. a respectful, obedient citizen.
   b. a judgmental, unfriendly leader.
   c. a wise and compassionate leader.

(Continues on next page)

4. The words on the pedestal show that the statue's subject
   a. was a king.
   b. felt few people had achieved more than he had.
   c. both of the above.

5. One of the poet's main points is that human vanity and pride
   a. were greater many years ago than they are today.
   b. stand up to the test of time.
   c. are ridiculous in the face of time and change.

B. Ten statements follow the textbook passage below. Check the *five* statements which are most logically supported by the information given.

    Suppose a man works six or seven days a week in a factory, trying to support his family, but never seems to be able to make ends meet. If he analyzed his situation rationally, he would probably blame the well-to-do generally and his employers specifically for failing to pay him an adequate wage. But these people have the power to cut off his income; to oppose them openly would be self-destructive. He could also blame himself for his financial problems, but this too makes him uncomfortable. Instead, he looks to the immigrants who have begun working in his factory. He doesn't really know them, but he suspects they're willing to work for low wages and that many other immigrants are eager to take his job. By a process of twisted logic, he blames these people for his poverty. Soon he is exchanging rumors about "them" with his cronies and supporting efforts to close the border. Hating immigrants makes the man and his friends feel a little better.

____ 1. People never blame themselves for their problems.

____ 2. Factory workers are not good at managing money.

____ 3. All factory workers are underpaid.

____ 4. Some people are reluctant to oppose their bosses.

____ 5. Immigrants are eager to take other people's jobs.

____ 6. The author feels that the man in the example is underpaid.

____ 7. Prejudice can be the result of wanting to blame someone for our problems.

____ 8. The man in the example would probably be violent against immigrants.

____ 9. The man in the example would probably oppose hiring more immigrants.

____ 10. Some people make themselves feel better by thinking less of others.

INFERENCES: Test 6

After reading each textbook selection, circle the letter of the best answer to each question.

A. In colonial America, anyone could become a physician merely by adopting the label. There were no medical schools or medical societies to license or regulate what was a free-for-all trade. Sometimes clergymen tried to provide medical care to their parishioners, and care of a sort was offered by all kinds of laypeople as well. Documents of the time record a doctor who sold "tea, sugar, olives, grapes, anchovies, raisins, and prunes" along with medicinals, and also tell of a woman who "Acts here in the Double Capacity of a Doctoress and Coffee Woman" (Starr 1982, p. 39). Training for medical practice, such as it was, was given by apprenticeship.

1. In comparison to today, a medical practice in colonial America
   a. must have been harder to establish.
   b. must have been more expensive to establish.
   c. probably required more study.
   d. was less likely to be full-time.

2. Considering the medical training of the time, we might conclude that
   a. most doctors did medical research.
   b. people were lucky to get good medical care.
   c. very few people would have been considered qualified to be medical apprentices.
   d. most colonial Americans were probably pretty healthy.

B. Urbanization is the process whereby large numbers of people leave the countryside and small towns in order to settle in cities and surrounding metropolitan areas. Thus, urbanization involves migration from sparsely populated regions to densely populated ones. The extent of this migration has been enormous in the twentieth century. In 1900, 86.4 percent of the world population lived in rural areas, whereas only 13.6 percent lived in cities. Today, only 37.5 percent of people are rural residents, whereas 62.5 are now city dwellers (Palen 1986). Densely populated urban regions have, in short, become a dominant feature of the modern landscape.

3. People probably migrate from rural areas to cities to find
   a. cleaner air.
   b. jobs.
   c. friendly neighbors.
   d. a safe environment.

(Continues on next page)

C. In the mid-1970s the networks tried to break down traditional viewing habits by introducing a new format, the mini-series. The idea was to get people hooked on the series in the first episode—usually broadcast on Sunday night—so they would tune in again the next several evenings. Mini-series have proven very popular and they are often scheduled during "sweep periods," when TV stations are monitored to determine audience sizes. (Sweeps are usually conducted three times a year—November, February and May—and are used to set advertising rates. High ratings means higher ad rates for the local stations and networks.)

The mini-series concept actually came from public broadcasting, which began showing BBC-produced serials such as *The Forsyte Saga* in 1969 and *Upstairs Downstairs*.

4. Since mini-series usually begin on Sunday nights, we can conclude that
   a. the first episode usually lasts an hour.
   b. mini-series appeal to the most religious Americans.
   c. many Americans watch TV on Sunday nights.
   d. there are usually fewer TV ads on Sunday nights.

5. From the passage, we can conclude that public broadcasting
   a. broadcasts ads during its mini-series.
   b. influenced the networks.
   c. has "sweep periods."
   d. would not begin its serials on Sunday nights.

PURPOSE AND TONE: Test 1

A. In the space provided, indicate whether the primary purpose of each sentence is to inform (**I**), to persuade (**P**), or to entertain (**E**).

_____ 1. The average dollar bill lasts about eighteen months.

_____ 2. Federal taxes must be raised so that we can afford a national health program.

_____ 3. Mac's idea of healthy eating is to have a double cheeseburger without putting any salt on it.

_____ 4. Every car built in America should have air bags on both the driver and the passenger side.

_____ 5. Among the Aztecs, a man could not get married until he'd graduated from school.

B. Each of the following passages illustrates one of the five different tones identified in the box below. In the space provided, put the letter of the tone that applies to each passage.

a. caring	b. critical	c. pessimistic
d. admiring	e. self-mocking	

_____ 6. What ever happened to the practice of saving up for what you want? It seems nobody has that kind of patience any more. Many Americans buy what they want when they want it and worry about paying for it later. The average American spends significantly more than he or she earns, much to the enjoyment of the credit-card companies. Apparently people need to reach a financial crisis before they realize that it's downright stupid to neglect to balance their budgets and to save for a rainy day.

_____ 7. Machines are complete mysteries to me, which has resulted in some embarrassing service calls at my home. For example, there was the time I called in a repairman because our refrigerator was too warm. Imagine my humiliation when he told me that the cause of the problem was a dirty filter, which I didn't know existed and therefore hadn't cleaned even once in the two years we owned the refrigerator. The best example of my brilliance with machines, however, has to be the time I called for someone to fix my washing machine. The repairman's solution was simply to put the plug back in the outlet,

(Continues on next page)

from which it had been jarred loose by the constant vibration of the washer.

_____ 8. I think Tina Turner is a terrific role model for anyone who thinks he or she cannot overcome obstacles early in life. Turner grew up in poverty, survived an abusive marriage, and dealt with dishonest business associates early in her career. Many people might have just given in at any point along the way. But Turner had the determination and inner strength to go in alone. Doing it her way, she first became a superstar when she was in her 40s, when she finally received the money, the acclaim and the respect she always deserved but had been deprived of. Not only is Turner talented and tough-minded, she has proved that beauty and sex appeal can be ageless. Way to go, Tina!

_____ 9. Research on rats shows that when animals live in crowded conditions they live disorderly, violent lives. Humans are no exception. Crowded inner cities are models of lawlessness; the crowded highways of Los Angeles encourage driver aggression and even shootings. As our urban areas continue to grow in population density, these types of problems will surely also grow. That means more family violence and more fighting over available resources. The American dream will become just that, only a dream.

_____ 10. Those addicted to drugs and alcohol probably feel terrible about themselves—even if they don't show it—and harsh judgments only worsen their self-image. What these people need are programs to help rid themselves of their addictions. It is also important that we all open our hearts and minds to these troubled people. Their addiction does not make them any less "children of God" or deserving to be stripped of the dignity that is the birthright of every human being. We must strive to create an environment of hope and help for those who so desperately need it.

PURPOSE AND TONE: Test 2

A. In the space provided, indicate whether the primary purpose of each sentence is to inform (**I**), to persuade (**P**), or to entertain (**E**).

_____ 1. The foundation of public education has always been reading, writing and arithmetic—the three "Rs." Yet the schools insist that students who have not mastered these fundamentals continue to take all the other subjects as well. What good does it do for young people to sit in on a history or science class if they can't read or calculate well? Schools ought to require students who are very behind in the fundamentals to devote all their time to the three Rs until they are at or near grade level.

_____ 2. One way to lose weight is to go on a scientific weight-loss program. These are widely advertised in those newspapers that are sold at supermarket check-out lines, the ones with headlines like: BURT REYNOLDS FINDS CANCER CURE IN UFO RIDE WITH PRINCESS DIANA. You should buy one of these magazines and flip through the pages until you see a full-page advertisement with a headline that says, "WOMAN LOSES 240 POUNDS IN 30 SECONDS." Under the headline are two pictures of a woman's head: in the first picture the head is on top of what appears to be an industrial boiler wearing a 1952 bathing suit; in the second picture, the head is on top of Bo Derek's body.

_____ 3. More and more elderly are turning to shared housing as a way to live more economically, more securely, and with more companionship. There are dozens of such projects around the country, including group homes in California, communes in Baltimore, and the "Share a Home" in Winter Park, Florida. While the latter includes 125 participants, a shared-housing project may involve only a few members. Most shared housing projects have full- or part-time help, but members often share in such chores as shopping for food and cooking.

(Continues on next page)

B. Each of the following passages illustrates one of the tones identified in the box below. In each space provided, put the letter of the tone that applies to the passage.

a. objective	b. optimistic	c. sarcastic
d. playful	e. angry	f. solemn

_____ 4. When I hired Atlas Carpets to install a new wall-to-wall carpet in my living room, I relied on your firm's excellent reputation for quality work. However, as I have told you repeatedly on the telephone, I am deeply dissatisfied with the dreadful job your clumsy workers did in my home. In one corner near the fireplace the carpeting is poorly fitted, and some of the flooring shows through. Some of the tacks are already coming loose, and I have had to hammer them in again myself even though I have a bad back. Moreover, one of your workmen stupidly put a hot cup down on my coffee table, leaving a stain for which I hold you responsible! If we cannot agree to a reasonable adjustment promptly, I will turn the whole matter over to my lawyer, as well as tell all my friends about my exasperating experience with Atlas.

_____ 5. Scientists say grilling meat creates cancer-causing substances that affect the meat in two ways. First, when fat drips onto the source of heat, the substances are formed and then carried up to the food by smoke. They are also formed when flames touch the meat. There are, however, a few ways that experts say will minimize the risk of grilling meat: (1) Use low-fat meats and non-fat sauces. (2) Partially cook meat before grilling. (3) Cover the grill with foil; punch holes in the foil to let fat drip down. (4) Avoid fire flare-ups, which cause harmful smoke. (5) Scrape off blackened material on the surface of meat before eating it. (6) Don't cook out every day.

Name _____

Section _____ Date_____

SCORE: (Number correct) _____ x 10 = _____ %

PURPOSE AND TONE: Test 3

A. Eight quotations in the story below are preceded by a blank space. Identify the tone of each italicized quotation by writing in the letter of one of these tones. (Two tone choices will be left over.)

a. sympathetic	b. straightforward	c. pleading	d. angry
e. superior	f. excited	g. depressed	h. scheming
i. curious	j. frightened		

The television reporter knocked on the door of the small row home. A woman opened the door.

_____ 1. *"My name is Tod Hunter," the reporter said. "I'm with Action News, and I'd like to talk to the woman who lost her daughter in the school fire last night."*

"Oh, I'm sorry, but she's not much in the mood for visitors."

"I understand," the reporter said. "Please tell her that we only want a moment of her time."

While the woman was gone, the reporter turned to his crew.

_____ 2. *"You could shoot from this angle," he whispered, "but let's try to get inside. If she's at all responsive to my questions, let's gradually move in through the doorway."*

Children in the neighborhood crowded around the TV crew.

_____ 3. *"Those are TV cameras!" some shouted, laughing. "Wow, real TV cameras!"*

_____ 4. *Pausing to look at the crew standing outside the house, passersby asked, "What do you suppose happened there?"*

Then the mother of the fire victim appeared at the door, looking drawn and exhausted. "What do you want?"

_____ 5. *"I'm really very sorry for your great loss, Ma'am."* Hunter continued, "I'm here for Action News. Do you know what caused the terrible fire?"

"Please, no interviews."

"Our viewers want to know about this awful fire."

_____ 6. *"The people can go to blazes," she shouted. "It's none of their business. It's none of your business, either, young man."*

_____ 7. *"Run! She's mad!" shouted the children as they raced away.*

_____ 8. *"All I want is two minutes," the reporter said. "Please, just two minutes of your time."*

(Continues on next page)

But the door had already slammed in his face.

"Let's get out of here," the frustrated reporter said to his crew. "I'm starved."

B. In the space provided, indicate whether the primary purpose of each passage is to inform (**I**), to persuade (**P**), or to entertain (**E**).

9. _____   Swollen glands can be uncomfortable, but they are a welcome sign that your body is working to defend itself. They are often associated with an illness such as mumps, German measles, a cold, or flu, but an insect bite or infected cut can also cause your glands to swell. A blocked duct in a salivary gland is another possible cause of a swollen gland. If swollen glands last more than a few days, they can be a sign of a serious illness, such as Hodgkin's disease.

10. _____   Puberty causes the changing of considerably more than your sheets. I remember that puberty inspired me to brush my hair so hard that I almost exposed the area where my brains should have been. The moment my glands kicked in, I began to brush my hair a hundred times a day so that not a single strand was out of place for the girls I now wanted to impress. I shined my own shoes, I cut the tiny hanging strings off the frayed parts of my collar, and, in a stunning blend of vanity and vapidness, I even began to flaunt my eyelashes, which were particularly long. Before puberty, I had actually trimmed these lashes because women had said I looked like a girl; but now I was grooming them with a toothbrush and wondering if girls would prefer them from the front or the side.

PURPOSE AND TONE: Test 5

This activity will give you practice in recognizing purpose and tone. Read each of the paragraphs below. Then carefully consider the questions that follow and circle the letters of the best responses.

A.   A successful doctor is scheduled to operate on a patient at 8 A.M., but it has snowed during the night, and driving is difficult. Do you think the doctor will stay home in bed? Not if he or she is professional. This attitude of professionalism is the key to being a successful college student, too. And it is within your reach, no matter how well or how poorly you have done in school up until now. You cannot undo the past, but you can adopt an attitude of professionalism from now on. All you have to do is intend to take school seriously, and the rest will follow. By attending classes, turning in assignments on time, and coming prepared for tests, you will gradually build your skills.

1. The primary purpose of this paragraph is to
   a. present facts on student behavior.
   b. persuade students to be responsible.
   c. entertain students with a dramatic story about professionalism.

2. In general, the tone of this paragraph can be described as
   a. critical.
   b. pessimistic.
   c. encouraging.
   d. praising.

B.   According to memory experts, there are ways you can improve your chances of remembering the names of people you meet. One way is to make associations between a person's name and looks. For example, if you meet a man named Baker, you might picture him wearing a baker's hat. If the name is a difficult one, ask for the spelling and visualize the letters mentally. It's also useful to repeat the person's name as you converse, keeping your mental images in mind. And when your conversation ends, repeat the person's name as you say goodbye.

3. The primary purpose of this paragraph is
   a. to inform.
   b. to persuade.
   c. to entertain.

4. The overall tone of this paragraph can be described as
   a. critical and angry.
   b. obviously humorous.
   c. doubtful.
   d. straightforward and instructive.

(Continues on next page)

C. Too many students treat school as a game in which they are the "good guys" and teachers are "the enemy." They turn in work far inferior to what they are capable of doing and then blame their teachers for their own failures. Such students feel assignments are annoyances and tests are punishments. They think school is an institution designed to divert them from having fun, not a place intended to help them grow.

5. The author of this paragraph intends
   a. to inform readers of facts about students.
   b. to persuade readers that many students' attitudes toward school is counterproductive.
   c. to entertain readers with colorful descriptions of student attitudes.

6. The tone of this paragraph can be described as
   a. tragic.
   b. critical.
   c. pessimistic.
   d. uncertain.

D. Like many children, Sarah had an invisible friend, a pet raccoon named "Orange." One day during a family drive, Sarah and her two sisters got into some intense sibling rivalry in the back seat of the compact car. At one point, Peggy, the oldest sister, pretended to grab Orange out of Sarah's arms. Sarah screamed and cried until their mother, out of desperation, ordered Peggy to return the raccoon to Sarah. Peggy refused to obey, and Sarah continued to cry until the parents reached their wit's end. Finally, the children's father stopped the car on the side of the road, got out, and opened the back door. He reached into the air between Peggy's arms and then dropped something unseen onto Sarah's lap. "There," he said. "Now you have Orange back. No more fighting!" Peggy looked stunned, Sarah grinned triumphantly, and Jenny, the youngest, just scratched her head.

7. The primary purpose of this paragraph is
   a. to inform.
   b. to persuade.
   c. to entertain.

8. The tone of this paragraph can be described as
   a. straightforward.
   b. critical.
   c. bitter.
   d. cheerful.

PURPOSE AND TONE: Test 6

This activity will give you practice in recognizing purpose and tone. Read each of the paragraphs below. Then carefully consider the questions that follow and circle the letters best responses.

A. It was about forty yards to the gallows. I watched the bare brown back of the prisoner marching in front of me. He walked clumsily with his bound arms, but quite steadily, with that bobbing gait of the Indian who never straightens his knees. At each step his muscles slid neatly into place, the lock of hair on his scalp danced up and down, his feet printed themselves on the wet gravel. And once, in spite of the men who gripped him by each shoulder, he stepped slightly aside to avoid a puddle on the path.

   It is curious, but till that moment I had never realized what it means to destroy a healthy, conscious man. When I saw the prisoner step aside to avoid the puddle, I saw the mystery, the unspeakable wrongness, of cutting a life short when it is in full tide. This man was not dying; he was alive just as we were alive. All the organs of his body were working—bowels digesting food, skin renewing itself, nails growing, tissues forming—all toiling away. . . His nails would still be growing when he stood on the drop, when he was falling through the air with a tenth of a second to live. His eyes saw the yellow gravel and the grey walls, and his brain still remembered, foresaw, reasoned—reasoned even about puddles. He and we were a party of men walking together, seeing, hearing, feeling, understanding the same world; and in two minutes, with a sudden snap, one of us would be gone—one mind less, one world less.

   1. The purpose of this passage (taken from the essay "A Hanging," by the British author George Orwell) is
      a. to inform readers about what executions are like.
      b. to persuade readers that executions are wrong.
      c. to entertain readers (in a broad sense) with a dramatic scene.
      d. to do all of the above.

   2. The tone of the passage can be described as
      a. detached and cruel.
      b. angry and revengeful.
      c. impassioned and distressed.
      d. loving and forgiving.

B. Al Smith, the Democratic candidate for President in 1928, was known for his ready wit and quick comebacks. Once he was heckled while making a campaign speech. "Tell 'em everything you know, Al," yelled the heckler. "It won't take very long."

   Al Smith answered with a grin, "I'll tell 'em everything we both know—it won't take any longer."

(Continues on next page)

305

3. The primary purpose of this passage is
    a. to inform readers about Al Smith's 1928 campaign.
    b. to persuade readers not to embarrass speakers.
    c. to entertain readers with an amusing story.

4. The tone of the paragraph can be described as
    a. forgiving.
    b. amused.
    c. bitter.
    d. disbelieving.

C. Three people were killed because a man was angry that his girlfriend wanted to break up with him. Now the state is planning to kill him, and that's as it should be. Some may argue that taking a life is always wrong, that two wrongs don't make a right. But there is nothing right about taxpayers having to give free room and board to a person who killed innocent people. And there's nothing right about putting such a dangerous person in prison, from which he will probably one day be released to again threaten society.

5. The primary purpose of this paragraph is
    a. to inform readers of facts about the death penalty.
    b. to persuade readers that the death penalty has merit.
    c. to entertain readers with a description of an interesting problem.

6. The overall tone of this paragraph can be described as
    a. impassioned.
    b. insulting.
    c. compassionate and sentimental.
    d. excited and joyous.

D. Part of the gap between thinking and feeling almost certainly comes from the lessons we learn while growing up. Usually without being aware of it, and almost inevitably, adults send message after message telling a child which emotions are acceptable and which aren't. In a house where angry words are taboo, the child gets the idea that anger is a "not OK" thing. If sex is never discussed except with great discomfort, then the child will learn to stop talking about—and even stop consciously feeling—emotions that center around the body. If the parents talk only about trivial subjects and never share their deeper feelings, the child's conversation and thinking will tend to follow the same path.

7. The primary purpose of this paragraph is
    a. to explain the author's point in detail.
    b. to persuade readers with research and personal experience.
    c. to entertain readers with fascinating descriptions.

8. The tone of this paragraph can be described as
    a. regretful.
    b. angry.
    c. playful.
    d. serious.

PROPAGANDA: Test 1

In each pair of sentences below, the first sentence does *not* illustrate a propaganda technique, but the second one does. On the line, write the letter of the propaganda technique used in the *second* sentence.

_____ 1. • Miami offers its residents several advantages.

• "I love Miami," says Dolphins' star George Raymond. "The fans here are great, and I recommend Miami as a wonderful place to live."

a. Plain folks   c. Name calling
b. Bandwagon   d. Testimonial

_____ 2. • Cheese Bits are good and economical.

• Home Town Cheese Bits taste just like the down-to-earth snacks at your local diner. You don't need expensive snacks, just simple, delicious food.

a. Testimonial   c. Name calling
b. Plain folks   d. Bandwagon

_____ 3. • Protect your teeth with sturdy Gordon's dental floss.

• Buy Gordon's dental floss, the official floss of the American space program. Protect your teeth the way the astronauts do.

a. Plain folks   c. Glittering generalities
b. Bandwagon   d. Transfer

_____ 4. • We hope you'll find that Choco-Chip Cookies are the best you've ever tasted.

• Try Choco-Chip Cookies—the cookies with goodness that doesn't quit.

a. Name calling   c. Testimonial
b. Glittering generalities   d. Plain folks

_____ 5. • Sea Fair cruises will be touring the Caribbean this summer.

• Don't miss out on this cruise of a lifetime enjoyed by thousands of knowledgeable travelers. Ask your agent for details about Sea Fair's very popular tour of the Caribbean.

a. Glittering generalities   c. Bandwagon
b. Transfer   d. Plain folks

(Continues on next page)

_____ 6. • Come to Smith's Carpets' spring sale.

• We cannot tell a lie—we honor America's Presidents with beauty and savings. Come see Cherry Tree Carpets to see the amazing quality and discounts at our Presidents' Day Sale.

a. Bandwagon
b. Name calling

c. Transfer
d. Plain folks

_____ 7. • The Falcon is designed to provide sports-car handling at an affordable price.

• As a test pilot, Susan Gibbs knows performance. "That's why I drive a Falcon," she says.

a. Bandwagon
b. Glittering generalities

c. Testimonial
d. Transfer

_____ 8. • A modern convention center will draw more conventions to our city.

• A stunning new convention center would be just what's needed to usher us into the twenty-first century.

a. Plain folks
b. Glittering generalities

c. Name calling
d. Bandwagon

_____ 9. • You can make a deal at Dave's Auto Dealership.

• Come early so you won't have to stand in line—because everyone knows you can make a deal with Dave and save.

a. Name calling
b. Transfer

c. Testimonial
d. Bandwagon

_____ 10. • We feel Cheesy Pizza is better than our competitors'.

• Al's Pizza is like the thick cardboard we use to wrap take-home orders of Cheesy Pizza. Eat Cheesy Pizza if you're a pizza lover; eat Al's if you love cardboard.

a. Name calling
b. Glittering generalities

c. Testimonial
d. Plain folks

PROPAGANDA: Test 2

A. Each of the passages below illustrates a particular propaganda technique. On the line next to the passage, write the letter of the technique being used.

_____ 1. The nitwits that make up City Council have created a real crisis in town. Instead of working together to create a permanent solution for our trash-disposal problem, these political clowns and incompetents spent all their time feuding with each other.

   a. Plain folks   c. Bandwagon
   b. Name calling   d. Testimonial

_____ 2. The U. S. Heritage Committee has selected Bubble-O as the official soft drink of the Heritage Celebration to be held in six major American cities this summer. Bubble-O: an important part of your heritage.

   a. Plain folks   c. Transfer
   b. Bandwagon   d. Name calling

_____ 3. Join your neighbors and friends in a massive protest against the proposed landfill. People from all walks of life are forming the overwhelming opposition to this dangerous project. Be a part of this important movement.

   a. Testimonial   c. Bandwagon
   b. Transfer   d. Name calling

_____ 4. James Oliver, the former star of *Avenue A*, is currently talking to kids across America about the dangers of drug addiction. "You don't want drugs," he says. "You don't need them, and remember, they can kill you."

   a. Glittering generalities   c. Transfer
   b. Testimonial   d. Plain folks

_____ 5. "We can work magic with your children," says Eileen of Eileen's Daycare Service. "Call upon us, and your children will be happy you did."

   a. Plain folks   c. Name calling
   b. Transfer   d. Glittering generalities

(Continues on next page)

_____ 6. Federal programs seem to be full of cheats and frauds, like the people who collect high salaries for doing no more than shuffling papers. These lazy good-for-nothings should be fired.

a. Glittering generalities   c. Name calling
b. Bandwagon   d. Transfer

_____ 7. Senator Bob Curren's rough-hewn manners and casual style are sure to be popular with the little guy. We think that the people of this country are ready for a down-to-earth candidate.

a. Plain folks   c. Glittering generalities
b. Name calling   d. Transfer

_____ 8. An Arnold Autofocus camera is the camera of your dreams. This delightful camera will make all your photography a pleasure. You'll love your new Arnold Autofocus.

a. Transfer   c. Bandwagon
b. Glittering generalities   d. Name calling

B. The following ads involve card stacking—in some way, they are too good to be true. Circle the letter of the important detail that the advertiser has intentionally omitted.

9. Congratulations, Ms. Kerr, you are among the finalists for the National Book Club's 10 Million Dollar Lottery.
   a. The ten million dollars will be split among several winners.
   b. There are several million other people who are also among the finalists.
   c. The company has sponsored lotteries for twenty years.

10. For only $25, Employment Education, Inc. will send you complete information on how to earn money stuffing envelopes at home.
   a. It is not difficult to stuff envelopes.
   b. The company also sells information on learning to type.
   c. Very few people are ever hired to stuff envelopes at home.

PROPAGANDA: Test 3

Read each of the passages below, and then circle the letter of the best answer to each question.

A. ¹First America Bank offers a remarkable protection plan for lost or stolen credit cards. ²For only fifteen dollars, you can buy credit card protection that covers your losses up to $10,000. ³Isn't this impressive guarantee worth the small yearly fee? ⁴Losing a credit card naturally causes some anxiety, but First America's protection plan frees you from needless worry. ⁵We notify your credit card company, and we cover your losses, all for one astonishingly low fee. ⁶Remember, First America Bank is as sound as the country it serves so well.

1. Which propaganda technique is used in sentence 6?
   a. Plain folks
   b. Transfer
   c. Bandwagon
   d. Testimonial

2. Which of the following missing details has the advertiser intentionally omitted?
   a. Federal law limits a card owner's legal responsibility for lost or stolen credit cards to fifty dollars.
   b. The First America protection plan covers no more than twenty credit cards.
   c. A lost or stolen credit card should be reported within forty-eight hours.
   d. The bank offers its own Red, White, and Blue Bank Card to members in the plan.

B. The idea that doctors should be able to sell the drugs they prescribe to their patients is outrageous. The current situation, in which patients take prescriptions from their doctors to their pharmacists, provides a check on doctors' greed. Doctors claim they want to make acquiring drugs more convenient for their patients, but they are clearly involved in a case of conflict of interest. What prevents doctors from prescribing unneeded drugs in order to improve their profit margins? Drug salespeople tempt doctors to enter this racket by promising increased profits of $30,000 to $50,000 a year. The greedy doctors in this country are hearing the cash registers ringing, but shouldn't they be keeping their minds on the oath they took when they entered their profession?

3. Which propaganda technique is being used in this paragraph?
   a. Bandwagon
   b. Name calling
   c. Testimonial
   d. Plain folks

(Continues on next page)

4. Which words are being used in that technique?
   a. Drug salespeople
   b. Current situation
   c. Their profession
   d. Greedy doctors

C.   [1]Wouldn't a hot cup of coffee taste great right now? [2]With a Dr. Zip coffee maker, a fresh cup like Mom has always made for Dad will be ready in minutes. [3]If you wish, you can even set Dr. Zip's automatic timer to prepare a heavenly pot of coffee to greet you first thing in the morning. [4]Dr. Zip has lots of convenient features, like the brew-strength lever that lets you decide how strong you want your coffee to be. [5]And you can make as many as twelve cups of coffee at one time with a Dr. Zip coffee maker. [6]Follow the lead of Richie Martz, basketball's highest scorer this season, who says, "Every morning, I'm a beast until I get my first delicious cup of coffee from Dr. Zip."

5. Which propaganda device is used in sentence 2?
   a. Testimonial
   b. Plain folks
   c. Name calling
   d. Transfer

6. Which of the following is a glittering detail?
   a. Ready in minutes
   b. Heavenly pot of coffee
   c. Automatic timer
   d. Brew strength lever

7. Which propaganda device is used in sentence 6?
   a. Testimonial
   b. Name calling
   c. Plain folks
   d. Bandwagon

8. Which of the following details has the advertiser intentionally omitted?
   a. It takes only four minutes for coffee to brew in a Dr. Zip coffee maker.
   b. The coffee maker allows you to make as few as two cups at a time.
   c. The twelve cups made by the coffee maker equal ten cups of other coffee makers.
   d. The Dr. Zip company also makes its own brand of coffee.

PROPAGANDA: Test 4

Read each of the passages below, and then circle the letter of the best answer to each question.

A. Try Mrs. Green's new Lite Line Cereals. We use only vegetables oils—and no animal fats at all! Try all of our new bright lites—Grandma's Granola, Tropical Wheat Flakes, and Nutty Nut Bran. True to its name, Tropical Wheat flakes contains coconut and the finest of coconut oil, and Nutty Nut Bran has more nuts per bite than any other cereal.

1. Which propaganda technique is probably the reason for the name "Grandma's Granola"?
   a. Bandwagon   c. Testimonial
   b. Glittering generalities d. Plain folks

2. Which propaganda technique describes the phrase "bright lites"?
   a. Transfer   c. Name calling
   b. Glittering generalities d. Bandwagon

3-4. Which *two* of the following details has the advertiser purposely omitted?
   a. Butter is an animal fat.
   b. Coconut oil is known to raise cholesterol levels.
   c. Nuts are very high-fat foods.
   d. Nuts are high in protein.

B. [1]You probably know many people who are constantly on a diet, starving themselves and yearning for forbidden hot fudge sundaes. [2]Did you know that at least ninety-five percent of the weight that is lost through all this effort is regained? [3]A new movement is based on the belief that the cycle of losing and regaining weight is worse for people than maintaining a stable (yet plump) weight. [4]Thousands of people are joining Roberta Rice, a champion of this splendid new cause, in the pledge, "I'll never diet again." [5]True, Miss Rice weighs much more than the vain models whose sickly thin thighs are displayed in fashion magazines. [6]But she is attractive, self-confident, and delighted with her role in the new movement. [7]She even reports that after she lost her obsession with food, she lost some weight.

5. Which propaganda technique is used in sentence 4?
   a. Name calling   c. Bandwagon
   b. Transfer   d. Plain-folks

(Continues on next page)

6. Which propaganda technique is used in sentence 5?
   a. Bandwagon
   c. Name calling
   b. Testimonial
   d. Glittering generalities

C. [1]Have you ever wondered why the prices at Broad Street Cameras are always lower than many of our competitors'? [2]Our magnificent discounts and amazing low prices are possible because of our wise policy. [3]That policy is to buy our products from independent importers who charge less than the companies that others choose as their official importers. [4]As a result, we pay less than many of our competitors, and so we charge less. [5]Our warehouse is fully stocked now with cameras, computers, and video equipment, so don't buy until you see us.

7. Which is a glittering detail?
   a. Lower than many of our competitors'
   b. Magnificent discounts
   c. Independent importers
   d. Warehouse is fully stocked

8. Which of the following details has the advertiser intentionally omitted?
   a. Broad Street Cameras' imported goods come with English-language instructions.
   b. The company sells both German and Japanese cameras.
   c. Companies that are not officially chosen as importers are still legitimate businesses.
   d. Goods not ordered from manufacturers' official importers do not have a manufacturer's U.S. warranty.

PROPAGANDA: Test 5

A. Below are descriptions of eight *actual* ads. On each line, write the letter of the main propaganda technique that applies to the ad.

a. Bandwagon	d. Plain folks
b. Testimonial	e. Name calling
c. Transfer	f. Glittering generalities

_____ 1. An ad for a Canon personal copier features a photo of television actor and sleight-of-hand card magician Harry Anderson. Anderson is quoted as saying, ". . . now, bingo, I'm knocking out clean, crisp copies on everything from business cards to . . . transparencies, faster than a three-handed card dealer."

_____ 2. A Ford ad states, "More repeat buyers than anyone, domestic or import" and "The Best-Selling Cars and Trucks Four Years Running."

_____ 3. An ad for Black Velvet Canadian Whiskey includes a large photo of a beautiful, sexy-looking blonde woman dressed in a strapless black velvet dress and gold jewelry. In the corner of the ad is a small picture of the whiskey.

_____ 4. An ad claims that Carlton cigarettes have "a taste that's right."

_____ 5. A Haggar slacks ad features a large photo of a smiling father holding a baseball mitt with one hand and holding his other arm around his smiling young son. The boy— wearing jeans a T-shirt, and a baseball cap—is holding a baseball bat and a mitt.

_____ 6. A Domino's Pizza ad says, "If Their Delivered Pizza Is So Hot, Why Do They Give You Reheating Instructions?" Under this question is a picture of a Pizza Hut box, which includes a message about "Reheating Instructions."

_____ 7. The Quaker Oats box features a picture of a man in Quaker dress. (The Quakers are a religious sect known for their honesty, integrity, and concern for others.) On the label is the slogan, "Quaker Oats. It's The Right Thing To Do."

_____ 8. A friendly-looking young man in a sweatshirt is pictured on an ad for AT&T Long Distance. The ad tells us his name is Nick Joost and that he's from Austin, Texas. Lines beneath the photos read, "My Daddy always had a saying—he said, 'Don't ever be afraid to buy the best. You'll always be happy with it.' So I did."

(Continues on next page)

B. The following ads involve card stacking—in some way, they are too good to be true. Circle the letter of the important detail that the advertiser has intentionally omitted.

9. An ad for a shaving gel for women claimed, "New Soft Sense Moisturizing Shave Gel with Vitamin E." It went on to say, "You've never shaved so soft." Circle the letter of the detail below that you think has been omitted:
   a. What the scent of the gel is like
   b. Whether or not vitamin E has been proven to moisturize well, or at all
   c. The percentage of women who have decided not to shave their legs at all

10. Bounty came out with a new roll of paper towels that carried the slogan "New! More Absorbent Than Ever." Circle the letter of the detail below that you think Bounty omitted:
    a. The new towels are 10% more absorbent than before.
    b. The new roll has fewer sheets of towels than before.
    c. The price has remained the same.

PROPAGANDA: Test 6

A. Below are descriptions of eight *actual* ads. On each line, write the letter of the main propaganda technique that applies to the ad.

a. Bandwagon   d. Plain folks
b. Testimonial   e. Name calling
c. Transfer   f. Glittering generalities

_____ 1. In an ad for Purina O·N·E dog food, actor Robert Urich is quoted as saying, "To me, there are two kinds of dog food. Purina O·N·E, and the rest."

_____ 2. "Sometimes the littlest people have the biggest coughs," says an ad for Robitussin with a picture of an average-looking mother reading to her child. Robitussin Pediatric Cough Suppressant, says the ad, is "Recommended by 'Dr. Mom.'"

_____ 3. A handsome young man applies Armor All car protectant to his car while an attractive blonde in a black mini-skirt walks by and admires his car's shine. An announcer's voice says, "Armor All—It keeps you looking good."

_____ 4. A TV ad shows a man trying frantically without success to find a place where he can use his American Express card to get some cash. The ad then points out that people with a MasterCard can get cash easily.

_____ 5. "How do you make something taste so fattening when it's at least 98% fat free?" asks an ad for Sara Lee low-fat baked products. "Make it 100% Sara Lee."

_____ 6. An ad for Scott Prints paper napkins states, "Our New Designs Are So Pretty, They're On Everyone's Lips."

_____ 7. An ad for Ultra Slim-Fast features before and after photos of six well-known people from various fields, including Los Angeles Dodgers coach Tommy Lasorda and former mayor of New York City Ed Koch. The caption says, "If We Can Do It, You Can Do It!"

_____ 8. An ad for Superslims cigarettes features a super-slim, beautiful and sexy woman relaxing with a Superslim cigarette.

(Continues on next page)

B. The following ads involve card stacking—in some way, they are too good to be true. Circle the letter of the important detail that the advertiser has intentionally omitted.

9. An MCI TV ad suggests you can save money with MCI by giving the company a list of people you often call long-distance. What information has the advertiser intentionally omitted?
   a. The program is relatively new.
   b. For you to save the money, the people you name must also join MCI.
   c. Competing companies have no such program.

10. The Kellogg's Corn Pops box explains that an ounce of Corn Pops (once called Sugar Pops) contains less sugar than an apple, a banana, or two pancakes with syrup. What information has the advertiser intentionally omitted?
   a. Corn Pops contains less sugar than cola drinks.
   b. Corn Pops can be eaten out of the box like a snack.
   c. Many people eat more than an ounce of Corn Pops for breakfast.

ARGUMENT: Test 1

A. In each of the following groups of statements, one statement is the point, and the other statement or statements are support for the point. Identify each point with a **P**, and identify each statement of support with an **S**.

Group 1

1. _____ Often you'll wait half an hour for a Route 27 bus, and then three will show up at once.

2. _____ Sometimes Route 27 buses will roar right past you at a bus stop, even though they aren't full.

3. _____ Route 27 seems to be assigned the oldest buses, ones that rattle and have broken seats.

4. _____ Whenever possible, people should not ride the Route 27 bus.

Group 2

5. _____ Cats refuse to learn silly tricks just to amuse people.

6. _____ Cats seem to be more intelligent than dogs.

7. _____ Dogs will accept cruel mistreatment, but if a cat is mistreated, she will run away.

Group 3

8. _____ At 29, Lincoln plunged into depression after the death of his first wife.

9. _____ Lincoln suffered another bout of depression around the time he was to marry Mary Todd.

10. _____ During the great Lincoln-Douglas debates, Lincoln had a depressive episode.

11. _____ The bout of depression Lincoln suffering during his presidency, when his son Willy died, was not his first.

(Continues on next page)

B. Each of the three points below is followed by six items, three of which logically support the point and three of which do not. In the spaces provided, write the letters of the three items that logically support each point.

Point: My old car is ready for the junkpile.
   a. The body has rusted through, and water trickles down on me if I drive it in the rain.
   b. The car is painted a particularly ugly shade of green.
   c. I've saved up enough to buy a much better car.
   d. My mechanic says its engine is too worn to be repaired, and the car isn't worth the cost of a new one.
   e. I never really did like that car very much.
   f. Its brakes are shot.

12–14. Items that logically support the point: _____ _____ _____

Point: Sunbathers should be careful to avoid excessive exposure to solar rays.
   a. In recent years, the sun has been particularly active in producing harmful rays.
   b. Beachgoers should also be aware of water pollution.
   c. Air pollution has destroyed some of the ozone in the atmosphere, which protects against solar rays.
   d. Too much exposure to the sun can lead to skin cancer.
   e. Protective suntan lotions can filter out many of the harmful rays.
   f. Other countries have stricter laws against air pollution.

15–17. Items that logically support the point: _____ _____ _____

Point: Our town diner is an unsanitary health hazard and ought to be closed down.
   a. Everything on the menu is high in fat, cholesterol, or both.
   b. The last time I ate at the diner I got food poisoning and was sick for two days.
   c. For the prices the diner charges, the food ought to be better than it is.
   d. The city inspector found roaches in the diner's kitchen.
   e. Most of the customers at the diner are a shabby, untidy lot.
   f. The toilet in the diner often backs up.

18–20. Items that logically support the point: _____ _____ _____

ARGUMENT: Test 2

A. In each of the following groups of statements, one statement is the point, and the other statement or statements are support for the point. Identify each point with a **P**, and identify each statement of support with an **S**.

Group 1

1. _____ Conditions in the workplace are tougher than they used to be.
2. _____ In many industries, workers have had to take wage cuts.
3. _____ If workers go on strike, they now may lose their jobs to replacement workers.

Group 2

4. _____ The biggest female stars make less than the most famous male stars.
5. _____ Very few good roles are written for older women.
6. _____ The film industry tends to treat women as second-class citizens.
7. _____ Only a handful of women have been allowed to direct major motion pictures.

Group 3

8. _____ I feel dread every time I sit down to take our Friday math quiz.
9. _____ During the math midterm, I "froze" and didn't even try to answer most of the questions.
10. _____ I'm a perfect example of someone who has "math anxiety."
11. _____ I turned down a salesclerk job because I would have had to figure out how much change customers should get back.

(Continues on next page)

B. Each of the three points below is followed by six items, three of which logically support the point and three of which do not. In the spaces provided, write the letters of the three items that logically support each point.

Point: Eating yogurt is healthy.
   a. Yogurt contains natural antibiotics that can prevent certain kinds of infection.
   b. Yogurt is available in nearly all food stores.
   c. Yogurt kills the bacteria that can cause diarrhea.
   d. You can substitute yogurt in many recipes calling for milk or sour cream.
   e. Yogurt is a staple of the diet in many Middle Eastern countries.
   f. Eating yogurt has been shown to lower cholesterol levels.

12–14.   Items that logically support the point: _____ _____ _____

Point: Selling cigarettes ought to be against the law.
   a. Cigarette smoking kills many more people than all illegal drugs combined.
   b. Today, tobacco growing is actually supported by government subsidies.
   c. Cigarette ads are aimed at young adults and promote smoking as glamorous.
   d. Alcohol is another legal drug that kills numerous Americans every year.
   e. Non-smokers are endangered by breathing the smoke from others' cigarettes.
   f. Tobacco is one of the most addictive of all drugs.

15–17.   Items that logically support the point: _____ _____ _____

Point: Religion is a powerful force in modern American life.
   a. The main religion in America is Christianity.
   b. Television evangelists are able to gather millions of dollars from contributors.
   c. Religious leaders are often influential voices on public issues in America.
   d. One of the fundamental principles of America is the separation between church and state.
   e. The Pilgrims came to America seeking religious freedom.
   f. Public opinion polls show that a majority of Americans consider religion personally important to them.

18–20.   Items that logically support the point: _____ _____ _____

ARGUMENT: Test 3

A. Circle the letter of the one sentence in each paragraph that does not support the point of the argument. The point (main idea) is set off in **boldface** type.

1. [1]**Short-term goals encourage self-discipline better than distant aims.** [2]For instance, dieters lose more weight by attempting to shed two pounds a week than by worrying about a total of twenty pounds or more. [3]Low-fat diets are another help for dieters. [4]Also, students who try to increase study time by a half-hour each day do better than those who think only about compiling straight "A" averages. [5]And alcoholics and drug addicts achieve more lasting recovery when they deal with their problems one day at a time.

    Which statement does not support the author's conclusion that short-term goals are better for will power than long-term goals?

    a. Sentence 2
    b. Sentence 3
    c. Sentence 4
    d. Sentence 5

2. [1]**There are some simple ways to make sure your home is a safer place.** [2]First, never run electrical cords across floors, where you can trip over them, or under rugs or carpets, where repeated footsteps can fray their protective coating. [3]Second, place non-skid mats or decals on the floor of your tub and/or shower. [4]Also, for greater comfort in the tub, buy one of those inflatable bathtub pillows. [5]Last, never cover the ventilation space around television sets, stereos or other vented appliances. [6]Even placing appliances up against, or too near, a wall can prevent proper ventilation. [7]The result can be an overheated appliance, which presents a fire hazard.

    Which statement does not support the author's conclusion that there are some simple ways to make your home safer?

    a. Sentence 2
    b. Sentence 3
    c. Sentence 4
    d. Sentence 5

(Continues on next page)

B. Check the conclusion that is best supported by the evidence in each group below.

Group 1

- The instructions for my new VCR might as well be written in Greek.
- When I try to tape a show, I get either nothing but "snow" or else I record the wrong channel.
- I have managed to ruin movies I've rented from the video store.

3. Which of the following is best supported by the evidence above?

___ a. The speaker doesn't know how to deal with any mechanical gadgets.

___ b. VCRs are a waste of money.

___ c. The speaker doesn't know how to use many of his VCR's features.

___ d. VCRs are too complicated for most consumers.

Group 2

- Under airline deregulation, one airline may have, for all practical purposes, a monopoly over air service to many cities.
- Since the airlines were deregulated, airline fleets have become older and maintenance standards have slipped.
- Airline deregulation has produced airline fares that are so confusing and complicated that even professional travel agents can't always figure them out.

4. Which of the following is best supported by the evidence above?

___ a. Deregulation of an industry is always a bad idea.

___ b. Airline deregulation has had some negative consequences.

___ c. Flying is now more dangerous than driving.

___ d. Travel agents earn more money than they're worth.

C. Circle the letter of the fallacy contained in the argument below.

5. A local association wants to establish a home in our neighborhood for retarded people. But the neighbors oppose the home; they don't want dangerous psychopaths roaming our streets.

a. Personal attack *(the argument shifts to irrelevant personal criticism)*

b. Circular reasoning *(a statement repeats itself rather than providing a real supporting reason to back up an argument)*

c. Straw man *(an argument is made by claiming an opponent holds an extreme position and then opposing that extreme position)*

ARGUMENT: Test 6

A. One sentence in each paragraph does not support the point of the argument. Answer each question by circling the letter of the sentence that does *not* support the argument.

1. [1]Everyone should have a living will, which is a legal document that states you do not want useless life-prolonging medical treatment when a major illness leaves no hope for recovery. [2]You can draw up your own living will, but because laws are complicated you should at least have an attorney review the will. [3]A living will means your wishes will be followed even if you become too ill to communicate. [4]That means you will be protected from being forced to painfully extend your death. [5]Without such an arrangement, your family is bound to suffer the financial and emotional stress of prolonging your death.

   Which of the following statements does *not* support the author's conclusion that everyone should have a living will?

   a. Sentence 2
   b. Sentence 3
   c. Sentence 4
   d. Sentence 5

2. [1]Renting a movie for a VCR makes much more sense these days than going to see a movie at a theater. [2]First of all, the large selection of video movies will always be many times greater than the available choices at all the neighborhood theaters and malls. [3]The rental stores even offer cassettes of made-for-television movies, foreign films, and classics like the legendary comedies of Charlie Chaplin. [4]Also, the low cost of film rental is well below the price of admission to a movie these days. [5]And you won't have to put up with noisy patrons drowning out the sound track with their personal conversations or comments on the action on the screen. [6]These ill-mannered moviegoers should be ejected from a theater when they create a disturbance.

   Which of the following statements does *not* support the author's conclusion that renting movies makes more sense than going to see movies at a theater?

   a. Sentence 3
   b. Sentence 4
   c. Sentence 5
   d. Sentence 6

(Continues on next page)

B. Check the letter of the conclusion that is best supported by the evidence in each group below.

Group 1

- Sex, or the lack of it, plays no role in the development of acne.
- Eating greasy foods and chocolate won't cause acne.
- Picking at or squeezing a pimple won't cause acne.

3. Which of the following conclusions is best supported by the evidence above?

___ a. Over-the-counter acne products don't work.

___ b. Greasy foods are not bad for you.

___ c. Everyone has acne sooner or later.

___ d. There are some widely believed myths about the cause of acne.

Group 2

- Vitamin C is not stored in the body fat like some other vitamins.
- Any vitamin C not used by the body is excreted within a few hours.
- In addition, vitamin C is an acid, and thus it's best not to take large doses of it on an empty stomach.

4. Which of the following conclusions is best supported by the evidence above?

___ a. Everyone should take supplemental doses of vitamin C.

___ b. For people who take vitamin C pills, it is more efficient to take one pill a day.

___ c. People should spread out vitamin C intake through the day.

___ d. People should never take any amount of vitamin C on an empty stomach.

C. Circle the letter of the fallacy contained in the argument below.

5. We'd never have all those wonderful synthetic fabrics without chemicals, so what's wrong with using plenty of chemicals on our farms?

a. False cause (*the argument assumes that the order of events alone shows cause and effect*)

b. False comparison (*the argument assumes that two things being compared are more alike than they really are*)

c. Either-or (*the argument assumes that there are only two sides to a question*)

COMBINED SKILLS: Test 3

After reading the paragraph, circle the letter of the best answer to each question.

[1]Little League baseball in its present form should be abolished. [2]For one thing, the pressure that children are put under to succeed may harm them more than help them. [3]One mother discovered her son taking Maalox tablets from the medicine chest whenever a game approached. [4]He explained that they helped relieve the stomach burn he would feel during the game. [5]Other children have been found taking tranquilizers. [6]Another drawback to today's Little League baseball is that some parents take the game too seriously and set a bad example for their children. [7]Recently, a disillusioned coach said, "At our field, we put the bleachers way back from the dugout where the players are. [8]That way, parents can't be hissing down advice to their children all the time and getting them upset." [9]A final reason Little League should be abolished is that it doesn't offer enough success to most players. [10]Instead, the game revolves around the more developed kids who are able to hit and throw the ball harder than the smaller children. [11]In one recent game, most of the batters were clearly afraid of the speed of the hardball, which was pitched by a boy bigger than many of the other players. [12]A viable alternative to Little League hardball would be lob-pitch softball. [13]The ball is pitched slowly and underhand and offers a high level of success to kids without a high level of ability. [14]Lob-pitch softball should get more children involved in the game, and help people remember that it *is* a game—not an adult arena where one is branded with success or failure.

1. In sentence 12, the word *viable* means
   a. dangerous.
   b. workable.
   c. impractical.
   d. professional.

2. According to the author, one advantage of lob-pitch softball is
   a. the ball's weight.
   b. the lesser degree of skill required.
   c. the field size.
   d. the players' ages.

3. The relationship of sentence 6 to the sentences that come before it is one of
   a. time.
   b. addition.
   c. contrast.
   d. comparison.

(Continues on next page)

4. Sentence 1 is a statement of
   a. fact.
   b. opinion.
   c. fact and opinion.

5. From the passage, you can conclude the author would agree with the idea that
   a. it's not whether you win or lose, it's how you play the game.
   b. competition in baseball helps prepare people for competition in life.
   c. children's games should imitate adults' games.
   d. sports should help children learn that there are winners and losers in life.

6. The author's main purpose is
   a. to inform.
   b. to persuade.
   c. to entertain.
   d. to predict.

7. What is the most appropriate title for this selection?
   a. The Pressures on Today's Children
   b. Lob-Pitch Softball
   c. Let's Reform Little League
   d. Sportsmanship in Baseball

8. The main idea of the passage is that
   a. some parents of Little League players are immature.
   b. Little League hardball should be abolished.
   c. bigger kids dominate Little League baseball in its present form.
   d. Lob-Pitch softball is easier than hardball baseball.

COMBINED SKILLS: Test 4

After reading the paragraph, circle the letter of the best answer to each question.

¹Earlier in this century, Halloween was a night when roving gangs (usually boys) played elaborate tricks on their neighbors. ²These tricks more closely resembled practical jokes than vandalism. ³For example, the boys might lift an outhouse off its foundations and move it to someone else's yard, or they might remove a screen door from its hinges and leave it on the owner's roof. ⁴Such tricks required skill and planning, and the victims were usually neighbors or relatives. ⁵Thus, Halloween was a night when adolescents took their "revenge" on adults in a way that was, for the most part, tolerated by the community.

⁶Today, the holiday mischief has degenerated into destructive vandalism, such as tire slashing and window breaking. ⁷These kinds of actions require no skill or intelligence. ⁸In addition, instead of the small offerings—an apple or a piece of cake—meant to be given in exchange for protection from practical jokes, trick-or-treaters demand bagfuls of commercial candy bars from the numerous people, many of them strangers, on a collection route. ⁹But the most alarming and repulsive aspect of the new Halloween combines evildoing and food in the worst way—now criminals insert pins into candy bars and razors into apples. ¹⁰Thus Halloween has been transformed into an event, not of harmless fun, but of greed, vandalism, and occasional terror.

1. Earlier in the century, children celebrated Halloween by
   a. committing vandalism.
   b. begging for candy bars.
   c. working for the community.
   d. playing practical jokes.

2. On the whole, the relationship between the two paragraphs is one of
   a. comparison.
   b. contrast.
   c. cause and effect.
   d. definition and example.

3. The words *these kinds of actions* in sentence 7 refer to
   a. holiday mischief.
   b. tire slashing and window breaking.
   c. trick-or-treaters demanding bagfuls of candy.
   d. taking "revenge" on adults.

(Continues on next page)

4. The author's attitude toward today's Halloween is
   a. sympathetic.
   b. critical.
   c. doubtful.
   d. unrealistic.

5. The author would probably agree with the idea that
   a. today, Halloween brings out some of our worst qualities.
   b. any kind of door-to-door solicitation is a form of begging.
   c. tire slashing is simple adolescent mischief.
   d. teenage boys are responsible for the change in Halloween.

6. From the passage you could conclude that earlier in this century
   a. children in effect bribed people to give them treats.
   b. holidays were more fun than they are now.
   c. girls never participated in the Halloween tricks.
   d. children had a sense of humor and pride about their Halloween tricks.

7. What is the most accurate title for this selection?
   a. Halloween: A Change for the Worse
   b. A Traditional Holiday
   c. Halloween Terror
   d. The Charm of the Past

8. Which statement best expresses the main idea of the passage?
   a. Halloween celebrations should be banned.
   b. Children today don't want to work for their rewards.
   c. Halloween has deteriorated into a time of greed and terror.
   d. Halloween is an event when adolescents are allowed to take their revenge on adults.

COMBINED SKILLS: Test 5

After reading the paragraph, circle the letter of the best answer to each question.

[1]Mary was watching a mystery on television. [2]The end of the movie was near, and she was totally engrossed. [3]Then her baby started crying. [4]She shouted at him to shut up. [5]His response was intensified crying. [6]Mary got angry and shook him. [7]The baby cried even louder. [8]In the meanwhile, the mystery's conclusion took place, and Mary missed it. [9]Angrily, she slapped her son's face. [10]In this situation, someone was pursuing a goal—seeing the end of a suspenseful television show. [11]But something happened to block the achievement of that goal. [12]The person thus became frustrated, anger built up, and direct aggression occurred.

[13]Aggression is not always aimed at the original frustrator. [14]For example, consider a businessman who has a hard day at the office. [15]He was about to close a deal with a client when his boss clumsily interfered and lost the sale. [16]On the way home in his car, the frustrated businessman blew his horn angrily at a car ahead when it didn't pull immediately away from a stoplight. [17]As he entered his home, his dog jumped up on him, only to receive a quick kick. [18]He then shouted at his wife during supper. [19]All these aggressive behaviors are examples of displaced aggression. [20]Aggression against the person who caused the original frustration can often be harmful. [21]In this case, assaulting or swearing at the boss could cost the businessman his job. [22]When the original frustrator has status and power over the frustrated person, aggression may be displaced onto a less threatening target, who may have nothing at all to do with the original frustration.

1. In sentence 2 of the passage, the word *engrossed* means
   a. absorbed.
   b. alone.
   c. lost.
   d. bored.

2. Aggression is more likely to be displaced if the original frustrator
   a. is a family member.
   b. has power over the frustrated person.
   c. is angry at the frustrated person.
   d. is unfair to the frustrated person.

3. The relationship between sentences 11 and 12 is one of
   a general idea and example.
   b. comparison.
   c. contrast.
   d. cause and effect.

(Continues on next page)

4. The main pattern of organization of *each* paragraph is
   a. list of items.
   b. contrast.
   c. comparison.
   d. cause and effect.

5. The second paragraph explains and illustrates the term
   a. aggression.
   b. direct aggression.
   c. indirect aggression.
   d. frustration.

6. The writer's main purpose in writing this selection is to:
   a predict how aggression influences relationships.
   b. inform readers about two types of aggression.
   c. persuade readers to be careful not to take out their aggression on the wrong people.
   d. entertain readers with dramatic anecdotes about aggressive behavior.

7. What is the best title for the selection?
   a Aggression
   b The Causes of Aggression
   c. Direct and Displaced Aggression
   d. Displaced Aggression

8. Which sentence best states the main idea of the selection?
   a. A great deal of frustration is aimed against family members.
   b. When frustration and anger build up, direct or displaced aggression may occur.
   c. Sometimes a frustrator may have a great deal more power or status than the person who is frustrated.
   d. Direct aggression is more satisfying than indirect aggression.

Part III

TEN READING SELECTIONS

1

The Yellow Ribbon
Pete Hamill

Preview

When is a yellow handkerchief like a pair of open arms? For the answer, read this selection, which first appeared in a *New York Post* newspaper column by Pete Hamill. The story became the inspiration for the popular song "Tie a Yellow Ribbon 'Round the Old Oak Tree." This moving article probably also describes the origin of using yellow ribbons as a symbol of America's wish to see her troops return home safely.

Words to Watch

cocoon (2): protective covering
bluntness (13): abruptness
exaltation (22): joy

They were going to Fort Lauderdale, the girl remembered later. There were six of them, three boys and three girls, and they picked up the bus at the old terminal on 34th Street, carrying sandwiches and wine in paper bags, dreaming of golden beaches and the tides of the sea as the gray cold spring of New York vanished behind them. Vingo was on board from the beginning.

As the bus passed through Jersey and into Philly, they began to notice that Vingo never moved. He sat in front of the young people, his dusty face masking his age, dressed in a plain brown ill-fitting suit. His fingers were stained from cigarettes and he chewed the inside of his lip a lot, frozen into some personal cocoon° of silence.

Somewhere outside of Washington, deep into the night, the bus pulled into a Howard Johnson's, and everybody got off except Vingo. He sat rooted in his seat, and the young people began to wonder about him, trying to imagine his life: Perhaps he was a sea captain, maybe he had run away from his wife, he could be an old soldier going home. When they went back to the bus, the girl sat beside him and introduced herself.

"We're going to Florida," the girl said brightly. "You going that far?"   4

"I don't know." Vingo said.   5

"I've never been there," she said. "I hear it's beautiful."   6

"It is," he said quietly, as if remembering something he had tried to forget.   7

"You live there?"   8

"I did some time there in the Navy. Jacksonville."   9

"Want some wine?" she said. He smiled and took the bottle of Chianti and took a   10
swig. He thanked her and retreated again into his silence. After a while, she went back to the others, as Vingo nodded in sleep.

In the morning they awoke outside another Howard Johnson's, and this time   11
Vingo went in. The girl insisted that he join them. He seemed very shy and ordered black coffee and smoked nervously, as the young people chattered about sleeping on the beaches. When they went back on the bus, the girl sat with Vingo again, and after a while, slowly and painfully and with great hesitation, he began to tell his story. He had been in jail in New York for the last four years, and now he was going home.

"Four years!" the girl said. "What did you do?"   12

"It doesn't matter," he said with quiet bluntness°. "I did it and I went to jail. If you   13
can't do the time, don't do the crime. That's what they say and they're right."

"Are you married?"   14

"I don't know."   15

"You don't know?" she said.   16

"Well, when I was in the can I wrote to my wife," he said. "I told her, I said,   17
Martha, I understand if you can't stay married to me. I told her that. I said I was gonna be away a long time, and that if she couldn't stand it, if the kids kept askin' questions, if it hurt her too much, well, she could just forget me. Get a new guy— she's a wonderful woman, really something—and forget about me. I told her she didn't have to write me or nothing. And she didn't. Not for three-and-half years."

"And you're going home now, not knowing?"   18

"Yeah," he said shyly. "Well, last week, when I was sure the parole was coming   19
through I wrote her. I told her that if she had a new guy, I understood. But if she didn't, if she would take me back she should let me know. We used to live in this town, Brunswick, just before Jacksonville, and there's a great big oak tree just as you come into town, a very famous tree, huge. I told her if she would take me back, she should put a yellow handkerchief on the tree, and I would get off and come home. If she didn't want me, forget it, no handkerchief, and I'd keep going on through."

"Wow," the girl said. "Wow."   20

She told the others, and soon all of them were in it, caught up in the approach of   21
Brunswick, looking at the pictures Vingo showed them of his wife and three children, the woman handsome in a plain way, the children still unformed in a cracked, much-handled snapshot. Now they were 20 miles from Brunswick and the young people took over window seats on the right side, waiting for the approach of the great oak tree. Vingo stopped looking, tightening his face into the ex-con's mask, as if fortifying himself against still another disappointment. Then it was 10 miles, and then five and the bus acquired a dark hushed mood, full of silence, of absence, of lost years, of the woman's plain face, of the sudden letter on the breakfast table, of the wonder of children, of the iron bars of solitude.

Then suddenly all of the young people were up out of their seats, screaming and   22
shouting and crying, doing small dances, shaking clenched fists in triumph and
exaltation°. All except Vingo.

Vingo sat there stunned, looking at the oak tree. It was covered with yellow   23
handkerchiefs, 20 of them, 30 of them, maybe hundreds, a tree that stood like a banner
of welcome blowing and billowing in the wind, turned into a gorgeous yellow blur by
the passing bus. As the young people shouted, the old con slowly rose from his seat,
holding himself tightly, and made his way to the front of the bus to go home.

BASIC SKILL QUESTIONS

Vocabulary in Context

1. The word *fortifying* in "tightening his face into the ex-con's mask, as if
   fortifying himself against still another disappointment" (paragraph 21)
   means
   a. strengthening.
   b. watching.
   c. hurrying.
   d. losing.

2. The word *acquired* in "the bus acquired a dark hushed mood" (paragraph
   21) means
   a. needed.
   b. took on.
   c. stopped.
   d. lost.

Central Point and Main Ideas

3. Which sentence best expresses the main idea of this selection?
   a. Prison sentences can ruin marriages.
   b. A bus ride to Florida can be an interesting experience.
   c. Vingo did not know what to expect.
   d. Vingo returned from prison to find that his wife still loved him.

4. Which sentence best expresses the main idea of paragraph 3?
   a. The bus stopped at a Howard Johnson's.
   b. The young people began to be curious about Vingo.
   c. Vingo might have been a sea captain.
   d. Everyone got off the bus except Vingo.

Supporting Details

5. __F__ TRUE OR FALSE? Vingo felt he should not have been put in prison.

Transitions

6. The relationship between the two sentences below is one of
   a. time.
   b. contrast.
   c. comparison.
   d. illustration.

   > ". . . I told her that if she had a new guy, I understood. But if she didn't, if she would take me back she should let me know." (Paragraph 19)

7. The transition words *as, when, after, now,* and *then,* which Hamill uses throughout this selection, all signal
   a. cause and effect.
   b. illustration.
   c. contrast.
   d. time.

8. The relationship expressed in the phrase "a tree that stood like a banner of welcome" (paragraph 23) is one of
   a. contrast.
   b. comparison.
   c. cause and effect.
   d. time.

Patterns of Organization

9. The main pattern of organization of paragraph 2 is
   a. cause and effect.
   b. comparison and contrast.
   c. list of items.
   d. time order.

10. The main pattern of organization of the entire selection is
    a. cause and effect.
    b. comparison and contrast.
    c. list of items.
    d. time order.

ADVANCED SKILL QUESTIONS

Fact and Opinion

11. In telling this narrative, Hamill
    a. stresses his own opinions.
    b. leaves out any of Vingo's opinions.
    c. leaves out any of the young people's opinions.
    d. includes some of Vingo's and some of the young people's opinions.

12. Judging by the first sentence of the selection, Hamill got some facts for this non-fiction narrative by
    a. observing everything as a passenger on the bus ride.
    b. only imagining what might have happened on such a ride.
    c. interviewing at least one passenger.
    d. using a tape recording of the bus ride.

Inferences

13. We can infer that the young people were going to Florida
    a. on business.
    b. to visit family.
    c. on vacation.
    d. to get married.

14. The author implies that Vingo thought
    a. he would someday be in prison again.
    b. there might be no yellow handkerchief on the tree.
    c. his wife was wrong for not writing to him in prison.
    d. his wife was sure to want him back.

15. __T__ TRUE OR FALSE? The statement that Vingo "rose from his seat, holding himself tightly" (last paragraph) implies that Vingo was trying to contain his emotions.

Purpose and Tone

16. The main purpose of "The Yellow Ribbon" is to
    a. inform readers that a convict's life can be rebuilt after prison.
    b. persuade readers to avoid a life of crime.
    c. entertain readers with a heartwarming story.

17. In paragraphs 17 through 21, the author's tone becomes increasingly
    a. bitter.
    b. amused.
    c. suspenseful.
    d. disbelieving.

Propaganda

18. The advertisement at the top of the next page (suggested by the reading) is an example of which propaganda technique?
    a. Bandwagon *(the appeal to do what many others are doing)*
    b. Testimonial *(use of a well-known spokesperson)*
    c. Name calling *(use of emotionally-loaded names or labels)*
    d. Transfer *(association with an admired symbol or image)*

On a Florida spring tourism TV ad, buses of students unload in Florida beach town. Then crowds of students are shown having fun on the beaches, and an announcer says, "During spring break, join the fun in the sun in Florida."

Argument

19. Which of the following points is well supported by the evidence below?
    a. Vingo was nervous about something.
    b. Vingo was on the verge of a nervous breakdown.
    c. Vingo had a hostile personality.
    d. Vingo disliked young people.

    [Vingo's] fingers were stained from cigarettes and he chewed the inside of his lip a lot, frozen into some personal cocoon of silence. (Paragraph 2)

20. Which of the following is *not* a reason for concluding that Vingo deserved the yellow handkerchiefs?
    a. He admitted his mistake.
    b. He paid for his crime by serving four years in jail.
    c. He probably caused his wife and children a lot of pain and embarrassment.
    d. He was forgiven by his wife.

SUMMARIZING

Following is an incomplete summary of "The Yellow Ribbon." Circle the letter (**a**, **b**, or **c**) of the item below that *best* completes the summary.

A man named Vingo had just been released from prison and was on a bus headed home. Some young people were also on the bus, and they got Vingo to tell his story. He said he had written to his wife when he went to prison to explain he would understand if she found another man. He hadn't heard from her since but still loved her very much. So he recently wrote to her, telling her to put a yellow handkerchief on a well-known oak tree in town if she wanted him to come home. If the handkerchief wasn't on the tree, he wouldn't get off the bus there. _____.

a. Vingo showed pictures of his wife and children to the young people, who got caught up in waiting to see the oak tree. As the bus got closer to Vingo's hometown, the bus became quiet and filled with suspense.
b. The young people got caught up in Vingo's situation. After a tense ride to his hometown, he and his fellow travelers finally got his wife's answer: not one, but scores of handkerchiefs fluttering on the tree.
c. Vingo would just continue on the bus to Florida, which is where the young people were going. He understood that while he was in prison, his wife might have started a new life for herself and their children.

DISCUSSION QUESTIONS

1. According to the information in the selection, what is Vingo's attitude toward his wife?

2. Has Vingo assumed responsibility for his crime, in your opinion?

3. While there is much we don't learn about Vingo in this very short narrative, Hamill does provide us with clues to some important aspects of his personality. What evidence is there that he is a decent man, a person who we could feel deserves a second chance?

4. Many people are thrilled, some even to tears, by this story. What makes "The Yellow Ribbon" have such a powerful effect on readers?

Check Your Performance   **THE YELLOW RIBBON**

Skill	Number Right	Points	Total
BASIC SKILL QUESTIONS			
Vocabulary in Context (2 items)	_____	x 4 =	_____
Central Point and Main Ideas (2 items)	_____	x 4 =	_____
Supporting Details (1 item)	_____	x 4 =	_____
Transitions (3 items)	_____	x 4 =	_____
Patterns of Organization (2 items)	_____	x 4 =	_____
ADVANCED SKILL QUESTIONS			
Fact and Opinion (2 items)	_____	x 4 =	_____
Inferences (3 items)	_____	x 4 =	_____
Purpose and Tone (2 items)	_____	x 4 =	_____
Propaganda (1 item)	_____	x 4 =	_____
Argument (2 items)	_____	x 4 =	_____
SUMMARIZING (1 item)	_____	x 20 =	_____

FINAL SCORE (OF POSSIBLE 100)   _____%

Enter your final score into the reading performance chart on the inside back cover.

2

Urban Legends
Beth Johnson Ruth

Preview

Did you hear the one about a woman who was looking through some Asian carpets and was bitten by a poisonous snake? Or was the story that the woman tried on a coat from Mexico, put her hand in the pocket, and found the snake there? These are just two versions of what folklorists call an urban legend. This selection explains what urban legends are and gives more examples of them.

Words to Watch

homicidal (3): murderous
legend (8): a story that can't be proven true
sophisticated (9): knowledgeable about the world
mint (15): brand-new
agonizing (18): painful

A group of college freshmen were sitting around in a friend's dorm room one night, eating popcorn and comparing notes on classes. Eventually the talk drifted away from academics and into the area of spooky stories. Tales of haunted houses were being giggled and shivered over when a girl from a small town in Michigan broke in. "I know a scarier story than any of those!" she announced. "And the scariest thing is, this one is true. It happened to a girl my sister knew."

She began her story. 2

"This girl went to babysit at a house way out in the country one evening. It was a 3
stormy night and she was feeling a little nervous anyway when the phone rang. When
she answered, a man said, 'Have you checked the children?' and laughed weirdly. She
was scared to death and ran to check the kids. They were all right, but a few minutes
later the guy called again and said again, 'Have you checked the children?' and laughed
like crazy. She called the operator to see if she could get the calls traced. A few minutes
later, the operator called back to say, 'Get out of the house! He's in the house with you!'
So she hurried and grabbed the kids and ran out into the rain just as the police pulled up.
They found this escaped homicidal° maniac in the parents' upstairs bedroom. She was
lucky to get out alive."

"Wow! What an awful story!" the girl's roommate exclaimed. 4

"But wait a minute!" called out another friend, this one from Iowa. "That didn't 5
happen in Michigan. It happened near my home town, back when my mother was in
high school. The guy had escaped from an asylum in Cedar Rapids."

"Well, it sounds an awful lot like something that happened a few years ago to a 6
friend of my cousin's in Colorado," said another freshman. "Only the guy actually
caught the babysitter."

What's going on here? How could the same event have happened to three different 7
babysitters in three different parts of the country at three different times?

Urban legend°is what's going on. 8

Urban legend is the modern-day equivalent of the Paul Bunyan story. We're too 9
sophisticated° these days to believe in Babe the blue ox or men who use pine trees to
comb their beards. But we haven't quite given up our need for scary stories that are a
little too good to be true. So we've developed our own type of slightly more believable
tall tales. They're modern. They sound real. They include a humorous, unexpected, or
frightening twist. And they probably never happened.

The deadly hairdo. Kentucky fried rats. The nude surprise party. 10

Do any of those ring a bell? Have you heard them told as true? Have you told 11
them as true? If you've believed them, don't be embarrassed. You've got lots of
company. And if you've helped spread them, well, you're just continuing a great
American folk tradition.

Urban legends have come in for some serious attention in the last couple of 12
decades. Their biggest fan is a University of Utah professor of English named Jan
Harold Brunvand. Professor Brunvand has devoted years to collecting, researching, and
analyzing urban legends all across the U.S. and even in other countries. He's written two
books, *The Vanishing Hitchhiker* and *The Mexican Pet*. These books are jam-packed
with the stories we love to tell and will swear are true—despite all evidence to the
contrary.

Americans love their automobiles, and so some of the most familiar urban legends 13
involve cars. One of the best-known is the classic story of teenagers parked late at night
in a lover's lane. The couple is listening to music on a car radio when a news bulletin
comes on: a dangerous maniac has escaped from a nearby mental asylum. (Escaped
madmen are common characters in urban legends.) Frightened, the girl demands to be
taken home. But when the boy tries to start the car, it won't run. The boy gets out, locks
the girl in the car, and walks off to find help.

The girl huddles in the cold car, becoming more and more frightened as minutes   14
and then hours go by with no sign of her boyfriend. Her fright turns to terror when she
begins to hear a soft "click, click" noise on top of the car. Finally, just as dawn breaks,
police cars arrive at the scene. Cops surround the car, help the girl out, and tell her, "Just
walk to the police car and get in. Don't look back." Naturally, though, she does look
back. Her boyfriend's body, suspended from a rope, is hanging upside down from a tree.
As he sways back and forth in the breeze, his class ring scrapes—"click, click"—against
the roof of the car.

But not all "car" urban legends are so horrible. "The Playboy's Car" tells of a man   15
who is in the market for a luxury sports car. He sees an ad in the newspaper for a nearly
new Porsche for $29.95. He figures the price is a mistake but goes to check it out
anyway. A woman greets him at the house, assures him that the price is correct, and
invites him to test drive the Porsche. He drives a few miles. The car is in mint°
condition. Hardly believing his luck, he hurries back to the house to close the deal. As
the ownership papers are changing hands, he blurts out, "I can't stand not knowing.
Why are you selling this car so cheap?" The woman smiles and answers, "My husband
left me and moved in with his secretary last week. He asked me to sell his Porsche and
send him the money."

How do these stories spread from coast to coast—and sometimes beyond? They   16
probably begin wherever people gather: slumber parties, bowling nights, breaks at the
office water cooler, transcontinental airplane flights. Eventually, they make their way
into our modern communications network: telephones, television, radio, and
newspapers. They sometimes even slip into local and national publications as true
events. The fact that the stories have shown up in the media convinces the public that
they must be true. People clip the articles and send them to friends and family and also
to columnists and radio and television talk-show hosts, who give them further publicity.
And the more the stories travel, the more realistic-sounding details they pick up, and the
more variations develop.

Another category of urban legends demonstrates, Brunvand believes, the great   17
American concern with cleanliness and health. "The Spider in the Hairdo," popular in
the 1950's and 1960's, told of the girl with a fashionable "beehive" hairdo. She rarely
washed her highly teased and sprayed hair. So—wouldn't you know it—a black widow
spider got in there, bit her, and she died. A sub-category of the "cleanliness" stories is
the set of "dreadful contamination" stories. These include tales about people finding
pieces of mice in their bottled soft drinks, or the poor girl who bit into an oddly shaped
piece of restaurant chicken, only to discover it was a batter-fried rat.

And then there are the stories concerning nudity. They sound familiar to any of us   18
who've ever had the agonizing° dream of being at work or on stage with no clothes on.
There's the man left naked by the roadside when his wife (not knowing he'd stepped
out) drove off with their trailer. Or the crafty host who gave his female guests bathing
suits that fell apart when they got wet. Or the poor woman who, feeling playful on her
birthday, came downstairs naked to surprise her husband—and walked into her own
birthday party.

What purpose do these stories serve? Why have they developed? They're part of a   19
long tradition that includes Aesop's Fables—remember the hare and the tortoise?—and
the morality plays of the Middle Ages, where "Truth"and "Virtue" were actual

characters. They are stories that touch some of our deepest fears and concerns. And they teach us lessons. Don't park on lonely lovers' lanes. Don't pick up strangers. Don't fool around on your spouse. Don't eat food you're not sure of. Bathe regularly. It's all the same stuff your parents told you, but it's told in a far more entertaining way.

One more story? Well, have you heard about the cement-truck driver who stopped 20 in to say hello to his wife during the day? When he got to his house, he found a brand-new Cadillac in his driveway. Becoming suspicious, he looked in the window and saw his wife and a strange man drinking coffee in the kitchen and laughing. Aha, he thought. So this is what she does all day. He could think of only one appropriate response. He backed his truck up to the Caddy, filled it full of cement, and then drove away.

When the truck driver got home that night, he found his wife hysterical. "Honey," 21 she sobbed. "I've been saving my money for twenty years to buy you a wonderful present. It came today, and when the man that delivered it left the house—well, just go *look* at your car!"

BASIC SKILL QUESTIONS

Vocabulary in Context

1. The word *equivalent* in "Urban legend is the modern-day equivalent of the Paul Bunyan story" (paragraph 9) means
   a. explanation.
   b. cost.
   c. story teller.
   d. equal.

2. The word *contamination* in "'dreadful contamination' stories. . . . include tales about people finding pieces of mice in their bottled soft drinks, or the poor girl who bit into an oddly shaped piece of restaurant chicken, only to discover it was a batter-fried rat" (paragraph 17) means
   a. impurity.
   b. disease.
   c. restaurant.
   d. bottling.

Central Point and Main Ideas

3. Which sentence best expresses the central point of the selection?
   a. Urban legends begin in unknown ways and then travel throughout the country.
   b. Urban legends are scary stories based on old superstitions.
   c. Urban legends are very interesting to scholars.
   d. Urban legends are modern tales that touch upon deep fears and concerns and that teach lessons.

4. Which sentence best expresses the main idea of paragraph 16?
   a. Urban legends are believed because they sound so realistic.
   b. Urban legends are often published in newspapers.
   c. Urban legends spread in various ways, gaining more realism and variations.
   d. Because of our modern communications network, information of all kinds can be spread over a wide area relatively quickly.

Supporting Details

5. According to the article, urban legends are
   a. always horrible and scary.
   b. very difficult to believe.
   c. usually started by college students.
   d. part of a long tradition of folk tales.

6. The author specifically mentions urban legends that are concerned with
   a. cars.
   b. sports.
   c. twins.
   d. none of the above.

Transitions

7. The relationship of the second sentence below to the first is one of
   a. addition.
   b. time.
   c. illustration.
   d. cause and effect.

   A group of college freshmen were sitting around in a friend's dorm room one night, eating popcorn and comparing notes on classes. Eventually the talk drifted away from academics and into the area of spooky stories. (Paragraph 1)

8. The relationship between the two parts of the sentence below is one of
   a. time.
   b. comparison.
   c. contrast.
   d. illustration.

   It's all the same stuff your parents told you, but it's told in a far more entertaining way. (Paragraph 19)

Patterns of Organization

9. The main pattern of organization of the selection is a version of
   a. time order.
   b. comparison/contrast.
   c. cause and effect.
   d. definition and examples.

10. The main pattern of organization of paragraph 3 is
    a. time order.
    b. comparison.
    c. cause and effect.
    d. definition and examples.

ADVANCED SKILL QUESTIONS

Fact and Opinion

11. The word that makes the sentence below an opinion is
    a. biggest.
    b. fan.
    c. Utah.
    d. named.

    Their biggest fan is a University of Utah professor of English named Jan Harold Brunvand. (Paragraph 12)

12. The statement below is
    a. fact.
    b. opinion.
    c. fact and opinion.

    [Urban legends] make their way into our modern communications network: telephones, television, radio, and newspapers. (Paragraph 16)

Inferences

13. The author implies that
    a. people should always check their food before eating.
    b. husbands should never be suspicious of their wives.
    c. throughout history people have told stories with morals.
    d. urban legends lack meaning and purpose.

14. From the selection we might conclude that urban legends are
    a. based upon European superstitions.
    b. worthy of serious study.
    c. not interesting to the average American.
    d. usually about true events.

Purpose and Tone

15. *Fill in the blank:* The author (*informs, persuades*) ___informs___ the reader about urban legends and illustrates with entertaining examples.

16. *Fill in the blank:* In general, the author's tone is (*formal, conversational*)

    ___conversational___.

17. The tone of the urban legend about the babysitter (paragraph 3) is
    a. playful.
    b. forgiving.
    c. threatening.
    d. mocking.

Propaganda

18. The advertisement below (suggested by the article) is an example of which propaganda technique?
    a. Bandwagon *(the appeal to do what many others are doing)*
    b. Transfer *(association with an admired symbol or image)*
    c. Plain folks *(showing candidates, company executives, or customers as ordinary folks)*
    d. Name calling *(use of negative, emotionally loaded language against a rival)*

    Flavor isn't the only reason to ask for Pepsi. After all, haven't you heard the story about a bottle of Cooler Cola that contained a mouse's tail? Maybe Cooler Cola should really be called "Rodent Cola."

Argument

19. The story about the man who assumed his wife was unfaithful is an example of what fallacy in thinking?
    a. Hasty generalization *(the argument makes a generalization based on insufficient evidence)*
    b. Personal attack *(the argument shifts to irrelevant personal criticism)*
    c. Straw man *(the argument is made by claiming an opponent holds an extreme position and then opposing that extreme position)*
    d. Either-or *(the argument assumes that there are only two sides to a question)*

20. Identify the one statement that does *not* support Brunvand's point that Americans are greatly concerned with cleanliness and health.
    a. Numerous Americans incorporate exercise into their lifestyles.
    b. Americans are buying increasing amounts of organic fruits and vegetables.
    c. There's a bewildering number of cleaning products on the market.
    d. More and more Americans are microwaving frozen dinners for their evening meals.

MAPPING

The map below divides the selection into three main parts. Complete the map by filling in the following four missing items.

• Gather more realistic details and variations as they travel

• The cement-truck driver's revenge

• What they are

• The playboy's car

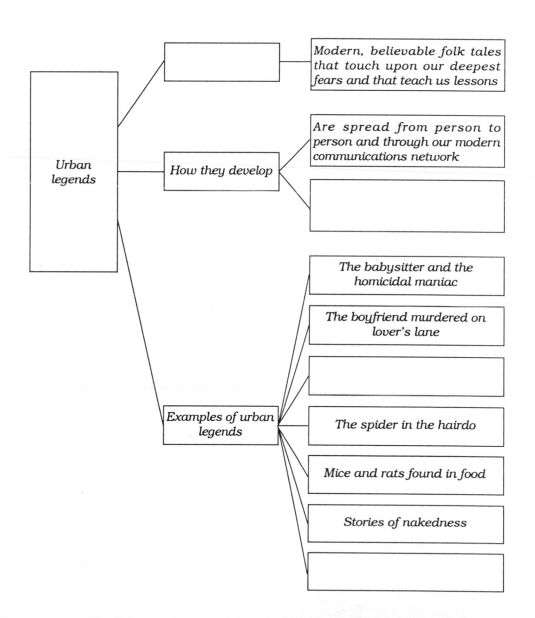

Urban legends

Modern, believable folk tales that touch upon our deepest fears and that teach us lessons

How they develop

Are spread from person to person and through our modern communications network

Examples of urban legends

The babysitter and the homicidal maniac

The boyfriend murdered on lover's lane

The spider in the hairdo

Mice and rats found in food

Stories of nakedness

DISCUSSION QUESTIONS

1. Ruth writes that urban legends "teach us lessons." Which of the stories in the article do you think teaches the most effective lesson?

2. Have you ever heard any of the stories described, but in slightly different form? Or have you heard any story that is so dramatic that you wonder if it is true or not? Retell any such story you have heard, as best as you can remember it.

3. Ruth claims that "we haven't quite given up our need for scary stories that are a little too good to be true." In our culture, where else besides urban legends do we find such stories?

4. Why do you think people enjoy being scared so much?

Check Your Performance   **URBAN LEGENDS**

Skill	Number Right	Points	Total
BASIC SKILL QUESTIONS			
Vocabulary in Context (2 items)	_____	x 4 =	_____
Central Point and Main Ideas (2 items)	_____	x 4 =	_____
Supporting Details (2 items)	_____	x 4 =	_____
Transitions (2 items)	_____	x 4 =	_____
Patterns of Organization (2 items)	_____	x 4 =	_____
ADVANCED SKILL QUESTIONS			
Fact and Opinion (2 items)	_____	x 4 =	_____
Inferences (2 items)	_____	x 4 =	_____
Purpose and Tone (3 items)	_____	x 4 =	_____
Propaganda (1 item)	_____	x 4 =	_____
Argument (2 items)	_____	x 4 =	_____
MAPPING (4 items)	_____	x 5 =	_____

FINAL SCORE (OF POSSIBLE 100)   _____%

Enter your final score into the reading performance chart on the inside back cover.

3

Shame
Dick Gregory

Preview

Upon receiving help, most of us feel grateful. But what if the help is given in an inconsiderate way? In this autobiographical piece, comedian and social activist Dick Gregory shows that the good intentions of a giver are not enough if they don't take the recipient's pride into account.

Words to Watch

complected (1): complexioned
stoop (2): an outside stairway, porch, or platform at the entrance to a house
mackinaw (28): a short, plaid coat or jacket
googobs (29): Gregory's slang for *gobs*, a large amount

I never learned hate at home, or shame. I had to go to school for that. I was about   1
seven years old when I got my first big lesson. I was in love with a little girl named Helene Tucker, a light-complected° little girl with pigtails and nice manners. She was always clean and she was smart in school. I think I went to school then mostly to look at her. I brushed my hair and even got me a little old handkerchief. It was a lady's handkerchief, but I didn't want Helene to see me wipe my nose on my hand. The pipes were frozen again, there was no water in the house, but I washed my socks and shirt every night. I'd get a pot, and go over to Mister Ben's grocery store, and stick my pot down into his soda machine. Scoop out some chopped ice. By evening the ice melted to water for washing. I got sick a lot that winter because the fire would go out at night before the clothes were dry. In the morning I'd put them on, wet or dry, because they were the only clothes I had.

Everybody's got a Helene Tucker, a symbol of everything you want. I loved her 2
for her goodness, her cleanness, her popularity. She'd walk down my street and my
brothers and sisters would yell, "Here comes Helene," and I'd rub my tennis sneakers on
the back of my pants and wish my hair wasn't so nappy and the white folks' shirt fit me
better. I'd run out on the street. If I knew my place and didn't come too close, she'd
wink at me and say hello. That was a good feeling. Sometimes I'd follow her all the way
home, and shovel the snow off her walk and try to make friends with her Momma and
her aunts. I'd drop money on her stoop° late at night on my way back from shining
shoes in the taverns. And she had a Daddy, and he had a good job. He was a paper
hanger.

I guess I would have gotten over Helene by summertime, but something happened 3
in that classroom that made her face hang in front of me for the next twenty-two years.
When I played the drums in high school it was for Helene and when I broke track
records in college it was for Helene and when I started standing behind microphones
and heard applause I wished Helene could hear it, too. It wasn't until I was twenty-nine
years old and married and making money that I finally got her out of my system. Helene
was sitting in that classroom when I learned to be ashamed of myself.

It was on a Thursday. I was sitting in the back of the room, in a seat with a chalk 4
circle drawn around it. The idiot's seat, the troublemaker's seat.

The teacher thought I was stupid. Couldn't spell, couldn't read, couldn't do 5
arithmetic. Just stupid. Teachers were never interested in finding out that you couldn't
concentrate because you were so hungry, because you hadn't had any breakfast. All you
could think about was noontime, would it ever come? Maybe you could sneak into the
cloakroom and steal a bite of some kid's lunch out of a coat pocket. A bite of something.
Paste. You can't really make a meal of paste, or put it on bread for a sandwich, but
sometimes I'd scoop a few spoonfuls out of the big paste jar in the back of the room.
Pregnant people get strange tastes. I was pregnant with poverty. Pregnant with dirt and
pregnant with smells that made people turn away, pregnant with cold and pregnant with
shoes that were never bought for me, pregnant with five other people in my bed and no
Daddy in the next room, and pregnant with hunger. Paste doesn't taste too bad when
you're hungry.

The teacher thought I was a troublemaker. All she saw from the front of the room 6
was a little black boy who squirmed in his idiot's seat and made noises and poked the
kids around him. I guess she couldn't see a kid who made noises because he wanted
someone to know he was there.

It was on a Thursday, the day before the Negro payday. The eagle always flew on 7
Friday. The teacher was asking each student how much his father would give to the
Community Chest. On Friday night, each kid would get the money from his father, and
on Monday he would bring it to the school. I decided I was going to buy a Daddy right
then. I had money in my pocket from shining shoes and selling papers, and whatever
Helene Tucker pledged for her Daddy I was going to top it. And I'd hand the money
right in. I wasn't going to wait until Monday to buy me a Daddy.

I was shaking, scared to death. The teacher opened her book and started calling 8
out names alphabetically.

"Helene Tucker?" 9

"My Daddy said he'd give two dollars and fifty cents." 10

"That's very nice, Helene. Very, very nice indeed." 11

That made me feel pretty good. It wouldn't take too much to top that. I had almost 12
three dollars in dimes and quarters in my pocket. I stuck my hand in my pocket and held
onto the money, waiting for her to call my name. But the teacher closed her book after
she called everybody else in the class.

I stood up and raised my hand. 13

"What is it now?" 14

"You forgot me." 15

She turned toward the blackboard. "I don't have time to be playing with you, 16
Richard."

"My Daddy said he'd. . . ." 17

"Sit down, Richard, you're disturbing the class." 18

"My Daddy said he'd give . . . fifteen dollars." 19

She turned around and looked mad. "We are collecting this money for you and 20
your kind, Richard Gregory. If your Daddy can give fifteen dollars you have no business
being on relief."

"I got it right now, I got it right now, my Daddy gave it to me to turn in today, my 21
Daddy said. . . ."

"And furthermore," she said, looking right at me, her nostrils getting big and her 22
lips getting thin and her eyes opening wide, "we know you don't have a Daddy."

Helene Tucker turned around, her eyes full of tears. She felt sorry for me. Then I 23
couldn't see her too well because I was crying, too.

"Sit down, Richard." 24

And I always thought the teacher kind of liked me. She always picked me to wash 25
the blackboard on Friday, after school. That was a big thrill, it made me feel important.
If I didn't wash it, come Monday the school might not function right.

"Where are you going, Richard!" 26

I walked out of school that day, and for a long time I didn't go back very often. 27
There was shame there.

Now there was shame everywhere. It seemed like the whole world had been inside 28
that classroom, everyone had heard what the teacher had said, everyone had turned
around and felt sorry for me. There was shame in going to the Worthy Boys Annual
Christmas Dinner for you and your kind, because everybody knew what a worthy boy
was. Why couldn't they just call it the Boys Annual Dinner, why'd they have to give it a
name? There was shame in wearing the brown and orange and white plaid mackinaw°
the welfare gave to three thousand boys. Why'd it have to be the same for everybody so
when you walked down the street the people could see you were on relief? It was a nice
warm mackinaw and it had a hood, and my Momma beat me and called me a little rat
when she found out I stuffed it in the bottom of a pail full of garbage way over on
Cottage Street. There was shame in running over to Mister Ben's at the end of the day
and asking for his rotten peaches, there was shame in asking Mrs. Simmons for a
spoonful of sugar, there was shame in running out to meet the relief truck. I hated that
truck, full of food for you and your kind. I ran into the house and hid when it came. And
then I started to sneak through alleys, to take the long way home so the people going
into White's Eat Shop wouldn't see me. Yeah, the whole world heard the teacher that
day, we all know you don't have a Daddy.

It lasted for a while, this kind of numbness. I spent a lot of time feeling sorry for 29
myself. And then one day I met this wino in a restaurant. I'd been out hustling all day,

shining shoes, selling newspapers, and I had googobs° of money in my pocket. Bought me a bowl of chili for fifteen cents, and a cheeseburger for fifteen cents, and a Pepsi for five cents, and a piece of chocolate cake for ten cents. That was a good meal. I was eating when this old wino came in. I love winos because they never hurt anyone but themselves.

The old wino sat down at the counter and ordered twenty-six cents worth of food. 30 He ate it like he really enjoyed it. When the owner, Mister Williams, asked him to pay the check, the old wino didn't lie or go through his pocket like he suddenly found a hole.

He just said: "Don't have no money." 31

The owner yelled: "Why in hell you come in here and eat my food if you don't 32 have no money? That food cost me money."

Mister Williams jumped over the counter and knocked the wino off his stool and 33 beat him over the head with a pop bottle. Then he stepped back and watched the wino bleed. Then he kicked him. And he kicked him again.

I looked at the wino with blood all over his face and I went over. "Leave him 34 alone, Mister Williams. I'll pay the twenty-six cents."

The wino got up, slowly, pulling himself up to the stool, then up to the counter, 35 holding on for a minute until his legs stopped shaking so bad. He looked at me with pure hate. "Keep your twenty-six cents. You don't have to pay, not now. I just finished paying for it."

He started to walk out, and as he passed me, he reached down and touched my 36 shoulder. "Thanks, sonny, but it's too late now. Why didn't you pay it before?"

I was pretty sick about that. I waited too long to help another man. 37

BASIC SKILL QUESTIONS

Vocabulary in Context

1. The word *pledged* in "Whatever Helene Tucker pledged for her Daddy, I was going to top it" (paragraph 7) means
   a. repeated.
   b. studied.
   c. promised to give.
   d. brought home.

2. The word *hustling* in "I'd been out hustling all day, shining shoes, selling newspapers, and I had googobs of money in my pocket" (paragraph 29) means
   a. complaining.
   b. relaxing.
   c. studying hard.
   d. working energetically.

Central Point and Main Ideas

3. Which sentence best expresses the central point of this selection?
   a. Dick Gregory had a long-standing crush on a girl named Helene Tucker.
   b. The charity Gregory received was given in a way that labeled him as poor, which made him ashamed.
   c. From both the giving and receiving ends, young Gregory learned that how something is given is as important as what is given.
   d. Gregory grew up in a fatherless, poor family.

4. Which sentence best expresses the main idea of paragraph 5?
   a. Gregory liked to eat paste.
   b. The teacher assumed Gregory was stupid.
   c. The teacher never realized that Gregory was hungry all the time.
   d. The teacher assumed Gregory was stupid and never realized his poor work was the result of hunger.

Supporting Details

5. _____ TRUE OR FALSE? Helene Tucker represented a way of life that Gregory wished he had.

6. After the teacher told him he was the type of person the Community Chest helped and that he was fatherless,
   a. Gregory never went back to school.
   b. Gregory felt sorry for himself for a while.
   c. Gregory stopped working.
   d. Gregory felt Helene Tucker did not feel sorry for him.

7. As support for his central point, the author uses several
   a. statistics.
   b. expert opinions.
   c. personal experiences.
   d. famous quotations.

Transitions

8. The relationship of the second sentence below to the first is one of
   a. addition.
   b. comparison.
   c. contrast.
   d. illustration.

   I stuck my hand in my pocket and held onto the money, waiting for her to call my name. But the teacher closed her book after she called everybody else in the class. (Paragraph 12)

9. The sentence below contains a
   a. contrast signal.
   b. comparison signal.
   c. illustration signal.
   d. cause-effect signal.

   I guess she couldn't see a kid who made noises because he wanted someone to know he was there. (Paragraph 6)

Patterns of Organization

10. The pattern of organization used in paragraphs 30-36 is
    a. list of items.
    b. time order.
    c. cause and effect.
    d. comparison.

ADVANCED SKILL QUESTIONS

Fact and Opinion

11. Which of the following is a statement of opinion?
    a. "I was sitting in the back of the room, in a seat with a chalk circle drawn around it."
    b. "Paste doesn't taste too bad when you're hungry."
    c. "She turned toward the blackboard."
    d. "Helene Tucker turned around, her eyes full of tears."

Inferences

12. _____ TRUE OR FALSE? In the classroom scene, the author implies that Helene is a sensitive girl.

13. In paragraph 5, the author implies that
    a. he is stupid.
    b. teachers understood him well.
    c. it was difficult for him to concentrate in school.
    d. he felt alone and ignored in school.

14. _____ TRUE OR FALSE? The author implies that the wino taught him a valuable lesson.

Purpose and Tone

15. _____ TRUE OR FALSE? One purpose of the author is to inform readers of how he learned the meaning of shame.

16. The word that best describes the tone of the last paragraph of the selection
is
   a. angry.
   b. objective.
   c. sentimental.
   d. ashamed.

Propaganda

17. The advertisement below (suggested by the reading) is a variation on what
propaganda technique?
   a. Testimonial *(use of a well-known spokesperson)*
   b. Transfer *(association with an admired symbol or image)*
   c. Plain folks *(showing candidates, company executives, or customers as
   ordinary people)*
   d. Glittering generalities *(use of an important-sounding but unsupported claim)*

   Don't neglect to make your annual contribution to the Campaign for the
   Homeless. After all, with bad luck, a homeless child could be your child
   or a mentally ill man or woman could be your relative. Yes, even a wino
   could be your uncle or brother.

Argument

18. _____ TRUE OR FALSE? The teacher's conclusion that Gregory was stupid
did not take into account all the relevant evidence.

19. Which evidence from the selection supports Gregory's statement that, after
the school incident, he felt shame everywhere?
   a. Gregory stuffed the plaid mackinaw in a garbage can.
   b. Gregory was always chosen to wash the blackboards on Fridays.
   c. Helene Tucker's eyes were full of tears.
   d. Gregory wanted to pay for the wino's dinner.

20. The argument below (suggested by the reading) would be an example of
what fallacy?
   a. Circular reasoning *(the statement repeats itself rather than providing a real
   supporting reason to back up the argument)*
   b. Personal attack *(the argument shifts to irrelevant personal attack)*
   c. Straw man *(the argument is made by claiming an opponent holds an extreme
   position and then opposing that extreme position)*
   d. Either-or *(the argument assumes that there are only two sides to a question)*

   Obviously, Gregory didn't think people should try to help children like
   himself. After all, he threw away a perfectly good mackinaw.

OUTLINING

The following outline of "Shame" is missing two major supporting details and three minor supporting details. Complete the outline by filling in the missing details, which are listed after the outline.

Central point: Young Gregory learned both the shame of being let down by those who were supposed to help him and the shame of letting down another person.

1. _____

   a. Intention to impress Helene Tucker by pledging to Community Chest

   b._____

   c._____

2. _____

   a. Earns a lot of money one day and goes to a restaurant for a good meal

   b. Sees wino being beaten for not being able to pay for his meal

   c._____

Items Missing from the Outline

- Offers to pay for meal, but too late
- Becoming ashamed of his own failure to help another
- Is humiliated by teacher
- Becoming ashamed of his poverty
- Leaves school and avoids it in the future

DISCUSSION QUESTIONS

1. Why did Gregory include both the classroom and the restaurant anecdotes in one piece? What is the difference between the shame he felt in the first incident and the shame he felt in the second? What are the similarities between the two incidents?

2. What does Gregory mean by the sentence "The eagle always flew on Friday" (paragraph 7)? What does this fact reveal about his world?

3. One type of irony is an event or an effect that is the opposite of what might be expected. In what ways are the following parts of "Shame" ironic?

    - I never learned hate at home, or shame. I had to go to school for that.

• If I knew my place and didn't come too close, she'd wink at me and say hello. That was a good feeling.

• I looked at the wino with blood all over his face and I went over. "Leave him alone, Mister Williams. I'll pay the twenty-six cents."

The wino got up. . . .He looked at me with pure hate.

4.   Has anyone ever tried to help you in a way that didn't take all your needs into account? If so, how did you feel toward that person? What are some ways activities that are meant to help people might also hurt them?

Check Your Performance   **SHAME**

Skill	Number Right	Points	Total
BASIC SKILL QUESTIONS			
Vocabulary in Context (2 items)	_____	x 4 =	_____
Central Point and Main Ideas (2 items)	_____	x 4 =	_____
Supporting Details (3 items)	_____	x 4 =	_____
Transitions (2 items)	_____	x 4 =	_____
Patterns of Organization (1 item)	_____	x 4 =	_____
ADVANCED SKILL QUESTIONS			
Fact and Opinion (1 item)	_____	x 4 =	_____
Inferences (3 items)	_____	x 4 =	_____
Purpose and Tone (2 items)	_____	x 4 =	_____
Propaganda (1 item)	_____	x 4 =	_____
Argument (3 items)	_____	x 4 =	_____
OUTLINING (5 items)	_____	x 4 =	_____

FINAL SCORE (OF POSSIBLE 100)   _____%

Enter your final score into the reading performance chart on the inside back cover.

4

The Bystander Effect
Dorothy Barkin

Preview

A few years ago, thirty-eight people witnessed a brutal attack—and hardly raised a finger to stop it. That kind of unwillingness to get involved is the topic of this article by Dorothy Barkin, who analyzes the confusion and lack of responsibility bystanders often feel when witnessing a crime or medical emergency. She begins by describing four crisis situations—and placing you right there at the scene. How would you react?

Words to Watch

intervene (2): interfere
phenomena (4): facts
apathy (23): indifference
paralysis (32): inability to act
diffusion (32): spreading

It is a pleasant fall afternoon. The sun is shining. You are heading toward the   1
parking lot after your last class of the day. All of a sudden, you come across the
following situations. What do you think you'd do in each case?

Situation One: A man in his early twenties dressed in jeans and a T-shirt is using a coat hanger to pry open a door of a late-model Ford sedan. An overcoat and camera are visible on the back seat of the car. You're the only one who sees this.

Situation Two: A man and woman are wrestling with each other. The woman is in tears. Attempting to fight the man off, she screams, "Who are you? Get away from me!" You're the only one who witnesses this.

Situation Three: Imagine the same scenario as in Situation Two except that this time the woman screams, "Get away from me! I don't know why I ever married you!"

Situation Four: Again imagine Situation Three. This time, however, there are a few other people (strangers to you and each other) who also observe the incident.

Many people would choose not to get involved in situations like these. Bystanders 2
are often reluctant to intervene° in criminal or medical emergencies for reasons they are well aware of. They fear possible danger to themselves or getting caught up in a situation that could lead to complicated and time-consuming legal proceedings.

There are, however, other, less obvious factors which influence the decision to get 3
involved in emergency situations. Complex psychological factors, which many are unaware of, play an important part in the behavior of bystanders; knowing about these factors can help people to act more responsibly when faced with emergencies.

To understand these psychological phenomena, it is helpful to look at what 4
researchers have learned about behavior in the situations mentioned at the beginning of this article.

Situation One: Research reveals a remarkably low rate of bystander intervention to protect property. In one study, more than 3,000 people walked past 214 staged car break-ins like the one described in this situation. The vast majority of passers-by completely ignored what appeared to be a crime in progress. Not one of the 3000 bothered to report the incident to the police.

Situation Two: Another experiment involved staging scenarios like this and the next situation. In Situation Two, bystanders offered some sort of assistance to the young woman 65 percent of the time.

Situation Three: Here the rate of bystander assistance dropped down to 19 percent. This demonstrates that bystanders are more reluctant to help a woman when they believe she's fighting with her husband. Not only do they consider a wife in less need of help; they think interfering with a married couple may be more dangerous. The husband, unlike a stranger, will not flee the situation.

Situation Four: The important idea in this situation is being a member of a group of bystanders. In more than fifty studies involving many different conditions, one outcome has been consistent: bystanders are much less likely to get involved when other witnesses are present than when they are alone.

Thus, membership in a group of bystanders lowers the likelihood of each member 5 of the group becoming involved. This finding may seem surprising. You might think there would be safety in numbers and that being a member of a group would increase the likelihood of intervention. How can we explain this aspect of group behavior?

A flood of research has tried to answer this and other questions about emergency 6 bystanders ever since the infamous case of the murder of Kitty Genovese.

In 1964 in the borough of Queens in New York City, Catherine "Kitty" Genovese, 7 twenty-eight, was brutally murdered in a shocking crime that outraged the nation.

The crime began at 3 A.M. Kitty Genovese was coming home from her job as 8 manager of a bar. After parking her car in a parking lot, she began the hundred-foot walk to the entrance of her apartment. But she soon noticed a man in the lot and decided instead to walk toward a police call box. As she walked by a bookstore on her way there, the man grabbed her. She screamed.

Lights went on and windows opened in the ten-story apartment building. 9

Next, the attacker stabbed Genovese. She shrieked, "Oh, my God, he stabbed me! 10 Please help me! Please help me!"

From an upper window in the apartment house, a man shouted, "Let that girl 11 alone!"

The assailant, alarmed by the man's shout, started toward his car, which was 12 parked nearby. However, the lights in the building soon went out, and the man returned. He found Genovese struggling to reach her apartment—and stabbed her again.

She screamed, "I'm dying! I'm dying!" 13

Once more lights went on and windows opened in the apartment building. The 14 attacker then went to his car and drove off. Struggling, Genovese made her way inside the building.

But the assailant returned to attack Genovese yet a third time. He found her 15 slumped on the floor at the foot of the stairs and stabbed her again, this time fatally.

The murder took over a half hour, and Kitty Genovese's desperate cries for help 16 were heard by at least thirty-eight people. Not a single one of the thirty-eight who later admitted to having witnessed the murder bothered to pick up the phone during the attack and call the police. One man called after Genovese was dead.

Comments made by bystanders after this murder provide important insight into 17 what group members think when they consider intervening in an emergency.

These are some of the comments: 18

"I didn't want my husband to get involved." 19

"Frankly, we were afraid." 20

"We thought it was a lovers' quarrel." 21

"I was tired." 22

The Genovese murder sparked a national debate on the questions of public 23 apathy° and fear and became the basis for thousands of sermons, editorials, classroom discussions, and even a made-for-television movie. The same question was on everybody's mind—how could thirty-eight people have done so little?

Nine years later, another well-publicized incident provided additional information 24 about the psychology of a group witnessing a crime.

On a summer afternoon in Trenton, New Jersey, a twenty-year-old woman was 25 brutally raped in a parking lot in full view of twenty-five employees of a nearby roofing company. Though the workers witnessed the entire incident and the woman repeatedly screamed for help, no one came to her assistance.

Comments made by witnesses to the rape were remarkably similar to those made 26 by the bystanders to the Genovese murder. For example, one witness said, "We thought, well, it might turn out to be her boyfriend or something like that."

It's not surprising to find similar excuses for not helping in cases involving a 27 group of bystanders. The same psychological principles apply to each. Research conducted since the Genovese murder indicates that the failure of bystanders to get involved can't be simply dismissed as a symptom of an uncaring society. Rather, the bystander effect, as it is called by social scientists, is the product of a complex set of psychological factors.

Two factors appear to be most important in understanding the reactions of 28 bystanders to emergencies.

First is the level of ambiguity involved in the situation. Bystanders are afraid to 29 endanger themselves or look foolish if they take the wrong action in a situation they're not sure how to interpret. A person lying face down on the floor of a subway train may have just suffered a heart attack and be in need of immediate medical assistance—or he may be a dangerous drunk.

Determining what is happening is especially difficult when a man is attacking a 30 woman. Many times lovers do quarrel, sometimes violently. But they may strongly resent an outsider, no matter how well-meaning, intruding into their affairs.

When a group of bystanders is around, interpreting an event can be even more 31 difficult than when one is alone. Bystanders look to others for cues as to what is happening. Frequently other witnesses, just as confused, try to look calm. Thus bystanders can mislead each other about the seriousness of an incident.

The second factor in determining the reactions of bystanders to emergencies is 32 what psychologists call the principle of moral diffusion. Moral diffusion is the lessening of a sense of individual responsibility when someone is a member of a group. Responsibility to act diffuses throughout the crowd. When a member of the group is able to escape the collective paralysis° and take action, others in the group tend to act as well. But the larger the crowd, the greater the diffusion° of responsibility, and the less likely someone is to intervene.

The more social scientists are able to teach us about how bystanders react to 33 emergencies, the better the chances that we will take appropriate action when faced with one. Knowing about moral diffusion, for example, makes it easier for us to escape it. If you find yourself witnessing an emergency with a group, remember that everybody is waiting for someone else to do something first. If you take action, others may also help.

Also realize that any one of us could at some time be in desperate need of help. 34 Imagine what it feels like to need help and have a crowd watching you suffer and do nothing. Remember Kitty Genovese.

BASIC SKILL QUESTIONS

Vocabulary in Context

1. The word *scenario* in "Imagine the same scenario as in situation two except that this time the woman screams, 'Get away from me! I don't know why I ever married you!'" (paragraph 1) means
   a. fight.
   b. relationship.
   c. suggested scene.
   d. quotation.

2. The word *ambiguity* in "First is the level of ambiguity involved . . . . Bystanders are afraid to endanger themselves or look foolish . . . in a situation they're not sure how to interpret" (paragraph 29) means
   a. argument.
   b. uncertainty.
   c. lack of interest.
   d. crowding.

Central Point and Main Ideas

3. Which sentence best expresses the central point of this selection?
   a. People don't want to get involved in emergencies.
   b. Kitty Genovese was murdered because no one helped enough.
   c. People don't care what happens to others.
   d. Understanding why bystanders react as they do in a crisis can help people act more responsibly.

4. Which sentence best expresses the main idea of paragraph 27?
   a. Bystanders always have the same excuses for not helping.
   b. There has been research on bystanders since the Genovese murder.
   c. The "bystander effect" is a symptom of an uncaring society.
   d. Research shows that a number of psychological factors, not a simple lack of caring, keeps bystanders from getting involved.

Supporting Details

5. Bystanders are most likely to help
   a. a woman being attacked by her husband.
   b. in any emergency when others are around.
   c. a woman being attacked by a stranger.
   d. when property is being stolen.

6. According to the author, when there is a group of bystanders,
   a. everyone is more likely to help.
   b. it is easier to understand what is happening.
   c. they are not influenced at all by each other.
   d. each is more likely to act after someone else takes action.

7. The author supports her statement that "bystanders are much less likely to get involved when other witnesses are present" with
   a. opinions.
   b. quotations from experts.
   c. research and examples.
   d. no evidence.

Transitions

8. The first word of the second sentence below serves as
   a. an addition signal.
   b. an illustration signal.
   c. a contrast signal.
   d. a cause-effect signal.

   Frequently other witnesses, just as confused, try to look calm. Thus bystanders can mislead each other about the seriousness of an incident. (Paragraph 31)

9. The relationship between the two parts of the sentence below is one of
   a. cause and effect.
   b. comparison.
   c. contrast.
   d. illustration.

   If you take action, others may also help. (Paragraph 33)

Patterns of Organization

10. The pattern of organization of paragraphs 7-16 is
    a. comparison/contrast.
    b. list of items.
    c. definition and example.
    d. time order.

ADVANCED SKILL QUESTIONS

Fact and Opinion

11. Which sentence is a statement of opinion?
    a. "The crime began at 3 A.M."
    b. "From an upper window in the apartment house, a man shouted, 'Let that girl alone!'"
    c. "Though the workers witnessed the entire incident and the woman repeatedly screamed for help, no one came to her assistance."
    d. "Two factors appear to be most important in understanding the reactions of bystanders to emergencies."

12. The following sentence is a statement of
    a. fact.
    b. opinion.
    c. fact and opinion.

    > In more than fifty studies involving many different conditions, one outcome has been consistent: bystanders are much less likely to get involved when other witnesses are present than when they are alone. (Paragraph 4)

Inferences

13. The reading suggests that people tend to believe
    a. theft is okay.
    b. loss of property is worse than bodily harm.
    c. bodily harm is worse than loss of property.
    d. rape is worse than murder.

14. From the article, we can conclude that Kitty Genovese's killer
    a. knew his victim.
    b. was unaware of the witnesses.
    c. stabbed her too quickly for her to get help.
    d. kept attacking when he realized no one was coming to help her.

15. From the article, we can conclude that of the following situations, the bystander is most likely to get involved when
    a. a man passes a house that is being burglarized.
    b. a high-school student sees a man collapsing on a street when no one else is present.
    c. a neighbor sees a father and son fighting in their yard.
    d. a softball team sees their coach angrily chasing his wife.

Purpose and Tone

16. The main purpose of this article is to
    a. inform readers about the bystander effect and the factors contributing to it.
    b. persuade people to be more helpful in emergency situations.
    c. both of the above.

17. The tone of the last paragraph of this article can be described as
    a. angry.
    b. confused.
    c. pleading.
    d. light-hearted.

Propaganda

18. Bystanders' influence on each other can be related to the success of which propaganda technique?
    a. Bandwagon *(the appeal to do what many others are doing)*
    b. Transfer *(association with an admired symbol or image)*
    c. Name calling *(use of negative, emotionally-loaded language against a rival)*
    d. Glittering generalities *(use of an important-sounding but unsupported claim)*

Argument

19. The argument below (suggested by the reading) would be an example of what fallacy?
    a. Circular reasoning *(the statement repeats itself rather than providing a real supporting reason to back up the argument)*
    b. False comparison *(the argument assumes that two things being compared are more alike than they really are)*
    c. Either-or *(the argument assumes that there are only two sides to a question)*
    d. Changing the subject *(the evidence sounds good but has nothing to do with the argument)*

    There are only two types of bystanders—those who are caring people and help out in an emergency and those who are uncaring people who think only of themselves.

20. Put a check by the item that does *not* support the following point: People must be more aggressive and courageous in taking action when witnessing an emergency.

    ___ a. Overcoming our psychological resistance to helping in a crowd requires extra effort.

    ___ b. Emergencies involving a man and woman probably often do involve a husband and wife or lovers.

    ___ c. It's better to interfere in what turns out to be a lovers' quarrel than to allow someone to be injured or killed.

    ___ d. Probably fewer thieves would be successful if bystanders were more willing to report ongoing theft to the police.

SUMMARIZING

Add the ideas needed to complete the following summary of "The Bystander Effect."

Witnesses to crisis situations are less likely to help when only property is at risk and when a woman is being attacked by a man who may be her husband. Numerous studies have shown that witnesses' resistance to helping is also increased when there are other _____

_____. A famous example is the case of Kitty Genovese, who was stabbed to death at 3 A.M. while returning to her apartment. The attack went on for over half an hour. Thirty-eight people listened to her cries for help, but _____

_____. In another example, employees of a roofing company ignored a rape taking place on a nearby parking lot. Two psychological factors seem to explain _____

_____. One is the level of uncertainty in the situation. If the bystanders don't know how to_____ a situation, they don't want to take action. The other factor is the principle of moral diffusion. The larger the crowd that is watching, the less responsibility _____.

Understanding these factors can help people be more useful in emergency situations.

DISCUSSION QUESTIONS

1. Have you ever been in a situation where the bystander effect played a part? Would your behavior be any different in light of what you have learned from this article?

2. The author states in paragraph 31, "Bystanders look to others for cues as to what is happening. Frequently other witnesses, just as confused, try to look calm." Why do you think witnesses would try to look calm during an emergency?

3. In paragraph 33, the author suggests that if you understand what causes "the bystander effect," you can act appropriately in an emergency: "If you take action, others may also help." If, say, you were in a group of onlookers while a fight was in progress, what could you do that would encourage others to intervene?

4. How does the conclusion of this article clarify the author's purpose for the reader? How does the article's beginning fit in with that purpose?

Check Your Performance   THE BYSTANDER EFFECT

Skill	Number Right	Points	Total
BASIC SKILL QUESTIONS			
Vocabulary in Context (2 items)	_____	x 4 =	_____
Central Point and Main Ideas (2 items)	_____	x 4 =	_____
Supporting Details (3 items)	_____	x 4 =	_____
Transitions (2 items)	_____	x 4 =	_____
Patterns of Organization (1 item)	_____	x 4 =	_____
ADVANCED SKILL QUESTIONS			
Fact and Opinion (2 items)	_____	x 4 =	_____
Inferences (3 items)	_____	x 4 =	_____
Purpose and Tone (2 items)	_____	x 4 =	_____
Propaganda (1 items)	_____	x 4 =	_____
Argument (2 items)	_____	x 4 =	_____
SUMMARIZING (5 items)	_____	x 4 =	_____

FINAL SCORE (OF POSSIBLE 100) _____%

Enter your final score into the reading performance chart on the inside back cover.

5

Preview, Read, Write, Recite
Gayle Edwards

Preview

Do you sometimes wonder if others know something about studying that you don't? Do they seem to have a successful system that helps them deal with reading assignments? In fact, there are methods of study that can make you a more productive student. If you have never learned one of those methods, this selection is your opportunity to do so.

Words to Watch

randomly (9): in a here-and-there way
disclose (11): make known
decipher (12): interpret
seethe (12): feel greatly upset
perceived (13): seen
inconsequential (14): unimportant
detrimental (14): harmful
paralinguistic (15): related to language
attributable to (27): considered to be caused by

Your idea of studying a textbook assignment may be to simply read it once or   1
twice. If so, you may be wondering why you have trouble understanding and remembering what you read. The PRWR system is an excellent way to boost your study power. By using it consistently, you'll become a better reader, you'll remember much more of what you read, and you'll be able to study effectively.

PRWR is an abbreviation of the system's four steps: 2

1. **P**review the reading.
2. **R**ead the material and mark important parts.
3. **W**rite notes to help you study the material.
4. **R**ecite the ideas in your notes.

You can put this system to work immediately. Each step is explained in detail   3
below, and a textbook selection is included for you to practice on.

STEP 1: PREVIEW THE READING

When you go to a party, you might look the scene over to locate the buffet, check   4
out the music, and see who's there. After getting an overview of what's happening,
you'll be more at home and ready to get down to the business of serious partying.
Similarly, a several-minute preview of a reading gives you a general overview of the
selection before you begin a careful reading. By "breaking the ice" and providing a
quick sense of the new material, the preview will help you get into the reading more
easily. There are four parts to a good preview:

• *Consider the title.* The title is often a tiny summary of the selection. Use it to help   5
you focus in on the central idea of the material. For instance, a selection titled
"Theories of Personality" will tell you to expect a list of differing theories of
personality.

• *Read over the first and last paragraphs of the selection.* The first paragraph or so   6
of a reading is often written as an introduction. It may thus present the main ideas,
giving you an overview of what's coming. The last paragraphs may be a summary
of a reading and thus give you another general view of the main ideas.

• *Note headings and their relationships.* Main headings tell you what sections are   7
about. They are generally printed in darker and/or larger type; they may be written
all in capital letters or in a different color. The main headings under the title
"Theories of Personality," for example, would probably tell you which theories
are being covered.

Subheadings fall under main headings and help identify and organize the material   8
under main heads. Subheads are printed in a way that makes them more prominent than
the text but less prominent than the main headings. A selection may even contain sub-
subheadings to label and organize material under the subheads. Here is how a series of
heads might look:

MAIN HEAD (at the margin in larger type)
   Subhead (indented and in slightly smaller type)
      Sub-subhead (further indented and in even smaller type)

Together, the headings may form a general outline of a selection. Note, for instance, the
main heading and subheads in this article.

• *Sample the text randomly°*. Read a few parts that seem likely to contain especially 9
significant information—the first sentence of some paragraphs, words set off in
italics or **boldface**, and visuals (pictures, diagrams, and graphs). Also keep an eye
out for prominent lists and definitions.

Does all this sound like a waste of time to you? You may wonder if it wouldn't be 10
better just to get on with reading the assignment. Well, don't reject previewing until
you've tried it a few times. The few minutes spent on previewing will help you to better
understand a selection once you do read it. To see how this works, take about three
minutes to preview the following textbook selection, taken from a popular college
textbook: *Communicate!* Sixth Edition, by Rudolph F. Verderber (Wadsworth, 1990).

DISCLOSING FEELINGS

An extremely important aspect of self-disclosure is the sharing of feelings. We all 11
experience feelings such as happiness at receiving an unexpected gift, sadness about the
breakup of a relationship, or anger when we believe we have been taken advantage of. The
question is whether to disclose° such feelings, and if so, how. Self-disclosure of feelings
usually will be most successful not when feelings are withheld or displayed but when they
are described. Let's consider each of these forms of dealing with feelings.

Withholding Feelings

Withholding feelings—that is, keeping them inside and not giving any verbal or nonverbal 12
cues to their existence is generally an inappropriate means of dealing with feelings.
Withholding feelings is best exemplified by the good poker player who develops a "poker
face," a neutral look that is impossible to decipher°. The look is the same whether the
player's cards are good or bad. Unfortunately, many people use poker faces in their
relationships, so that no one knows whether they hurt inside, are extremely excited, and so
on. For instance, Doris feels very nervous when Candy stands over her while Doris is
working on her report. And when Candy says, "That first paragraph isn't very well
written," Doris begins to seethe°, yet she says nothing— she withholds her feelings.

Psychologists believe that when people withhold feelings, they can develop physical 13
problems such as ulcers, high blood pressure, and heart disease, as well as psychological
problems such as stress-related neuroses and psychoses. Moreover, people who withhold
feelings are often perceived° as cold, undemonstrative, and not much fun to be around.

Is withholding ever appropriate? When a situation is inconsequential°, you may well 14
choose to withhold your feelings. For instance, a stranger's inconsiderate behavior at a
party may bother you, but because you can move to another part of the room, withholding
may not be detrimental°. In the example of Doris seething at Candy's behavior, however,
withholding could be costly to Doris.

Displaying Feelings

Displaying feelings means expressing those feelings through a facial reaction, body 15
response, and/or paralinguistic° reaction. Cheering over a great play at a sporting event,
booing the umpire at a perceived bad call, patting a person on the back when the person
does something well, or saying, "What are you doing?" in a nasty tone of voice are all
displays of feelings.

Displays are especially appropriate when the feelings you are experiencing are 16 positive. For instance, when Gloria does something nice for you, and you experience a feeling of joy, giving her a big hug is appropriate; when Don gives you something you've wanted, and you experience a feeling of appreciation, a big smile or an "Oh, thank you, Don" is appropriate. In fact, many people need to be even more demonstrative of good feelings. You've probably seen the bumper sticker "Have you hugged your kid today?" It reinforces the point that you need to display love and affection constantly to show another person that you really care.

Displays become detrimental to communication when the feelings you are 17 experiencing are negative—especially when the display of a negative feeling appears to be an overreaction. For instance, when Candy stands over Doris while she is working on her report and says, "That first paragraph isn't very well written," Doris may well experience resentment. If Doris lashes out at Candy by screaming, "Who the hell asked you for your opinion," Doris's display no doubt will hurt Candy's feelings and short-circuit their communication. Although displays of negative feelings may be good for you psychologically, they are likely to be bad for you interpersonally.

Describing Feelings

Describing feelings—putting your feelings into words in a calm, nonjudgmental 18 way—tends to be the best method of disclosing feelings. Describing feelings not only increases chances for positive communication and decreases chances for short-circuiting lines of communication, it also teaches people how to treat you. When you describe your feelings, people are made aware of the effect of their behavior. This knowledge gives them the information needed to determine whether they should continue or repeat that behavior. If you tell Paul that you really feel flattered when he visits you, such a statement should encourage Paul to visit you again; likewise, when you tell Cliff that you feel very angry when he borrows your jacket without asking, he is more likely to ask the next time he borrows a jacket. Describing your feelings allows you to exercise a measure of control over others' behavior toward you.

Describing and displaying feelings are not the same. Many times people think they 19 are describing when in fact they are displaying feelings or evaluating.

If describing feelings is so important to communication effectiveness, why don't 20 more people do it regularly? There seem to be at least four reasons why many people don't describe feelings.

1. *Many people have a poor vocabulary of words for describing the various* 21 *feelings they are experiencing.* People can sense that they are angry; however, they may not know whether what they are feeling might best be described as annoyed, betrayed, cheated, crushed, disturbed, furious, outraged, or shocked. Each of these words describes a slightly different aspect of what many people lump together as anger.

2. *Many people believe that describing their true feelings reveals too much* 22 *about themselves.* If you tell people when their behavior hurts you, you risk their using the information against you when they want to hurt you on purpose. Even so, the potential benefits of describing your feelings far outweigh the risks. For instance, if Pete has a nickname for you that you don't

like and you tell Pete that calling you by that nickname really makes you nervous and tense, Pete may use the nickname when he wants to hurt you, but he is more likely to stop calling you by that name. If, on the other hand, you don't describe your feelings to Pete, he is probably going to call you by that name all the time because he doesn't know any better. When you say nothing, you reinforce his behavior. The level of risk varies with each situation, but you will more often improve a relationship than be hurt by describing feelings.

3.   *Many people believe that if they describe feelings, others will make them feel*   23 *guilty about having such feelings.* At a very tender age we all learned about "tactful" behavior. Under the premise that "the truth sometimes hurts" we learned to avoid the truth by not saying anything or by telling "little" lies. Perhaps when you were young your mother said, "Don't forget to give Grandma a great big kiss." At that time you may have blurted out, "Ugh—it makes me feel yucky to kiss Grandma. She's got a mustache." If your mother responded, "That's terrible—your grandma loves you. Now you give her a kiss and never let me hear you talk like that again!" then you probably felt guilty for having this "wrong" feeling. But the point is that the thought of kissing your grandma made you feel "yucky" whether it should have or not. In this case what was at issue was the way you talked about the feelings—not your having the feelings.

4.   *Many people believe that describing feelings causes harm to others or to a*   24 *relationship.* If it really bothers Max when his girlfriend, Dora, bites her fingernails, Max may believe that describing his feelings to Dora will hurt her so much that the knowledge will drive a wedge into their relationship. So it's better for Max to say nothing, right? Wrong! If Max says nothing, he's still going to be bothered by Dora's behavior. In fact, as time goes on, Max will probably lash out at Dora for other things because he can't bring himself to talk about the behavior that really bothers him. The net result is that not only will Dora be hurt by Max's behavior, but she won't understand the true source of his feelings. By not describing his feelings, Max may well drive a wedge into their relationship anyway.

If Max does describe his feelings to Dora, she might quit or at least try to quit biting   25 her nails; they might get into a discussion in which he finds out that she doesn't want to bite them but just can't seem to stop, and he can help her in her efforts to stop; or they might discuss the problem and Max may see that it is a small thing really and not let it bother him as much. The point is that in describing feelings the chances of a successful outcome are greater than they are in not describing them.

To describe your feelings, first put the emotion you are feeling into words. Be   26 specific. Second, state what triggered the feeling. Finally, make sure you indicate that the feeling is yours. For example, suppose your roommate borrows your jacket without asking. When he returns, you describe your feelings by saying, "Cliff, I [indication that the feeling is yours] get really angry [the feeling] when you borrow my jacket without asking [trigger]." Or suppose that Carl has just reminded you of the very first time he brought you a rose. You describe your feelings by saying, "Carl, I [indication that the feeling is yours] get really tickled [the feeling] when you remind me about that first time you brought me a rose [trigger]."

You may find it easiest to begin by describing positive feelings: "I really feel elated 27
knowing that you were the one who nominated me for the position" or "I'm delighted that
you offered to help me with the housework." As you gain success with positive
descriptions, you can try negative feelings attributable to° environmental factors: "It's so
cloudy; I feel gloomy" or "When the wind howls through the cracks, I really get jumpy."
Finally, you can move to negative descriptions resulting from what people have said or
done: "Your stepping in front of me like that really annoys me" or "The tone of your voice
confuses me."

If you have previewed the above selection carefully, you already know a bit about 28
it—without even having really read much. To confirm this to yourself, answer these
questions:

- What is the selection about?

- Which are three ways of dealing with our feelings?

- What are four reasons why many people don't describe feelings?

STEP 2: READ THE MATERIAL AND MARK IMPORTANT PARTS

After previewing a selection, take the time to read it through from start to finish. 29
Keep reading even if you run into some parts you don't understand. You can always
come back to those parts. By reading straight through, you'll be in a better position to
understand the difficult parts later.

As you read, mark points you feel are especially significant. This will make it easy 30
for you to find them later when you take study notes. The goal is to mark the most
important ideas of a selection. They include:

- Definitions

- Helpful examples

- Major lists of items

- Points that receive the most space, development, and attention

Because you noted some of these ideas during the preview, identifying them as you read
will be easier.

Ways to Mark

Here are some ways to mark off important ideas: 31

- Underline definitions and identify them by writing *DEF* in the margin.

- Identify helpful examples by writing *EX* in the margin.

- Number 1, 2, 3, etc. the items in lists.

- Underline obviously important ideas. You can further set off important points by
  writing *IMP* in the margin. If important material is several lines long, do not
  underline it all, or you will end up with a page crowded with lines. Instead, draw a
  vertical line along side the material, and perhaps underline a sentence or a key few

words. If you're not yet sure if material merits marking, simply put a check by it; you can make your final decision later.

As you mark a selection, remember to be selective. Your markings should help 32 you highlight the most significant parts of the reading; if everything is marked, you won't have separated out the most important ideas. Usually you won't know what the most important ideas are in a paragraph or a section until you've read all of it. So it's good to develop a habit of reading a bit and then going back to do the marking.

STEP 3: WRITE STUDY NOTES

After reading and marking a selection, you are ready to take study notes. 33 *Notetaking is the key to successful learning.* In the very act of deciding what is important enough to write down, and of then writing it down, you begin to learn and master the material.

Here are some guidelines to use in writing study notes: 34

1. After you have previewed, read, and marked the selection, reread it. Then write out the important information on 8 and 1/2 by 11 inch sheets of paper. Write on only one side of each page.

2. Write clearly. Then you won't waste valuable study time trying to decipher your handwriting.

3. Use a combination of the author's words and your own words. Using your own words at times forces you to think about and work at understanding the material.

4. Organize your notes into a rough outline that will show relationships between ideas. Do this as follows:

   a. Write the title of the selection at the top of the first sheet of notes.
   b. Write main headings at the margin of your notes. Indent subheads about half an inch away from the margin. Indent subsubheads even more.
   c. Number items in a list, just as you did when marking important items in a list in the text. Be sure each list has a heading in your notes.

Try preparing a sheet of study notes for the material on feelings. Here is a start for 35 such a sheet of study notes:

Three Ways of Dealing with Feelings

A. *Withholding feelings—keeping them inside and not giving any verbal or non-verbal clues to their existence.*
   Ex.—poker player with a "poker face."

The activity of taking notes will help you see how useful it is to write out the important information in a selection.

STEP 4: RECITE THE IDEAS IN YOUR NOTES

After writing your study notes, go through them and write key words in the 36
margin of your notes. The words will help you study the material. For example, here are
the key words you might write in the margin of notes taken on the material about
disclosing feelings.

3 ways of dealing with feelings
Def and ex of withholding feelings
Def and ex of displaying feelings
Def and ex of describing feelings
4 reasons many don't describe feelings
3 steps to describing feelings

To study the material, turn the words in the margin into questions. First ask 37
yourself, "What does *describing feelings* mean?" Then recite the answer until you can
say it without looking at your notes. Then ask yourself, "What are the four reasons
many people don't describe their feelings?" Then recite that answer until you can say it
without looking at your notes.

Then—and this is a key point—go back and review your answer to the first 38
question. Test yourself—see if you can say the answer without looking at it. Then test
yourself on the second answer. *As you learn each new bit of information, go back and
test yourself on the previous information.* Such repeated self-testing is the real key to
effective learning.

In summary, then, this article describes a simple but extremely helpful study 39
system that you can use to learn textbook material. On a regular basis, you should
preview, read, write, and recite your college reading assignments. By doing so, and by
reciting and learning your classroom notes as well, you will be well prepared to deal
with college exams.

BASIC SKILL QUESTIONS

Vocabulary in Context

1. The word *merits* in "If you're not yet sure if material merits marking,
   simply put a check by it; you can make your final decision later"
   (paragraph 31) means
   a. forbids.
   b. deserves.
   c. illustrates.
   d. provides.

2. The word *selective* in "As you mark a selection, remember to be selective.
   Your markings should help you highlight the most significant parts of the
   reading" (paragraph 32) means
   a. colorful in marking.
   b. neat.
   c. careful in choosing.
   d. quick in making choices.

Central Point and Main Ideas

3. Which sentence best expresses the central point of the selection?
   a. Some people have trouble understanding their textbooks.
   b. PRWR is a four-step system that improves textbook study skills.
   c. There are systems that can improve study skills.
   d. The PRWR system begins with previewing the reading.

4. The main idea of paragraph 31 is best expressed in its
   a. first line.
   b. second line.
   c. third line.
   d. last sentence.

Supporting Details

5. When previewing a selection, you should *not*
   a. look at the title.
   b. read the first and last paragraphs.
   c. read every word.
   d. check the headings and their relationships.

6. _____ TRUE OR FALSE? According to the author, as you read through a selection for the first time, you should stop to reread parts you don't understand.

7. Study notes
   a. focus your attention on the important parts of a reading.
   b. should be written on both side of the paper.
   c. should always be taken word for word from the text.
   d. should be written before the selection is marked.

Transitions

8. The relationship of the second sentence below to the first is one of
   a. time.
   b. addition.
   c. comparison.
   d. illustration.

   Main headings tell you what sections are about. . . .The main headings under the title "Theories of Personality," for example, would probably tell you which theories are being covered. (Paragraph 7)

Patterns of Organization

9. The main pattern of organization of paragraph 34 is
   a. definition and example.
   b. cause and effect.
   c. list of items.
   d. comparison.

10. The main pattern of organization of the PRWR system (and thus of the selection) is
    a. time order.
    b. comparison.
    c. cause and effect.
    d. contrast.

ADVANCED SKILL QUESTIONS

Fact and Opinion

11. The statement below is
    a. a fact.
    b. an opinion.
    c. both fact and opinion.

    Each step [of PRWR] is explained in detail below, and a textbook selection is included for you to practice on. (Paragraph 3)

12. The statement below is
    a. a fact.
    b. an opinion.
    c. both fact and opinion.

    The PRWR system is an excellent way to boost your study power. (Paragraph 1)

Inferences

13. _____ TRUE OR FALSE? From the first paragraph, we can conclude that for study purposes, one or two readings are not enough.

14. From the selection, we can conclude that the PRWR system
    a. is used by all good students.
    b. is too difficult for some students.
    c. is a relatively new approach to study.
    d. can help you improve your grades.

Purpose and Tone

15. Which purpose or purposes best apply to this selection?
    a. To inform and persuade
    b. To inform and entertain
    c. To inform

16. The tone of the selection is
    a. light-hearted.
    b. scolding.
    c. helpful.
    d. annoyed.

Propaganda

17. The advertisement below (suggested by the article) is an example of which propaganda technique?
    a. Testimonial *(use of a well-known spokesperson)*
    b. Transfer *(association with an admired symbol or image)*
    c. Plain folks *(showing candidates, company executives, or customers as ordinary people)*
    d. Glittering generalities *(use of an important-sounding but unsupported claim)*

    "The PRWR system has certainly helped me study better," says Homer Jackson, college senior and star halfback.

18. The advertisement below (suggested by the article) is an example of which propaganda technique?
    a. Testimonial *(use of a well-known spokesperson)*
    b. Transfer *(association with an admired symbol or image)*
    c. Bandwagon *(the appeal to do what others are going)*
    d. Glittering generalities *(use of an important-sounding but unsupported claim)*

    Join the ranks of students all across the country who are benefiting from PRWR.

Argument

19. Check the one item that does *not* support the point that the PRWR system is probably a helpful study system:

    ____ a. Repetition is known to help students remember information.

    ____ b. The system provides for a thorough reading of assigned material.

    ____ c. Some students would rather simply read an entire selection without previewing it first.

    ____ d. The system provides for carefully organized study notes.

20. The statement below, based on the selection, expresses which fallacy?
   a. Changing the subject *(the evidence sounds good but has nothing to do with the argument)*
   b. False cause *(the argument assumes that the order of events alone shows cause and effect)*
   c. False comparison *(the argument assumes that two things being compared are more alike than they really are)*
   d. Either-or *(the argument assumes that there are only two sides to a question).*

   Students must use the PRWR system, or they'll never do well in school.

MAPPING

Complete the following map of "Preview, Read, Write, Recite." You will find headings and lists in the selection helpful. Note that the map does not include the reading on disclosing feelings.

Central Point: PRWR, a helpful textbook study system, involves four steps.

Step 1: Preview the Reading

a. _Look at title_

b. Read over the first and last paragraphs of the selection.

c. Note headings and their relationships.

d. _sample text_

Step 2: Read the Material and Mark Important Parts

a. Read the selection from start to finish.

b. Mark significant parts.

c. Use various ways of marking.

Step 3: Write Study Notes

a. Reread selection and write out important information.

b. _organize notes_

c. Use a combination of the author's and your own words.

d. _____

Step 4: Recite the Ideas in Your Notes

a. Write key words in the margins of your notes.

b. Turn key words into questions, and recite the answers.

c. _self-test_

DISCUSSION QUESTIONS

1. What study system or approach to study do you use? How does it compare or contrast with the PRWR approach?

2. Do you plan to use all or part of the PRWR system? (Be honest.) Why or why not?

3. In what ways has Edwards organized her article so that it can be studied with the PRWR system?

4. Why does Edwards write that "notetaking is the key to successful learning"? Why isn't merely reading and marking a selection enough?

Check Your Performance   **PREVIEW, READ, WRITE, RECITE**

Skill	Number Right		Points	Total
BASIC SKILL QUESTIONS				
Vocabulary in Context (2 items)	_____	x	4 =	_____
Central Point and Main Ideas (2 items)	_____	x	4 =	_____
Supporting Details (3 items)	_____	x	4 =	_____
Transitions (1 item)	_____	x	4 =	_____
Patterns of Organization (2 items)	_____	x	4 =	_____
ADVANCED SKILL QUESTIONS				
Fact and Opinion (2 items)	_____	x	4 =	_____
Inferences (2 items)	_____	x	4 =	_____
Purpose and Tone (2 items)	_____	x	4 =	_____
Propaganda (2 items)	_____	x	4 =	_____
Argument (2 items)	_____	x	4 =	_____
MAPPING (5 items)	_____	x	4 =	_____

FINAL SCORE (OF POSSIBLE 100) _____%

Enter your final score into the reading performance chart on the inside back cover.

6

The No-Fat Nation
James Fallows

Preview

Many Americans rely on working out to improve health and to feel good. It is hard, then, for us to imagine a country in which few people exercise. We might expect such a country to be full of unhealthy people struggling with weight problems. Yet James Fallows, the author of this article from *Atlantic* magazine, found almost no fat people in Japan, where exercise is the exception rather than the rule. Why are people who rarely exercise so healthy—and so slim? In this article based on his experiences in Japan, Fallows provides his answer.

Words to Watch

longevity (3): long life
cardinal (6): basic, fundamental
sedentary (7): characterized by much sitting
vigor (9): energy
omnipresent (9): constant
bestirring (10): making oneself take energetic action
frugal (10): thrifty
atavistic (12): backsliding
stupefying (14): astonishing
girth (16): fatness
satiation (18): a condition of extreme fullness

This may seem a small thing, but it sums up many of the differences between us   1
and the Japanese: they can live practically forever in circumstances that Americans have come to regard as fatal.

I'm not talking about the threat of beriberi or industrial wastes or anything so exotic—only about exercise. Most Japanese, judging by the ones I have seen during a four-and-a-half-month stay in Tokyo, live in happy ignorance of aerobics, health clubs, and Nautilus machines—and they live, and live, and live. Last summer the government released the latest set of statistics showing that Japanese people are living even longer than they used to, and easily longer than we are. The average life expectancy for Japanese women is now more than 80 years, and for men it's in the mid-70s. Yet during those long years the average Japanese person will rarely work up a sweat.   2

I should perhaps explain why this mystery is so intriguing to me. I have reached a stage in life (I've just turned 37) at which practical steps toward longevity° are more interesting than they used to be. For 20 or so years before arriving in Japan I'd placed my hopes for health and heartiness where many other Americans have: on exercise and sports. Long ago I played on school tennis teams and ran cross-country. He-man activities these may not be, but I enjoyed them, and kept on enjoying them until a few months ago. I also thought it must do at least some good to be out there, breathing hard, several times a week. Wasn't that, in fact, precisely what all the health experts recommended?   3

The only thing I'm now sure of is that exercise used to make me feel better. These days I don't get any, and I feel like hell. In Japan I walk a lot—to and from train stations, up and down the endless subway stairs—but almost never run, swim, play tennis or basketball, or engage in any other forms of exercise that tax lungs and sweat glands. Last month, on a trip to Hiroshima, I rowed my family around in a little boat. Three months ago I sneaked onto the British Embassy's tennis court and played tennis for half an hour—mixed doubles. That's about it.   4

The reason for my new indolence is perfectly simple: Tokyo is so crowded that it doesn't have space for sports. I once read that Frank Shorter, the famous marathoner, never missed a day of running, even when on the road. He'd change his clothes in an airport bathroom and head outside to put in a few miles. No doubt he would have found a way to make even Tokyo into a sports paradise. I frequently see a few people like him—Westerners, mainly, who push their way down the jammed sidewalks as they attempt to "run" a few miles.   5

Conceivably I could have followed their example—running late at night after my trip home on the train. My wife could theoretically have gone swimming, if she'd been willing to wait in line several hours at the pool built for the 1964 Olympic Games. We could have tried harder, could have joined the foreign madmen dodging down the street, could have shown more of that cardinal° Japanese virtue, fighting spirit. My point is that most Japanese—who, after all, are going to outlive us—take Tokyo's limits for granted and don't even try.   6

The few exercise clubs that exist in Tokyo are well beyond the reach of the average Japanese family. One extremely well-off Japanese friend told me that he had recently joined a swimming club with a $10,000 initiation fee. The club has 1,500 members, who compete for use of one 25-meter pool. When they stop working and are ready to have a good time, most Japanese still prefer more or less sedentary° activities—purposeful drinking, fancy restaurant meals, parties to view the cherry blossoms or maple leaves or even the new-fallen snow. Teenage girls in Tokyo have lately favored carrying black nylon tennis-racket bags, labeled Dunlop or Donnay, as fashion accessories and statements of self. From the way they hang on the girls'   7 shoulders and feel when they jab into my kidneys on the subway car, I assume that the bags actually contain rackets. But I would bet that most of them have never been used—unless, of course, being carried and admired is in fact their primary function.

Many Japanese youngsters take up gymnastics, *kendo,* or other aerobic activities, but as grown-up "salarymen" or housewives, they tend to leave these childish pursuits behind. In America I often talked sports with my friends—not sports we watched so much as sports we played. In Japan I've had many conversations about the sumo *bashos* (tournaments) and Japan-league baseball, but the only friends who have mentioned their own athletic interests are those who have lived in America and come to think of exercise as something they "should" have.   8

So why are they all so healthy? Why, even before outliving us, do they look so much fresher and less shopworn than Westerners of similar age? (My rule of thumb when meeting a Japanese man is to guess his age by Western standards of wrinkles and hair loss—and then add 10 years to come up with his real age. The misjudgment runs the other way, too: people here are always guessing that I am older than I am.) Maybe they look so young because Tokyo's cheerless climate spares them the withering effects of the sun. But there must be more to Japanese vigor° and longevity than the near omnipresent° cloud cover over Tokyo, which has a copious annual rainfall.   9

The answer, of course, is the Japanese diet. By living so long while bestirring° themselves so little, the Japanese prove that their diet is healthier than ours—and that diet matters more than exercise does. But there is an emotional significance to this statement that is hard to appreciate until you've lived it. Japanese food is on the whole superb, one of the adornments of the culture. Yet merely by eating it one begins to feel part of a society that is frugal°, competitive, keen-edged.   10

Like most other Americans, I've heard for years that our national cuisine contains too much fat. But I never took this personally until I came to Japan. For the first month or two after arrival my wife and children and I felt constantly famished—even after we had gotten over the price shock that at first made us reluctant to buy anything at all. Although it took us a while to realize it, we were being starved for fat: a meal couldn't leave us feeling really full unless it laid down a rime of fat globules in our mouths and stomachs. (Let's not talk about our arteries.) Japanese food is varied and flavorful, and when accompanied by mounds of rice it can even seem filling. But for us it lacked staying power, because it had so little fat.   11

A week or two after arrival we suddenly grasped what was wrong when we passed one of Tokyo's countless McDonald's outlets and, overcome by atavistic° cravings, turned back and rushed in. We ate Big Macs and drank milkshakes, felt the grease on our lips and fingers, and carried a full feeling with us the rest of the day.   12

We've adjusted more gracefully after our several months here. We live on rice, fish, pickles, noodles, and miso soup, made from soybeans. Most of the time we feel satisfied. We tell ourselves that Japan is making us healthier, even though we puff and trudge when we climb subway steps and generally feel like we're falling apart. But the idea that fat distinguishes the two cultures stays with us, like the fat from an order of fries.   13

It's not that the Japanese are uninterested in greasy, fat-drenched food. They are wild about McDonald's, Kentucky Fried Chicken, Mr. Donut, and other American-style fat mines. Their own cuisine features one cheap, popular item that approximates the hot dog in nutritional value: *ton katsu,* a fatty pork cutlet, breaded and prepared like a Texas   14 chicken-fried steak. I need hardly add that the local *ton katsu* outlet is my family's favorite haunt. Sushi eaters pay a premium for *toro*, the oiliest part of the tuna. Some of the most expensive food to be had in Japan (which is saying something) is its domestic beef, which is so thickly marbled with fat that every bite is a swirl of red and white. For sheer stupefying° obesity, the biggest Japanese sumo wrestlers, at 400 pounds and up, make William "The Refrigerator" Perry look like an overpublicized fake.

But while recognizing that fat has its place, and even according it some dignity, 15 the Japanese somehow avoid getting carried away. After we'd been going to a local public bath for several weeks, one of my sons looked around the room, inspecting the bodies one by one. Then he asked, in his loudest voice, "Daddy, why aren't there any fat people in Japan?" His question made me realize why I felt so at home in the baths. In America the typical locker-room situation always made me think of myself as an underdeveloped weakling. Here I was merely tall.

About a month later I visited Yokosuka, a port town south of Tokyo where the 16 U.S. Navy has a base. For the first time in Japan I saw dozens of American families on the street, not just the scattered businessmen and consultants of Tokyo. I stared goggle-eyed at my countrymen, amazed not at how tall they were or what a variety of colors they came in but at how many of them were fat. How do they do it? I found myself wondering. How can they possibly eat enough to become so much fatter than the Japanese? (The Japanese Ministry of Agriculture says that there's no mystery at all about the difference in girth°. The average American is said to ingest 800 calories a day more than a Japanese—3,393 calories versus 2,593.)

Because fat in America runs along class lines, it should not be surprising that 17 sailors' wives were fatter than the downtown sharpies from IBM. Still, I marveled at us as Americans, regardless of class. Every tank town in America has better sports facilities than can be found practically anywhere in Japan—but we take it for granted that we and our friends will get bigger and heavier with each passing year. Why did this happen to us? How do the cooped-up Japanese remain so fit?

Primitive cultures attach moral and political significance to body size—powerful 18 chiefs had better look well fed—and I'm afraid that I am starting to do the same thing. Forty years ago the physical contrast between Americans and Japanese was between the tall, strong victors and the short, weak vanquished. Now it looks to me like a contrast between a soft culture and a hard one—between people who eat to satiation° and those whose portions are small.

The Japanese do permit themselves excesses: each night on the subway I see 19 businessmen who are fall-down, throw-up drunk. But they generally curb their appetites and channel their energies into production, not mere exercise. On a trip outside Japan I watched a bodybuilder from UCLA work out in a hotel gym. I thought about the hours of hard work his physique had cost him. There are very few who resemble him in Japan. His counterparts spend their time not in the gym but with the work group.

Some Japanese friends tell me that things are changing. Kids are overeating now; 20 adults are starting to worry about weight. I don't believe it, but I take heart from their concern. When *Jane Fonda's Workout Book* becomes a best-seller in Japan, we'll know that our industries have a chance.

BASIC SKILL QUESTIONS

Vocabulary in Context

1. The word *indolence* in "The reason for my new indolence is . . . Tokyo . . . doesn't have space for sports" (paragraph 5) means
   a. activity.
   b. laziness.
   c. conditioning.
   d. anger.

2. The word *famished* in "my wife and children and I felt constantly famished. . . . we were being starved for fat" (paragraph 11) means
   a. very hungry.
   b. satisfied.
   c. stuffed.
   d. poor.

3. The word *copious* in "But there must be more to Japanese vigor and longevity than the near omnipresent cloud cover over Tokyo, which has a copious annual rainfall" (paragraph 9) means
   a. small.
   b. rare.
   c. welcome.
   d. plentiful.

Central Point and Main Ideas

4. Which sentence best expresses the central point of the selection?
   a. There are no fat people in Japan.
   b. Though the Japanese rarely exercise, they live longer lives than Americans because of their low-fat diet.
   c. The average Japanese eats 800 calories a day less than the average American.
   d. Exercising in Tokyo is difficult because it is so crowded and health clubs are very expensive.

5. Which sentence best expresses the main idea of paragraph 2?
   a. The Japanese exercise less but live longer than Americans.
   b. Japanese men live until their mid-70s.
   c. Japanese women live until their 80s.
   d. Most Japanese exercise rarely.

Supporting Details

6. Many Japanese exercise
   a. in health clubs.
   b. when they are young.
   c. by jogging.
   d. by wrestling and playing baseball.

7. According to the article, the Japanese combination of long life, little exercise and a low-fat diet proves
   a. exercise is harmful.
   b. exercise makes no contribution to health.
   c. diet is more important to good health than exercise.
   d. watching sports is better than playing them.

Transitions

8. The relationship between the two sentences below is one of
   a. time.
   b. contrast.
   c. comparison.
   d. cause-effect.

   Japanese food is on the whole superb, one of the adornments of the culture. Yet merely by eating it one begins to feel part of a society that is frugal, competitive, keen-edged. (Paragraph 10)

Patterns of Organization

9. The main pattern of organization of paragraph 8 is
   a. cause and effect.
   b. definition and example.
   c. comparison/contrast.
   d. time order.

10. The overall pattern of organization of the reading is a combination of
    a. time order and definition/example.
    b. list of items and definition/example.
    c. comparison/contrast and cause/effect.
    d. time order and comparison.

ADVANCED SKILL QUESTIONS

Fact and Opinion

11. The sentence below is a statement of
    a. fact.
    b. opinion.
    c. both fact and opinion.

    The average American is said to ingest 800 calories a day more than a Japanese—3,393 calories versus 2,593. (Paragraph 16)

12. Which of the following is a statement of fact?
    a. "Maybe they look so young because Tokyo's cheerless climate spares them the withering effects of the sun."
    b. "Japanese food is on the whole superb, one of the adornments of the culture."
    c. "Last month, on a trip to Hiroshima, I rowed my family around in a little boat."
    d. "When *Jane Fonda's Workout Book* becomes a best-seller in Japan, we'll know that our industries have a chance."

Inferences

13. The author implies that the Japanese diet is
    a. a reflection of the nature of the Japanese people.
    b. inexpensive.
    c. made up of food that is less tasty than American food.
    d. easy for Americans to adjust to.

14. __T__ TRUE OR FALSE? The author implies that the Japanese people have less time for leisure activities than Americans.

15. __T__ TRUE OR FALSE? The author implies that it takes time to adjust to a low-fat diet.

Purpose and Tone

16. The author's main purpose is to
    a. inform Americans about the Japanese culture.
    b. entertain readers with amusing stories of his Japanese adventures.
    c. persuade Americans that a low-fat diet is more important to good health than exercise.

17. In general, the author's tone is
    a. angry but understanding.
    b. self-pitying and hopeless.
    c. critical and ridiculing.
    d. serious but good-humored.

Propaganda

18. The advertisement below (suggested by the article) is an example of which propaganda technique?
    a. Testimonial *(use of a well-known spokesperson)*
    b. Bandwagon *(the appeal to do what many others are doing)*
    c. Plain folks *(showing candidates, company executives, or customers as ordinary people)*
    d. Transfer *(association with an admired symbol or image)*

    Try our new Japanese-style diet and join the millions of Japanese who are eating right.

Argument

19. Which of the following statements is a valid conclusion based on the information in paragraph 14?
    a. All Japanese love McDonald's food.
    b. Fatty foods are expensive in Japan because foreigners increase the demand for them.
    c. Chain restaurants selling Japanese fast food would certainly be successful in the United States.
    d. The Japanese eat some food that is high in fat.

20. Which of the following evidence does *not* support the author's conclusion that the Japanese are healthier than we are?
    a. "[The Japanese] can live practically forever in circumstances that Americans have come to regard as fatal."
    b. "The few exercise clubs that exist in Tokyo are well beyond the reach of the average Japanese family."
    c. "But while recognizing that fat has its place . . . the Japanese somehow avoid getting carried away."
    d. "Last summer the government released the latest set of statistics showing that the Japanese people are living even longer than they used to, and easily longer than we are."

OUTLINING

Following is an incomplete outline based on "The No-Fat Nation." Complete it by filling in the missing major and minor details. The details appear in random order below the outline.

Central Point: In contrast to Americans, the Japanese rarely exercise, yet they live longer, healthier lives because of their low-fat diets.

A.   The Japanese way of life
    1. Little exercise for adults

       a. ~~Look~~ *No space in Tokyo*
       b. Expense of health clubs
    2. Low-fat diet
    3. Effects on health

       a. *healthier looks*

       b. *" lives*
B.   *American way of life*
    1. Belief in regular exercise for adults
    2. High-fat diet

    3. *effects on life*
       a. Look older than Japanese
       b. Shorter lives than Japanese

Items Missing from the Outline

- Healthier looks than Americans
- Lack of space in Tokyo
- Effects on health
- Longer lives than Americans
- The American way of life

DISCUSSION QUESTIONS

1.   What facts does Fallows give to show that the Japanese are healthier than Americans? Has he left anything out?

2.   While the Japanese diet is central to Fallows' essay, he doesn't mention it until paragraph 10. Why do you think he didn't mention diet earlier in the article?

3.   Besides the facts that the Japanese live longer than Americans, don't exercise much, and eat a low-fat diet, what do we know about life in Japan after reading "The No-Fat Nation"?

4.   Should all Americans be asked to read this article? Why or why not?

Check Your Performance   THE NO-FAT NATION

Skill	*Number Right*	*Points*	*Total*
BASIC SKILL QUESTIONS			
Vocabulary in Context (3 items)	_____	x 4 =	_____
Central Point and Main Ideas (2 items)	_____	x 4 =	_____
Supporting Details (2 items)	_____	x 4 =	_____
Transitions (1 item)	_____	x 4 =	_____
Patterns of Organization (2 items)	_____	x 4 =	_____
ADVANCED SKILL QUESTIONS			
Fact and Opinion (2 items)	_____	x 4 =	_____
Inferences (3 items)	_____	x 4 =	_____
Purpose and Tone (2 items)	_____	x 4 =	_____
Propaganda (1 item)	_____	x 4 =	_____
Argument (2 items)	_____	x 4 =	_____
OUTLINING (5 items)	_____	x 4 =	_____

FINAL SCORE (OF POSSIBLE 100)   _____%

Enter your final score into the reading performance chart on the inside back cover.

7

Death on the Road
Albert R. Karr

Preview

Do you consider yourself a better-than-average driver? If you do, you have plenty of company, according to this article from the *Wall Street Journal*. In fact, most drivers consider their skills to be above average. Then what is the cause of all the accidents? And what can be done to improve traffic safety? The answers in this selection may surprise you.

Words to Watch

reverting (2): returning
ingrained (2): deep-seated
proneness (6): tendency
inducing (8): causing
embargo (9): ban on trade

In 1904, the story goes, there were just two automobiles in Kansas City, Mo. 1
They crashed into each other at an intersection.

Many of today's 155 million U.S. drivers continue to have trouble avoiding 2
collisions, and traffic-safety experts continue to search for ways to make driving safer.
After an emphasis on improving the designs of cars and roads in recent years, the auto-safety focus now is reverting° to what used to be called "the nut behind the wheel." But it isn't easy to improve the ingrained° behavior of drivers, whom some analysts blame for more than 90% of all traffic accidents.

The problem is that pinpointing which drivers are to blame for crashes, why 3
accidents happen and how to stop them remains elusive. For example, drivers with the worst accident or violation records do account for more than their share of accidents, but their numbers are relatively few, and they cause only a small percentage of all crashes.

"The largest part of the traffic-accident problem has been shown to involve lapses by normal drivers rather than errors by just a few problem cases," according to Theodore Forbes, a Michigan State University psychology professor and highway-safety research adviser.

Changing driver habits is so difficult partly because "people just don't take 4 driving seriously," says Frank Kramer, an accident investigator for the California Highway Patrol. "They grow up with it and take it as second nature. They never stop to think they're driving 3,000 to 4,000 pounds of steel down the road at 40 to 50 miles per hour."

The leading cause of accidents, an Indiana University study concluded, is failure 5 to look for or see hazards before pulling into traffic, changing lanes or passing. Other causes include excessive speed; improper evasive action in an emergency, such as locking the brakes instead of steering around an obstacle; inattention; and distractions within the car. (Distraction from stereo tapes rose steadily during the four-year period studied.)

According to General Motors Corp. researchers, following other cars too closely 6 is an important factor in accident proneness°. And it's estimated that 40% to 50% of fatal traffic accidents involve drinking drivers.

Combination of Causes

What prevents easy solutions is the fact that although various unsafe acts, such as 7 speeding or tailgating, can lead to a collision, they usually don't. Other things generally have to be wrong, too: poor judgment or slow reactions by more than one driver, car-design features that impair a driver's vision or otherwise increase the hazard, or perhaps a tricky road. A number of these problems combine to produce an accident.

Many safety experts say the car and the road play bigger roles than often realized 8 in inducing° bad driving and are easier to improve than driver behavior. Nevertheless, a new wave of driver-training programs is springing up around the country to teach traffic-law violators and others to drive more safely. More states are cracking down on drunk drivers. And the federal government is pushing driver-related programs.

Ironically, the most effective driver-control measure has been one aimed at saving 9 fuel rather than lives—the 55-mile-per-hour national speed limit first imposed during the 1974 Arab oil embargo°. The speed limit is cited as the major factor in a drop in U.S. traffic fatalities from a peak of 54,600 in 1972 to a recent low 44,500 in 1975. One reason is that between 45 and 60 mph, the chances of death in a crash double, and they double again from 60 to 70 mph.

Concerned that compliance with the law has slipped, many states are renewing 10 efforts to enforce the 55-mph limit. In Missouri, for example, speeding citations climbed from 51,000 in 1973 to 182,000 in 1974 after the new speed limit was imposed, and highway deaths fell 26% to 1,075. But later, as speeds crept up, so did fatalities. Thus, a new effort was begun in 1978, using aircraft and other means, along with a lot of publicity, to show that the crackdown was "serious," says Lt. Ralph Biele, a Missouri Highway Patrol spokesman. The crackdown, along with a recent campaign against drunk driving, has helped cut road deaths again, by 14% between 1978 and 1981.

Enforcement of the 55-mph limit, however, is facing resistance in many states, 11 especially Western states, where road speeds have long been high. Safety experts warn that reduced speeding penalties could increase highway fatalities; indeed, when Maryland troopers seeking a pay raise engaged in a ticket-writing slowdown for several months last year, road deaths climbed. Since 1975, federal figures show, most of the U.S. increase in deaths has occurred in the West.

A growing number of states also are stepping up highway enforcement and 12 passing laws requiring stiffer penalties to combat drunk driving. In the past, however, such efforts haven't permanently reduced alcohol-related fatalities substantially. One reason might be that in many crashes with alcohol involvement, bad-driving practices that aren't tied to alcohol are also involved.

Undoubtedly, police traffic-law enforcement keeps roads safer than they would be 13 without it. But the kind of driving—such as tailgating—that can lead to serious accidents often differs from driving that produces traffic violations. So, in Chicago, police are cracking down on tailgating as a major case of fatalities, says Paul L. Tasch, the commander of the Chicago Police Department's traffic-enforcement division. "It's a difficult charge to enforce," he says, "but we've zeroed in on it and are trying to increase the number of arrests."

Mixed Results

Other driver-related programs have produced mixed results. Many states and localities 14 have installed government and private driver-improvement programs for frequent traffic violators, older drivers and others. These programs include the National Safety Council's "defensive driving" course and an attitude-mending, eight-hour session offered in about a dozen states by the National Traffic Safety Institute, a Salem, Ore., company formed in 1975.

Studies of such programs frequently show a small improvement in violators' 15 safety records and sometimes a reduction in traffic convictions; but accident frequency changes little. In California, an improvement program for frequent violators trims accidents and violations about 10% for six months after the sessions, says Raymond Peck, a California Department of Motor Vehicles research specialist. But the effect on road safety is "very minor," he concedes—preventing about 1,200 accidents a year, or only 0.2% of the state's yearly reported total.

Longstanding high-school driver-education courses also have fallen short of safety 16 planners' goals. A recent four-year federal demonstration project in Georgia's DeKalb County, which includes Atlanta, was designed to assess whether an advanced driver-ed course could clearly result in safer driving. But the analysis so far shows that although traffic violations by the course's graduates were lower than for others, there was little reduction in accidents—a typical result for many driver-improvement programs.

Educational Hazard?

Some studies conclude that high-school driver-education actually reduces highway 17 safety by encouraging the licensing of high-risk young drivers and putting them on the road earlier than otherwise. Leon Robertson, a Yale University safety researcher, found that when Connecticut eliminated financing for driver-ed and nine school systems dropped the courses, licensing and crash involvement of 16-year-olds and 17-year-olds dropped sharply.

Predictions Difficult

Though some drivers have more traffic violations and accidents than others, past records 18
often are of little help in predicting who will have accidents. Most offenders in any one
year invariably turn out to be crash- and violation-free for, say, the next three years, and
for the previous three years, too. Studies show that if an "accident-prone" group can be
identified and millions of persons screened out from being licensed, those who would
actually have accidents would be a small part of that group.

Other studies show that most drivers involved in crashes blame others for the 19
accidents and that 90% of those surveyed consider their driving to be better than
average. The difficulty of changing such attitudes prompts some experts to conclude that
more significant safety gains can be made by making cars more protective or by
designing highways that make safe driving easier.

"We have no empirical evidence that trying to change the behavior of the driver is 20
effective, and we have a lot of evidence that improving the vehicle and the highway is
very effective," says David Klein, a professor of social science at Michigan State
University and a veteran highway-safety analyst.

Even those who advocate increased attention to the driver, such as Mr. Knaff of 21
the federal traffic-safety agency, concede that any gains will come slowly. "There's no
such thing," he says, "as a silver bullet."

BASIC SKILL QUESTIONS

Vocabulary in Context

1. The word *elusive* in "The problem is that pinpointing . . . why accidents
   happen and how to stop them remains elusive" (paragraph 3) means
   a. difficult to grasp.
   b. clear.
   c. critical.
   d. alone.

2. The word *empirical* in "We have no empirical evidence that trying to
   change the behavior of the driver is effective, and we have a lot of
   evidence that improving the vehicle and the highway is very effective"
   (paragraph 20) means
   a. unreliable.
   b. strange.
   c. discouraging.
   d. proven as fact.

Central Point and Main Ideas

3. Which sentence best expresses the central point of this article?
   a. Accidents are caused by unsafe actions.
   b. Most traffic accidents are caused by poor vehicle and highway design.
   c. Drunk drivers may be involved in as many as half of fatal traffic accidents.
   d. There seems to be no easy solution to the problem of driver error, the main cause of traffic accidents.

4. Which sentence best expresses the main idea of paragraph 16?
   a. According to one study, driver-education courses for high-school students have not significantly reduced accidents.
   b. The federal government sponsored an advanced driver-education course in DeKalb County, Georgia.
   c. Graduates of the federal driver-education project in Georgia committed fewer traffic violations than others.
   d. A four-year federal demonstration project analyzed an advanced driver-ed course.

Supporting Details

5. ___T___ TRUE OR FALSE? Accidents are usually caused by a combination of problems.

6. According to the article, the 55-mile-per-hour speed limit
   a. was originally designed to save lives.
   b. eliminates crashes.
   c. has resulted in fewer fatal crashes.
   d. has always been fully enforced.

7. According to a California accident investigator, drivers
   a. are not mindful of the fact that they drive up to 4,000 pounds of steel at highway speeds.
   b. easily change their driving habits.
   c. take driving very seriously.
   d. are usually aware of the potential dangers of driving a large vehicle at high speeds.

8. The central point of this article is supported by
   a. opinions.
   b. statistics.
   c. factual examples.
   d. all of the above.

Transitions

9. The relationship between the two sentences below is one of
   a. cause and effect.
   b. time.
   c. illustration.
   d. contrast.

   > Many safety experts say the car and the road . . . are easier to improve than driver behavior. Nevertheless, a new wave of driver-training programs is springing up. . . . (Paragraph 8)

Patterns of Organization

10. In paragraph 10, the author presents
    a. a definition and example about driving (definition and example).
    b. a listing of many programs enforcing the 55-mph speed limit (list of items).
    c. a comparison of states' enforcement programs (comparison).
    d. the results of one state's efforts to enforce the 55-mph speed limit (cause and effect).

ADVANCED SKILL QUESTIONS

Fact and Opinion

11. The following is a statement of
    a. fact.
    b. opinion.
    c. fact and opinion.

    > In Missouri, for example, speeding citations climbed from 51,000 in 1973 to 182,000 in 1974 after the new speed limit was imposed, and highway deaths fell 26% to 1,075. (Paragraph 10)

12. Which of the following is a statement of opinion?
    a. "According to General Motors Corporation researchers, following other cars too closely is an important factor in accident proneness."
    b. "More states are cracking down on drunk drivers."
    c. "One reason might be that in many crashes with alcohol involvement, bad-driving practices that aren't tied to alcohol are also involved."
    d. "Longstanding high-school driver-education courses also have fallen short of safety planners' goals."

Inferences

13. ___✓___ TRUE OR FALSE? From the article, we can conclude that driving will undoubtedly be much safer by the year 2000.

14. The author implies that driver-training programs
    a. succeed only with older drivers.
    b. are producing disappointing results.
    c. are growing because of their great success in improving driver behavior.
    d. are more effective than the 55-mile-per-hour speed limit.

Purpose and Tone

15. The purpose of this article is
    a. to inform.
    b. to persuade.
    c. to entertain.

16. The tone of this article can be described as
    a. pleading.
    b. objective.
    c. annoyed.
    d. optimistic.

Propaganda

17. The phrase "the nut behind the wheel" might be considered a form of
    a. transfer *(association with an admired symbol or image).*
    b. plain folks *(showing candidates, company executives, or customers as ordinary people).*
    c. name calling *(use of negative, emotionally-loaded language against a rival).*
    d. glittering generality *(use of an important-sounding but unsupported claim).*

Argument

18. Check the statement that is the point of the following argument. Note that two other statements support the point, and that one statement is neither the point nor the support of the argument.

    _____ The results of high school driver-education courses have been disappointing.

    __✓__ Improving driving habits is difficult.

    _____ There's a lot of evidence that improving the vehicle and the highway can lower the number of automotive accidents.

    _____ Such programs as the National Safety Council's "defensive driving" course have little impact on accident frequency.

19. According to information in the article, the statement below would be an example of what fallacy?

    a. Changing the subject (*the evidence sounds good but has nothing to do with the argument*)

    b. Straw man (*the argument is made by claiming an opponent holds an extreme position and then opposing that extreme position*).

    c. False cause (*the argument assumes that the order of events alone shows cause and effect*).

    d. False comparison (*the argument assumes that two things being compared are more alike than they really are*).

    School board members trying to eliminate driver education clearly care more about the budget than about safety on the road.

20. Check the statement that is the *point* of the following argument. Note that two other statements support the point, and that one statement is neither the point nor the support of the argument.

    _____ When speeding citations rose greatly in Missouri after the new speed limit was imposed, highway deaths fell 26 percent.

    _____ The most effective driver-control measure is the 55-mile-per-hour speed limit.

    _____ It's estimated that drinking drivers are involved in 40 to 50 percent of fatal traffic accidents.

    _____ As speeds crept up in Missouri, so did fatalities.

SUMMARIZING

Below is the first part of a summary of "Death on the Road" followed by three different ways of completing it. Circle the letter (**a, b,** or **c**) of the best ending to the summary.

> Improving driving behavior—the leading cause of highway accidents— is not easy. So many factors are involved in accidents, including carelessness, poor driver attitudes, and non-driver-related elements like a poor road, that experts cannot predict or control driver behavior very well. Nevertheless, there is an increasing emphasis on driver-related programs. The most effective so far has been the 55-mile-an-hour speed limit.

a. Many states are now strictly enforcing this limit with notable success. In Missouri, for example, an increase in speeding tickets combined with a campaign against drunk driving cut road deaths by 14 percent within about three years.

b. However, there is much resistance to this law, especially in the Western states. In contrast to the speed limit, driver-improvement and driver-education programs have had mixed and limited success. Some experts feel that because of the poor results with most driver-related programs, the emphasis should be on improving car and road design.

c. Because of the difficulty of predicting just who will cause an accident, however, one program that is not being attempted is the refusing of licenses to accident-prone drivers. Because so much more has been learned about improving cars and highways, some experts feel efforts in those areas should be emphasized.

DISCUSSION QUESTIONS

1. Why did Karr begin with the brief anecdote about two automobiles in Kansas City, Missouri? What point is he making? How effectively does that anecdote pull the reader into the article?

2. Think about the accidents you have been in, have witnessed, or have heard about. What factors were involved in causing each accident?

3. Karr writes, "The difficulty of changing such attitudes prompts some experts to conclude that more significant safety gains can be made by making cars more protective or by designing highways that make safe driving easier." In what ways could cars and highways be improved?

4. According to accident investigator Frank Kramer, "People just don't take driving seriously." Do you agree? Why or why not?

Check Your Performance   DEATH ON THE ROAD

Skill	Number Right	Points	Total
BASIC SKILL QUESTIONS			
Vocabulary in Context (2 items)	_____	x 4 =	_____
Central Point and Main Ideas (2 items)	_____	x 4 =	_____
Supporting Details (4 items)	_____	x 4 =	_____
Transitions (1 item)	_____	x 4 =	_____
Patterns of Organization (1 item)	_____	x 4 =	_____
ADVANCED SKILL QUESTIONS			
Fact and Opinion (2 items)	_____	x 4 =	_____
Inferences (2 items)	_____	x 4 =	_____
Purpose and Tone (2 items)	_____	x 4 =	_____
Propaganda (1 item)	_____	x 4 =	_____
Argument (3 items)	_____	x 4 =	_____
SUMMARIZING (1 item)	_____	x 20 =	_____

FINAL SCORE (OF POSSIBLE 100)   _____%

Enter your final score into the reading performance chart on the inside back cover.

8

Lie Detectors: Foolproof or Fraudulent?
Diane E. Papalia and Sally Wendkos Olds

Preview

If you were falsely accused of a crime, would you trust a lie detector to prove your innocence? Or if you were a crime victim, would you trust a lie detector to prove the guilt of the person who committed the crime? A logical response to these questions would have to be based on how well you thought lie detectors work. So don't make such a decision until you read this selection, which is taken from the college textbook *Psychology,* Second Edition (McGraw-Hill, 1988).

Words to Watch

> *fraudulent* (title): deceptive
> *consequent* (1): resulting
> *justifiable* (1): defensible
> *persistent* (2): continuing
> *irrelevant* (5) not related to the case at hand
> *elicit* (5): bring out
> *physiological* (7): being of the body's processes
> *emotionality* (7): a state of great emotion
> *skepticism* (9): doubt
> *validity* (9): effectiveness

Your chances of being hooked up to a lie detector at some point are greater now than they were several years ago. Increasing numbers of government agencies and private employers have been requiring job applicants and current employees to take polygraph tests, and law enforcement agencies have turned to them more and more to help solve crimes. The consequences of "failing" a lie-detector test may include being   1 fired from a job (with a consequent° reputation for lying or theft); being refused government security clearance (with this fact going on one's record): or indictment on a criminal charge, a trial, and perhaps a prison term. What should you do if you're asked to take such a test? Are these tests useful and ethically justifiable°? Let's look at the evidence.

Suppose that Ms. A., the owner of Scooper Dupers, an ice cream parlor, finds a   2 persistent° shortage in the cash register—a discrepancy between the amount of ice cream being sold and the cash taken in. She questions her 12 employees and is unable to figure out who is either stealing money or giving away ice cream. She administers lie-detector tests to all 12. Six "fail" the test and are fired. The question is: Have the real culprits been fired?

People selling such tests often tell prospective customers that psychologists have   3 proved that they work. This is not true. What psychologists have found is that on a probability basis, they "detect" more people who are lying than people who are not. In any particular instance, however, the tests are not foolproof. (This is like the probability that when we toss a coin, we don't know on any given toss whether heads or tails will come up, but we do know that if we toss enough coins, we'll turn up half heads and half tails.)

Because results of lie detector tests have a high error rate, Ms. A. is likely to be   4 firing one or more honest employees. To see how this could be, let's see how these tests, called polygraph tests, work.

The examiner reminds the subject of his or her right not to take the test and has   5 the person sign a consent form testifying that the test is taken "voluntarily." (An important ethical issue here is how voluntary such a step can be when the subject feels that refusing to take the test will make him or her the object of suspicion.) The examiner then discusses the questions that will be asked. Some are irrelevant° ("Are you in the United States?"), some are designed to elicit° an emotional response ("Besides what you told me about, have you ever stolen anything?"), and some are related to the specific purpose of the test ("What color was the envelope containing the stolen money?").

Before the examiner actually asks the questions—usually no more than 12   6 questions over a time period of 3 to 4 minutes—devices are attached to the subject's body. These measure breathing rate, blood pressure, and electrodermal response (EDR), an index that detects changes in the resistance of the skin to the passage of a very weak electric current. This last measure, EDR, is the most accurate. The subject cannot see either the examiner or the machine's record of his or her responses.

The tests do show that certain physiological° responses reflect a high level of   7 emotionality°. But they don't necessarily prove that the emotions are linked to lying. The theory underlying these tests is that persons who are guilty of whatever wrongdoing the tests is being given to uncover will respond emotionally to the key questions and that these measures can correctly identify emotional responses. Often this is so: people show greater changes from their baseline scores (the scores they show when they're answering irrelevant questions) when they're lying than when they're telling the truth.

There are, however, many factors that affect a person's score on a test. Some   8 people react emotionally to certain words or phrases even when they're telling the truth. Those who believe that the lie detector is effective in detecting lies are more likely to receive accurate readings from it than people who don't (probably because they'll be more nervous about being found out when they lie than people who don't think that lie detectors work). It's also possible to reduce detectability in a number of ways.

Laboratory studies have shown that it's harder to detect lying by subjects who have taken tranquilizers, people who are not paying close attention to the questions, habitual liars, those of the same ethnic group as the examiner, and those who were later-born children in large families.

The principle underlying polygraph testing is that people who show anxiety are   9
lying. Yet, as the authors of a recent review of the psychological literature on these tests have pointed out, anxiety can stem from many causes other than lying (for example, the anxiety some people feel just from having to take the test). They conclude that the tests can sometimes detect deception at rates that are better than chance, especially when the test is conducted by an experienced examiner who asks narrowly focused questions of a subject who believes in the test. These psychologists point out, however, that the tests often indicate that a truthful person is lying or that a liar is telling the truth, thus giving rise to scientific skepticism about them. Such skepticism° was voiced in a recent resolution adopted by the American Psychological Association, maintaining that the scientific evidence for the validity° of polygraph tests to detect deception is unsatisfactory, and that if the test is to be given at all, it should be administered only in narrowly defined situations and by well-trained examiners. At present, civil liberties organizations are trying to ban the use of polygraph tests and are counseling people who have been asked to take them.

BASIC SKILL QUESTIONS

Vocabulary in Context

1. The word *discrepancy* in "Ms. A. . . . finds a persistent shortage in the cash register—a discrepancy between the amount of ice cream being sold and the cash taken in" (paragraph 2) means
   a. reason.
   b. scoop.
   c. customer.
   d. lack of agreement.

Central Point and Main Ideas

2. Which sentence best expresses the central point of the selection?
   a. People who sell polygraph tests often claim that psychologists have proved that they work.
   b. Government agencies and private employers have been checking up more on employees and job applicants.
   c. Using lie detectors is unjustified except, perhaps, when given by well-trained examiners in certain situations.
   d. Civil liberty organizations are trying to ban the use of polygraph tests.

3. The main idea of paragraph 8 is expressed in its
   a. first sentence.
   b. second sentence.
   c. third sentence.
   d. last sentence.

4. Which sentence best expresses the main idea of paragraph 9?
   a. Since polygraph tests can detect anxiety and since people who lie are often anxious, the tests are used to detect lying.
   b. A great deal more research must be done on polygraphs to perfect their reliability in detecting lies.
   c. Anxiety can be caused by many other things than just lying.
   d. Since polygraph tests are often not reliable, psychologists feel their used should be limited, and civil liberties organizations are trying to ban them.

Supporting Details

5. The supporting details of paragraph 8 are
   a. people's scores on lie detector tests.
   b. emotional reactions to certain words or phrases.
   c. results of laboratory studies showing that tranquilizers make it harder to detect lying.
   d. factors that affect how people score on lie-detector tests.

6. Lie detectors can
   a. usually detect lying.
   b. never detect lying.
   c. sometimes detect lying.
   d. always detect lying.

7. The scientists judging the effectiveness of lie detectors are
   a. physicians.
   b. psychologists.
   c. crime researchers.
   d. biologists.

Transitions

8. The relationship of the second sentence below to the first is one of
   a. addition.
   b. time.
   c. contrast.
   d. comparison.

   In any particular instance, however, the tests are not foolproof. (This is like the probability that when we toss a coin, we don't know on any given toss whether heads or tails will come up . . . .) (Paragraph 3)

9. The relationship of the second sentence below to the first is one of
   a. example.
   b. time.
   c. contrast.
   d. comparison.

The tests do show that certain physiological responses reflect a high level of emotionality. But they don't necessarily prove that the emotions are linked to lying. (Paragraph 7)

Patterns of Organization

10. The pattern of organization of paragraph 8 is
    a. steps in a process.
    b. a list of items.
    c. comparison/contrast.
    d. a definition and examples.

ADVANCED SKILL QUESTIONS

Fact and Opinion

11. Judging by the second sentence of paragraph 1, the first sentence is
    a. an opinion.
    b. a fact.

12. The reading is
    a. mainly factual.
    b. mainly opinion.
    c. an equal mix of fact and opinion.

Inferences

13. Why might psychologists prefer that narrowly focused questions be used with polygraph tests?
    a. Because the answers will always be less emotional.
    b. Because the subject's answer will more clearly be the truth or a lie, nothing in between.
    c. Because narrowly focused questions may take less of the examiner's time.
    d. Because broad questions make it harder to lie.

14. We can conclude from the selection that the authors
    a. are polygraph examiners.
    b. are members of civil liberties organizations.
    c. would agree to take a lie-detector test for any purpose.
    d. are probably in favor of banning lie-detector tests.

15. Civil liberties organizations are probably against polygraph tests because people who take the tests may be
    a. too young.
    b. unfairly judged.
    c. charged too much.
    d. caught in their lies.

Purpose and Tone

16. ___T___ TRUE OR FALSE? The main purpose of this selection is to to persuade readers that lie detectors are not foolproof.

17. The tone of the reading can be identified as
    a. chatty and playful.
    b. bitter and sarcastic.
    c. solemn and gloomy.
    d. concerned and analytical.

Propaganda

18. The salespeople who claim psychologists have proved that lie detectors work are using which propaganda technique?
    a. Bandwagon *(the appeal to do what many others are doing)*
    b. Plain folks *(showing candidates, company executives, or customers as ordinary folks)*
    c. Name calling *(use of negative, emotionally loaded language against a rival)*
    d. Card stacking *(purposeful omission of important, relevant information)*

Argument

19. Which of the following does *not* support the point that lie detectors are undependable?
    a. Emotional reactions detected by the tests don't necessarily result from lying.
    b. It's hard to detect lying by habitual liars.
    c. Some of a polygraph examiner's questions are irrelevant.
    d. It's hard to detect lying in people on tranquilizers.

20. Based on the information in the reading, the statement that anyone who fails a lie-detector test is a liar can be considered
    a. circular reasoning *(the statement repeats itself rather than providing a real supporting reason to back up the argument).*
    b. a personal attack *(the argument shifts to irrelevant personal attack).*
    c. a hasty generalization *(the argument makes a generalization based on insufficient evidence).*
    d. a false comparison *(the argument assumes that two things being compared are more alike than they really are).*

SUMMARIZING

1. Circle the letter of the statement that best summarizes paragraph 1.
    a. Your chances of being hooked up to a lie detector are greater now than ever.

    b. The consequences of failing a lie detector test are sometimes being fired from a job.

    c. Lie detector tests are being used more and more, so it's important to determine how useful they are.

2. Circle the letter of the statement that best summarizes paragraphs 2-4.

    a. The owner of an ice cream parlor may use a lie-detector test to figure out who is stealing money and ends up firing the six employees who "fail" the test.

    b. Lie detectors don't always detect lying, so an employer who uses the test to catch a thief may end up firing someone innocent.

    c. When we toss a coin, we don't know on any given toss whether heads or tails will come up.

3. Circle the letter of the statement that best summarizes paragraph 4 (a transition paragraph) through paragraph 6.

    a. There are several steps to a polygraph test, which measure various biological responses.

    b. A polygraph examiner usually asks no more than twelve questions over a period of three to four minutes.

    c. The most accurate measure in a lie detector is the EDR—the electrodermal response, an index that detects changes in the resistance of the skin to a very weak electric current.

4. Circle the letter of the statement that best summarizes paragraphs 7-8.

    a. Often people show greater changes from their baseline scores when they're lying than when they're telling the truth.

    b. Although lie-detector tests do measure emotionality, there are other reasons for emotion beside lying and there are other factors that affect test scores.

    c. According to laboratory studies, it is harder to detect lying by certain categories of subjects.

5. Circle the letter of the statement that best summarizes the concluding paragraph.

    a. The idea behind polygraph testing is that people who show anxiety are lying, yet anxiety can result from many causes other than lying.

    b. A recent resolution adopted by the American Psychological Association states that the scientific evidence for the soundness of lie detector tests is unsatisfactory, and if the tests are to be given at all, they should be administered only in certain circumstances by well-trained examiners.

    c. Some psychologists conclude that the tests only sometimes detect lying at rates that are better than chance, especially under certain circumstances. Such skepticism about the tests have led to some opposition to the tests.

DISCUSSION QUESTIONS

1. The authors state, "Increasing numbers of government agencies and private employers have been requiring job applicants and current employees to take polygraph tests." What reasons might employers have for asking applicants and employees to take such tests?

2. Why do you think lie-detector examiners ask test subjects some irrelevant questions (as stated in paragraph 5)?

3. Under which circumstances do you think you would or would not take a lie detector test?

4. Do you think lie detector tests should be banned? If not, would you limit their use in any way?

Check Your Performance   **LIE DETECTORS**

Skill	Number Right	Points	Total
BASIC SKILL QUESTIONS			
Vocabulary in Context (1 item)	_____	x 4 =	_____
Central Point and Main Ideas (3 items)	_____	x 4 =	_____
Supporting Details (3 items)	_____	x 4 =	_____
Transitions (2 items)	_____	x 4 =	_____
Patterns of Organization (1 item)	_____	x 4 =	_____
ADVANCED SKILL QUESTIONS			
Fact and Opinion (2 items)	_____	x 4 =	_____
Inferences (3 items)	_____	x 4 =	_____
Purpose and Tone (2 items)	_____	x 4 =	_____
Propaganda (1 item)	_____	x 4 =	_____
Argument (2 items)	_____	x 4 =	_____
SUMMARIZING (5 items)	_____	x 4 =	_____

FINAL SCORE (OF POSSIBLE 100)   _____%

Enter your final score into the reading performance chart on the inside back cover.

9

Nonverbal Communication
Anthony F. Grasha

Preview

When we think of communication, we usually think of language. But a great deal of human communication takes place without speaking. When we are angry, we may make a fist. When we are happy, our faces give us away. The extent to which we reveal our feelings without words, however, goes much further than we are often aware of. In this excerpt from a college textbook titled *Practical Applications of Psychology*, Second Edition (Scott, Foresman/Little, Brown, 1983), Anthony F. Grasha provides an overview of just how much we really say without words.

Words to Watch

> *enhance* (1): strengthen
> *norms* (2): normal standards
> *culprit* (6): guilty one
> *manipulate* (7): use
> *utterances* (7): verbal expressions
> *quivering* (8): trembling

The way we dress, our mannerisms, how close we stand to people, eye contact, touching, and the ways we mark our personal spaces convey certain messages. *Such nonverbal behaviors communicate certain messages by themselves and also enhance° the meaning of our verbal communications.* Pounding your fist on a table, for example, suggests anger without anything being spoken. Holding someone close to you conveys the message that you care. To say "I don't like you" with a loud voice or waving fists increases the intensity of the verbal message. Let us examine the concepts of *personal space* and *body language* to gain additional insights into the nonverbal side of interpersonal communication.

1

Nonverbal Messages: The Use of Personal Space

Edward Hall notes that we have personal spatial territories or zones that allow   2
certain types of behaviors and communications. We only allow certain people to enter or
events to occur within a zone. Let us look at how some nonverbal messages can be
triggered by behaviors that violate the norms° of each zone. The four personal zones
identified by Hall are as follows:

1   Intimate distance. This personal zone covers a range of distance from body   3
contact to one foot. Relationships between a parent and child, lovers, and close friends
occur within this zone. As a general rule, we only allow people we know and have some
affection for to enter this zone. When someone tries to enter without our permission,
they are strongly repelled by our telling them to stay away from us or by our pushing
them away. Why do you think we allow a doctor to easily violate our intimate distance
zone?

2   Personal distance. The spatial range covered by this zone extends from one to   4
four feet. Activities like eating in a restaurant with two or three other people, sitting on
chairs or on the floor in small groups at parties, or playing cards occur within this zone.
Violations of the zone make people feel uneasy and act nervously. When you are eating
at a restaurant, the amount of table space that is considered yours is usually divided
equally by the number of people present. I can remember becoming angry and generally
irritated when a friend of mine placed a plate and glass in my space. As we talked I was
visibly irritated, but my anger had nothing to do with the topic we discussed. Has this
ever happened to you?

3   Social distance. Four to twelve feet is the social distance zone. Business   5
meetings, large formal dinners, and small classroom seminars occur within the
boundaries of the social distance zone. Discussions concerning everyday topics like the
weather, politics, or a best seller are considered acceptable. For a husband and wife to
launch into a heated argument during a party in front of ten other people would violate
the accepted norms for behavior in the social zone. This once happened at a formal party
I attended. The nonverbal behaviors that resulted consisted of several people leaving the
room, others looking angry or uncomfortable, and a few standing and watching quietly
with an occasional upward glance and a rolling of their eyeballs. What would violate the
social distance norms in a classroom?

4   Public distance. This zone includes the area beyond twelve feet. Addressing a   6
crowd, watching a sports event, and sitting in a large lecture section are behaviors we
engage in within this zone. As is true for the other zones, behaviors unacceptable for
this zone can trigger nonverbal messages. At a recent World Series game a young male
took his clothes off and ran around the outfield. Some watched with amusement on their
faces, others looked away, and a few waved their fists at the culprit°. The respective
messages were, "That's funny," "I'm afraid or ashamed to look," and "How dare you
interrupt the game." What would your reaction be in this situation?

Nonverbal Messages: The Use of Body Language

Body language refers to the various arm and hand gestures, facial expressions,   7
tone of voice, postures, and body movements we use to convey certain messages.
According to Erving Goffman, they are the things we "give off" when talking to other
people. Goffman notes that our body language is generally difficult to manipulate° at

will. Unlike our verbal utterances°, we have less conscious control over the specific body gestures or expressions we might make while talking. Unless we are acting on a stage or purposely trying to create a certain effect, they occur automatically without much thought on our part.

Michael Argyle notes that body language serves several functions for us. *It helps* 8 *us to communicate certain emotions, attitudes, and preferences.* A hug by someone close to us lets us know we are appreciated. A friendly wave and smile as someone we know passes us lets us know we are recognized. A quivering° lip tells us that someone is upset. Each of us has become quite sensitive to the meaning of various body gestures and expressions. Robert Rosenthal has demonstrated that this sensitivity is rather remarkable. When shown films of people expressing various emotions, individuals were able to identify the emotion correctly 66 percent of the time even when each frame was exposed for one twenty-fourth of a second. *Body language also supports our verbal communications.* Vocal signals of timing, pitch, voice stress, and various gestures add meaning to our verbal utterances. Argyle suggests that we may speak with our vocal organs, but we converse with our whole body. *Body language helps to control our conversations.* It helps us to decide when it is time to stop talking, to interrupt the other person, and to know when to shift topics or elaborate on something because our listeners are bored, do not understand us, or are not paying attention.

BASIC SKILL QUESTIONS

Vocabulary in Context

1. The word *convey* in "the ways we mark our personal space convey certain messages" (paragraph l) means
   a. prevent.
   b. communicate.
   c. entertain.
   d. deny.

2. The word *repelled* in "When someone tries to enter without our permission, they are strongly repelled by our telling them to stay away from us" (paragraph 3) means
   a. greeted.
   b. turned away.
   c. encouraged.
   d. ignored.

Central Point and Main Ideas

3. Which sentence best expresses the central point of the selection?
   a. It is difficult to communicate without words.
   b. People communicate with each other in various ways.
   c. Nonverbal behavior both communicates messages and emphasizes verbal messages.
   d. The way we use personal space can trigger nonverbal messages.

4. Which sentence best expresses the main idea of paragraph 7?
   a. We must plan our body language.
   b. It is hard to control body language.
   c. Actors use body language to create an effect.
   d. Body language refers to the nonverbal ways we communicate, usually without conscious control.

5. The main idea of paragraph 8 is expressed in
   a. the first sentence.
   b. the second sentence.
   c. the next-to-last sentence.
   d. the last sentence.

Supporting Details

6. According to Rosenthal's work, we
   a. frequently understand body language.
   b. rarely understand body language.
   c. always understand body language.
   d. never understand body language.

7. To support his central point, the author uses
   a. examples.
   b. research.
   c. opinions of other experts.
   d. all of the above.

Transitions

8. The signal word at the beginning of the sentence below shows
   a. emphasis.
   b. comparison.
   c. contrast.
   d. time.

   Unlike our verbal utterances, we have less conscious control over the specific body gestures or expressions we might make while talking. (Paragraph 7)

Patterns of Organization

9. The pattern of organization of paragraph 3 (as well as 4, 5, and 6) is
   a. time order.
   b. cause and effect.
   c. definition and example.
   d. list of items.

10. On the whole, paragraph 8
    a. compares and contrasts body language to verbal expression.
    b. lists the functions of body language.
    c. defines body language and gives examples of it.
    d. uses time order to narrate an incident about body language.

ADVANCED SKILL QUESTIONS

Fact and Opinion

11. The sentence below is
    a. totally factual.
    b. only opinion.
    c. both fact and opinion.

    When shown films of people expressing various emotions, individuals were able to identify the emotion correctly 66 percent of the time even when each frame was exposed for one twenty-fourth of a second. (Paragraph 8)

Inferences

12. _____ TRUE OR FALSE? Just as body language generally occurs automatically, so does the use of personal space.

13. Goffman's ideas on body language (paragraph 7) imply that
    a. we usually are aware of our own body language.
    b. our body language might reveal emotions we wish to hide.
    c. we can never manipulate our body language.
    d. we should learn to manipulate our body language.

14. From the reading and our experience, we might conclude that outwardly expressive people will usually
    a. have more noticeable body language.
    b. have less noticeable body language.
    c. purposely control their body language.
    d. try to eliminate body language.

15. Two students reviewing together for a test would be working within
    a. an intimate distance.
    b. a personal distance.
    c. a social distance.
    d. a public distance.

Purpose and Tone

16. The author's primary purpose in this selection is to
    a. inform.
    b. persuade.
    c. entertain.

17. On the whole, the author's tone is
    a. humorous.
    b. objective.
    c. scornful.
    d. enthusiastic.

Propaganda

18. Which propaganda technique (suggested by the reading) is illustrated in the following ad?
    a. Bandwagon *(the appeal to do what many others are doing)*
    b. Testimonial *(use of a well-known spokesperson)*
    c. Plain folks *(showing candidates, company executives, or customers as ordinary people)*
    d. Transfer *(association with an admired symbol or image)*

    Order your copy today of *Body Language in Business*. Like the thousands of other executives who have read this book, you will learn to have the extra edge—because you will know what others are thinking.

19. Which propaganda technique (suggested by the reading) is illustrated in the following ad?
    a. Bandwagon *(the appeal to do what many others are doing)*
    b. Testimonial *(use of a well-known spokesperson)*
    c. Plain folks *(showing candidates, company executives, or customers as ordinary people)*
    d. Glittering generalities *(use of an important-sounding but unsupported claim)*

    Corporate kingpin David Danner advises, "Get this book. It will give you the winning edge."

Argument

20. Check the statement that is the *point* of the following argument. Note that two other statements support the point, and that one statement expresses another point.

    ___ a. I became angry and generally irritated when a friend of mine placed a plate and glass in my space.

    ___ b. As we talked I was visibly irritated, but my anger had nothing to do with the topic we discussed.

   ___ c. Business meetings take place within the boundaries of the social distance zone.

   ___ d. Violations of the personal zone make people feel uneasy and act nervously.

OUTLINING

Complete the following outline of "Nonverbal Communication" by using the information in the boldface headings, italics, and numbers in the selection.

Central Point: Our use of personal space and body language communicates meaning and emphasizes verbal communication.

A. _____

   1. Intimate distance
   2. Personal distance

   3. _____

   4. _____

B. Nonverbal messages: the use of body language
   1. Definition and explanation of body language
   2. Functions of body language

      a. _____

      _____

      b. _____

      c. Helps control our conversations

DISCUSSION QUESTIONS

1. What are your answers to the following questions from the selection? Why do you think the author included these questions?

   • Why do you think we allow a doctor to easily violate our intimate distance zone?

   • I can remember becoming angry and generally irritated when a friend of mine placed a plate and glass in my space.... Has this ever happened to you?

   • What would violate the social distance norms in a classroom?

2. This selection includes headings, italics, labels and numbered items. How are these related to the author's purpose?

3. What are some examples of a dating or business situation in which someone's body language might contradict his or her verbal communication?

4. Give examples from your own experience of all four types of personal space.

Check Your Performance   NONVERBAL COMMUNICATION

Skill	Number Right	Points	Total
BASIC SKILL QUESTIONS			
Vocabulary in Context (2 items)	_____	x 4 =	_____
Central Point and Main Ideas (3 items)	_____	x 4 =	_____
Supporting Details (2 items)	_____	x 4 =	_____
Transitions (1 item)	_____	x 4 =	_____
Patterns of Organization (2 items)	_____	x 4 =	_____
ADVANCED SKILL QUESTIONS			
Fact and Opinion (1 item)	_____	x 4 =	_____
Inferences (4 items)	_____	x 4 =	_____
Purpose and Tone (2 items)	_____	x 4 =	_____
Propaganda (2 items)	_____	x 4 =	_____
Argument (1 item)	_____	x 4 =	_____
OUTLINING (5 items)	_____	x 4 =	_____

FINAL SCORE (OF POSSIBLE 100)   _____%

Enter your final score into the reading performance chart on the inside back cover.

10

Preindustrial Cities
Rodney Stark

Preview

"What was it like in London and Paris when they had only 40,000 to 50,000 residents and before they had factories or freeways, subways or suburbs?" asks Rodney Stark in his popular college textbook (*Sociology*, Third Edition, Wadsworth, 1989). If you think problems in big cities are modern "inventions," this excerpt from Stark's book may surprise you. In it, he discusses the uncleanliness, crowding, and crime that existed in "big" cities before machines and electricity changed society.

Words to Watch

densely (2): closely
virtually (5): for all practical purposes
ravaged (7): violently destroyed
trenches (8): ditches
strewn (9): scattered
radius (14): a line from the center of a circle to its edge
lurked (16): hid, ready to attack
incentive (18): motivation
vital (18): essential
innovations (19): things that are newly introduced
enticed (20): tempted
rampant (20): widespread
condoning (20): forgiving or overlooking
exalted (21): high
replenished (22): resupplied

Let us go back into history and examine what life was like in the famous cities of preindustrial times. What was it really like in ancient Athens and Rome? What was it like in London and Paris when they had only 40,000 to 50,000 residents and before they had factories or freeways, subways or suburbs? 1

PREINDUSTRIAL CITIES

Until very recently, cities were small, filthy, disease-ridden, densely° packed with people, and disorderly, and they were dark and very dangerous at night. If that description is unlike your image of Athens during the Golden Age of Greek civilization, that is because history so often leaves out the mud, manure, and misery. 2

Typically, preindustrial cities contained no more than 5,000 to 10,000 inhabitants. Large national capitals were usually smaller than 40,000 and rarely larger than 60,000. Few preindustrial cities, such as ancient Rome, grew as large as 500,000 and then only under special circumstances. Moreover, these cities rapidly shrank back to a much smaller size as slight changes in circumstance made it impossible to support them. 3

Limits on City Style

A major reason why cities remained small was poor transportation; food had to be brought to feed a city. With only animal and human power to bring it, however, food could not be transported very far. Therefore, cities were limited to the population that could be fed by farmers nearby. The few large cities of preindustrial times appeared only where food could be brought long distances by water transport. Ancient Rome, for example, was able to reach the size of present-day Denver (and only briefly) because it controlled the whole Mediterranean area. Surplus food from this vast region was shipped by sea to feed the city's masses. 4

However, as the power of the empire weakened, Rome's population declined as the sources of food supplies dwindled. By the ninth century, the sea-power of Islam had driven nearly all European shipping from the Mediterranean, and the cities of southern Europe, including Rome, were virtually° abandoned. In fact, Europe had practically no cities during the ninth and tenth centuries. 5

Disease also checked the size of cities. Even early in the twentieth century, cities had such high mortality rates that they required a large and constant influx of newcomers from the countryside just to maintain their populations. As recently as 1900, the death rate in English cities was 33 percent higher than that in rural areas (Davis, 1965). A major reason for the high mortality in cities was the high incidence of infectious diseases, which are spread by physical contact or by breathing in germs emitted by coughs and sneezes. Disease spreads much more slowly among less dense rural populations. 6

Disease in cities was also caused by filth, especially by the contamination of water and food. Kingsley Davis (1965) pointed out that even as late as the 1850s, London's water "came mainly from wells and rivers that drained cesspools, graveyards, and tidal areas. The city was regularly ravaged° by cholera." 7

Sewage treatment was unknown in preindustrial cities. Even sewers were uncommon and what sewers there were consisted of open trenches° running along the streets into which sewage, including human waste, was poured from buckets and chamber pots. Indeed, sewage was often poured out of second-story windows without any warning to pedestrians below. 8

Garbage was not collected and was strewn° everywhere. It was hailed as a major step forward when cities began to keep a municipal herd of pigs, which were guided through the streets at night to eat the garbage dumped during the day. Of course, the pigs 9 did considerable recycling as they went. Still, major cities in the eastern United States depended on the pigs for their sanitation services until the end of the nineteenth century.

Today we are greatly concerned about pollution, especially that produced by 10 automobile exhausts and factories. But the car and the factory cannot match the horse and the home fireplace when it comes to pollution. It is estimated that in 1900 horses deposited 26 million pounds of manure and 10 million gallons of urine on the streets of New York City every week.

London's famous and deadly "fogs" of previous centuries were actually smogs 11 caused by thousands of smoking home chimneys during atmospheric inversions, which trapped the polluted air. Indeed, the first known air-quality law was decreed in 1273 by England's King Edward I. It forbade the use of a particularly smoky coal. The poet Shelley wrote early in the nineteenth century that "Hell is a city much like London, a populous and smokey city." In 1911, coal smoke during an atmospheric inversion killed more than a thousand people in London, and this incident led to the coining of the word *smog*.

Pedestrians in preindustrial cities often held perfume-soaked handkerchiefs over 12 their noses because the streets stank so. They kept alert for garbage and sewage droppings from above. They wore high boots because they had to wade through muck, manure, and garbage. And the people themselves were dirty because they seldom bathed. Not surprisingly, they died at a rapid rate.

Population density also contributed to the unhealthiness of preindustrial cities. 13 People were packed closely together. As we saw in Chapter 13, whole families lived in one small room. The houses stood wall to wall, and few streets were more than 10 to 12 feet wide.

Why was there such density when the population was so small? First of all, for 14 most of its history, the city was also a fortress surrounded by massive walls for defense. Once the walls were up, the area of the city was fixed (at least until the walls were rebuilt), and if the population grew, people had to crowd ever closer. Even cities without walls were confined. Travel was by foot or by hoof. Cities did not spread beyond the radius° that could be covered by these slow means of transportation, and thus the city limit was usually no more than 3 miles from the center.

Second, preindustrial cities could not expand upward. Not until the nineteenth 15 century, when structural steel and reinforced concrete were developed, could very tall structures be erected. Moreover, until elevators were invented, it was impractical to build very high. By expanding upward, people could have much greater living and working space in a building taking up no greater area at ground level. This could, of course, have meant that cities would become even more crowded at street level. They did not, however, because even modern high-rise cities have much more open space than did preindustrial cities, and, as we shall see, newer cities have expanded primarily outward rather than upward.

Preindustrial cities were not only dirty, disease-ridden, and dense but also dark 16 and dangerous. Today we sometimes say people move to the city because they are attracted by the bright lights, and we joke about small towns where they "roll up the sidewalks by 9 P.M." The preindustrial city had no sidewalks to roll up and no electricity to light up the night. If lighted at all, homes were badly and expensively illuminated by candles and oil lamps. Until the introduction of gas lamps in the nineteenth century, streets were not lighted at all. Out in the dark, dangerous people lurked°, waiting for victims. To venture forth at night in many of these cities was so dangerous that people did so only in groups accompanied by armed men bearing torches. Many people today fear to walk in cities at night. Still, it is much safer to do so now than it used to be.

Why Live in Such Cities?

Knowing what preindustrial cities were like, one must ask why anyone willingly lived there and why a large number of newcomers were attracted to cities each year from rural areas.   17

One reason was economic incentive°. Cities offered many people a chance to increase their incomes. For example, the development of an extensive division of labor, of occupational specialization, virtually required cities. Specialists must depend upon one another for the many goods and services they do not provide for themselves. Such exchanges are hard to manage when people live far apart. Thus skilled craftsmen, merchants, physicians, and the like gathered in cities. Indeed, cities are vital° to trade and commerce, and most early cities developed at intersections of major trade routes.   18

In addition to economic attractions, cities drew people because they offered the prospect of a more interesting and stimulating life. As Gideon Sjoberg (1965) noted, "new ideas and innovations° flowed into [cities] quite naturally," as travelers along the trade routes brought ideas as well as goods from afar. Moreover, simply by concentrating specialists in an area, cities stimulated innovation not just in technology but also in religion, philosophy, science, and the arts. The density of cities encouraged public performances, from plays and concerts to organized sporting events.   19

Cities undoubtedly also enticed° some to migrate from rural areas in pursuit of "vice." The earliest writing we have about cities includes complaints about rampant° wickedness and sin, and through the centuries cities have maintained the reputation for condoning° behavior that would not be tolerated in rural communities (Fischer, 1975). In part, this may be because from the beginning cities have been relatively anonymous places. Preindustrial cities may have been even more anonymous, given their size, than modern cities.   20

Consider that cities relied on large numbers of newcomers each year just to replace the population lost through mortality. As a result, cities tended to abound in people who were recent arrivals and who had not known one another previously. Before modern identification systems, many people in cities were not even who they claimed to be—runaway sons and daughters of peasants could claim more exalted° social origins. The possibility of escaping one's past and starting anew must have drawn many to the cities. But this also meant that cities then were even less integrated by long-standing interpersonal attachments than modern cities.   21

In any event, it was primarily adventuresome, single, young adults who constantly replenished° city populations. E. A. Wrigley (1969) has computed that in the years from 1650 to 1750, London needed 8,000 newcomers each year to maintain its population. The newcomers averaged 20 years of age, were unmarried, and came from farms. Most of these newcomers came from more than 50 miles away—at least a two-day trip at that time.   22

For all our complaints about modern cities, industrialization did not ruin city life. 23
Preindustrial cities were horrid. Yet for many young people on farms, the prospect of
heading off to one of these miserable cities seemed far superior to a life of dull toil.
Then as the Industrial Revolution began, the idea of going off to the city suddenly
appealed not just to restless young people but also to whole families. Soon the
countryside virtually emptied, as people flocked to town.

BASIC SKILL QUESTIONS

Vocabulary in Context

1. The word *dwindled* in "Rome's population declined as the sources of food
   supplies dwindled" (paragraph 5) means
   a. increased.
   b. decreased.
   c. remained the same.
   d. became less expensive.

2. The word *checked* in "A major reason why cities remained small was poor
   transportation. . . . Disease also checked the size of cities" (paragraphs 4
   and 6) means
   a. encouraged.
   b. predicted.
   c. limited.
   d. increased.

Central Point and Main Ideas

3. Which sentence best expresses the central point of the selection?
   a. Poor transportation and fortress walls kept cities from becoming too
      large.
   b. Preindustrial cities had major disadvantages, but they still attracted
      people.
   c. Until structural steel, reinforced concrete and elevators were invented, it
      wasn't possible or practical to build high buildings.
   d. Life in earlier times was very different from life today.

4. The main idea of paragraph 6 is best expressed in its
   a. first sentence.
   b. second sentence.
   c. third sentence.
   d. fourth sentence.

5. Which sentence best expresses the main idea of paragraphs 17-21?
   a. Despite the great disadvantages of preindustrial cities, people were drawn to the cities for economic reasons.
   b. Despite the great disadvantages of preindustrial cities, people were drawn to the cities for several reasons.
   c. Cities held many attractions for adventuresome single rural men and women.
   d. Our earliest knowledge of cities includes complaints about widespread vice, and cities have kept the reputation for allowing behavior that would not be tolerated in rural communities.

Supporting Details

6. _____ TRUE OR FALSE? According to the author, preindustrial cities, on the whole, were more crowded and dangerous than modern cities.

7. The major supporting details of paragraphs 14 and 15 are
   a. 1) travel by foot or horse and 2) elevators.
   b. crowding of 1) preindustrial cities and 2) modern-day cities.
   c. the limits on city size caused by 1) city walls and 2) lack of construction technology.
   d. 1) cities with walls and 2) cities without walls.

Transitions

8. The relationship between the two sentences below is one of
   a. addition.
   b. time.
   c. contrast.
   d. illustration.

   A major reason why cities remained small was poor transportation . . . Disease also checked the size of cities. (Paragraphs 4 and 6)

9. The relationship between the two sentences below is one of
   a. comparison.
   b. time.
   c. cause and effect.
   d. illustration.

   . . . cities relied on large numbers of newcomers each year just to replace the population lost through mortality. As a result, cities tended to abound in people who were recent arrivals and who had not known one another previously. (Paragraph 21)

Patterns of Organization

10. The main pattern of organization of paragraph 4 is
    a. time order
    b. list of items.
    c. cause and effect.
    d. definition and example.

ADVANCED SKILL QUESTIONS

Fact and Opinion

11. Paragraph 6 is made up of
    a. facts.
    b. opinions.
    c. both facts and opinions.

12. The reading "Preindustrial Cities"
    a. is mainly made up of facts.
    b. is mainly made up of opinions.
    c. includes many facts and many opinions.

Inferences

13. From paragraph 4, we can conclude that cities probably grew significantly larger after the invention of
    a. elevators.
    b. trains.
    c. bicycles.
    d. antibiotics.

14. The author implies that today's cities
    a. are as dirty as preindustrial cities were.
    b. are better places to live than preindustrial cities.
    c. shouldn't have so many tall buildings.
    d. are very safe places at night.

15. Reread paragraph 21; from that paragraph, we can conclude
    a. people's social class influenced how others treated them.
    b. it was easy in preindustrial times to check on people's pasts.
    c. both of the above.
    d. neither *a* nor *b*.

Purpose and Tone

16. The author's main purpose is
    a. to inform.
    b. to persuade.
    c. to entertain.

17. The overall tone of the selection is
    a. amused.
    b. disappointed.
    c. objective.
    d. critical.

Propaganda

18. The advertisement below (suggested by the reading) is an example of what propaganda technique?
    a. Bandwagon *(the appeal to do what many others are doing)*
    b. Testimonial *(use of a well-known spokesperson)*
    c. Transfer *(association with an admired symbol or image)*
    d. Glittering generalities *(use of an important-sounding but unsupported claim)*

    Join the thousands of rural citizens who have left their nosy rural neighbors to start a new life in the city.

Argument

19. To support the statement that "the car and the factory cannot match the horse and the home fireplace when it comes to pollution," the author provides in paragraphs 10 and 11
    a. facts about how cars and factories pollute.
    b. facts about how horses and home fireplaces pollute.
    c. both of the above.

20. Complete the following argument by adding a statement of support.

    Point: Preindustrial cities were not better than our cities.

    Support: Preindustrial cities had worse environmental pollution.

    Support: _____

MAPPING

Complete the map of the selection by filling in the missing major and minor details scrambled in the following list:

- Population density
- Opportunity to start a new life
- Disease limited size of city
- Reasons people were attracted to them
- Not being able to expand upward

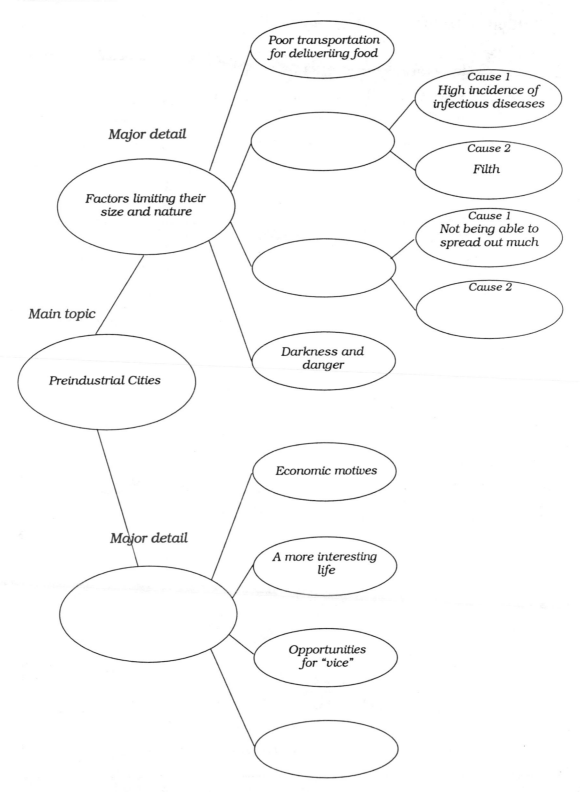

DISCUSSION QUESTIONS

1. If you had lived in preindustrial days, do you think you would have chosen to live in a city or in a rural area? Why?

2. What draws people to or keeps them in big cities today? Compare these reasons to those which attracted newcomers to preindustrial cities.

3. The radius of preindustrial cities was "usually no more than 3 miles from the center." What factors have allowed today's huge cities and their suburbs to exist?

4. According to the reading, preindustrial city dwellers had to protect themselves from the filth and crime in big cities. How are problems of city dwellers today the same or different?

Check Your Performance   **PREINDUSTRIAL CITIES**

Skill	Number Right	Points	Total
BASIC SKILL QUESTIONS			
Vocabulary in Context (2 items)	_____	x 4 =	_____
Central Point and Main Ideas (3 items)	_____	x 4 =	_____
Supporting Details (2 items)	_____	x 4 =	_____
Transitions (2 items)	_____	x 4 =	_____
Patterns of Organization (1 item)	_____	x 4 =	_____
ADVANCED SKILL QUESTIONS			
Fact and Opinion (2 items)	_____	x 4 =	_____
Inferences (3 items)	_____	x 4 =	_____
Purpose and Tone (2 items)	_____	x 4 =	_____
Propaganda (1 item)	_____	x 4 =	_____
Argument (2 items)	_____	x 4 =	_____
MAPPING (5 items)	_____	x 4 =	_____

FINAL SCORE (OF POSSIBLE 100)   _____%

Enter your final score into the reading performance chart on the inside back cover.

Limited Answer Key

An Important Note: To strengthen your reading skills, you must do more than simply find out which of your answers are right and which are wrong. You also need to figure out (with the help of this book, the teacher, or other students) *why* you missed the questions you did. By using each of your wrong answers as a learning opportunity, you will strengthen your understanding of the skills. You will also prepare yourself for the review and mastery tests, for which answers are not given here.

ANSWERS TO THE PRACTICES IN PART I

1   Vocabulary in Context

Practice 1

1. Example: *only a spoonful of rice and a few beans*; a
2. Examples: *The TV is talking to them, others can steal their thoughts*; a
3. Examples: *What sign are you? How do you like this place? You remind me of someone*; b
4. Examples: *gardening, long-distance bike riding*; a
5. Examples: *two heads, webbed toes*; c

Practice 2

1. Synonym: *a person who habitually postpones doing things*
2. Synonym: *carefully examine*
3. Synonym: *practical*
4. Synonym: *isolating infected patients to prevent their diseases from spreading*
5. Synonym: *mercy-killing*

Practice 3

1. Antonym: *great wealth*; c
2. Antonym: *long, vague*; a
3. Antonym: *openly*; b
4. Antonym: *weak*; c
5. Antonym: *decorated plainly*; b

Practice 4

1. c
2. b
3. a
4. b
5. c

2   Main Ideas

Practice 1

1. Topic: c; Main Idea: b
2. Topic: a; Main Idea: d
3. Topic: c; Main Idea: c
4. Topic: d; Main Idea: d

Practice 2

Group 1. a. SD
         b. SD
         c. T
         d. MI

Group 2. a. SD
         b. T
         c. SD
         d. MI

Group 3. a. SD
         b. T
         c. SD
         d. MI

Group 4. a. T
         b. SD
         c. MI
         d. SD

Practice 3

A. 1
B. 4
C. 2
D. 1, 5

Practice 4

1. b
2. b
3. c

Practice 5

The implied main ideas may be stated in various ways, including the following:

1. Many commonly held beliefs about sleepwalking are not true.
2. Being an only child is not as great a privilege as people think it is.
3. There are benefits to watching television.

3   Supporting Details

Note: Wording may vary throughout these practices.

Practice 1

Group 1

(The order of points a. and b. may vary.)

1. Bad location
2. Poor advertising
   a. Relied on word of mouth
   b. No display ad in Yellow Pages
3. a. Unexpected rise in wholesale prices
   b. High salaries for workers

Group 2

Missing minor details under "Substitutes for high-fat dairy products": Skim milk instead of whole milk; Yogurt instead of sour cream.

Missing second major detail: Substitutes for fats.

Missing third major detail: Substitutes for high-fat meats.

Missing minor details under "Substitutes for high-fat meats": Ground turkey breast instead of ground beef; Boiled ham instead of bacon.

Practice 2

1. Missing minor detail under "Sports addicts": Summer: focus is baseball, golf, tennis.
   Missing second major and minor details: Television—Flip on television as soon as they get home; Schedule much of their lives around favorite shows.
   Missing third major detail: Love
2. Main idea: Animals open their mouths for several reasons besides hunger.
   1. To warn an intruder away
      Examples: Lizards and fish threaten by opening their mouths.

Bears and wolves show their teeth before attacking.

2. To quiet aggression
Example: Lions yawn to distract other lions that may want to fight.

3. To get their teeth clean
Example: The crocodile opens to let little birds eat leftover food off its teeth.

4. To signal an interest in the opposite sex
Example: Open beaks are part of the penguin's court-ship dance.

Practice 3

1. serious depression?
   a. A change in sleep patterns
   b. Abnormal eating patterns
   c. A general feeling of hopeless-ness

2. What simple steps can drivers take to prevent car theft?
   a. Lock all valuables in the trunk or glove compartment.
   b. Park in the middle of the block on a busy, well-lighted street.
   c. Always lock the car and take the keys.

Practice 4

A. 1. b
   2. a
   3. c
   4. They can undo complicated bolts on gates.
   5. c
B. 6. c
   7. shipping them out of the country.
   8. witches or possessed by the devil.
   9. punishing the mentally ill.
   10. c

4 Transitions

Answers to some of these exercises may vary.

Practice 1

1. also
2. First of all
3. In addition
4. Finally
5. third

Practice 2

1. After
2. Then
3. during
4. before
5. while

Practice 3

1. Although
2. in contrast
3. but
4. in spite of
5. Nevertheless

Practice 4

1. Similarly
2. like
3. in the same way
4. In like manner
5. Just as

Practice 5

1. For example
2. such as
3. To illustrate
4. For instance
5. For example

Practice 6

1. Because
2. as a result
3. Since
4. Consequently
5. therefore

5 Patterns of Organization

Wording will vary throughout these practices.

Practice 1a

Main idea: The 1960s were a time of turmoil and change in America.
1. Assassination of President Kennedy depressed the country.
2. Urban riots brought out the issue of racial equality.
3. Anti-war protests spread across the country.

Practice 1b

Main idea: There are several steps to remembering your dreams
2. Put a pen and notebook near your bed.
3. Turn off alarm and wake up gradually.
4. Write down any dream you remember before you get out of bed.

Practice 2

1. Number of items: 3
   Type of item: Advantages to children of owning a pet
2. Number of items: 3
   Type of item: Ways to be an active listener

Practice 3

A. Comparison; 1. Mysteries, 2. Science fiction
B. Contrast; 1. Government's role in society 2. Journalists' role in society (in relation to their attitudes toward secrecy)

Practice 4

A. 1. Cause: late spring freeze
      Effect: poor Florida orange crop
   2. Cause: Mr. Coleman's compulsive gambling
      Effect: Mr. Coleman's bankruptcy
   3. Cause: I slipped and fell on a patch of ice
      Effect: I twisted my ankle
   4. Cause: Linda's new boss not appreciating her excellent work habits
      Effect: Linda's work became careless
B. 5. Uncontrolled high blood pressure: cause
      Stroke: effect
      Heart attack: effect
   6. Valid objection: cause
      Thrown-out evidence: effect
      Dismissed case: effect
   7. Ammunition was low: cause
      Food supplies were low: cause
      The general surrendered: effect
   8. A study schedule: cause
      Tonia's better grades: effect
      Not going out on weeknights: cause
C. 9. Inability to listen carefully all the time: effect
      Message overload: cause
      Preoccupation with personal concerns: cause
      Surrounding noise: cause
   10. Meditation: cause
      Decrease or elimination of drug use: effect
      Cardiovascular improvements: effect
      Stress relief: effect

Practice 5

A. Definition: 1   Example: 2
B. Definition: 2   Example 1: 5
                    Example 2: 7

Practice 6

1. b   4. c
2. c   5. c
3. a

6   Fact and Opinion

Practice 1

1. F
2. F+O
3. F
4. F+O
5. F
6. F
7. F
8. F+O
9. F
10. F+O

Practice 2

1. F
2. O
3. F
4. O
5. O
6. F
7. O
8. F
9. F
10. O

Practice 3

1. O
2. F
3. F+O
4. F+O
5. O
6. F
7. O
8. F
9. F+O
10. O

Practice 4

1. O
2. F+O
3. O
4. F
5. F

7   Inferences

Practice 1

1. c
2. c
3. a
4. c
5. d

Practice 2

1. c
2. b
3. b
4. c
5. b

Practice 3

1, 6, 8

Practice 4

1. c
2. c
3. b
4. a
5. c
6. c
7. b
8. b
9. b
10. c

8   Purpose and Tone

Practice 1

1. I
2. P
3. E
4. P
5. I
6. I
7. E
8. P
9. E
10. I

Practice 2

1. P
2. E
3. I

Practice 3

A. 1. admiring
   2. sympathetic
   3. critical
   4. objective
   5. ironic
B. 6. straightforward
   7. ironic
   8. threatening
   9. self-pitying
   10. sympathetic

Practice 4

1. h
2. f
3. c
4. e
5. d

9 Propaganda

Practice 1

2, 5

Practice 2

2, 4

Practice 3

2, 3

Practice 4

1, 5

Practice 5

2, 4

Practice 6

1, 5

Practice 7

1. c
2. c
3. b

10 Argument

Practice, page 187

1. S, P
2. S, P
3. S, S, S, P
4. P, S, S, S
5. S, S, P, S

Practice, pages 188-189

1. a, d, e
2. a, c, f
3. a, c, f
4. b, d, f

Practice 1

1. c
2. c

Practice 2

2

Practice 3

1

Practice 4

4

Practice 5

Group 1: d
Group 2: a

Practice 6

3

Practice 7

4

Practice 8

1

Acknowledgments

Baker, Russell, Excerpt from *Growing Up*. Copyright © 1982 by Russell Baker. Published by St. Martin's Press, Inc.

Barkin, Dorothy. "The Bystander Effect." Copyright © 1991 by Trend Publications. Reprinted by permission.

Barry, Dave. Selections on pages 152, 297, and 302. Reprinted by permission.

Cosby, Bill. Selection on page 300. From *Love and Marriage*. Copyright © 1989 by Bill Cosby. Reprinted by permission of Doubleday, a division of Bantam, Doubleday, Dell Publishing Group, Inc.

De Leon, Clark. "Bird Girl." Reprinted by permission.

Ellerbee, Linda. Excerpt from *Move On*. Reprinted by permission of The Putnam Publishing Group. Copyright © 1991 by Linda Ellerbee.

Ephron, Delia. "Coping with Santa Claus," from *Funny Sauce* by Delia Ephron. Copyright © 1982, 1983, 1986 by Delia Ephron. Used by permission of Viking Penguin, a division of Penguin Books USA Inc.

Fallows, James. "The No-Fat Nation." Copyright © 1986 by James Fallows. Reprinted by permission of the *Atlantic Monthly* and James Fallows.

Grasha, Anthony F. "Nonverbal Communication," from *Practical Applications of Psychology*, 3rd ed., pp. 248-250. Copyright © 1987 by Anthony F. Grasha. Reprinted by permission of Scott, Foresman/Little, Brown College Division.

Gregory, Dick. "Shame," from *Nigger: An Autobiography*. Copyright © 1964 by Dick Gregory Enterprises, Inc. Used by permission of the publisher, Dutton, a division of Penguin Books USA Inc.

Hamill, Pete. "The Yellow Ribbon." Reprinted by permission.

Karr, Albert R. "Death on the Road." Reprinted by permission of the *Wall Street Journal*. Copyright © 1982 by Dow Jones & Company, Inc. All rights reserved worldwide.

Lester, Julius. Excerpt from "Being a Boy," which originally appeared in *Ms.* magazine. Reprinted by permission of Julius Lester.

Light, Donald, Suzanne Keller, and Craig Calhoun. "Communities and Cities," from *Sociology*, 5th ed. Copyright © 1989 by Alfred A. Knopf, Inc. Reprinted by permission of McGraw-Hill, Inc.

Orwell, George. Excerpt from "A Hanging," from *Shooting an Elephant and Other Essays*. Copyright © 1945, 1946, 1949, 1950 by Sonia Brownell Orwell; renewed 1973, 1974 by Sonia Orwell. Published by Harcourt Brace Jovanovich, Inc.

Papalia, Diane E., and Sally Wendkos Olds. "How Parents' Child-Rearing Styles Affect Their Children," from *Psychology*, 2nd ed. Copyright © 1988 by McGraw-Hill, Inc. Reprinted by permission of McGraw-Hill, Inc.

Papalia, Diane E., and Sally Wendkos Olds. "Lie Detectors: Foolproof or Fraudulent?" from *Psychology*, 2nd ed. Copyright © 1988 by McGraw-Hill, Inc. Reprinted by permission of McGraw-Hill, Inc.

Popkin, Roy. "Night Watch." Originally appeared in *The National Observer*. Reprinted by permission of Dow Jones & Company, Inc. Copyright © 1964 by Dow Jones & Company, Inc. All rights reserved worldwide. Also reprinted with permission from the September 1965 *Reader's Digest*.

Rhodes, Richard. Excerpt from *A Hole in the World*. Copyright © 1990 by Richard Rhodes. Published by Simon and Schuster.

Roberts, Paul. Excerpt from "How to Say Nothing in 500 Words." From *Understanding English* by Paul Roberts. Copyright © 1958 by Paul Roberts. Reprinted by permission of HarperCollins Publishers.

Robinson, Edwin Arlington. "Richard Cory," from *The Children of the Night*. Published in New York by Charles Scribner's Sons, 1897.

Roth, Philip. Excerpt from *Goodbye Columbus*. Copyright © 1959 by Philip Roth. Reprinted by permission of Houghton Mifflin.

Sherry, Mary. "In Praise of the F Word," A *My Turn* column in the May 6, 1991 issue of *Newsweek*. Used with the permission of Mary Sherry.

Sifford, Darrell. "How People Rise and Fall." Reprinted by permission from *The Philadelphia Inquirer*.

Stark, Rodney. "Preindustrial Cities," from *Sociology*, 3rd ed. Copyright © 1989 by Wadsworth, Inc. Reprinted by permission of the publisher.

Verderber, Rudolph E. "Disclosing Feelings," from *Communicate!* 6th ed. Copyright © 1990 by Wadsworth, Inc. Reprinted by permission of the publisher.

Wilkins, Roger. "I Became Her Target." Reprinted by permission.

Index